MAN OF
THE PEOPLE

MAN OF THE PEOPLE

THE LIFE OF JOHN McCAIN

PAUL ALEXANDER

John Wiley & Sons, Inc.

Published by John Wiley & Sons, Inc., Hoboken, New Jersey.
Published simultaneously in Canada.

For general information on our other products and services, or technical support,
please contact our Customer Care Department within the United States at
(800) 762-2974, outside the United States at (317) 572-3993 or fax (317) 572-4002.

Wiley also publishes its books in a variety of electronic formats. Some content that
appears in print may not be available in electronic books.

For more information about Wiley products, visit our web site at www.wiley.com.

Library of Congress Cataloging-in-Publication Data:

Alexander, Paul, 1955-
  Man of the people : the life of John McCain / by Paul Alexander.
    p. cm.
  ISBN 0-471-22829-X (alk. paper)
  1. McCain, John, 1936- 2. Legislators—United States—Biography. 3.
United States. Congress. Senate—Biography. I. Title.
  E840.8.M26 A44 2002
  328.73′092—dc21

                                                          2002014898

Printed in the United States of America.

10 9 8 7 6 5 4 3 2 1

MAR 1 3 2003

once again, for Lauren Elizabeth Alexander
and for my family

Freedom is never more than one generation away from extinction. We didn't pass it to our children in the bloodstream. It must be fought for, protected, and handed on for them to do the same, or one day we will spend our sunset years telling our children and our children's children what it was once like in the United States where men were free.

—Ronald Reagan
Phoenix, Arizona
March 30, 1961

. . . that we here highly resolve that these dead shall not have died in vain—that this nation, under God, shall have a new birth of freedom—and that government of the people, by the people, for the people, shall not perish from the earth.

—Abraham Lincoln
The Gettysburg Address
November 19, 1863

PREFACE

Born in Birmingham, Alabama, in 1955, I grew up in the Deep South at a time when that region of the country was still dominated by the "yellow-dog Democrat," a person who would vote for a yellow dog if the dog was a Democrat. In the late 1960s, Nixon devised his Southern strategy; even later, the Reagan Democrat emerged. But in the early to mid-1960s, when I was first becoming aware of politics, the Southern political landscape featured giants like Congressman Hale Boggs of Louisiana; Senator John Sparkman of Alabama; Speaker of the House Sam Rayburn of Texas, whose lasting influence on the Congress following his death in November 1961 would be so profound that a Capitol Hill office building now bears his name; Senator John Stennis of Mississippi; and, of course, the giant of the giants, Lyndon Baines Johnson. In Alabama, as the world came to know, we had a complicated character for governor by the name of George Wallace—a famously self-avowed racist who got more than 90 percent of the African-American vote the last time he ran for office, a man so worshipped by Alabama voters he once ran his wife, Lurleen, for governor, when he was term-limited out, and she won. My grandmother kept a framed photograph of Governor Lurleen B. Wallace hanging on her living room wall. When Lurleen Wallace died of cancer before she finished her term in office, I remember my grandmother crying as she watched the state funeral on television.

When you're a yellow-dog Democrat, these are your frames of reference. All of this would change when George McGovern ran for president in 1972, since the South fell behind Nixon. That the South went for Jimmy Carter in 1976 was an illusion; Southerners voted for him because he was a native son. As it turned out, he was not at all in the tradition of Johnson and Rayburn, so the South, almost all of it, drifted back to Reagan in 1980. It was there solidly for Reagan in 1984, and for George H. W. Bush in 1988. It took two native sons, Bill Clinton and Al Gore, to bring the South back to the Democrats in 1992 and 1996, but the party's hold on the region was so tenuous that Gore lost important Southern states, most notably his home state of Tennessee, when he ran for president in 2000. Had Gore won just Tennessee—forget Florida—he would be president today.

By the time I began my career as a journalist in the late 1980s, versions of the Southern Democratic figures with which I had grown up were more or less gone. There were some throwbacks to the yellow-dog Democrats—Senator Sam Nunn of Georgia or Congressman Tom Bevill, the champion of working people whose niece I had gone to school with in Alabama—but not many. Perhaps that's why, when I first started writing nonfiction, I avoided politics, even though I had been obsessed with the subject for most of my life. How could I not, coming from a state that was once run by Governor Lurleen B. Wallace?

I wrote a book about the American poet Sylvia Plath. I wrote a book about the Hollywood icon James Dean. I wrote a book about the myriad scandals surrounding the Andy Warhol Foundation for the Visual Arts. I also wrote numerous articles for an array of magazines, but I did not write about politics. Then, in 1995, an editor I knew, Elizabeth Mitchell, called and asked if I would like to write an article for the first issue of *George*, the political magazine being started by John F. Kennedy Jr. I lept at the chance, and the article, "The War on Time Warner," a piece as much about Bob Dole running for president as it was about gansta rap, appeared in the issue with Cindy Crawford on the cover. It was during the writing of the *George* piece that I decided to focus my writing on politics.

Over the ensuing years, I did a number of articles for *George*. I wrote about attempts to get Colin Powell to join the Dole ticket in

1996. I wrote about NASA, the organization closely associated with John's father. The last piece I did for *George* was a profile of Georgette Mosbacher called "Little Red Georgette." When John saw Georgette Mosbacher at an event in Washington not long after the article appeared, he told her how proud he was of the piece and how happy he was to include it in his magazine. Later, once I found out about the exchange, I was pleased, since by the time I learned of the remark, John had died. I was delighted to know the last piece I wrote for his magazine was one he admired.

In the meantime, I had also started writing for *Rolling Stone*. My piece on George W. Bush that appeared in the summer of 1999— "All Hat, No Cattle"—is still the longest magazine article to be published on him to date. Afterward, I went on to write about other politicians, among them John Kerry, James Jeffords, and, as it happened, John McCain.

I first encountered John McCain on the campaign trail in 2000, when he was running for president. In the fall of 1999, I remember watching on C-SPAN as he conducted in New Hampshire one of the town hall meetings for which he would become famous. On this outing, he was talking about returning the government to the people, and I flashed back to all of the speeches I had heard by the populist Southern politicians—those yellow-dog Democrats—with whom I had grown up. He was not talking about a Republicanism I had come to understand, one where the bottom line always has to do with corporate America. He was preaching old-time, grass-roots populism, and his audience was loving it. When I got to see him on the trail up close—from New England to New York to South Carolina—I witnessed firsthand how he connected with his audience. He was not your run-of-the-mill politician. He was a true believer who wanted to change the very way Washington had come to function. He was a visionary. He was dangerous. His followers adored him.

Throughout the fall and the winter of the presidential race, the number of McCainiacs grew tremendously. In New Hampshire,

McCain went from tracking in the five percent range in the polls to winning the Republican primary by a landslide. At the same time, he created just as many enemies as he did supporters; specifically, he became a threat to the hardline establishment of the Republican Party. That was why, in a phrase, he had to be taken out. And he *was* taken out in the Republican primary in South Carolina, in one of the most brilliant, effective, and ugly political assassinations ever seen in American politics. It was at this point that McCain's relationship with his party became even more tenuous than it had been before. He knew what had happened to him. He had ceased to be a party maverick and had become a threat who had to be crushed. He was.

When I sat down to interview him one-on-one in the spring of 2001 for *Rolling Stone*, after the man who had vanquished him, George W. Bush, had become president, McCain was still bitter, though he was careful to deal with his emotions the way he often does with details in a life that has been full of tragedy—with humor. He relished the chance to tell me the story of how he and Cindy had gone to the White House to have dinner with George and Laura Bush—and the two food tasters. The joke, which he told over and over in the spring of 2001, was funny, but telling. Regardless of what they said, regardless of the fact that McCain even campaigned for Bush in the general election, McCain and Bush didn't like each other. Period.

The animosity was still there later in 2001 when I talked with McCain, in September. We spoke so long during this meeting, which became the basis for "The *Rolling Stone* Interview with John McCain" that was published in late August, that the rough draft of the interview was 22,000 words. Over and over in our conversation, McCain's unhappiness with the Bush Administration and its policies came through. During the fall of 2000 and throughout 2001, I had also interviewed McCain for the radio show I co-host with John Batchelor, *Batchelor & Alexander*. Each time I asked McCain about his relationship with his party, he gave me the same answer: He was happy to be a Republican. This seemed odd when so much of his political rhetoric indicated he was *not* happy with his party. Finally, in the fall of 2001, I asked one of his longtime political advisers what I thought was a flip question: "How long is the Senator going to tell me that he cannot envision a way to leave the Republican Party?" His adviser answered, "Until he tells you he *can* envision a way to leave the Republican Party."

That's where we are today. I entitled this book *Man of the People* because, even though he arrived in Washington in 1983 a Reaganite, McCain has evolved over his 20-year political career into the one current politician who best articulates the hopes and dreams of the common man, the citizen out there in Kansas or Oklahoma or Alabama who wants to see a return to populism in America. That he is an authentic American hero because of his service in Vietnam, though he himself will never admit he is, only underscores the authority he has to say what he does. If my grandmother were alive today, residing as she did in Cordova, Alabama, she would have a framed photograph of John McCain hanging on her living room wall.

PAUL ALEXANDER

New York, New York
August 2002

ACKNOWLEDGMENTS

For their help in the preparation of this book, I would like to thank Congressman Gary Ackerman, Everett Alvarez, Tom Arrasmith, Mike Briggs, Joyce Campbell, Senator Thad Cochran, Karen Cook, Eugene Corey (of *Brave New Words*), Craig Crawford, Monica Crowley, Ben Davol, Beth Day, Colonel George ("Bud") Day, Patricia Duff, Senator John Edwards, Congressman Eliot Engel, Kevin Fogerty, Frank Gaffney, Paul Galanti, Robert Giuffra, Jonathan Goldberg, Jordon Goldis, Betsy Gotbaum, Mike Guy, Gordon Hamel, Senator Gary Hart, Ann Hassinger (of the United States Naval Institute), Edward W. Hayes, Susie Gilder Hayes, William Haynes, George Hiltzik, Charles Hooff, Arianna Huffington, Richard Johnson, Senator John Kerry, Congressman Peter King, Arthur Klebanoff, Katie Levinson, Carolyn Licht, Beverly Lyall (of the Department of the Navy), Malcolm Matheson, Linda Mellon, Maggie Melson (of the Episcopal High School), Gary Meltz, Tim Meyer, Georgette Mosbacher, Meredith Mosley, Captain Chuck Nash, James Ortenzio, Phil Pulizzi, Governor Ann Richards, Cindy Rinfret, Peter Rinfret, Ken Ringle, Steve Sadicario, Richard Sementa, Congressman Christopher Shays, Richard Shepard, George Shipley, Senator Alan Simpson, Carl Smith, Erik Smulson, Kalman Sporn, Michael Steinhardt, Admiral James Stockdale, Roger Stone, Gene Suhir, Orson Swindle, Harry Thomas, Dick Thomsen, Rip Torn, Amanda Vaill, General Paul Vallely, Jack Van Loan, Michael Vlahos, David Wade, Senator John Warner, John Weaver, Bill White, Daniel White, Robert Whittle, Angie Williams, Carl Wilson, Robert W. Wilson, David Winters, and Patrick Woodson. I was also helped enormously by Mark Juszczak, to whom I am grateful.

This book grew out of the pieces I did on McCain for *Rolling Stone*, a magazine for which I have happily written now for several years. Besides Senator McCain and his wife Cindy, I thank Rebecca Hanks, Nancy Ives, Mark Salter, Mark McKennon, Lawrence Pike, James Pinkerton, Ed Rollins, Greg Stevens, Roger Stone, and John Weaver for information that contributed to those pieces. I was also helped in the writing of this book by an article I did for the magazine about Senator James Jeffords titled "The Reluctant Revolutionary." For that piece, I would like to thank Senator Jeffords, Senator Lincoln Chafee, Senator Patrick Leahy, Susan Russ, Erik Smulson, and Bill Richardson. At *Rolling Stone*, I have had the good fortune to work with Jann Wenner, Robert Love, Will Dana, and Erika Fortgang Casriel.

I would never have written *Man of the People* if not for Pamela van Giessen of John Wiley & Sons. During a telephone conversation one day, she asked me to name a person who deserved a biography. When I answered "John McCain," she signed me up on the spot.

I would also like to acknowledge John McConnell and Timothy McCarthy at the ABC Radio Network and Thomas Henriksen, Henry I. Miller, and Abraham Sofaer at the Hoover Institution at Stanford University.

I could not have written this book without the friendship and support of two people—Iris Rossi and John Batchelor.

P. A.

CONTENTS

PROLOGUE

Just before eight o'clock on the morning of March 27, 2002, President George W. Bush sat at his desk in the Oval Office and did something he didn't want to do. He signed into law campaign finance reform legislation. For years, the legislation had been so hotly debated—in Congress, the media, and the political world in general—that it had been given abbreviations. It was called "CFR" or, just as often, "McCain-Feingold," the name of the Senate version of the bill. "McCain," of course, was John McCain, the Arizona senator who had made CFR the cornerstone of his presidential campaign in 2000. In that campaign, he and Bush had clashed over CFR. McCain believed that significant campaign finance reform was needed to hold in check the special-interest groups that increasingly controlled Washington. McCain-Feingold bans "soft" money—unlimited contributions by corporations to politicians and political parties—and represents the most sweeping reform of the political system since the changes brought about by the Watergate scandal in the mid-1970s. Bush believed, as did groups on both the right and the left of the political spectrum, that the First Amendment protected an entity's right to give money to a politician or a political party. In the wake of the Enron debacle, the Senate and the House of Representatives had passed CFR—the House had passed it twice during the late 1990s—so Bush was in an odd position. He could either veto the bill—and appear to be insensitive to the issue of corporate corruption—or sign a bill he didn't like. After weighing the pros and cons, he signed the bill, which would become effective on November 6, 2002.

The signing was done with as little pomp and circumstance as possible. Normally, when signing a noteworthy law, the president invites the principal sponsors of the bill in the House and the Senate, hordes of appropriate onlookers, and, naturally, the media to the White House. The president uses numerous pens when signing a law, and each of the bill's cosponsors receives a pen as a keepsake of the momentous day. With CFR, Bush did none of this. In the quiet of the Oval Office—before most reporters were awake, much less at the White House—Bush simply signed his name to the bill. His audience was tiny: Vice President Dick Cheney and Condoleezza Rice, Bush's close friend and national security adviser. To make clear his opposition to the legislation—he believed it would be deemed unconstitutional by the Supreme Court—Bush left the White House, boarded Air Force One, and flew first to South Carolina and then to Georgia to attend fund-raisers for two Senate candidates. He spent the day raising the very soft money he had just banned.

The White House announced the signing of the bill by releasing a written statement. The public was told that even though parts of the bill "present serious constitutional concerns," making it "far from perfect," the legislation "will improve the current financing system for federal campaigns," which was why Bush signed it. At his daily press briefing, Ari Fleischer, the spokesperson for the White House, fielded questions about the legislation and why Bush signed it in an almost clandestine way. "The ceremony the White House chose," Fleischer said, "is reflective of the president's thoughts on the legislation. It would be inconsistent to have a Rose Garden ceremony for a bill which on balance improves the system, but contains what the president views as several important flaws." Bush himself was coy about the bill. "I wouldn't have signed it if I was really unhappy with it," he told reporters later that day. When asked about his decision then to go out and raise soft money, which he had just banned (effective on the day after the midterm election), Bush said flatly, "I'm not going to lay down my arms. These Senate races are very important for me. I want the Republicans to take control of the Senate."

McCain learned that Bush had signed the legislation when a midlevel staffer at the White House called him at home and told him the bill had been signed. McCain knew immediately what this meant. By refusing to hold a ceremony at the White House, Bush was underscoring his feeling that the law was unworthy. By having a midlevel staffer call McCain at home to give him the news, Bush was sending McCain a message: *You* are unworthy of my respect. According to sources, McCain was furious at Bush for the way he handled the signing. The one-sentence statement McCain released through his office in Phoenix hinted at his anger: "I am pleased that President Bush signed campaign finance reform legislation into law." By the time he spoke to reporters that day, McCain had decided to handle Bush's snub with humor. "He didn't promise me a rose garden," McCain quipped.

The events on the morning of March 27 serve as a glimpse onto Washington's ugliest political battle: the feud between McCain and Bush. The animosity between them grew out of the 2000 presidential race, when McCain dared to challenge his party's chosen candidate, Governor George W. Bush of Texas, the son of a former president. When the insurgent candidate McCain upset the frontrunner Bush in a landslide victory in the New Hampshire primary, the full force of the Republican Party was brought to bear on McCain to knock him out of the race. The awfulness of that assault profoundly affected McCain. In the early days of the Bush presidency—and even more so as the months passed—McCain went out of his way in Congress to challenge Bush and the legislation the president wanted. He was often successful.

McCain and his fight to pass campaign finance reform grew to be so important that venerable Washington journalist Elizabeth Drew wrote a book, *Citizen McCain*, about the struggle. Bush—and, presumably, the Republican Party—purposefully insulted McCain when his CFR bill was signed into law. This was just the latest round in a war that had been raging since late 1999 and had often been personal. "Here's the question," says one Washington insider. "Just how will the feud end? After all, neither of them is going away." That's true. One is president of the United States. The other is the person most feared—and for good reason—by that president's men. If McCain were to run for president as a Republican in the primaries in 2004, he could damage Bush's candidacy beyond repair, much as Ted Kennedy destroyed a sitting president, Jimmy Carter, in 1980. If McCain were to run as a Democrat (or even as an Independent), he could win.

1

ADMIRAL McCAIN

On September 5, 1945, during a peaceful and beautiful evening in the San Diego area, Vice Admiral John Sidney McCain settled into his home in Coronado, California. His wiry frame had become dangerously slim—he weighed just over 100 pounds—and his face was weather-beaten from his years at sea. McCain, nicknamed "Slew" by his fellow officers and "Popeye" by the sailors he commanded, was exhausted. Dragged down by a cold, he may have also suffered an undetected heart attack within the previous few months. The summer, which had finally brought the end of World War II, had been especially hard on him. He had commanded the Second Carrier Task Force, Pacific Fleet, since August 1944. In the final year of the war, operating in conjunction with the Third Fleet under the command of Admiral William F. Halsey, McCain's Task Force 38 "spearheaded the drive in the Philippines," to quote from his official naval biography, "supported the capture of Okinawa, and rode rampant through the Western Pacific from the Indo-China Coast to the Japanese home island. The force knew only one word—'Attack!'"

Task Force 38's motto certainly fit its commander. Slew McCain was gruff, hard-edged, quick-tempered, frequently profane, sometimes suspicious, always hardworking, and prone to sullenness. He also liked to slam down bourbon, play the horses, shoot craps, and roll his own Bull Durham cigarettes. He was unwaveringly patriotic, stubbornly ambitious, and brilliant. Most important, he was a leader. In the last six months of the war in the Pacific, McCain's Task Force 38 was cited for damaging or destroying 6,000 Japanese airplanes and either sinking or damaging an estimated 2,000,000 tons of Japanese warships. The task force's airplanes once sank 49 Japanese ships in a single day. Between July 10 and August 14, 1945, McCain's planes destroyed some 3,000 grounded Japanese planes. All in all, McCain's accomplishments were nothing short of phenomenal.

Indeed, Slew McCain, with his trademark ill-fitting sailor cap (hence the Popeye reference), had established a reputation that would become nearly mythic in naval lore. The legend centered around one fact: McCain was a fighter. He refused to back off—ever. Regarding the Japanese, he once proposed "killing them all—painfully." Even after the Allied forces had won the war, McCain was ready to keep going. At the signing of the peace accords on the battleship *Missouri* in Tokyo Bay on September 2, 1945—a ceremony that Halsey insisted McCain had to attend, even though he was sick and anxious to go home—McCain glared at the deck, unable to bring himself even to look at his just-defeated enemy. "The Jap warlords are not half licked yet," he said after the ceremony, a comment that made headlines. "They're going to take a lot more killing in the future. I don't like the look in their eyes."

That same day, he also made his point with authentic "McCain" humor. "He went from group to group [on the *Missouri*]," one newspaper reported, "greeting old acquaintances, and announced he was at work on the concoction of three new drinks, the 'Judy,' the 'Grill,' and the 'Zeke,' each named after a Japanese plane. 'Each time you drink one you can say, "Splash one Judy" or "Splash one Zeke,"' he explained." His colorful commentary on the enemy was not new. During an earlier radio appearance, the interviewer asked him what should be done about a particular Japanese island that had not yet been attacked by the Allied forces. "Oh, let the little"—McCain mumbled what was surely an expletive—"stay there," he quipped. "They're the type that eat themselves."

The last year of the war had not been without tragedy for McCain. Besides fighting a formidable enemy in the Japanese, McCain and Halsey had to contend with the horrendous forces of nature and their profound effects on both admirals' careers. On December 17, 1944, Halsey and McCain's fleet of ships was hit by a typhoon. In the lead ship, Halsey—tired, and focused on fighting the Japanese, not the weather—had failed to anticipate the approaching storm. He was also given insufficient warning about meteorological conditions by the central command in Pearl Harbor. The result was catastrophic. The overwhelming waves capsized and sank three destroyers—the *Hull*, the *Spence*, and the *Monahan*—and damaged six other ships, killing 778 men in all. As more and more equipment—guns, radar facilities, and the like—had been added to the ships during the war, they had become top-heavy and were at risk in a powerful storm. In addition, 146 airplanes were destroyed when they were swept overboard.

Later in December, at a board of inquiry held in Hawaii, Halsey defended his decisions. Admiral Chester Nimitz, one of the navy's power brokers, personally lobbied Secretary of the Navy James Forrestal to keep him from relieving Halsey of his command. It is believed that it took no less than Chief of Naval Operations Ernest King to prevent the board of inquiry from trying to make McCain the fall guy. With the war in the Pacific going so well, it made no sense, it was argued, to remove either Halsey or McCain from their commands. They were, after all, two main reasons for the navy's success.

Recommendations Halsey made as a result of the disaster were obvious enough. The navy, he said, should take steps to improve its weather-tracking methods; it should also beef up its communications links to Pearl Harbor. The navy failed to act on either recommendation. Six months later, on June 2, 1945, when Halsey and McCain again found themselves in severe weather conditions, they were unprepared for the second typhoon that hit their fleet. The storm damaged 33 ships, destroyed 76 airplanes, and killed six men. More questions were asked but the navy still took no action against Halsey or McCain. However, it was decided that McCain should come in from the sea and take a job in Washington—specifically, he was to become an assistant to General Omar Bradley in the Bureau of Veterans' Affairs—but the war ended before his orders were activated. McCain witnessed the historic surrender ceremony on the deck of the *Missouri* in Tokyo Bay. Then he began a well-deserved leave at his home in California.

He was born on August 9, 1884—not quite two full decades after the end of the Civil War—in Teoc, Mississippi, a tiny town in rural Carroll County. The son of John Sidney and Elizabeth-Ann Young McCain, he grew up on a plantation. The McCains of this era even owned slaves, as reporters would later reveal. McCain attended high school in Carrollton, then matriculated at the University of Mississippi. After his freshman year, he entered the United States Naval Academy in Annapolis, Maryland, on September 25, 1902. When he graduated on February 12, 1906, *The Lucky Bag*, the academy's yearbook, listed his nicknames as "Mac," "Lentz," "Lintsey," and "Bucket Shop." His quotation of choice came from John Milton: "That power which erring men call chance." The yearbook described McCain this way: "The skeleton in the family closet of 1906. A living example of the beneficial course of physical training in the N.A. having gained 1⅝ ounces since he entered. A man of exemplary habits which make him very popular, his 'den' having been a favorite resort for 'all hands' ever since the days of plebe rough-houses. Laughs with an open-face movement that reminds one of the Luray Cane. Furnishes all kinds of innocent amusement for the children. A Mississippi watermelon who would make a good floor manager at a hop. Out for the class banner."

Social, fun-loving, and often mischievous, he was as big of spirit as he was slight of build. In 1909, Ensign McCain served on the battleship *Pennsylvania* and the cruiser *Washington*. On August 9 of that year, in Colorado Springs, Colorado, he married Katherine Daisy Vaulx, a beautiful and personable woman from Arkansas and a daughter of an Episcopalian minister. The couple had three children—Catherine Vaulx McCain, James Gordon McCain, and John Sidney McCain Jr., who was born on January 17, 1911, in Council Bluffs, Iowa. Slew McCain's son—nicknamed "Junior" and "Mac" but most often called "Jack"—was born in Council Bluffs because his father, during an extended tour of duty on the *San Diego*, was sailing around the southern tip of South America, and Katherine had traveled to Iowa to stay with a sister who had moved there.

In 1918, the year World War I ended, McCain was still stationed on the *San Diego*, which was performing escort duty in the Atlantic Ocean. Between 1918 and 1927, he served in various capacities on a number of other ships—among them, the *Maryland* and the *New Mexico*. He traveled constantly, often to far destinations, but when he was stateside, he usually worked in Washington at the Department of the Navy. His family, for the most part, was raised in Washington, not far from the Capitol. "My mother was the real parental control," Jack McCain would say later, "because my father was gone part of the time that I was growing up. When my father was home . . . he was there a big part of the time, too, but most of his time was spent down at the navy department."

Describing the pride he felt about his father, Jack was unequivocal. "My father," he would say, "was a great leader, first, and people loved him, and he knew how to lead. He also knew when the time came to be a strict disciplinarian, versus the time to be a more easygoing commanding officer. And he had an intense and keen sense of humor. My mother used to say about him that the blood of life flowed through his veins, he was so keenly interested in people. . . . [H]e was also, amongst other things, extraordinarily well read. Now, by that I mean as a boy he had read such things as Shakespeare and all the rest of these things that they try—or did at the time, anyway—to encourage young people to engage in. So this gave him an outstanding command of the English language, which will stand you in good stead, I can assure you, as time moves on. I don't have to tell you about the fact that he was a man of great moral and physical courage. The fact that he had the first carrier task force under Halsey bears witness to that."

In September 1927, as his father had before him, Jack McCain entered the Naval Academy, which was his goal "from the time that I was old enough to begin to realize there was such [a place]." He had attended, first, Central High School in Washington and, finally, Columbia Preparatory School, which featured a nine-month program that got boys ready for either West Point or Annapolis. Before he entered the academy, he spent two weeks with his father, who was the executive officer on the *New Mexico*, which was in the Bremerton Navy Yard for overhaul, as a "final and farewell gesture before I went into the Naval Academy." When he got to his father's alma mater, Jack, having just turned sixteen, discovered he was among the youngest students in his class—and one of the few to enter with a presidential appointment. "I went in there at the age of sixteen, and I weighed one hundred and five pounds," he would say, referring to another trait he shared with his father—a decidedly puny build. "I could hardly carry a Springfield rifle, which they used to drill us with extensively, and also particularly when it came time for cutter drill. Getting out there and holding an oar was another unique experience in my life. But the whole training system at the Naval Academy was good." Perhaps because he was so much smaller and physically weaker than his classmates, Jack seemed to go out of his way to break academy rules. He routinely got into scuffles and amassed a daunting number of demerits.

When he graduated on May 1, 1931, his yearbook citation avoided the behavior issue: "Mac was born with one weakness which he strives in vain to conquer: his liking for the fair sex. After each leave period he resorts to reading the philosophy of the ancients in order to calm his fluttering heart and always emerges after a short period of time with his old equilibrium. . . . 'An officer and a gentleman' is the title to which he pays absolute allegiance. Sooner could

Gibraltar be loosed from its base than could Mac be loosed from the principles which he has adopted to govern his actions. . . . Beneath his external shell of fun and good fellowship is a big heart which has easily enveloped his classmates."

Upon graduation, Jack sought advice from his father, who told him simply, "The only thing I say to you is to make a good job of it"— whatever he chose to do. Jack decided to pursue a naval career that focused on submarines. Beginning in June 1931, as his first post-academy assignment, Jack served on the *Oklahoma*. At its home port—Long Beach, California—he met Roberta Wright, a daughter of Archibald Wright, a rich and strong-willed oil wildcatter. Originally from Mississippi, Wright had retired from his business in Oklahoma and Texas and moved his family to Los Angeles for a better life.

Roberta and her twin sister Rowena, born on February 7, 1912, in Muskogee, Oklahoma, were their father's darlings. Each summer, the family escaped the heat in Oklahoma by coming to the West Coast. Los Angeles became their permanent home in 1924, the year Archie had retired so he could spend all of his time with his daughters. Roberta's mother, Myrtle, was horrified that one of her daughters would take up with a sailor, so when Jack and Roberta decided to marry, over the objections of Roberta's parents, the couple eloped to Tijuana, Mexico. They were married on January 21, 1933, at Caesar's Bar. "Not exactly in the bar," Roberta would later say. "It was really sort of upstairs." Naturally, as Rowena would put it, their mother "had a cat fit." But there was little she could do. Jack and Roberta went about their lives—they survived the Long Beach earthquake that occurred not long after their return from Mexico—and Jack tried to find humor in their lives whenever he could. "Asked once how he could tell his beautiful wife from her identical twin," the *Washington Post* would one day write, "[Jack McCain] replied . . . : 'That's their problem.'"

In July 1933, Jack reported to the Naval Submarine Base in Groton, Connecticut, to follow his interests and study submarines. At about the same time, Rowena married John Luther Maddox—who later founded an airline that eventually became part of TWA—and settled down in Los Angeles. In December, Jack graduated and took up his first of numerous submarine assignments.

In June 1935, Slew McCain, now age 51, decided to return to school and reported to the Naval Air Station in Pensacola, Florida, to study flight training and aviation. On August 19, 1936, having been designated a naval aviator, Slew was appointed Commander of Aircraft Squadrons and Attending Craft at the Coco Solo Air Base in the Panama Canal Zone. Jack happened to be stationed there; he and Roberta were awaiting their first child. Ten days into Slew's new command, Roberta entered a navy hospital. On August 29, she gave birth to a son. In keeping with the McCain family tradition, he was named John Sidney McCain III. Jack's son, too, would be given a nickname, just as Jack and Slew had been before him. This John Sidney McCain would be known as "Johnny."

Slew McCain remained at Coco Solo until May 1937. Next, he commanded the *Ranger* but then was named commander of the Naval Air Station in San Diego, California, a post he held from July 1939 until January 1941. (In 1939, Rowena's husband, John Maddox, died; years later, she married an investment counselor.) When Slew assumed the command of Aircraft Scouting Training on January 23, 1941, he was promoted to rear admiral. During these years, Jack was advancing in his assignments as well. He taught in the Department of Electrical Engineering at the Naval Academy from June 1938 to May 1940. Then he served on the submarine *Shipjack* until, in April 1941, he was made commanding officer of the *USS O-8*, which was being recommissioned in the Philadelphia Navy Yard. While he held this post, Jack's family—which now included another son, Joseph, and a daughter, Jean—lived in New London, Connecticut, where the submarine command headquarters was located. Johnny was five years old when the Japanese attacked Pearl Harbor. When news of the attack came, Jack rushed to the base at once. His family rarely saw him for the next four years.

During World War II, Jack McCain tried his best to live up to his father's reputation. He commanded the submarine *Gunnel*, which was part of the naval armada involved in D-Day, and the submarine *Dentuda*, which was on patrol in the Pacific when the cease fire was announced on August 14, 1945. The first U.S. submarine had been designed and built by David Bushnell in 1776; the first contract submarine, known as the Plunger, appeared in 1896, with a steam engine for surface propulsion. By World War II, submarines were equipped with sonar and radar technologies. Still, submarines accounted for only approximately two percent of the entire U.S. fleet. Even so, submarines were vital for tactical purposes. As Admiral Chester W. Nimitz once put it, "We shall never forget that it was our submarines that held the lines against the enemy while our fleets replaced losses and repaired wounds." No one knew this better than Jack McCain.

As a submarine commander during the war—McCain was in charge of three subs altogether—he sank, according to one published report, "twenty thousand tons of Japanese shipping" and "once spent 72 hours on the ocean bottom, riding out a depth charge attack. 'It gives you a new outlook on life,' [McCain] said of the experience." For his service during the war, Jack McCain received the Silver Star Medal (for "conspicuous gallantry and intrepidity in action as Commanding Officer of a submarine in enemy Japanese-controlled waters . . . [in which he] succeeded in sinking an important amount of Japanese shipping, including a destroyer," the citation said) and the Bronze Star Medal with Combat "V" (for "sinking an enemy vessel of 4,000 tons and damaging two small crafts totaling 350 tons"). He was also awarded two Letters of Commendation.

As for Slew, he served, at the beginning of World War II, as Commander of Air Forces for the Western Sea Frontier and the South Pacific Force. He was named Chief of the Bureau of Aeronautics in October 1942, and, in August 1943, became a vice admiral in his capacity of Deputy Chief of Naval Operations (Air). While in Washington, he refused to use the intercom in his office, but kept his door open and shouted instructions to his secretary, as if he were barking orders to a subordinate on one of the ships he had commanded. Obviously, McCain much preferred sea duty to the Washington bureaucracy, so, in 1944, he returned to the Pacific Theater to command Task Force 38, which became infamous by the war's end. As Task Force 38's leader, he received the Navy Cross and Gold Stars in lieu of the Second and Third Distinguished Service Medals. The citation that accompanied the award reflected Slew McCain's lust for fighting: "[H]e devised techniques and procedures to locate and destroy grounded enemy planes, accounting for 3,000 planes smashed throughout his sustained attacks against Japan's home islands with only one of our destroyers damaged during the intensive operations between July 10 and August 15 [1945]. . . . He hurled the might of his aircraft against the remnants of the once-vaunted Japanese Navy to destroy or cripple every remaining major hostile ship by July 28 . . . [and] maintained a high standard of fighting efficiency in his gallant force while pressing home devastating attacks which shattered the enemy's last vital defensive hope."

The historic drama of the last months of the war in the Pacific— the relentless fighting, the around-the-clock anxiety, the never-ending presence of death—had taken a toll on Slew McCain. On September 5, 1945, his first day back home in California, he had greeted his wife Katherine and then gone to a navy doctor who had voiced concern about McCain's fragile health. But McCain didn't want to dwell on the negative. He wanted to look to the future, when he would be reporting once again for duty in Washington and would then submit to the Chief of Naval Operations, Admiral Ernest J. King, a white paper he and a friend, Admiral John Thach, had written. The landmark McCain-Thach report argued that navy air power should be used to support troop action in the coordinated air–ground effort that would become commonplace in the future. That first day, Slew spent much time with Katherine, whom he had badly missed during his long months away at sea. He especially enjoyed telling her about a lunch he had had with Jack on the submarine *Proteus* in Tokyo Bay just after the peace accords were signed. Although Slew could not have known it at the time, the meeting had left a lasting impression on his son.

Admiral Charles Lockwood gave the luncheon that both McCains attended on board the *Proteus*. "During the process of the luncheon," Jack would recall, "I got my father off to one side, and I said to him that I would like to talk to him alone in that little state-room they used to give commanding officers on submarine tenders when they had command of a submarine that was tied up alongside. And we went back there, and we talked for a little while. . . . And my father said to me at that time, he said, 'Son, there is no greater thing than to die for the principles—for the country and the principles that you believe in.' I considered myself very fortunate to have had a chance to see him at that particular moment."

On Slew's second day home, September 6, Katherine had arranged a welcome-home party for him. As he stood in a room packed with friends and naval personnel, Slew was the picture of the vaunted warrior having returned home from victory, but he did appear tired and subdued. Everyone there was thrilled the war was finally over—a spirit of thankfulness and optimism filled the room—and most people who noticed Slew's lack of energy chalked it up to the stress he had experienced during the preceding months. Then, as the party roared noisily around him, Slew approached his wife to tell her he didn't feel well; this said, he suddenly collapsed to the floor. A doctor attending the party rushed to his side but Slew was already dead. His heart had simply stopped beating. It was all too apparent that the war he had just finished fighting had killed him. At the time of his death, Slew McCain was 61 years old.

McCain's body was flown to Washington, D.C., with full honor guard. Secretary of the Navy James Forrestal had made jesting comments to the press before McCain's death. "Oh, I think John Sidney ought to stay out there and see the Japanese surrender," he had said in answer to McCain's desire to return stateside immediately after the end of the war, "[since he] certainly has it coming to him." When McCain died, Forrestal made a conscious effort to put McCain's naval career into perspective. "His conception of the aggressive use of fast carriers as the principal instrument for bringing about the quick reduction of Japanese defensive capabilities," Forrestal said, "was one of the basic forces in the evolution of naval strategy in the Pacific War."

On September 10, following a funeral service, McCain was buried in Arlington National Cemetery with full military honors. His first namesake, Jack, was a navy commander; his second namesake, Johnny, was nine years old. They stood in the grey haze of the cemetery and watched the proceedings in silence—the 21-gun salute, the presentation of the folded flag to the widow, the last rites given by the navy chaplain. In the immediate wake of McCain's death, which was deemed significant enough that President Truman sent condolences to the family and the *New York Times* ran his obituary on the front page, the United States Congress moved to recognize McCain's considerable achievements in World War II by posthumously awarding him a fourth star, a reward the navy, no doubt, would have bestowed on him had he lived.

The *Times* obituary, which had as its subhead "Commander of Task Force 38 Had Just Returned from Tokyo Bay Surrender," captured McCain's military achievements and their importance to the American victory in World War II. "Admiral McCain's groups were called the world's most powerful task force," it read, "and the destruction they wrought upon Japanese military installations and armament centers played a vital role in reducing [that] country's ability to fight and bringing about final victory. . . . In a single day in an attack upon Saigon, his air groups caught four convoys, sank forty-one ships and damaged twenty-eight others. Eight of the ships sunk were tankers. The score was 127,000 tons sunk, 70,000 tons damaged, a total of 197,000 tons, which he believed was the all-time record for a one-day strike by fleet carriers."

In the years after World War II, with the example of his father urging him on, Jack McCain continued to excel in the navy his father had loved so much. In November 1945, to take a break from the many months he had spent at sea during the war, Jack assumed the position of Director of Records for the Bureau of Naval Personnel in the Department of the Navy in Washington. "They brought me back and put me in charge of the records activity," Jack McCain would recall. "And there was something like one million enlisted men records, and I forget how many officer records, see. But there was a backlog of filing of papers into these records in the neighborhood of several million sheets. And when you get into several million of anything, you're getting into real problems of management. . . . I had a team up there of five hundred sailors, three or four hundred waves [women sailors]. . . . I must admit it's an interesting job because you read all sorts of strange things about people that you don't ordinarily get your hands on."

McCain held that post until January 1949. In those three years, he spent a good deal of time with his family in Washington. Then he was again ordered to go to sea, this time to command two different submarine divisions (Seventy-One for eleven months and Fifty-One for two months). In February 1950, he was made executive officer of the heavy cruiser *St. Paul* and held that post until November, when he was sent back to Washington to become the Director of the Undersea Warfare Research and Development Branch of the Office of the Deputy Chief of Naval Operations. In July 1951, he was named commander of the *Monrovia*.

By the 1950s, the McCain name had become famous in the navy, and revered in Mississippi. "We were all steeped in the tradition and history of the McCain legacy," Senator Thad Cochran of Mississippi recalls. "I trained as a naval reserve officer (NROTC) in McCain Hall at the University of Mississippi. That was where we would go to classes. I knew all about the family history. It was the first Admiral McCain who the building was named for at the University of Mississippi. We would also have a McCain Field, where the army national guard would train, not too far from the McCain homestead."

In the early 1950s, Jack's son Johnny was poised to enter the family business by first attending Slew's and Jack's alma mater—the Naval Academy. In four years, Jack McCain would earn the rank of admiral. Before his career ended, his promotion to four-star admiral made the McCains the only family in American history to have both a father and a son reach that rank. But that distinction came much later. In the summer of 1954, as he prepared to enter the Naval Academy, Johnny McCain already felt enormous pressure to live up to the remarkable accomplishments of his father and grandfather. The McCain legacy was not about mere success; it was about the devotion Slew and Jack—and other McCain family members—felt for the navy, the one organization that had given focus and meaning to their lives. Throughout his early years, it never occurred to Johnny McCain that he could choose *not* to go into the navy. He was, simply, born to be a sailor.

2

ANCHORS AWAY

If there was ever a military brat, it was Johnny McCain. He was born in a navy hospital in the Panama Canal Zone while his father was stationed there, but that was just the beginning of the long, odd childhood of a boy who grew up under the pressure of being the son and grandson of navy brass. From 1936 until 1946, Jack McCain held posts that took him from New London, Connecticut, to Pearl Harbor and the Pacific Ocean battle areas where he fought during World War II. He served on—or so it seemed—countless ships and submarines. With his father's active duty defined by such a rapid rate of reassignment, Johnny would barely get used to one home before his family would be uprooted and assigned to the next. His education was gained in whatever school happened to be on the base where his family was living at any given time. More than once he found himself in a "combined class" attended by students of varying ages. Routinely, naval-base schools did not have the facilities needed to achieve even the most basic education standards.

As a young boy, Johnny exhibited one behavior trait about which he would often comment as an adult—a hair-trigger temper that could be set off by even the slightest provocation. When he was a toddler and young child, it was not unusual for him to become so mad he would hold his breath until his brain was deprived of

oxygen and he passed out on the floor. As his body developed, another notable factor emerged. Although he was healthy, robust, and
athletic even at an early age, he was still slight of build, as were his
father and his grandfather. Johnny compensated for his lack of size
by exhibiting a determined and aggressive drive not merely to com-
pete but to conquer.

In the early years of his life, Johnny's parents made one decision
about which they would be unwavering: When Johnny grew up, he
would follow the family model and attend the Naval Academy and
would then enter the navy. Jack and Roberta used a subtle tactic to
make Johnny's future life known to him. Neither parent ever told
Johnny directly that he had been born with a life plan over which
he had little if any control. Instead, they simply talked about his
future as though the plot for it were a fait accompli. "You know,
Johnny is going to the Academy one day," Jack would say to a
friend. Or Roberta would simply state at a family gathering, "Naturally, Johnny is going to be a midshipman." They echoed the way
parents discuss plans for a child who will some day take over the
family business, as if that business were a law firm or bank. It never
occurred to Jack or Roberta to ask Johnny what *he* wanted to do
with his life.

The first demonstrative move Jack and Roberta made toward realizing their goal came in September 1946; they enrolled Johnny,
then 10 years old, in St. Stephen's School in Alexandria, Virginia.
When Jack had returned to Washington after the war, the family had
settled down in northern Virginia. To make Johnny ready academically for acceptance into the Naval Academy, an institution of higher
learning that required more than minor scholastic ability, Jack and
Roberta had to remove him from the inferior educational system
provided by the nation's naval bases. At the time, St. Stephen's was a
relatively new, up-and-coming private day school, but it was surely
an improvement over the schools Johnny had been attending.

Founded in 1944, only two years before Johnny arrived there,
St. Stephen's, located on Russell Road in Alexandria, originally had

just 97 students spread between the third and eighth grades. One of the church schools in the Diocese of Virginia, the all-boys institution was established by Reverend Edward E. Tate, who became the school's first headmaster. "St. Stephen's was in its formative years," says Charles Hooff, who was enrolled there at the school's beginning. "It wasn't much of a school, really. It was very small. But it was filling a void in the immediate postwar era." Malcolm Matheson, another early student of St. Stephen's, says of his alma mater: "If you were in Alexandria, it was the place to go." Of McCain, Matheson notes: "John was a little guy but tough. He came from his father and his grandfather."

At the end of the 1948–1949 school year, McCain left St. Stephen's so he could spend the next two years traveling with his family as his father held positions of command on submarines. Then, for the fall of 1951, with acceptance into the Naval Academy looming only three years away, Jack and Roberta decided to send Johnny to boarding school. They did not want him to have to rely on the influence of his legacy to get into the Academy; they hoped he would be accepted for his ability as a student and his potential as a midshipman. This time, taking into account both his emotional and intellectual developmental needs, Jack and Roberta chose for Johnny one of the most famous all-boys boarding schools in the South: the Episcopal High School in Alexandria, Virginia.

"Episcopal was one of the better prep schools in the South," says Dick Thomsen, Episcopal's principal from 1951 until 1967. "It was always ranked with the best schools in New England. The two Southern schools that stood out with Andover, Exeter, Groton, and so on, were Episcopal and Woodberry, the two rival schools in Virginia. Academically, Episcopal was good. Our students were very bright because the South was beginning to rise again . . . at least economically, and people there were looking for better schools. We were getting boys from major Southern centers like Charlotte, Charleston, and Atlanta, as well as leading cities in Virginia."

Jack and Roberta were enrolling Johnny in a school that empha-
sized his Southern heritage, which was traceable to his grandfather's
early years on a plantation in Mississippi. Episcopal was so completely associated with the South that, from Virginia to Louisiana, it
was often referred to simply as "The High School." Located just
across the Potomac River from Washington, on a sprawling campus
that featured rolling green lawns, Episcopal marked its beginning in
1839, the year when 35 boys attended school on an 80-acre piece of
land under the directorship of the Reverend William Nelson
Pendleton. Headmaster Pendleton stressed the school's religious
bearings and his own understanding of the true nature of boys of an
age he intended to educate when he wrote, "[W]e do not flatter ourselves that boys will cease to be boys and subside into lambs under
the broad wings of the Gospel."

Because it was the first high school in Virginia, Episcopal's student body expanded to 100 within a year. Only the Civil War could
stop its growth. In 1861, after Union troops occupied Alexandria,
the school shut down and served as an army hospital for Union soldiers during the next four years. When the school reopened in 1866,
a memorial was constructed in Pendleton Hall to commemorate the
68 Episcopal alumni who had been killed fighting for the Confederate cause during the war. With Launcelot Minor Blackford serving as
principal—he held the post from 1870 until 1913—the school became a formidable educational institution. Early in Blackford's
tenure, Episcopal adopted an honor code that became synonymous
with the school itself. The code was deceptively simple. In theory,
however, it spoke for each Episcopal student by stating: "I will not
lie. I will not cheat. I will not steal. I will report the student who
does so."

When McCain arrived at Episcopal in the fall of 1951, he found
a place steeped in heritage and traditions that demanded rigid adherence to social and cultural codes, as exemplified by the honor
code. By then, the 275 boys who comprised the student body lived
on a campus that had grown to 130 acres to accommodate large

athletic facilities, especially playing fields for football, baseball, and track. The boys spent a good deal of their time on sports; in fact, a student's day could be divided into two parts. The morning and early afternoon were taken up with rigorous academic pursuits; each boy was required to select a college-preparatory core curriculum plus electives. From mid-afternoon on, the students retired to the sports fields for mandatory athletics. The weekly schedule, which ran from Tuesday to Saturday—Sunday and Monday were off days—was intense, by calculation.

"In a word, it was brutal," says Charles Hooff, who, like McCain, had moved from St. Stephen's to Episcopal. "You were allowed off the campus only three weekends a year. You could leave the campus one Monday a month. We went to school on Saturday and were off on Monday because Sunday was a pious day and they didn't want you studying on Sunday. If there were Monday classes, you'd be studying Sunday night. You had mandatory chapel every morning and mandatory church on Sunday. On Saturday night, you could go down to Fairlington [a neighborhood in Alexandria]—they had a movie theater there. You could go after dinner but you had to be back by a certain hour. And they checked you many times a day to make sure you were on campus. You might as well have been on Parris Island.

"The school was built on the old tradition of hazing. There weren't a lot of masters—30 at the most. The school was really run by the monitors and the seniors. They handed out all of the discipline, and it was swift and severe. They wouldn't physically abuse you; they would mentally abuse you. Now, occasionally they might work you over, but the hazing and punishment were mostly verbal. I mean, you were 14 and they were 18. They intimidated you. It was the seniors going after the freshmen. Some kids absolutely collapsed under the pressure. There was a real requirement to conform. John McCain had a problem with this at first, but then he grew into being a leader in that area, when he was a senior."

In this constricting environment, each boy also dealt with living conditions that were less than luxurious. A contemporary of

McCain, Ken Ringle, later wrote: "We lived in curtained alcoves like hyperglandular adolescent monks; slept in sagging pipeframe beds; drank milk drawn from some dairy where, it seemed, the cows grazed on nothing but onions; and amused ourselves at meals by covertly flipping butter pats with knives onto the ceiling, where they would later melt free to drop on other, unsuspecting skulls." Ringle and McCain lived in the same building. "It had been used by the Union during the war and hadn't been renovated since then," Ringle says. "There were cockroaches in there. One day, they swarmed in, and you couldn't see the floor. The curtained alcoves we slept in were like the pictures you see of hospitals in the Civil War."

Almost from the start of his first year there, McCain had trouble fitting into Episcopal's environment. More a navy brat than a "good old boy," he found it easier to embrace his family's military background than its Southern heritage. He had spent significantly more time on naval bases than on his family's homestead in Mississippi, so he looked on the customs and traits of the vast majority of Episcopal's student body, full of echoes of the mores of the Old South, as strange and anachronistic. Besides, McCain, intense and edgy, stood in stark contrast to the average Episcopal boy, who tended to be mannerly and genteel. As a sophomore, he didn't like the seniors bossing him around. Indeed, in his first year at Episcopal, he did more than his share of rebelling against both the school's traditions and the practice of intimidation against the freshmen (and any sophomores experiencing their first year at Episcopal). The new comers were called "rats" and the intimidation was carried out daily by the seniors. McCain did excel in wrestling; in his first year at the school, he accomplished what few others were able to achieve: He lettered in the sport. He was also voted "freshest rat."

Before long, the brash and in-your-face McCain had earned the nickname "Punk." He seemed to go out of his way to underscore that characterization by wearing a funky-looking overcoat and smoking cigarettes. This was McCain's idea of being a punk: Clad in blue jeans, motorcycle boots, and his overcoat, and smoking a cigarette that dangled from his lips, he'd sneak into Ninth Street in Washington, go to Waxy Maxy, and buy the latest record by Elvis Presley or Stick McGee. Or, if he was feeling lucky, he'd slip into a bar and try to buy a beer. "There was illegal smoking at Episcopal and the one way to do the illegal smoking was to sneak off to the woods," Ringle recalls. "His coat was a sign that he was always skipping off, because in the winter it was cold out there. McCain also skipped off into Washington where he would go to places and drink occasionally. Not drinking, really; just grab a beer. Beer was a forbidden thrill. At that time Washington had a lot of good jazz places." So when McCain was not picking up records at Waxy Maxy, he was grooving at a jazz club like The Little Mirror where, for him, getting served was a big deal.

"As headmaster, I actually saw very little of him," Dick Thomsen says, "because I mostly dealt with cases that needed special attention. While he was not what you'd call a happy camper, in the sense that he was not devoid of problems, he was never so bad he came to me as a student to deal with. My impression of him was: I knew he walked around with his jacket and tie all messed up. The tie would be at half-mast and the jacket collar turned up. He'd have this sort of surly look on his face, that 'Don't tread on me' type of expression. He traveled with a gang that was, I guess you could say, dissidents. He may have broken every rule in the book but he got away with most of them. On the other hand, he wasn't a bad student. Not outstanding; a good student. He was small but a good athlete. He was an excellent wrestler—a tough competitor on the wrestling mat. He won a number of matches."

During his junior year, he was voted runner-up to "Sloppiest," and in his senior year, he got runner-up to "Thinks he's hardest." He certainly cut a "hard" image. One way he did this was to show off in his job as waiter. "That was another subculture, being a waiter," Ringle says. "We got paid a little something for it. It was kind of a macho thing. Every waiter waited on two tables. Each table had 14 people. You brought out platters and plates. At the end of the meal, the rats who sat in the middle of the table had to scrape the plates, and then the waiters took them off. They carried them out to the kitchen on this oval aluminum tray they balanced on their shoulder. If you were a waiter, one of the big deals was if you could balance the tray and go out kind of swinging it a little bit, with a swagger. If you were strong, you could lift this thing off your shoulder—28 of these plates and all of the silverware. On Sundays, we had salad too. So we had what you called 28 and 28. And if you were strong enough to lift—to press—28 and 28, you were a heavy mother. I think McCain could get 28 and 28 up, even though he was a fairly small guy. He may have been small but he was very muscular." There were other details about McCain too. He slept in his underwear and made his rat—Ken Ringle—wake him up at the very last moment before he had to be at breakfast.

By his senior year, McCain had gotten in line enough to collect his share of achievements. He lettered a second time in wrestling, starred on the junior varsity football team, played on the tennis team, and participated in the Dramatic Club and the E-Club. He served on the staffs of the school newspaper, The Chronicle, and the yearbook, Whispers. He spent time on athletic and extracurricular activities, but McCain was able to maintain an academic performance good enough to position himself for acceptance into the Naval Academy—a goal he had to achieve because that's what his family wanted him to do. During his three years at Episcopal, whenever he was not racking up demerits for his often bad behavior or the general sloppiness of both his appearance and his dormitory room, McCain made a concerted effort to sneak off campus whenever he could—and not just to Ninth Street in Washington. This was an especially egregious act since the rules about leaving campus were clear and unnegotiable. Still, if McCain saw the opportunity to leave, off he would go.

"They called my uncle, for whom I am named, 'Herr Whittle' because he taught German," Robert Whittle says. "He was Mr. Chips. He was a bachelor teacher who taught at Episcopal for over 50 years. He also taught Latin. Anyway, once John McCain was off campus bending the rules. He was in Fairlington visiting a girlfriend when Herr Whittle and a colleague happened to walk by and spy him. Needless to say, he hightailed it back to school. That passed for scandal in 1954—sitting on the front porch sipping lemonade with a girl when you're not supposed to be off the grounds."

With his youthful, handsome face; his taut, muscular body; his aggressive, hard-charging ways, McCain had more than ample appeal to teenage girls; he was, in a word, a stud. So it was not surprising that McCain would want to see whatever girlfriend he happened to have at the moment. It was incumbent on faculty members like Robert Whittle to monitor students like McCain. Indeed, at Episcopal, McCain had a handful of masters he would remember as being influential. Although he was brash, McCain, because of his age, was still readily impressionable. Years later, he would single out one master who played a meaningful part in shaping his character: William B. Ravenel, who devoted his life and career to teaching young men. The effort Ravenel expended on McCain was profound: He tried to make McCain become a better person.

"William Ravenel was a leader of men," Robert Whittle recalls. "Mostly, he used a sense of humor instead of force. He was a guy you knew was smarter than you and funnier than you. He used both traits to move you along. He coached football and taught English. Specifically, he had a wry sense of humor. He understood what you were going through as a 16- or 17-year-old, and he turned it around and used it on you. You were very cynical, if you were at a boarding school. And he let you know he was more cynical than you were. He used that positively. He was, simply, a wonderful English teacher. Fundamentals were very important to him. *The Gray Gospel* was a nickname for a book he wrote on punctuation and grammar; the book was actually named *ERB* [short for *English Reference Book*] but it was gray in color—hence the nickname. If you wanted to know where to put a comma or how to use parentheses, he was your man."

In the end, Ravenel was one of the main reasons why McCain matured as much as he did at Episcopal. Ultimately, McCain left the school more seasoned than the 15-year-old who had arrived there, but he was still full of the fire and contentiousness he would have with him for the rest of his life. McCain's citation in his school yearbook would attest to that fact. Underneath his senior portrait, McCain, whose home address was listed as 540 New Hampshire Avenue in Norfolk, Virginia, was described as follows: "It was three fateful years ago that 'Punk' first crossed the threshold of the High School. In this time he has become infamous as one of our top-flight wrestlers, lettering for two seasons. His magnetic personality has won for him many lifelong friends. But, as magnets must also repel, some have found him hard to get along with. John is remarkable for the amount of grey hair he has; this may come from his cramming for Annapolis or from his nocturnal perambulations on Ninth Street. The Naval Academy is his future abode—we hope he will prosper there."

As it happened, McCain *did* prosper there, almost from the start—or so it appeared. "Following his first summer at the Naval Academy," Dick Thomsen remembers, "John came back to the Episcopal campus during the opening days of school. He was dressed in his midshipman uniform and looking absolutely spit-and-polished. Everything was in order—necktie up, the very model of the modern midshipman." That day, McCain sought out Thomsen with a purpose. "Sir," McCain said to his former principal, "I know I gave you a lot of trouble while I was here at the school, and I'm sorry for that. But some of my buddies from last year are still here and I wonder if you'd like me to talk to them and try to get them to have a little bit better senior year than they might have otherwise."

Thomsen was thrilled. "John," he said, "I'd be delighted for all the help I can get. So be sure to talk to them and see if you can give them a straight year ahead."

McCain did. He sought out his old classmates—his fellow punks, as it were—and he talked to them man-to-man. Impressed,

Thomsen thought to himself, "Boy, can the Naval Academy really straighten a young man out!"

Eventually, Thomsen got the real story. "About a year or so later," Thomsen recalls, "I learned McCain was one of the greatest hell raisers the Naval Academy ever had. He was always about one or two demerits removed from dismissal from the Academy."

M cCain entered the Naval Academy in Annapolis, Maryland, when he was 17 years old. Right from the start, he displayed a bad attitude. "I was basically told when I was young," McCain says, "that I was going to the Naval Academy. And that caused resentment in me—and obviously affected some of my wild behavior. Or *caused* some of my wild behavior." He had been rambunctious at Episcopal. "I would fight at the drop of a hat" because "I was very defensive of my individuality—much too much so." That behavior didn't let up at the Academy. During his years there, his conduct earned him so many demerits that, as the *Los Angeles Times* later reported, "by the end of his sophomore year he had marched enough extra duty to go from Annapolis to Baltimore and back 17 times."

He certainly couldn't have been unhappy with his surroundings. The Naval Academy, laid out handsomely in the quaint town of Annapolis, looks as if it has come alive from a picture postcard. The campus is known as "The Yard." Its French Renaissance influence creates a charming, almost European feel. The green lawns blend flawlessly with the Academy's many buildings and related facilities. Walking across the campus is a pleasant and peaceful experience for visitors, but it offers the midshipmen only an atmosphere that is in sharp contrast to the tension and anxiety caused by the school's academics and traditions. For McCain, all of the nervousness, tumult, and anger he felt did not necessarily come from an outside influence. It came from within.

"He had a little bit of internal conflict," Frank Gamboa, one of his Naval Academy roommates, would say later. "His legacy weighed heavy on him. I was there because I wanted to be there. He was there because it was the family business. He felt he didn't have a choice. He was very proud of his father and of the navy—and he felt comfortable—but at the same time his lack of freedom, of choosing his own way, bothered him." Another roommate, Jack Dittrick, saw a troubled but mature young man. Even though he dressed shoddily, left his room a wreck, and had a generally bad disposition a good part of the time, McCain knew what he was doing. He was hardheaded but aware of his hardheadedness. "He just wouldn't back down," Dittrick recalled. "He was very mature. He had been around the world . . . and he seemed to understand everything about the United States Navy."

In his first year—"Plebe Year"—at the Academy, McCain often engaged in insubordinate behavior, such as the time he and other plebes gathered in his room and, wearing only their underwear, had a water-balloon fight. He also found a way to keep a contraband television set hidden in his room. But these were nothing compared to the rituals of Plebe Year with which McCain had to deal—the traditions that had been firmly established at the school through the years. "The plebe will be barked at, shouted at, forced to memorize and recite at all times," John Karaagac, an authority on military matters, later wrote. "He will be ordered to stand in that demeaning and exaggerated attention known as 'the brace.' His first year will comprise an extended test of memory and endurance, of conspicuous obedience to the thousands of wearisome chores and indignities that make up the hazing process. His superiors will judge who can take the abuse and who cannot, who reacts well under pressure and who breaks. . . . The plebe will grow accustomed to the timetable, punctuated by bells, that dominates his whole existence; he will grow accustomed to drill and marching and quickly eating in the cavernous mess hall; he will, by degrees, accommodate himself to the constant inspection of room and uniform—aggressive, probing, minute inspection. Above all, he will learn the reality of sleep deprivation and come to dread the shrieking alarm raising him from his sweet slumber at half past six on cold, cruel, and dark mornings."

McCain survived Plebe Year and went on to make his way through his sophomore and junior years. He consistently struggled academically, but somehow got by; he excelled in sports and became a standout in boxing. When he sailed off on his first-class cruise in June 1957, he was looking forward to his senior year. One highlight of the cruise was a nine-day stay in Rio de Janeiro. McCain and some of his friends rented an apartment there. "The next four days," one journalist later wrote, "were a blur, involving liquor, women, and nightclubs, everything except sleep, as Rio embraced McCain and his pals in its many charms, X-rated and otherwise." Then, through an invitation from a fashion designer, McCain met a Brazilian model and spent five days escorting her to various Rio social events.

When he returned to Annapolis for his senior year, McCain was looking to the future. He would do what his grandfather and father had both done—join the navy with the intention of being a "lifer." At Christmas break, he spent four days with the fashion model in Rio. Then he returned to the Academy for his final semester, which proceeded like those before it. When McCain's graduation was imminent, he discovered that, of the 894 midshipmen graduating, he was fifth from the bottom. Nevertheless, he proudly attended his graduation exercises—held on the Yard, under a beautifully clear sky, on June 4, 1958—and received his bachelor of science degree. The audience listened carefully as President Dwight D. Eisenhower delivered the commencement address.

McCain's yearbook citation was telling: "John, better known as Navy's John Wayne, was always reputed to be one of our most colorful characters. Following his family forbears to our sacred shores, he thought the Navy way was the only way. A sturdy conversationalist and party man, John's quick wit and clever sarcasm made him a welcome man at any gathering. His bouts with the Academic and Executive Departments contributed much to the stockpile of legends within the hall. His prowess as an athlete was almost above reproach. . . . John looks forward to a long and successful career in the Navy; he is a natural and will not need the luck we wish him."

U pon graduation, McCain was commissioned an ensign. He spent part of the summer in Europe, where he dated an heiress to a tobacco fortune. In August 1958, he reported to Pensacola, Florida, to commence his training as a naval aviator. (For four years, the Pensacola base had been the home of the Blue Angels, the navy's world-famous precision flying unit.) While in Pensacola, McCain lived the life of a navy playboy, driving about town in a Corvette, partying around the clock when he was not in training, and dating a bevy of women, including an exotic dancer headlined as "Marie, the Flame of Florida."

For the next two-and-a-half years, McCain attended flight school. A meaningful part of that time was spent at the Naval Air Station in Corpus Christi, Texas, where he continued to train as a pilot. One Saturday, as he was making a practice run, his engine died. Unable to get back to the landing strip, he crashed the plane into Corpus Christi Bay. The plane sank to the bottom of the bay, and McCain, having been knocked out temporarily when the plane slammed into the water, came to and somehow broke the canopy, wedged his way out of the cockpit, and swam up to the surface of the bay. When he was examined by doctors at the base hospital, it was determined that he had escaped the crash—which could have killed him—with no major injuries, just some bumps and bruises.

Eventually, he graduated from flight school in Corpus Christi and was awarded his wings as a naval aviator. During the Cuban Missile Crisis in October 1962, he was a navy flier stationed in the Caribbean. By 1964, he had returned to Pensacola and entered into a relationship that would be life-changing. While he was at Annapolis he had known a young woman named Carol Shepp. She was originally from Philadelphia and had dated a fellow midshipman whom she eventually married. The couple had two sons, Douglas and Andrew, but, like many first marriages, the union ended in divorce. Carol was tallish, rail-thin, and dark-haired, and her air of sophistication and class appealed to McCain. She was also intelligent and independent-minded—traits that were captivating to McCain as well.

Soon after he and Carol reconnected, McCain was transferred to Meridian, Mississippi, where he served at McCain Field, which was named for his grandfather. McCain continued with his partying ways, but the longer he stayed in Mississippi the more he became serious about Carol, who still lived in Philadelphia. In time, McCain was flying up to Pennsylvania on weekends to see her. He was a pilot, so flying himself anywhere was not a problem. The couple married on July 3, 1965, in Philadelphia, at the home of Connie and Sam Bookbinder, who were close friends of Carol. A reception followed at the Bookbinders' famous restaurant. As soon as he could, McCain adopted Carol's two sons from her first marriage and the new family settled into their life in Mississippi.

McCain continued to fly himself to destinations around the country. A trip in the autumn of 1965 almost ended in disaster. He had flown to Philadelphia to see the Army-Navy football game. On his way back, as he was flying to Norfolk, Virginia, where he planned to stop before proceeding to Mississippi, he had just started his descent when his plane's engine failed. He tried to re-crank the engine three times—with no luck. As the plane headed toward the ground and an inevitable crash, McCain ejected at 1,000 feet. The plane crashed in a wooded area and he floated peacefully to the earth. Because he had radioed ahead to tell the Norfolk tower what was happening, McCain was soon picked up by a helicopter. For the second time, he had survived a plane crash that occurred through no fault of his own. He had to wonder how many more times he could crash a plane and survive.

The next year, on September 2, 1966, Carol gave birth to the couple's first child, a daughter they named Sidney Ann McCain. While Sidney would be the only child McCain would have with

Carol, it *seemed* he had three children with her since he always treated Doug and Andy as if they were his own. Soon after Sidney's birth, McCain was transferred to Jacksonville, where he joined a squadron scheduled to go to Vietnam. In the spring of 1967, the squadron set out for Vietnam on the carrier *Forrestal*. (The ship was named for James Forrestal, the former navy secretary who had known McCain's grandfather.) Because McCain's parents were stationed in London, Carol decided to move to Europe and live there while McCain served his tour in Vietnam. As it happened, his tour on the *Forrestal* was shorter than planned, and his tour in Vietnam became much longer than he could ever have imagined.

On November 9, 1958, McCain's father, Jack, had been made a rear admiral. On August 10, 1960, he was named Commander Amphibious Group Two. Less than a year later, on May 26, 1961, he became Commander Amphibious Training Command, Atlantic Fleet. By late 1963, he had been promoted to vice admiral for his duties as Commander Amphibious Force, Atlantic Fleet. In this capacity, he was involved in a crisis in the Dominican Republic.

"When Admiral McCain was commander of the amphibious forces, the symbol was an alligator," says Tom Arrasmith, McCain's aide. "An amphibian that's mean! One of the ships brought him back a real alligator from the Okefenokee Swamp once. I tried to talk him out of it, but he thought it was a great public relations thing. So we ended up traveling with an alligator. The sailors loved it. They thought it was the coolest thing in the world. It was about two and a half feet long. It was a mean, cold-blooded bastard. You cannot make friends with an alligator. We would take him to sea. The sailors would take the alligator for a walk on the deck. The alligator was in a tool locker in the stern of the ship. We built a little box for him and somebody donated a sun lamp. We had it suspended so that when the ship rolled he didn't lose his water. He moved fast too. You bet your ass he bit. You would be surprised. I have a number of scars on me that would prove that. By the way, his name was Spike.

"Admiral McCain was in charge of an operation in the Dominican Republic. When it was wrapping up, the Organization of American States said it would take over and manage it. The Brazilians are tough nuts. The general in charge of the Brazilians was not someone you would want to meet on a dark night. He came out to visit the admiral and pay his respects, and the admiral said, 'Tom, bring Spike out here.' So we brought Spike out and the general, being very macho, said, 'Oh, yes, we have lots of these. Our children play with them.' The admiral said, 'You want to play with him?' He replied, 'There's nothing to it.' I took the top off the box and Spike looked at the general and the general looked at Spike and the general said, 'I believe I will have a cup of coffee.'"

On May 1, 1967, Jack McCain was named Commander-in-Chief, United States Naval Forces, Europe, which was why he was living in London when Carol and the children moved to Europe. Jack McCain would hold that post until July 1968, when he became Commander-in-Chief, Pacific.

3

VIETNAM

For Lieutenant Commander John McCain, July 29, 1967—a Saturday—started out like any other day he had spent as a naval aviator assigned to fly missions against the enemy: the North Vietnamese. He awoke at his normal time, ate a standard breakfast, dressed in his flight gear, and attended the mid-morning preflight briefings in preparation for the mission that was to begin promptly at 11:00 o'clock. Since Tuesday of that week, the *Forrestal*, the carrier on which he had served for eight months, had been in Yankee Station in the Gulf of Tonkin, 175 miles north of the city of Da Nang. After tours in the Mediterranean and the Atlantic, the *Forrestal* had been assigned to join in the American bombing of North Vietnam. To sustain this ongoing bombing campaign, carrier-based airplanes had been flying between 30 and 40 missions a day. During the past several months, a sense of routine had come to identify the entire process for the American airmen, and McCain was becoming a part of that routine.

Each day, like clockwork, American jets took off from the carriers in the Gulf: the *Oriskany*, the *Bon Homme Richard*, and now the *Forrestal*. On average, the North Vietnamese shot down 21 planes a month—a statistic that McCain tried to put out of his mind as he got ready for the day's bombing mission. The high number of losses was one reason pilots loved routines; reassurance came from the sameness of the days. Like many other pilots, McCain was superstitious. He always stuck to a certain sequence, no matter what. Before each flight, as one detail of his routine, McCain had his parachute rigger clean his helmet visor. It was a minor task, but it was important to McCain. Had a person been prone to superstition, he might have been troubled on Thursday when, barely 48 hours into the *Forrestal*'s new assignment in the Gulf, two small fires broke out on the ship—one below deck and one in an airplane. The fires had been put out quickly, but there they were—bad omens. It's never good when any fire breaks out on an aircraft carrier. There's just too much fuel and armament on board.

On the morning of July 29, between 10:15 and 10:30, McCain left a lower deck and proceeded upstairs to the flight deck. It was a beautiful, crystal-clear day on the Gulf; a 40-mile-per-hour wind blowing from north to south gave the day a cool and spring-like feel. The hot mugginess of the Vietnamese jungles seemed a world away. McCain walked over to his plane, an A-4 Skyhawk, which was parked near the carrier's island about halfway from either end of the ship's 1,000-feet-plus flight deck. Carefully, McCain climbed into his fighter jet. A dozen or so other pilots were boarding their planes to get ready for the day's bombing missions.

When he was strapped down and buckled into the cockpit, McCain pulled shut the plane's canopy and cranked the engine. With the deafening roar of the engine engulfing him, he went through the preflight procedure—a careful check of all gauges and instrument settings. It was not yet 10:55 and the first plane was scheduled to take off at 11:00, so McCain settled back and tried to calm his nerves by using the mental sequence he invoked before he started any flight. Then, as he sat quietly in the cockpit, noting how the peaceful blue waters of the Gulf stretched out as far as he could see, all hell broke loose. Only later did he learn what happened. While the planes were idling on the flight deck waiting to take off, a plane that was parked several positions down from

McCain's jet experienced what naval aviators call "a wet start." A large burst of flame shot out of the plane and ignited a missile on a nearby aircraft. The missile then zoomed across the deck and crashed into either McCain's plane or the one parked to his right. The resulting explosion, which masked any identification of the plane the missile actually hit, shocked McCain. All around him, the deck was almost instantly consumed in flames.

His survival instincts took over. McCain disengaged himself, climbed out of the cockpit, carefully stepped onto his plane's refueling pipe, jumped onto the burning deck, rolled quickly through the flames, and came out on the other side of the inferno. Miraculously, he was relatively unscathed; he had sustained only minor burns and bruises. As he ran away from his plane, he saw that another pilot, about 50 feet away, had also jumped from a plane, but his clothes had caught fire when he rolled through the flames on the deck. McCain turned and started running to the pilot's aid, but then a nearby bomb exploded with such force that McCain was catapulted backward and the pilot he had hoped to rescue was blown up.

This was just the beginning of a long nightmare for the ship's enormous crew. While McCain watched helplessly, the fire rapidly consumed much of the four-acre flight deck and spread quickly to the areas immediately below, setting off bomb after bomb. If the sailors below the deck didn't know better, they would have thought the *Forrestal* was under attack by North Vietnamese fighter jets. Instead, the might of the American military, at least in the form of this one carrier and the aircraft on board, had been unleashed on itself. The ordeal was horrific.

In no time, half of the carrier's flight deck was overtaken by flames as airplanes caught fire and bombs exploded. Eyewitness accounts later described how sailors were running from the fire with their clothes aflame; several jumped into the sea, 70 feet below. Some crewmen shoved planes and bombs overboard, hoping to prevent more deadly explosions; others used trucks to push planes off the ship. In the chaos, individual dramas unfolded. When a chief petty officer tried to put out a flame near a bomb, the bomb exploded and killed him. Lieutenant Otis Kight, a 130-pound Oklahoman, lifted a bomb twice his weight and threw it overboard. Two sailors, trapped by flames, leaped into the Gulf, were rescued and brought back on board, and resumed the battle against the fire. Before long, roughly two-thirds of the ship's 4,800 crew members were involved in the effort to contain the fire.

Of all the descriptions of the hellish blaze, this one, provided by Lieutenant James J. Campbell, was especially chilling: "I saw so many guys running from the planes, all on fire. Then there were yellow shirts, brown shirts, blue shirts—all jumping on them, trying to smother the flames. They were burning head to foot, screaming. A guy ran past me with no clothes left, burnt off, and not much skin left. I saw two guys with a fire hose. Then there wasn't any more water. A bomb went off. Then they weren't there any more, just the stump of the hose, flopping around."

The fire, officially recorded as having started at 10:53 in the morning, raged all day and into the night. At 8:30, almost 10 hours after it began, the fire was finally brought under control, but the last flame was not put out until 12:20 A.M. on Sunday. Even then, as the carrier made its way to Subic Bay in the Philippines before proceeding to the United States for repairs, fires continued to break out. In all, four massive holes had resulted from the explosions on the deck of the ship, and four more holes had to be cut in the deck to fight the fires below. In total, 26 planes were lost—either blown up or shoved overboard—and 31 planes and three helicopters were damaged. The total cost of the lost or damaged aircraft was $85 million, and the ship's repair would require another $50 million. But the most devastating statistic was the casualties: 135 men died in the tragedy, while countless others were injured. Had it not been for the herculean efforts of the crew, the ship itself would have sunk. As it were, the New York Times described the fire on the Forrestal as "the worst calamity to strike a United

States navy ship since World War II and constituted one of the darkest hours in the history of carrier operations."

Naturally, press coverage of the fire was extensive. One of the front-page stories in the *Times* featured a striking photograph of McCain. His eyes, dark and foreboding, were looking away from the camera, and his face reflected shock and anguish. The article, "Start of Tragedy: Pilot Hears a Blast As He Checks Plane," described McCain as having "a disarming disregard for formal military speech or style," adding, "He is wiry, prematurely gray and does not take himself too seriously."

"We're professional military men and I suppose it's our war," McCain told the *Times* reporter, "and yet here were enlisted men who earn $150 a month and work 18 to 20 hours a day—and I mean manual labor—and certainly would have survived had they not stayed to help the pilots fight the fire. I've never seen such acts of heroism."

Years later, he would still be haunted by the horror of the fire on the *Forrestal*. "I was first in Vietnam on the *USS Forrestal*," McCain would write. "We had a horrible fire that began when a rocket was fired from an aircraft by mistake from across the flight deck and punched through the fuel tank in my A-4 aircraft. Huge fire ensued. Bombs went off and we lost 135 brave young American sailors who fought that fire as would be fought in hand-to-hand combat. These young people literally saved the *Forrestal*. Following that, the ship went back to the Philippines, then had to return to the United States. I made one of the several tactical blunders that I made in my life, and that was when the recruiters came over from the *USS Oriskany* and said they were looking for volunteers because they'd lost a number of pilots. And for reasons I still can't explain, my arm shot up and I found myself on the *USS Oriskany* in a very famous squadron, VA-163. The air wing on the *Oriskany*, I'm told, had the highest losses of any air wing in the war. Part of that was because the *Oriskany* was in the middle of the escalation that took place in the summer and fall of 1967."

That escalation, of course, was not devoid of controversy. It had already become obvious to many of the military personnel involved in the Vietnam War that the United States did not have in place a tactical agenda directed toward winning the conflict. Perhaps the greatest source of their frustration was their belief that Washington was not allowing them to do what they needed to do to win. Politics was getting in the way of the war. The most constant criticism centered on President Lyndon B. Johnson, who had become so concerned about provoking a nuclear conflict with either China or the Soviet Union that he, or rather a committee he controlled, had to approve all designated targets in North Vietnam before they were bombed by American planes. This led to weird developments. Some targets worth hitting—for example, a strategically located dam without which the Vietnamese would not be able to grow food—were off limits. Others—a less important dam, for instance—were approved. Many targets—a bridge here, a road there—were bombed repeatedly because they were on an approved list and a certain number of missions to bomb a certain number of targets had to be recorded on a given day.

"It was dumb the way we were doing it," says Roger W. Smith, who served in the air force in Vietnam at that time. "I wasn't sure there was any value to what we were doing, but I was the commander and we were losing a lot of people. I was responsible to encourage the pilots to get the job done and do it the best way we could, even if the target seemed like it wasn't worth the risk. I even changed the way we did things to try to hit targets better at a somewhat increased risk. But it had no real impact. You had to be an idiot not to know that, because nothing changed. Nothing at all changed. And we knew, better than the protesters back home, the fact of what was going down and how ineffectual it was. We had rules of engagement that put us at greater risk in order to not put the enemy at greater risk—like rolling in over Hanoi. We did not want to have collateral damage from a stray bomb, which is kind of strange when you think about it. Think of World War II. We were bombing all over Berlin, and here we were going to Hanoi, their capital, and we were told to keep the bomb and pull up on a run if a little cloud rolls over in front of you.

"I had guys who puked before every mission. There was one young fellow, a really scared guy. He threw up every time and finally said he couldn't sleep. He just couldn't do it. I said, 'If you want to quit, I will see what I can do to let you resign from this. But you're a young man, and for the rest of your life you will look in the mirror at the coward you see before you. If you can live with that, you're a different kind of guy than most of us. So you think about it.' He came back and said he wanted to keep going. He did, and some halfway through his tour—50 missions or so—they requested one of our pilots with experience to move down to the HQ and I got him that assignment, because what he did in 50 missions was more than I'd ever do in 2,000 missions. He was just fighting a demon."

Many members of the American military blamed the United States' unsuccessful approach to the war on Robert McNamara (in later years, McCain insisted on calling him by his full name: Robert Strange McNamara), who was secretary of defense under President Johnson. Their complaint about McNamara was straightforward: He made uninformed decisions that directly affected the war effort because he did not understand the military and he would not listen to those who did. "I was an aide to a general," says Paul Vallely, a veteran of Vietnam who eventually retired from the army as a major general. "My boss and Admiral McCain cut the ribbons on Cameron Bay in 1965—I believe, in August. Admiral McCain was highly respected. A very good man. His relationship with Robert McNamara, the defense secretary, was not very good. My boss's relationship with McNamara was negative too, because McNamara wouldn't listen to anybody. He knew it all. He knew more than the generals and the admirals. When my boss picked up McNamara at Cameron Bay later that summer and took him out on the border, he wouldn't even listen to him. My boss was telling him the North Vietnamese were using Cambodia and Laos as a sanctuary and, if we were serious, we needed to take them out but McNamara wouldn't even listen." It was not until 1968 that Johnson replaced McNamara with Clark Clifford.

McCain continued to fly bombing missions throughout August and September and on into October 1967. Back home, as the war dragged on, the antiwar forces had become increasingly organized—and more vocal. Indeed, an actual movement was asserting itself on the national political scene. One of the highlights of that movement occurred on October 22, 1967, when protesters from around the country gathered in Washington for a March on the Pentagon. Thousands of marchers surrounded the building and, in an obvious attempt at irony—or at least what would pass for irony when one is dealing with issues of war and peace—tried to concentrate, en masse, so strongly that they would be able to levitate the building. Of course, the Pentagon did not leave the ground, but the point of the protest was made: A huge and noteworthy segment of the population wanted an end to a war that had never been declared.

During this political and military maelstrom in the summer and fall of 1967, John McCain was flying bombing missions over Vietnam. After the fire on the *Forrestal*, he had chosen to volunteer to fly bombing missions with VA-163 off the *Oriskany*. He could have chosen to go to the *Intrepid*, the carrier that had replaced the *Forrestal* following the fire—he had been stationed on the *Intrepid* twice before and had enjoyed the tours—but McCain joined the *Oriskany* attack squadron because that was where the action was. McCain had come to Vietnam to fly combat missions. The *Forrestal* fire was not going to stop him, although, because he was a superstitious person, it had shaken him up. Over the years, McCain had walked away from other near-disasters. He was about to conclude that what he had going for him, more than anything else, was luck—pure dumb luck. Otherwise, there was no way to explain how he kept finding himself in the middle of calamities—two plane crashes and then the historic fire on the *Forrestal*—and surviving them unscathed.

Four days after the March on the Pentagon, on the morning of October 26, on the other side of the world, Lieutenant Commander John McCain climbed into his A-4 Skyhawk to fly his twenty-third bombing mission. (On average, a pilot flew about 100 missions during a year-long tour of duty and then was reassigned.) McCain's plane was one of 24 aircraft that were catapulted off the *Oriskany* that morning. They headed away from the carrier and formed their flight pattern as they started toward Hanoi. None of his earlier missions had taken McCain over the center of Hanoi, so he was more than a little apprehensive as he flew above the blue waters of the Gulf.

McCain's mission required flying over downtown Hanoi because his target was the Hanoi Thermal Power Plant, a vital installation worth the risk he would have to take to bomb it. By now, the issue of targets had become sensitive to a number of pilots, McCain among them. Since the Johnson Administration was deeply worried about hitting civilian and other inappropriate targets, the president had become aggressive about having the selected bombing sites preapproved by his advisory committee. Combat pilots like McCain believed it made no sense to have the bombing of North Vietnam masterminded, for all intents and purposes, by the White House. But that was what was happening. Because Washington wanted the bombing to continue, American pilots, on many days, were risking their lives to bomb installations they had bombed and destroyed the day before. The level of absurdity in this process infuriated those charged with fulfilling the war effort, but military personnel must follow orders, especially when they originate with the commander-in-chief. Therefore, the pilots flew their missions, regardless of what they thought about some of them.

Knocking out a power plant at least made some sense. So, as McCain was flying the number-three aircraft in the first division of his strike group, he was anxious to conduct his mission. Before long, the American planes arrived over Hanoi, a city that had become, because of its long siege, one of the most guarded cities in recent history. Day after day, air-raid sirens wailed as civilians ran to bomb shelters and the North Vietnamese military personnel manned anti-aircraft artillery to defend the city. American pilots who flew over Hanoi were aware that they would meet a more or less constant barrage of surface-to-air missiles (SAMs), which the North Vietnamese were buying from the Soviets. The pilots feared the huge SAMs—each missile was the height of a telephone pole—because any plane hit by a SAM was probably going to crash. Also, the Vietnamese anti-aircraft crews had gained some success in shooting down American planes; a loss of two or three planes a day was not unusual.

So far, McCain's twenty-third mission seemed like it was going to be successful, though the planes were encountering more than their share of surface-to-air missiles. As he flew over the city, McCain spotted his target. The power plant, 4,500 feet below, was just waiting to be hit, so McCain cut his steering wheel and rolled into a dive. The dive was quick and effective; he released his bombs. Then, just after the release, the unthinkable happened. BAM! A SAM came out of nowhere and smashed into his plane's right wing. The explosion blew the wing off completely. Immediately, the plane twisted into an inverted, straight-down spiral as it plunged toward the ground.

McCain had no choice but to eject, even though the plane was upside-down and hurtling downward. When he pulled the cord, the force of the ejection knocked him unconscious. He could not know it at the time, but the ejection had broken his right leg at the knee, his left arm, and his right arm (in three different places). The knee break had occurred because his leg crashed into the control panel as his body shot out of the cockpit. The jerk of the parachute had probably broken his arms. While his limp body drifted toward the ground, McCain regained consciousness only to discover himself hanging precariously in midair, underneath his parachute. With much noise, his airplane crashed before he was completely aware of what was happening. Then, glancing down, McCain could see he was dropping steadily toward a body of water. As luck would have it, he had been shot down over the largest urban area in North Vietnam, yet he was going to land in water—apparently a lake. Later, he would learn its name: Truc Bach Lake.

The fall to earth seemed to take forever; in reality, only seconds passed as McCain glided through the air and plunged into the lake. The shock of landing in the water helped him to regain further consciousness; then he faced another problem. His helmet and oxygen mask had been blown off during the ejection, but because he still had 50 pounds of equipment strapped to his body, he began to sink. Somehow he rose up to the surface, yet no sooner had he taken a gulp of air than he started to descend again. He tried to swim—to no avail; his right arm and right leg could not respond. Miraculously, he resurfaced again; but when he sank the third time, he went to the bottom of the lake, which was about 15 feet deep. Unable to use his arms or legs enough to save himself, McCain was in danger of drowning. Finally, he was able to bite the toggle of his life preserver with his teeth and pull it free.

Quickly, the life vest inflated, and McCain floated to the surface. As he shot out of the water, he gasped for air. Then he began bobbing in the middle of the lake. Needless to say, the spectacular sight of a plane being shot down and a pilot parachuting to earth drew some attention. North Vietnamese onlookers had begun to gather on the edge of the lake. One of the Hanoi locals who had watched the American pilot shot from the sky—a sight not as uncommon as one might think (on this day, three American planes were shot down)—was a young man who worked as a storeroom clerk at the Department of Industry. His name was Mai Van On.

This day, On had left work and gone home to have lunch, which he normally didn't do. The day was sunny and cool, and he wanted to enjoy the weather. On lived in a small thatched-roof house on the shore of the lake, and he had just gotten home when the sirens signaled that another American bombing mission was imminent. On knew what to do. He ran to a nearby bomb shelter, where he found dozens of other people taking refuge. The bombs were exploding all around them. On was standing near the shelter's door, watching the sky fill with a deluge of antiaircraft artillery and SAMs. Then, suddenly, in the sky, high above the city, a SAM hit an American plane—BOOM! The explosion blew a wing off the plane, forcing the aircraft into a violent and deadly dive. On watched as the pilot ejected and, after his parachute deployed, started to descend helplessly toward the lake. When On tried to get out of the shelter, intending to run to the lake and save the pilot, others tried to stop him. It was dangerous, they said. "Why do you want to go out and rescue our enemy?" one asked. Others cursed him. Ignoring them all, On grabbed a bamboo pole and headed for the lake.

When he got there, he swam out to where McCain was floating in the water. With the weighty equipment pulling McCain under, more of his body was under the water than above it. Also, McCain was all tangled up in his parachute cords. The first thing On did was to pull the upper part of McCain's body out of the water. "His head was drooped and his eyes were closed," On later said. "They gradually opened, and I saw a look of relief that he was still alive." With the pole engaged among the parachute cords, On pulled McCain toward the shore. When they were drawing close to the lake's edge, a neighborhood teenager, Le Tran Lua, swam out to help On bring McCain the rest of the way. In the shallower water, On could see that, under his badly ripped flight suit, McCain was wearing a chain around his neck. On could not have known that it was McCain's good-luck charm.

Once On and Lua had pulled McCain near the shore, a group of locals came out to bring him in the rest of the way. On could not stave off the crowd of 40 or more people who moved in to curse and spit at the downed pilot. McCain, so crippled he was unable to move, could not defend himself. Soon after, some of the mob stripped McCain of his clothes until he wore only his underwear. The Vietnamese did this to make sure that captured Americans were not concealing any hidden weapons. As others in the mob kicked him, McCain looked down at his leg. His right foot was resting at a 90-degree angle against his left knee. Horrified at how badly his leg was broken, McCain shouted, "My God, my leg! My leg!" And when he said this, the mob, for reasons that were never clear, became infuriated.

A Vietnamese soldier slammed his rifle butt into McCain's shoulder, crushing it. Another soldier stuck a bayonet first into his left foot, then into his groin. In unfathomable pain, McCain lay on the ground unable to move or to do anything but hope the assault would soon stop. He was at the mercy of a mob that seemed intent on killing him, and, in his condition, it would not have taken much. Then, out of nowhere, the Hanoi police arrived, forced the crowd to back off, and prepared to transport McCain to the place where they took all American pilots who had been shot down over Hanoi. Positioning him on a stretcher, they put McCain's crumpled body in a car and drove him across town to Hoa Lo Street, the only thoroughfare in Hanoi that had just one address on it. Hoa Lo Street was the site of Hoa Lo Prison, a place the Americans had nicknamed the Hanoi Hilton.

The next day, when Mai Van On arrived for work at the Department of Industry, his coworkers began applauding and shouting, "You saved the pilot! You saved the pilot!" For John McCain, the fact that a storeroom clerk named On had saved his life held no promise. In those first dark and disturbing hours in the Hanoi Hilton, McCain could never have even imagined what fate awaited him.

"I was taken into a cell and put on the floor," McCain later wrote. "I was still on the stretcher, dressed only in my skivvies, with a blanket over me." For the next four days, McCain remained in that spot. Periodically, one interrogator or another would come into the room and try to get military information from him. McCain would give up only his name, rank, serial number, and date of birth—the procedure stipulated in the military Code of Conduct for prisoners of war. When McCain refused to provide military information, the interrogator would slap him around, but McCain was so injured that if he was hit too hard, he blacked out. This happened on several occasions. Indeed, during the four days, McCain was in such unbearable pain he repeatedly lapsed in and out of consciousness. All the while, the North Vietnamese made his status clear: He would get medical attention if—and only if—he gave them military information. "You will not receive any medical treatment," McCain was told by one interrogator, "until you talk." He was also given little food and water. To the Vietnamese, McCain and other Americans who were captured were regarded as war criminals, not POWs.

One day, two guards came in and pulled back the sheet to look at McCain's body. When they did, McCain saw his knee for the first time. He was shocked to see that it had swollen to the size of a football. Realizing how bad his knee was, McCain said to one of the guards, "Get the interrogator." Before long, a man arrived whom the prisoners would call The Bug. McCain later described him as "a psychotic torturer, one of the worst fiends that we had to deal with."

Calmly, McCain said to The Bug, "Look, take me to the hospital, give me some treatment, and then maybe we can talk about military information."

The Bug left but soon returned with the camp doctor, whom the prisoners called Zorba. Zorba looked McCain over, took his pulse, and spoke to The Bug in Vietnamese.

"Are you going to take me to the hospital?" McCain asked The Bug.

"It's too late," The Bug said.

McCain tried to bargain. "Take me to the hospital," he said, "and we'll talk about military information. If you take me to the hospital, I'll get well."

Ignoring McCain, The Bug repeated, "It's too late. It's too late." Then he and Zorba left. In the dead silence of the room, McCain lay motionless, his body so broken he could barely move a muscle. A quiet despair came over him as he weighed what he could do next—if anything. That was the problem: There was nothing he could do. He was at the mercy of his captors.

A few hours later, The Bug burst back into the room. "Your father is a big admiral," he said, so excited he was almost shouting. "Now we're going to take you to the hospital." More than once, in his excited speech, The Bug referred to McCain as the "Crown Prince."

Men soon came and took McCain to the hospital where, for the next three or four days, he was given blood and plasma, which probably saved his life. His guard was a 16-year-old boy, a new arrival from the rice paddies. He frequently hit or slapped McCain, and he ate nearly all the food he was supposed to feed him. Each day McCain was in the hospital, he got little more than a few spoonfuls of soup; the boy ate all the rest of the food. Eventually, the doctors tried to administer some medical treatment. After being placed on a rolling stretcher, McCain was taken to a room where a doctor attempted to put a cast on his right arm. The bone was broken in three places, and the doctor had a problem getting the bone pieces into proper alignment. For three excruciating hours, without the benefit of a sedative or novocaine, McCain endured the doctor's fumbling attempt to fit the pieces of bone together. Repeatedly, McCain passed out from the indescribable pain. Finally, the doctor gave up and simply placed the arm in a cast.

When the doctor finished, McCain was rolled into a clean, white room where he was placed in a bed. Exhausted by the ordeal, he felt as if he had no energy left in his body. An hour or so later, a man the prisoners called The Cat came in, accompanied by a man known as Chihuahua, who seemed to function as The Cat's assistant. McCain later learned that The Cat, a neatly dressed, lithe, well-mannered man, was the supervisor of all the POW camps in Hanoi. The Cat showed McCain the identification card of Colonel

John Flynn of the air force, who had been shot down on the same day as McCain. The Cat, it seemed, wanted McCain to know that the Vietnamese had captured another senior officer. The Cat told McCain he had to speak to a journalist, but McCain refused.

The Cat threatened, "You need two operations and if you don't talk to him, then we will take your cast off and you won't get any operations. You will say that you're grateful to the Vietnamese people, and that you're sorry for your crimes."

Before McCain knew what was happening, they were joined in the room by a French journalist—one could have suspected he was a communist—and a two-man television crew. The journalist, a congenial man named Chalais, asked McCain a number of questions, some of which McCain answered.

At one point, Chalais asked McCain to describe how he was being treated, and McCain said his treatment was satisfactory. The Cat, standing behind Chalais and alongside Chihuahua, told McCain to say he was grateful for the lenient and humane treatment he was receiving from the North Vietnamese, but McCain refused. The Cat insisted that he must say it, but again McCain refused. Finally, Chalais turned to The Cat and said, "I have enough." Only then did The Cat back off. As soon as the filming was over, McCain was taken back to his filthy and unsanitary room, where the young guard continued to treat him badly and eat his food.

Before long, it became evident that the North Vietnamese intended to use the capture of McCain for propaganda purposes. On Saturday, November 11 (Armistice Day in the U.S.), the *New York Times* ran an article entitled "Hanoi Says McCain's Son Terms U.S. 'Isolated'"—a story that repeated comments attributed to McCain that had just appeared in the North Vietnamese press. In the article, McCain, who was identified as "son of Admiral John S. McCain Jr., commander of United States naval forces in Europe," was said to have given an interview to North Vietnamese journalists in which he said: "The morale of the Vietnamese people is very high, the Vietnamese people are very strong, present events are moving to the advantage of North Vietnam, and the United States appears to be isolated." To make the comment sound plausible, the Hanoi press had included information about, and remarks presumably made by, another American serviceman, John Flynn. The Hanoi press reports said, according to the *Times*, that both McCain and Flynn had mentioned the effectiveness of the antiaircraft artillery being used by the North Vietnamese to guard Hanoi. "The papers quoted Colonel Flynn," the *Times* noted, "as having said that the young pilots at the Korat base [a United States base in Thailand that was Flynn's home base], despite an outward show of bravado, were frightened at the idea of having to fly over North Vietnam, and particularly Hanoi."

Two weeks after the surgery on his right arm, McCain was subjected to a second operation, this one on his leg. (Never treated, his left arm healed on its own.) During the second operation, which was filmed for propaganda purposes, the doctors cut the ligaments and the cartilage in his knee. However, in the days following the operation, McCain's condition worsened. His spirits were not lifted when the doctors told him his leg needed two more operations but they were not going to perform them because he had a "bad attitude." Finally, one day, when it was obvious McCain was not improving, The Bug visited him and asked what could be done to make him feel better. "Well," McCain said, "I would get better if I was put with some Americans who would take care of me."

Six weeks had passed since the Vietnamese moved McCain from the Hanoi Hilton to the hospital. In that time, he had endured two operations that did not seem to improve his medical condition at all. Indeed, it looked as if, should his state not change soon, he was going to die. He weighed a mere 100 pounds; in those six weeks, he had lost 55 pounds.

That night, McCain was taken by truck to a nearby prison that the Americans had named The Plantation. He was placed in a cell with two other American POWs—Major George ("Bud") Day and Major Norris Overly, both of the air force. Day was a character in his own right; he had tried to escape once but was shot and returned to prison. Day himself was in pretty bad condition. His right arm was broken in three places, he had been shot in the leg and the hand, he had shrapnel in his right and left legs, and his left knee had been badly sprained. At first, neither Day nor Overly was sure McCain was going to make it. His condition was so life-threatening that Day didn't think he'd last a week. But Day and Overly did all they could to care for him; they fed him, bathed him, and attended his wounds. Finally, after several days in their care, McCain began to perk up and Day and Overly decided that McCain might make it after all. Years later, McCain was clear about what happened: Day and Overly saved his life.

"When they brought John in," says George ("Bud") Day, "I'd say he probably weighed around 100 pounds. He was just horribly skinny. He was in this huge cast that was wearing a hole in his elbow. He was really very tender. And, of course, he had this white hair. I knew he was quite a bit younger than he looked, so I was really astonished at his appearance. My first thought was that they had dumped him on us to die.

"He was also filthy. He hadn't been washed, I don't think, since he had been shot down. He had a bunch of food in his hair, and a beard, and he just smelled like he was rotten. So Overly started cleaning him up and washing him up and taking care of him. John was determined to live. Overly also started getting some food in him. Soon John started gaining some weight and doing better. I sensed very quickly that I was dealing with a remarkably brilliant guy."

After Christmas, the three Americans were moved to another room in The Plantation. In early February, Overly was released, along with David Matheny and John Black. They were the first three POWs freed by the North Vietnamese. "When Overly left, John and I were alone," Day says. "By then, John was doing wonderfully. He'd probably gained about seven or eight pounds. We got really well acquainted. We talked about everything imaginable. We had the same kind of interests in our career pattern, and we had a lot of common interests. I was a lawyer. I'd been around the world in the military in World War II and Korea. John was a young guy, but he'd been around the world. We were also both a couple of boozers who had tried to run the babes."

In March—the month in which President Johnson announced an end to bombing north of the twentieth parallel, and W. Averell Harriman was dispatched to Paris to prepare for peace negotiations with the Vietnamese, scheduled to begin on May 10—McCain's condition had improved so much the Vietnamese moved Day to another cell. McCain was then kept permanently in solitary confinement. "I was not allowed to see or talk to or communicate with any of my fellow prisoners," McCain would write. "My room was fairly decent sized—I'd say it was about 10 by 10. The door was solid. There were no windows. The only ventilation came from two small holes at the top in the ceiling, about six inches by four inches. The roof was tin and it got hot as hell in there. The room was kind of dim—night and day—but they always kept on a small light bulb, so they could observe me. I was in that place for two years."

One day in mid-June, McCain was taken to an interrogation room that was much larger than the others he had seen. He was met there by The Cat and another guard whom the POWs nicknamed The Rabbit. For two hours, The Cat spoke randomly to McCain about subjects that, quite frankly, seemed meaningless. Then, out of the blue, The Cat asked flatly, "So you want to go home? The doctor says your condition is still very poor. Would you like to go home?"

McCain knew exactly what The Cat was up to. If the North Vietnamese released him, this son of a famous American admiral, they could use the episode for propaganda that would yield untold political gain. After a moment, McCain said, "Well, I'll have to think about it back in my room." That response allowed McCain to buy some time so he could decide what to do next. He was suffering from a case of dysentery that had terribly debilitated his system, so The Cat's offer was tempting, even though he knew in his heart that he would not be able to go home. For he was familiar with the military Code of Conduct: Prisoners could be released only in the order in which they were taken prisoner. Many POWs—Everett Alvarez and James Stockdale, to name only two—had been there much longer than McCain.

The other POWs were aware that McCain was being pressured to leave. Sometimes it seemed the North Vietnamese were intentionally trying to provoke McCain, who was often more than willing to strike back. "I was in a cell that was catty-corner from the cell block that John, Norris Overly, and Bud Day were in," says Jack Van Loan, who had been shot down on May 20, 1967. "The only way we could communicate with those guys was when they were in the shower. We'd get down on our hands and knees, and we'd whisper in the shower drain. The Vietnamese very conveniently built a drain that was handy to talk into. That's how I first heard about John McCain. After they let Overly go, that left Bud in there with a bad arm, and John who was all busted up. In time, they moved Bud too.

"Then one day I was peeking out through a little hole that I had in my door and I saw this group of what obviously were high-rankers coming down through the courtyard of The Plantation. They had with them one of the really good English speakers. He and one or two of the senior guys went into the cell block that John was in and they in essence told him, we found out later, that they had a plane out there waiting and all John had to do was say he had been treated well and he could go home.

"Immediately John started to yell, which you could hear all over the camp. Let me tell you, I picked up a couple of new words that day, because he called them everything in the book. Now this was really dangerous stuff. I mean, it really was. To start calling them what he was calling them was unacceptable by any standard. I was just standing in my cell cringing, thinking, 'For God's sake, what are you doing?'

"Of course, John was telling them, in so many words: 'I'm not going home early, I'm going home in turn, and you can take this whole thing and shove it where the sun don't shine.' When he was finished, they came out of there just like tumbleweed. I mean, it was funny. It was frightening, but funny. I mean, they could have killed him right there. They could have said: 'Okay, take him and shoot him on the spot.' But Ho had told them these were valuable blue chips, so John got away with it."

Three days after the earlier meeting, McCain was brought back to the interrogation room. The Cat and The Rabbit were waiting for him; they would try to achieve what the high-rankers had not been able to. The Cat got right to the point. "Did you think about our offer?" he said. "Do you want to go home?"

"Yes," McCain said, fully in control of his emotions. "I can't accept that offer."

"Why?" The Cat said.

"Our code of conduct says you go home by order of those who have been shot down first, then the sick and injured."

"But you're injured," The Cat said.

"Yeah, but I'm going to survive."

"President Johnson has ordered that you go home."

"Show me the orders."

"We don't have them."

"Show me the orders and I will believe it."

"The doctors say you cannot live if you do not go home."

McCain said calmly, "The prisoners must be sent home in the order in which they were captured, starting with Alvarez."

With this, the interrogation session ended abruptly. The Cat was clearly unhappy with McCain. A few days later, McCain was brought in for a third session with The Cat, but he was too weak from dysentery and had to return to his cell. Finally, on the morning of the Fourth of July, the day on which McCain's father was named the commander-in-chief of the United States forces in the Pacific (McCain did not know this at the time, nor did he know when his father assumed the command on July 31), McCain was taken into another interrogation room where he again encountered The Cat and The Rabbit. McCain sat down and The Rabbit didn't waste any time. Their drawn-out attempt to get McCain to agree to go home, an effort that had so far failed miserably, was beginning to infuriate them.

"Our senior officer wants to know your final answer," The Rabbit said, as if the officer didn't already know it.

McCain looked at The Cat, who sat there silently fiddling with an ink pen and a copy of the *New York Herald Tribune.*

"My final answer is the same," McCain said. "It's 'no.'"

"That is your final answer?" The Cat said, seemingly unable to believe what he was hearing.

"That is my final answer."

Then, as McCain stared at him, The Cat, becoming more and more angry, suddenly snapped the ink pen in half, splattering ink in all directions. Standing up, The Cat kicked the chair over as he said to McCain in a voice electric with fury—and in English that was unusually precise for him—"They taught you too well. They taught you too well." Turning, he stalked out of the room, slamming the door behind him. He was as frustrated as his superiors had been.

An ugly uneasiness filled the air. McCain was not sure what was going to happen next. Finally, The Rabbit said, using a tone clearly meant to send a warning, "Well, you better go back to your cell. Things will be very bad for you now."

The Rabbit was right. For the next year and a half, McCain lived through nothing short of hell.

The Vietnamese were acting especially cocky because they believed they were winning the war. During the Vietnamese lunar New Year (known as Tet) in mid-1968, the North Vietnamese started an offensive against 31 of South Vietnam's 44 provinces. Saigon and Hue were both attacked. The fighting went on until February 24, 1969, when South Vietnamese forces recaptured The Palace at Hue. North Vietnam lost but showed the world how much its forces were willing to fight. Along the way, they had contributed toward having the commander of the United States forces in South Vietnam, General William Westmoreland, fired, and they had helped derail President Johnson's plans to run for reelection. Hubert Humphrey, his vice president, ran instead—and lost to Richard Nixon. The North Vietnamese also believed, based on news coverage of the antiwar movement in the United States, that most Americans were now against the war. This meant that Americans back home were siding with them.

In August 1968, the North Vietnamese had decided McCain was a war criminal who must apologize to the Vietnamese people for what he had done. One night in August, a guard the prisoners had named Slopehead took him into a room where 10 other guards were gathered. "You have violated all the camp regulations," Slopehead said. "You're a black criminal. You must confess your crimes." Specifically, Slopehead wanted McCain to sign a statement saying he was sorry for the crimes he had committed against the Vietnamese people, and thanking his captors for treating him well as a prisoner of war.

When McCain refused, Slopehead said, "Why are you so disrespectful of the guards?"

"Because the guards treat me like an animal," McCain said.

At this response, the guards attacked him viciously. They knocked him to the floor and beat him. "After a few hours of that," McCain later wrote, "ropes were put on me and I sat that night bound with ropes. Then I was taken to a small room. For punishment, they would almost always take you to another room where you didn't have a mosquito net or a bed or any clothes. For the next four days, I was beaten every two to three hours by different guards. My left arm was broken again and my ribs were cracked."

The beatings continued, with one goal: The Vietnamese wanted McCain to sign the statement, which of course they intended to use for propaganda purposes. McCain knew this, so he refused to comply. "I held out for four days," McCain would later write. "Finally I reached [my] lowest point. . . . I was at the point of suicide, because I saw that I was reaching the end of my rope. I said, 'Okay, I'll write for you.'"

McCain was taken to another room where, for 12 hours, he worked on a statement with an interrogator. The interrogator wrote the final statement, which McCain signed. "It was in their language," McCain would write, "and spoke about black crimes, and other generalities. It was unacceptable to them. But I felt just terrible about it. I kept saying to myself, 'Oh, God, I really didn't have any choice.' I had learned what we all learned over there: Every man has his breaking point. I had reached mine."

After he signed the statement, McCain was allowed to rest for two weeks. But because the Vietnamese decided they could not use the statement he had signed, they tried to break him again and make him sign another one. This time, he was both physically and mentally strong enough to resist. He never signed the document they wanted—in fact, he never signed anything else for the Vietnamese. Because of this, the beatings continued, sometimes two or three a week. During this time, when two prisoners tried to escape, all of the prisoners were punished. Also, McCain was singled out for punishment when he was caught trying to communicate with other POWs by tapping on the wall. The POWs had devised a sophisticated system of tapping that allowed them to "talk" to one another. As soon as a new POW arrived in the prison, he was taught the system so that he could communicate with the others.

When McCain refused to sign a statement telling American pilots to stop flying bombing missions over North Vietnam, he was forced to stand for days on end. A guard also crushed his knee, which forced him to get around on crutches. The severe treatment went on until October 1969. In August of that year, Navy Lieutenant Robert F. Frishman, along with Air Force Captain Wesley Ramble and Seaman D. B. Hegdahl, had been released. On September 2, in a press conference held at Bethesda Naval Medical Center, Frishman and Hegdahl detailed the abuse they had suffered as POWs in North Vietnam.

Frishman had been shot down on a bombing mission over Hanoi on October 24, 1967. In the crash, his elbow was crushed, but instead of treating his injury the Vietnamese doctors simply removed the elbow, leaving him disabled. The doctors had also *not* removed missile fragments in his arm, so the wound became severely infected. Frishman had been imprisoned, he said, in a 10-foot-by-11-foot room with a tin roof, which became excruciatingly hot in the tropical heat. Hegdahl, who had been captured when he fell overboard from his ship, had been kept in solitary confinement for a year. One chilling moment of the press conference occurred when Frishman described how the North Vietnamese had tortured Lieutenant Commander Richard Stratton by pulling out his fingernails and burning him with cigarettes.

The testimony of the former POWs so disturbed Secretary of Defense Melvin Laird—who had replaced Clark Clifford following Nixon's victory over Humphrey in November 1968—that he released a statement, that day, which included this sentence: "There is clear evidence that North Vietnam has violated even the most fundamental standards of human decency." In the coverage published in the *New York Times* article, "Ex-POWs Charge Hanoi with Torture," Frishman was quoted talking about McCain. "It's bad enough just being in solitary confinement," Frishman said of McCain, "but when you're wounded like John, it's harder." Starting in October, as a result of the news conference and subsequent bad publicity, the treatment for all the POWs in Hanoi improved significantly.

One morning during Christmastime, the guards came and told McCain, "We're going to take you to a Christmas service." At first enthusiastic, McCain became furious when his guards escorted him into a room that had been fully equipped with five or six television cameras. Obviously, the Vietnamese were going to film the POWs holding a Christmas church service to try to make the world believe that the Americans were receiving excellent treatment at the hands of the North Vietnamese. The guards had barely gotten McCain inside the room before he shouted, "What the hell is this?" Soon, his yelling included foul language, and when he was forced to sit down in one of the pews, he said loudly to the man beside him, "Hi, my name's John McCain; what's yours?" Throughout the episode, which was entirely staged for the cameras, McCain continued with his noisy speech laced with vulgar obscenities. Single-handedly, McCain had all but ruined the attempt made by the North Vietnamese to create a propaganda tool. "That was the fun part," McCain later wrote. "They let me enjoy the rest of Christmas day but the next few weeks were pretty rough. That was sort of the way I acted towards them. You had to stand up because they wanted to take your dignity and if they got your dignity and your pride, then they could make you do what they wanted."

As part of the Vietnamese reaction to McCain's Christmas antics, he was removed from The Plantation and sent back to the Hanoi Hilton, his first prison when he was shot down. Specifically, within the Hanoi Hilton, he was placed in an area called Las Vegas. He could not have known it at the time, but, even though the extreme abuse had ended, years would pass before he was allowed to leave the prison he later described as, "the hotel where they didn't leave a mint on your pillow."

"He had landed in that Ho Chi Min pond," says Admiral James Stockdale, who had been a prisoner since September 1965, and knew both McCain and his father. "Without having the guts and kicking himself off the bottom, he would still be down there. After that, he probably got a bit mellower. But he was no mellow guy then. He wasn't going to give anybody anything. As a result, I don't think anybody got beaten up as much as John McCain. He was obstreperous, and he hated people that tried to work him over. He was contemptuous of those goddamned gooks and he let them know it. Being the son and grandson of navy admirals, he knew more than most that when you get into prison camp, the story changes. He knew the rules of the game, and he was not about to kiss ass to get out of there. In fact, the last thing you want to be is cooperative. He conducted himself as a belligerent, and that is the only way to go. He wasn't trying to make a deal. He wouldn't accept favors. They wanted to kiss him because he was the prince of an admiral. He told those gooks to go screw themselves. He wasn't there for that. He was there to keep his mouth shut and get out of prison when the war was over. He was also involved in screwing up religious services and doing other good things like that. When I heard about it later, I gave him an 'atta-boy.'

"What they had was really an extortion prison, where you were expected to make pacifistic comments or take a beating. And anybody who was anybody was taking beatings. There was no such thing as a calmed-down prisoner. It was an outrage. I beat myself up, had lots of bruises. I learned how to protect myself from propaganda, and that was: self-disfiguration. That was an art. I beat myself over the head with stools. I cut myself with razors they gave me. I would emerge into the room ready for assignment with deluges of blood running down my face. That was the way it went."

"My first encounter with John McCain was through a wall between Rooms Six and Seven in the Hanoi Hilton," says Orson Swindle, who had been taken prisoner on November 11, 1966. "I was put in Room Six adjacent to John. We started communicating through the wall. I was tapping, 'Who is this?' 'John McCain,' he replied. Then he told one of these really lousy jokes. 'How can you identify an Italian airline?' 'I have no idea,' I tapped back. 'It's the one with the hair in the wheel wells.' This guy has been shell-shocked or something, I thought."

At the time, the Hanoi Hilton held about 450 POWs. Many of them, like Swindle and McCain, had come to know the history of the facility well. Construction of the Hoa Lo Prison had been finished by the French in 1945. In Vietnamese, *hoa lo* means "portable earthen stove." The structure had been built on a site once occupied by local families who made earthenware hibachis, known as "hoa lo." Throughout the prison, there were leg shackles in the cells so that the prisoners could be chained to their beds. The steel doors had peepholes for spying on the prisoners. The first American POWs had landed in the Hanoi Hilton in August 1964. Over time, as more and more Americans arrived, the place developed a folklore that included labels provided by the POWs. The prison's sections had names like Camp One, Camp Unity, Heartbreak Hotel, New Guy Village, and Las Vegas. Some of the larger areas had subdivisions. The Las Vegas section had areas named after Las Vegas hotels: the Thunderbird, the Stardust, the Riviera, the Desert Inn, and the Golden Nugget. When he arrived there in late 1969, McCain was put in the Golden Nugget, a sub-area consisting of only three rooms.

McCain remained in solitary confinement in the Golden Nugget until March 1970. John Finley, an air force colonel, then lived with him for the next two months. In May, the Vietnamese wanted McCain to meet with an antiwar group that was visiting the prison. (This new phenomenon of antiwar groups coming to see the American POWs had started in 1969.) McCain refused. In June, because of his unwillingness to meet with any of these groups, McCain was moved into a room called Calcutta, a six-foot-by-two-foot enclosure with no ventilation. The tiny space was incredibly hot, and McCain quickly came down with another case of dysentery. In September 1970, when he was moved to the Riviera, he was able to communicate with other prisoners by tapping on the wall in code. He remained in the Riviera until December, when he was moved to a huge space called the Thunderbird. On Christmas night, he was transferred to Camp Unity. For the first time since he was brought to the Hanoi Hilton a year ago, he was in a part of the prison outside Las Vegas.

"In late 1970," McCain later wrote, "there was a change in our treatment. Ho Chi Minh died. We were put into large cells of two or three together in each cell. I was put in a cell with Admiral Stockdale, Robinson Risner, the other famous ones. But it didn't last very long because [in March 1971] we had a riot over having church services. The Vietnamese wouldn't let us have a church service. The Vietnamese came and selected 36 of us, and we were taken out to a punishment camp called Skid Row." Those who were left that day started singing "The Star-Spangled Banner."

"Once we engaged in a little bit of resistance effort," Orson Swindle says, "they singled out about 30 of us and moved us to a place on the outskirts of Hanoi that I named Skid Row. I called it that because it was a single long building with about 36 cells and a long dark walkway in front of us. They told us we were the bad apples in the barrel and they were isolating us there. The first thing we did was establish who was there, because we were taken out there in typical fashion: blindfolded and handcuffed. Instinctively, we knew that we were put in cells. We started peeking through doors and cracks, and soon we concluded that there were no guards in the area and the doors were closed. But we could whisper, talk, or bounce our voices across the wall in front of us. We learned all these ingenious ways of communicating.

"John is a compulsive communicator. As soon as we got there, he said, 'Hey, Orson, it's John McCain. I am down in Room Nine. Orson,' he continued, 'I wanted to tell you this when we started tapping through the wall the other day. Ever since I graduated from the Naval Academy in '58, I wanted to be a marine in the worst way.' 'That's interesting, John,' I said. 'Why weren't you?' 'I was going to apply,' John said, 'but they told me I wasn't qualified.' 'How can that be possible?' I said. 'You're a Naval Academy graduate. Why weren't you qualified?' 'Well,' John answered, 'my parents were married, so therefore I wasn't qualified.' Those were his first words to me in Skid Row."

McCain and the group remained in Skid Row from March until August. They returned to Camp Unity for one month because Skid Row flooded, but then were sent back to Skid Row until November.

"Finally," Swindle says, "in November 1971 they moved us back to the Hilton. They moved about 25 of us into a room together. John and I ended up sleeping side by side on this stone pedestal." It was the first time McCain had been kept with a large group of Americans since he had arrived at the Hanoi Hilton four years earlier. "Believe it or not," McCain would write, "we had a wonderful time in that cell. We played cards. We had church services. I taught a history course. We had a choir. Our choir director was a guy named Quincy Collins who had been the choir director at the Air Force Academy Glee Club. We had guys with wonderful voices. When people say how terrible it was in prison, this was wonderful, especially after what we had just gone through."

"We had hours upon hours of time to talk and get to know each other in infinite detail," Orson Swindle says. "We talked about everything we ever did in sports personally, and all of our heroes from the great sports events we had witnessed or listened to on the radio. We talked about books. John is one of the most well-read people I've ever met. He has an incredible memory. John and I tried to put together a history of the English and American novels. We tried to recollect the sequence of the novels as they were written, going back to *Robinson Crusoe* and *Moll Flanders*. We just made up what we didn't remember. We pulled in other guys and asked them what they remembered about this or that book.

"John would also tell movies by narrating them from memory. We would have 'Monday Night at the Movies,' 'Tuesday Night at the Movies,' and so on. There was a Hemingway movie made in the early 1960s about the adventures of a young man, Nick Adams. A biography of Hemingway, really. We told it with all the sequences of the punch-drunk fighter. One of the best things John did was tell stories of Damon Runyon. He could imitate the dialect of the New York bookies. He told us all about the Harvards and the Yales playing football, and going up to Saratoga. John was a great entertainer."

In 1971, the POWs were finally able to have a proper church service on Christmas because, after numerous requests from prisoners, the Vietnamese belatedly found a copy of the Bible. Because he had gone to Episcopal High School, which required attendance at chapel each morning as well as on Sunday, McCain was selected by the group to be their chaplain—a profound irony, considering the more-than-occasional use of profanity that peppered his normal speech. McCain copied passages from the Bible before he returned it to the Vietnamese, and, on Christmas Day, the POWs were able to hold a church service during which scriptures from the Bible were read. "[T]he choir would sing a hymn, and then I would read from that part of the story of the actual birth of Christ," McCain later wrote. "The choir sang 'Silent Night.' I looked around that room and there these guys were with tears in their eyes. In some cases streaming down their cheeks. The tears were not of sorrow and homesickness. They were tears of joy that for the first time, in the case of some who had already been there seven years, we were able to celebrate Christmas together. It was one of the most, if not the most, remarkable experience of the time that I was in prison."

In May 1972, the U.S. bombing resumed, so junior officers, including McCain, were taken up to a prison called Dogpatch, near the China border, for a few weeks. At Dogpatch, McCain's health finally improved. Not long after the group was brought back to the Hanoi Hilton, the Vietnamese caught a POW named Mike Christian in violation of prison rules. Christian—a quiet and respectful young man originally from Selma, Alabama—had been shot down in 1967, the same year as McCain. Unknown to the guards, Christian, using red and white thread and a bamboo needle, had sewn an American flag into the back of a blue shirt. The POWs had used the flag to say the Pledge of Allegiance each morning. When the guards found the shirt-flag, they took Christian out of the cell and, within hearing distance of the other POWs, beat him severely. In the assault, they punctured his eardrum and broke several ribs. Then they returned him, bleeding and almost unconscious, to his cell. The homemade flag, the beating, and the actions Mike Christian took next would stay with McCain for the rest of his life.

As McCain was enduring his fifty-sixth month of captivity, events in Hanoi, outside of the Hanoi Hilton, would focus worldwide attention on the war and the plight of American POWs, creating a controversy that, in some circles in the United States, lasted for decades. On July 8, 1972, after establishing a reputation for being not only an accomplished actress but also a passionate social critic, Jane Fonda landed in Hanoi for a two-week visit as a guest of the North Vietnamese Government. Her stay would generate sensational headlines around the world and change Fonda's life for good. Only weeks before, she had won the Academy Award for Best Actress for her performance in *Klute,* so her supporters could not argue that she didn't know the power of the image. It's hard to imagine that she didn't understand what she was doing when, just days into her visit, as she was being given a tour of North Vietnamese military equipment, she was asked to pose in a tank and, after strapping on a helmet, readily complied.

"The government guides took Miss Fonda on a tour of the environs of Hanoi and some of us reporters were allowed to accompany her," one Czech journalist would say years later, recalling the events of that day. "We stopped for lunch, where there were a lot of toasts in Russian wine and Hungarian *slivoritz.* Then they took her to an antiaircraft battery. She had this fixed smile on her face as they moved her toward one of the antiaircraft guns. They said that this was one of the heroic weapons that was protecting the city from the barbaric American air bombardment. Someone put a soldier's steel helmet on her head and she joked that this was just like a Hollywood publicity opportunity, except that her hair didn't look right. One of the guides, a woman, then fixed her hair so that it was arranged correctly around the edge of her helmet. They asked her to climb up into the gun mount, which she did, sitting in the gunner's seat. Everybody laughed, including Miss Fonda. I don't know whether or not she realized a camera crew was filming every moment of the incident." Of course, if there was one person in the group who *did* know about a camera—and when it was or was not rolling—it would have been Jane Fonda.

When they were released by the North Vietnamese Government, the images of Fonda, laughing as she cavorted in a Vietnamese
tank, stunned the American public. Days later, what she had to *say*
proved to be equally controversial. In a gesture that earned her a
comparison to Tokyo Rose, Fonda delivered, on Hanoi Radio, an attack on President Nixon and a defense of the actions of the North
Vietnamese. "Tonight, when you're alone, ask yourselves, 'What are
you doing?'" Fonda said, in a direct address to the members of the
American military in Vietnam. "[A]s human beings, can you justify
what you are doing? Do you know why you are flying these missions, collecting extra pay on Sunday? . . . The people beneath your
planes have done us no harm. They want to live in peace. They
want to rebuild their country. They cannot understand what kind of
people could fly over their heads and drop bombs down there. . . . I
know that if you saw and if you knew the Vietnamese under peaceful conditions, you would hate the men who are sending you on
bombing missions."

During her visit, Fonda toured homes, state buildings, and hospitals. She was shown the Red River delta, famous for its dikes. One
day, she met with a group of seven captured American pilots. "The
day before, these guys were cleaned up, given clean pajamas, haircuts, and all that good stuff," says William Haynes, who was serving
as a military pilot in Vietnam at the time. "They were lined up and
they knew they would be meeting Jane Fonda. So they got together
and decided, 'Hey, we've got to do something. Some of our families
don't even know we're here.' They came up with the scheme that
they would have tiny little slips of paper with their Social Security
numbers written on them. They figured they'd try to get them to
Jane Fonda because they didn't believe she was really in support of
North Vietnam. When she went down the line and shook their
hands, they gave her these little slips of paper in the handshake, and
she promptly palmed them. At the end of the whole thing—and this
is all a photo-op, of course—when all of the cameras were off, she
calmly walked over to the head of the North Vietnamese delegation,

handed him the papers, and said, 'This is what these people did.' The POWs couldn't believe it. They absolutely couldn't believe it. They were beaten severely. The story I heard—and I was told this from guys who were present—is that one guy died from the beating."

On July 20, Fonda made a speech for which many members of the American military, and their families, would never forgive her. She misrepresented the conditions under which American POWs were being held. "They are all in good health," she said about the pilots. "We exchanged ideas freely. They asked me to bring back to the American people their sense of disgust of the war and their shame for what they have been asked to do. . . . They all assured me that they are well cared for. They listen to the radio. They receive letters. They are in good health. . . . I'm sure that with the studying and reading they've been doing here, those pilots will go home better citizens than when they left."

The American POWs were horrified by Fonda's actions and comments. "We were absolutely dismayed when Jane Fonda showed up over there," Jack Van Loan says. "Because she went on Hanoi radio and told our young people in the South to lay down their arms and desert, she committed treason. That's what we thought. We knew right away when she was doing it too because they played Hanoi radio for us. The way she conducted herself was absolutely inexcusable. Years later, I would get a picture—a big picture—of her posing in front of a flak battery, simulating shooting down American airplanes."

One of the pilots Fonda had hoped to meet in Hanoi, before she left North Vietnam on July 22, was John McCain. McCain, aware of the flood of propaganda that was sure to follow after a trip made by such a famous American, refused to meet with her.

The years 1971 and 1972 had been comparatively quiet. Then, on December 18, 1972, the United States forces resumed their bombing of North Vietnam. Hanoi was targeted right away. "The bombs were dropping so close that the building would shake,"

McCain later wrote. "The SAMs were flying all over and the sirens were whining—it was really a wild scene. When a B-52 would get hit—they're up at more than 30,000 feet—it would light up the whole sky. There would be a red glow that almost made it like daylight, and it would last for a long time, because they'd fall a long way." When the bombing missions were resumed, there was an influx of new POWs. More important, what these men brought to McCain and the others was news from back home, a commodity that was in short supply in the Hanoi Hilton.

"We had a loudspeaker in the cell, and they would play a program that we called 'Hanoi Hannah,'" McCain recalls. "That was a propaganda program that supposedly was beamed to the South, although I never talked to a soldier that heard it. But it was sort of like Tokyo Rose. It was a lot of the slanted stuff. I found it kind of entertaining. There was never any newspapers or magazines. After Johnson stopped the bombing of North Vietnam in October 1968, there were no new POWs coming in. Then when we resumed the bombing a year and a half, two years, later, new POWs came in. We would get in contact with them eventually through tapping on the walls. Then they would give us information."

McCain learned a great deal about the war. At the end of October 1968, the month before Nixon's election to the presidency, Johnson ordered an end to the bombing of North Vietnam. Then, early in November 1969, Nixon announced what he called his policy of "Vietnamization," a plan that would turn over the fighting of the war to the South Vietnamese. Thus began the gradual withdrawal of American troops from Vietnam, a reduction process that continued during the next several months. In April 1970, Nixon announced that U.S. troops would join up with South Vietnamese troops for an invasion of Cambodia because it had been decided—at last—that the North Vietnamese had been setting up supply bases in Cambodia. The allied assault would target the destruction of those bases. The reaction of the American public was negative; people saw this effort as an escalation of the war. Two months later, Nixon had to change his position.

He declared that, from then on, the United States would provide only air cover to the South Vietnamese, who were continuing their ground assault.

In March 1972, the North Vietnamese began to attack installations in the demilitarized zone. On April 15, 1972, for the first time in four years, the United States resumed bombing Hanoi and the strategically important port city of Haiphong. But that action was nothing, compared to what was about to come. In May, Nixon ordered the mining of Haiphong's harbor. On August 12, the last of the American troops left Vietnam by departing Da Nang, leaving some 43,500 troops in the country as a support force. The number was reduced to 16,000 by December, the month in which the United States began the worst bombing of the entire war. In September 1972, McCain's father had ended his tour as commander-in-chief of U.S. troops in the Pacific. McCain may still have been the crown prince, but his father, the admiral, no longer had the lead role that he had once played on the war's stage.

From December 18 until December 30, 1972, North Vietnam was subjected to relentless bombing that was unprecedented in recent memory. Finally, after 12 days of unremitting hell, it was announced that the on-again-off-again peace talks would resume in Paris on January 8, 1973. Now, all sides—especially the Americans, because of political pressure at home, and the North Vietnamese, because of the threat of another history-making bombing campaign—were motivated to reach an agreement once and for all. Given the possibility that the peace accords could be reached and would allow the United States to exit the war for good, the POWs in North Vietnam began to sense that they might be able to go home.

As this geopolitical drama unfolded, everyday life went on for the American POWs. "John is very competitive," Orson Swindle says. "He doesn't like to lose. In January, the guards were pretty much leaving us alone. We made a deck of cards out of some old cardboard so we could play bridge, and we had these little bridge games. One time, Bob Wagoner and John were playing together;

Jimmy Bell and I were their opponents. In one hand, John was dealt a really poor hand to our seven no-trump. Jim and I just took our time playing each trick and harassing the living hell out of John. He was seething. We just kicked his butt. We just dragged it out. He pouted about it for a day or two. He would walk around the room, stiff-legged, and I would say, 'John, want to play a little bridge today?' We were merciless. He really scowled about this damn thing.

"Then, within a day or two, the guards came around one night and told us to roll up and get ready to move. It became almost immediately apparent, by who they were calling, that this thing might be over. The bombing had stopped and there were lots of reasons to be optimistic. They separated us by date of shoot-down and told us to roll up and get out. I was in the first group so I went back and started rolling up my kit—rice mat and silly-looking pajamas. John ran up, grabbed me from behind and said, 'Orson, I have been a real prick. You know you're my best friend. I have really been acting foolish here. I am just really sorry, and I hate to see you go. We got to get together when we get home.' And I said, 'You little, shanty Irish bastard, I don't want to talk to you. You're such a poor loser.' John's jaw just dropped. He couldn't believe what I just said. I turned around and walked away, then I turned back, grinned, and said, 'I'll see you at home.' I left a few weeks later to be stationed in Jacksonville, Florida. When John arrived in Jacksonville himself, after I did, I was standing at the bottom of the stairs waiting for him as he got off the plane."

There were a few plot points between Swindle's telling McCain goodbye in Vietnam and his greeting him in Florida. On January 20, 1973, McCain was moved from the Hanoi Hilton to The Plantation. For the first time, the POWs were now hopeful that the war might be ending. The peace accords were signed in Paris on January 23, 1973, by Henry Kissinger and Le Duc Tho. President Nixon announced to the world that there would be "peace with honor," and a cease-fire would come as a preamble to withdrawal of U.S. troops and release of all POWs. McCain would not know it until later, but while Kissinger was in Paris to sign the peace agreement, the North Vietnamese offered him the chance to take McCain with him. "[A]fter I got back," McCain would write, "Henry Kissinger told me that when he was in Hanoi to sign the final agreements, the North Vietnamese offered him one man that he could take back to Washington with him, and that was me. He, of course, refused, and I thanked him very much for that, because I did not want to go out of order."

After the accords were signed, American POWs knew it was only a matter of time before they would be released. They could hardly control their emotions. Still, most did not allow themselves to become too hopeful—not until they were told to get on an airplane that would fly them out of Hanoi. That day came for John McCain on March 14, 1973. Along with 106 pilots and one civilian, McCain was taken to Gia Lam Airport. When the Americans were lined up on the tarmac and ready to board the plane in the order of their capture, The Rabbit was there to see them off. "When I read your name off," The Rabbit said, "you get on the plane and go home." As McCain later wrote, "There was no way I can describe how I felt as I walked toward that United States air force plane." Soon after he boarded, the plane, full of POWs, took off and headed for Clark Air Force Base in the Philippines. As the plane climbed into the air, McCain did not look back. His had been an ordeal through which few would ever live. It would be one of the defining periods, if not *the* defining period, of his life. For his service in Vietnam, McCain would eventually be awarded the Legion of Merit, a Silver Star, a Bronze Star, a Purple Heart, the Distinguished Flying Cross, and the Vietnamese Legion of Honor.

McCain would struggle for years with what the Vietnam War had meant to him. "I think history will judge the Vietnam War in two perspectives," McCain says. "One is that it was the most divisive conflict, besides the Civil War, in our history and caused deep divisions within American society. We saw a tragic loss of thousands of young Americans. I think the second way it will be viewed concerns what we learned from that war. And we learned, hopefully, never to make those kinds of errors again—never, in other words, to find ourselves in a conflict without a clear, definable goal [or one] that doesn't have the support of the majority of the people. In short, there was a fundamental reform of the military— and our strategic thinking—as a result of the Vietnam War.

"Looking back, I am proud to have served my country in a cause that I believe was just—Vietnam. I am saddened by the way that it was conducted, which caused the tragic sacrifice of so many inno-cent young lives. I think the average age of those killed in Vietnam is nineteen and a half. That grieves me beyond description."

In fact, many in prison in Vietnam knew this back then. "We had time to analyze what we perceived to be the pattern that led us to Vietnam," Swindle says, "the mistakes that were made and whether or not we should have been there. I think John and I both agreed that we had a great cause. America just screwed it up royally by hav-ing too much political control over the process of the war. The mil-itary generals did not have the balls to stand up and say, 'Damn it, let us run the war or let's get out of here.'" As for John, "He was an incredibly courageous guy," Swindle says. "He shouldered a burden. We all were tortured. He had these injuries. That was bad enough. He had the additional burden of being *who* he was. That carried with it enormous liability, since he could be used. He steadfastly re-fused to be used. He did everything he could. He couldn't be some-one he wasn't. He was who he was. And the North Vietnamese were going to exploit it if they could. He just did a marvelous job."

Others agreed. "John was a hero because of what he could have done," Jack Van Loan says. "We were told nobody was to seek an early release; nobody was to go home early. John could have, but he didn't. We all did the same thing, including John." Paul Galanti, an-other American POW, adds: "John was the toughest of the tough.

He was offered a way out, and he told them to go pound sand. He did it for a lot of reasons, but the biggest, I think, was he knew they were trying to embarrass his father. But what they did to him afterward was awful. And he knew it was coming. They kept trying to convince him to accept early release. And he finally said: 'No, I'm not going to do it.' And they said: 'You will regret that decision.' He got hammered as bad as anybody did after that, and he had a whole lot less to work with, because he was so badly banged up."

Ultimately, then, McCain's heroism came from the fact that he conducted himself as if he were not special, even though he was. "His father may have been commander-in-chief of the Pacific forces," says Everett Alvarez, who was shot down in August 1964, "but, other than that, there was nothing else to distinguish John from any of the rest of us. He was one of the guys. He went through everything we did."

4

COMING HOME

"Other guys would have snapped," Richard Nixon would one day say, "but McCain never did. Those guys were really something. Everyone who served in Vietnam had guts. They could have ducked it; who wants their ass shot off? But McCain went, and once he became a POW—you know, the North really got a propaganda bonanza with him—he just never gave up."

That's how President Nixon described McCain years later. At the time of McCain's release, Nixon was just happy that the war had ended and the American POWs were returning home. Not long after McCain arrived in the United States, Nixon hosted a reception at the White House to honor the POWs who were now back. One picture taken on that occasion would become famous. In it, Nixon is extending a handshake to McCain who, crippled, on crutches, and clad in his navy dress-white uniform, has hobbled up to meet his commander-in-chief.

"That night at the White House John looked so good," George Day says. "He had put on some weight. He was in a white uniform and had a haircut and a good shave. I was delighted to see how young he looked. He probably looked 10 years younger. He looked marvelous." Many of the POWs would remember the reception at the White House as being one of the highlights of the first months they were back in the United States. Coming home was difficult for many of them; Nixon's tribute helped. Of course, Nixon, himself under political fire, was cheered by the event as well. Paul Galanti remembers: "Each of the POWs was invited along with a guest. We had the run of the White House. They even let people on the second floor. I mean, Nixon was ebullient. He was just bubbling. And he said: 'You want to go up and see the living quarters? Go ahead.' The Secret Service had a conniption, but he was the boss. So we went up."

"When Nixon held his welcoming ceremony for the POWs," says Monica Crowley, who served as Nixon's aide during the last four years of his life, "McCain stood before the President of the United States as he commended him for his service, unashamed of that service and proud of his uniform and his country, at the same time so many others were ridiculing those very things. McCain's defiance resonated with Nixon. The resilience, fortitude, and determination that helped McCain survive the Hanoi Hilton were the same qualities Nixon prided in himself. Indeed, Nixon admired McCain for one particularly dramatic reason: He had been held captive in Hanoi during the war, tortured, starved, beaten, and yet he never gave his captors the information they wanted. He never gave up his fellow soldiers. He never asked for preferential treatment, even though his father was Nixon's Pacific commander. He never asked for an early release. He never broke."

What he did have to do, though, was what all POWs had to do: readjust to civilian life back in the United States. For McCain, the transition from prison life to a normal existence was easy. "It took me about 40 minutes to adjust to freedom," McCain says. "That was the time of the flight from Hanoi to get over the water. You see, I was 30 years old when I was shot down, so I was pretty well formed. The ones that suffered the most from the Vietnam War were the 18- and 19-year-old kids." By the time he was reunited with Carol and his children in Jacksonville, he was more than ready to resume the life they had enjoyed before he left for Vietnam.

One fact was especially difficult to deal with: Carol's physical condition. At Christmastime in 1969, while McCain was imprisoned in Vietnam, Carol was almost killed in a car crash. "Carol had taken the kids to her parents' house for the holidays," McCain later wrote. "After dinner on Christmas Eve, she drove to our friends, the Bookbinders, to exchange gifts. It had begun to snow by the time she started back to her parents, and the roads were icy. She skidded off the road, smashed into a telephone pole, and was thrown from the car. The police found her some time later in shock, both legs fractured in several places, her arm and pelvis broken, and bleeding internally.

"Several days passed before she was out of immediate danger. It would be six months and several operations before she was released from the hospital. Over the next two years, she would undergo many more operations to repair her injured legs. By the time the doctors were finished, she would be four inches shorter than she was before the accident. After a year of intense physical therapy, she was able to walk with the aid of crutches." Carol's new appearance was one of the more shocking details McCain had to deal with during his period of adjustment; quite simply, Carol was a different person from the one she was when he left. Then again, Carol could say the same about him.

A first step McCain took to readjust to ordinary life was to write about his years in captivity. On May 14, 1973, two months after his release, McCain published a long and riveting account of his five and a half years in prison in Vietnam in *U.S. News & World Report*. Entitled "How the POWs Fought Back," McCain also addressed the reception the POWs received on coming home, as well as his own future plans. "The outpouring on behalf of us who were prisoners of war is staggering," McCain wrote, "and a little embarrassing because basically we feel that we are just average American Navy, Marine, and Air Force pilots who got shot down. Anybody else in our place would have performed just as well. My own plans for the future are to remain in the navy, if I am able to return to flying status. That depends on whether the corrective surgery on my arms and my leg is successful. If I have to leave the navy, I hope to serve the Government in some capacity, preferably in Foreign Service for the State Department. I had a lot of time to think over there and came to the conclusion that one of the most important things in life— along with a man's family—is to make some contribution to his country."

But first he had to deal with his medical problems. Over the next several months, McCain underwent three operations; for six months he also submitted himself to grueling physical therapy twice a week in an attempt to regain movement in his leg, since his shattered knee had left the leg frozen. "They said, 'You're never going to fly again,'" recalls Carl Smith, a navy pilot who became a close friend of McCain in the early years after his return home. "He said, 'I can do it, I can do it.' He underwent ghastly physical therapy—where they just bent and pushed and stretched and stretched till he was ready to scream—in order to restore enough flexibility that he could fly. The problem was doing the brakes. You have got to be able to put your feet on the pedals and press up at the top of the pedals. Those are your toe brakes. He just didn't have the dexterity at that point because of the injuries. He said, 'No, whatever it takes I am going to do it.' And he kept at it until he finally could do it. So they put him back in there."

The physical therapy was conducted by a brilliant and gifted woman named Ann Lawrence. McCain would later credit her with performing a virtual miracle on him. She worked with him until he was able to achieve the unthinkable: be a pilot again. The operations and the physical therapy allowed him to become mobile enough to get back into the cockpit, but there were certain functions that he would never again be able to perform since he had been given such bad medical attention by the North Vietnamese. Because of the injuries to his arms, McCain would not be able to type on a keyboard or tie his shoes. He could not raise his arms above his head to comb his hair, and he would never be able to throw a baseball or a football again. Naturally, even though he could fly, he was never as limber as he was before he was shot down. Without the full use of his arms and legs, working the gears in the cockpit was hard for him. He also had trouble maneuvering the steering wheel. McCain knew that if he was never able to regain his complete physical abilities, he would not advance to the higher ranks in the navy. He would most certainly never gain the rank of four-star admiral—a tradition that had been well established in his family.

During the academic year 1973 to 1974, as he focused on getting the medical treatment he needed, McCain attended the National War College in Washington. At the end of 1973, he was featured in *U.S. News & World Report*, six months after he had written the article that had received tremendous notoriety and made him even more of a celebrity in the world of the military. "The last two years that we were there the treatment was relatively mild," McCain was quoted as saying in the article published on December 31, 1973, as he discussed his readjustment to life in America. "If we had come out, say, in late 1969, the problems of readjustment would have been far more severe. Starting in 1971, the food improved considerably. We were allowed to be together more and set up educational programs, and work out some simple entertainment and do a lot of things for each other, to keep our minds active." According to McCain, he had had few problems adjusting to normal life. "The only thing," he said, "that has been somewhat of an adjustment is the difference in the pace of living now, as compared to in prison. There, the big event of the day usually was when it came your turn to go out of your cell to bathe. I still seem not to have enough time to do all the things that I want to do—or have to do."

Finally, in the article, McCain discussed the major political story that had unfolded since he had returned: the controversy that had surrounded President Nixon as a result of the Watergate scandal. "It has certainly made me sad that this situation should have arisen," McCain said about the man who had welcomed him home only a few months earlier. "However, I feel that, in the context of history,

Watergate will be a very minor item as compared with the other achievements of this Administration, particularly in the area of foreign affairs. I do hope that this country will get over Watergate and get going again on the very serious problems that we're facing today." Clearly, McCain had misjudged the impact that would come from Watergate and how it would define, for at least the remainder of the twentieth century, Nixon's presidency.

Because of his national reputation, McCain was approached for his opinion on issues that were important to veterans, especially those who had been in Vietnam. "During this period," says Senator John Warner, who was secretary of the navy from 1969 until 1974, "I had the extraordinary challenge of deciding how to dispose of allegations against several prisoners who allegedly, should we say, worked with the North Vietnamese in a manner that was detrimental to other prisoners and . . . , in some cases, benefited themselves. I remember one case came to the point where we were about to file general court martial charges, and I sought John's advice as to the reaction of himself and other prisoners, were the case to go to full trial and be scrutinized publicly. His advice was very helpful to me. The record shows that the Department of the Navy made the decision to deal certain punishments to these individuals, short of bringing court martial."

McCain finished his year at the War College in August 1974, right around the time President Nixon was forced to resign from office to avoid impeachment by the Congress. The navy then officially approved McCain's return to pilot status. His remarkable recovery was accomplished because he was willing to put himself through excruciating pain during his physical therapy sessions. With his physical state now drastically improved, McCain undertook, in the late fall of 1974, a trip that he hoped would help him emotionally as well. He may have had few problems adjusting to life back home, but he was not sure how he felt about the world of Vietnam he had left behind. Nine months after he had flown out of

North Vietnam on an air force plane, McCain joined a group of guests who flew to South Vietnam to celebrate what turned out to be the country's last National Day.

The American troops had left some time back, but the war between North and South Vietnam continued to grind on. When McCain arrived in South Vietnam, he was surprised to see protests raging against the government. Nguyen Van Thieu was in what became the final days of his presidency. While there, McCain attended a reception for former POWs, hosted by a Thieu aide. When he spoke to the group who had attended the reception, the aide said Vietnam could never repay the American POWs for what they had done for his country. If there was anything the government could do, the aide said—anything at all—they should let him know. McCain, sitting among the others at the gathering, raised his hand and suggested one way he could be repaid. "You can take me to Con Son," he said, referring to the most brutal facility in South Vietnam's prison system. It was easily on a par with the Hanoi Hilton; among other things, it featured tiger cages in which prisoners were kept.

The aide was stunned by McCain's request; he was noncommittal about whether a trip to Con Son could be arranged. Finally, on the last day of his visit, McCain was taken to the island, 50 miles off the southern coast, where Con Son was located. It seemed to do McCain some good. He reported later, to friends, that the South Vietnamese had prison facilities just as gruesome and inhumane as those of the North Vietnamese.

One veteran who joined McCain on the trip was Jim Thompson, the longest-held American POW in Vietnam. (He was captured by the Viet Cong in South Vietnam on March 26, 1964, and held until his release in 1973, when he would be described as a "skeleton with hair.") "I had heard legendary stories of Jim's fierce resistance to his captors," McCain would write about Thompson, "and of his heroic endurance under conditions that would have killed many men. Our trip together afforded me a welcome opportunity to get to know him. Never will I forget the love of country that accompanied his surviving the prison camps, his extraordinary test of patriotism, or the evident damage that years of concerted cruelty had done to this good and decent man."

After he returned to the United States, McCain reported to his new assignment in the navy: He was a member of Attack Squadron 174, stationed in Jacksonville, Florida. When he resumed active duty, he was named the executive officer (XO) of the squadron. (Many of the men who had been held as POWs were promoted to higher ranks, to make up for the service time they had lost in Vietnam.) While he went about his life at the base in the state that had once been home to him before he went to Vietnam, McCain was fully aware of military and political events. He watched as, on April 30, 1975, the Vietnam War finally ended with the defeat of South Vietnam by North Vietnam. On March 4, 1976, two friends, James Stockdale and George ("Bud") Day, were awarded the Medal of Honor by President Gerald Ford at the White House. And as the country tore itself apart during the first presidential race ever to take place after a president had resigned from office, he saw Jimmy Carter defeat Gerald Ford for the presidency. On July 1, 1976, McCain got good news: He was named commanding officer (CO) of the squadron. Formerly XO, he was now promoted to CO. This would be his chance to show the kind of leader he could be.

"At the time, VA-174 was the largest aviation squadron in the navy, with 70-some aircraft," says Carl Smith, who served under McCain in Jacksonville. "The job of the squadron was to train the replacement pilots that were being assigned to the fleet. The whole squadron had become rather stagnant. It was at a time when, because of the post-Vietnam defense budgets, there really wasn't enough money to maintain the aircraft properly. As a result, a lot of practices were followed that were not optimal; cannibalization is the best example. You could routinely take from one airplane to keep another airplane flying. Realizing this was a bad practice, the navy implemented a policy that prohibited cannibalizing any airplane that had been down for 60 days or longer. Those were called SPINTAC aircraft.

"When McCain became the CO, it was his squadron to run and he could put his mark on it. He immediately began making changes. He fired people, and he replaced people at the top, both senior officers and senior enlisted, whom he thought were not being as effective as he wanted them to be. He wanted real leadership. He wanted the squadron to come to life. It was an incredible transformation—what happened over the next six to nine months.

"We had at any given time one-third of our aircraft in that SPINTAC category. McCain said, 'All right, let's get these airplanes up and running.' The decision was reached that said McCain would write a letter to the authorities in AIRLANT in which he said, 'If you will give me permission to cannibalize the SPINTAC aircraft, then I will commit to getting every one of these aircraft up and flying, save two.' That was essentially putting his career on the line because there were a lot of guys back then who thought McCain was all show and no go.

"What we saw next was an example of leadership. McCain would say, 'You guys in the maintenance department, here's what I want you to do: I want you to get those airplanes up and flying. Give me a schedule and tell me how long it is going to take.' He was perfectly comfortable delegating. Now they had a goal and a challenge, and they had permission to do the cannibalization on the SPINTACs. They got that permission in response to McCain's letter. The enthusiasm in the maintenance department was magnificent after that. It went from being a stagnant, mediocre squadron to being a highly motivated, highly achieving organization.

"Let me just tell you what happened. What McCain would do was go around to each one of those shop spaces every day and motivate people. It was wonderful to see how he picked up the morale of the place that had just been dragging along. He would do it by giving his personal attention to individuals. Just by going there and talking to them, kidding with them, just showing them he knew what was going on. To cut to the chase: We finally got down to where we were approaching the change of command, and it was either the day before or the day of the change of command that we flew our last SPINTAC. And I mean our *last*. When he turned that squadron over, it was SPINTAC free. We didn't even have the two left. Every airplane in that squadron was off the SPINTAC list.

"We had had zero accidents. Six months after John left, the next CO had a fatal accident. And the SPINTAC numbers came back. It was strictly a function of leadership—John's leadership. It was bad before him. It was bad after him. And it was great while he was there. As a result of his leadership, the squadron was awarded the navy's meritorious unit commendation for the first time in its history."

In his stint in Jacksonville, McCain left a lasting impression on many of the men he commanded. "I'll never forget the first time I saw John McCain," says Chuck Nash, who was a young pilot in training in VA-174 when McCain was the commanding officer (Nash would retire a captain). "A member of a new class, I was sitting at a table in a training room. We had listened to all of these guys tell us how hard our training was going to be for the next six months. Then we were told the skipper was coming in. The door opened, we all stood at attention, and McCain entered. He had a slight limp, and you could tell his arm was not effective. 'Carry on,' he said as he sat down with us pilots at the table. 'Welcome,' he said, and then proceeded to tell us how hard our training was going to be but how we were going to get through it. After all the gloom and doom we had heard from others, here was a real pep talk.

"Everyone knew what McCain and the other POWs had been through over there. We all knew. To us, they were heroes. They were gods."

During the fall of 1977, in the wake of his success in Jacksonville, McCain was assigned to a Washington post that his father had once held: the navy's liaison to the Senate. The minute

McCain got there, the liaison office changed, just as the attack squadron had changed when he took it over. "The Senate Liaison Office had been a backwater office of no particular consequence before McCain arrived," says Carl Smith, who remained close to McCain even after he moved to Washington. "Suddenly, the electricity around the place was attracting people. It became alive. It became a center for people to come after-hours and just shoot the breeze with John McCain."

Specifically, it was McCain's job to be the face of the navy in dealings with the Senate. His job included planning trips abroad for senators—trips on which McCain often accompanied the Senate delegation. Another main function was dealing with lobbyists, a duty McCain sometimes found difficult to bear. "In the late 1970s," Carl Smith says, "Grumman, who manufactured the A-6, was aggressively lobbying to get some increased capabilities added to the A-6 at some expense, and Congress had expressed some misgiving about whether or not this program was really worthwhile. A retired admiral, who was a lobbyist for Grumman, once went to see McCain, and McCain was basically sticking to the navy line, which was not all that enthusiastic about the airplane and what Grumman was proposing to do. There this retired admiral was, leaning rather heavily on McCain, trying to get him to commit to supporting his project. Finally, the guy went too far, and McCain abruptly told him, 'Look, I don't work for Grumman in general, and I don't work for you in particular.'" That was the end of the meeting."

McCain was also asked to perform other duties for the navy. One was too much for him to accept. "Shortly after John came back to Washington, he came to a party at my house," says Ken Ringle, who had remained a friend of McCain since they were students together at Episcopal. "He told me that President Carter had been talking about opening up preliminary negotiations for establishing normal relations with North Vietnam. They were going to send a delegation from Congress. John said to me, 'They want me to go. Sometimes this country just asks too much of you. Can you believe that the navy expects me to go? Can you believe they would even ask me?' He was really bitter about this." It had been one thing for McCain to return to South Vietnam to celebrate the national holiday of one of our allies, the people for whom we were fighting. But being friendly with the North Vietnamese was another matter altogether. McCain could not sit down and be cordial toward the very enemy that had almost killed him not very many years ago. Needless to say, he did not go to North Vietnam.

Mostly, in those years, he worked directly with the senators and their staffs; among the senators who became good friends were John Tower of Texas (a Republican), William Cohen of Maine (a Republican), and Gary Hart of Colorado (a Democrat). "I think John went on two or three of those trips I was involved in," Gary Hart says, "and as you might expect, traveling together you begin to bond. Whereas he was always very respectful of us and our titles, being of roughly the same age, and observing the protocol of us being in the Senate and him being a navy officer, we nevertheless got to be friends. John had very strong opinions—and not only on military matters. He was not reticent. He was clearly a conservative, traditional Republican in many respects, but also clearly a free-thinker. When he did take a position, he wasn't just spouting a party line or an orthodox position. He would back up his views with his own arguments." In particular, Hart admired McCain's sense of humor. "It was a raucous, military, masculine, occasionally profane sense of humor," Hart says. "When talking about the navy, he would quote Churchill, who said of the navy, 'Rum, sodomy, and the lash!' So John would joke, 'I love the navy! Rum, sodomy, and the lash!'"

Then again, McCain often saw irony in his daily life. "Senator 'Scoop' Jackson and his party were traveling by train into one of the hinterlands of China," says Frank Gaffney, a defense industry insider and a longtime friend of McCain, "and as they rolled along, passing through cornfields, the senator remarked to the Chinese liaison how he had a great deal of corn in his home state of Washington. The senator said he was personally very fond of corn and expressed the desire to have some with dinner that night. As John tells the story, the Chinese liaison was amused by the request, but fairly anxious to please Senator Jackson. So he contacted the appropriate authorities to make it happen. Sure enough, that night they got to dinner and along with one-hundred-year egg and stewed eye of dog, they had corn on the cob. Senator Jackson apparently bit into the ear that was in front of him with considerable gusto and never let on that it was corn for forage, not for human consumption. Dutifully, his foreign policy adviser and John McCain proceeded to do so as well. Senator Jackson even had a second ear just to demonstrate how pleased he was and how polite he was to his Chinese host."

When he was not traveling, McCain was always present in his office in the Russell Senate Office Building. Since the office was down the hall from the suite of offices occupied by John Tower, a powerhouse on the Senate Armed Services Committee (not to mention a proud navy veteran), McCain and Tower soon became good friends. "Tower took a natural liking to him for two reasons," says Carl Smith, who followed McCain to Washington and got a job on the Senate Armed Services Committee, thanks to McCain. "First, Tower was navy, but, second, Tower greatly respected intelligent people. He enjoyed being around intelligent people who were well informed, and John was—and is—extremely well informed. He has an incredible appetite for reading, and after Vietnam he had this need to read everything he could get his hands on—books, magazines, newspapers. Carol loved to read too. Every night, they would end the night by reading. McCain was truly a voracious reader. He once gave me a book to read just after he had come back from China. It was a very insightful book about the causes of the Chinese revolution. It was that interest, that facet of his intelligence, that made him so attractive to John Tower because Tower was truly a global and strategic thinker. McCain is the same."

While McCain was making more and more new friends and connections through his job in the Senate, he and Carol were also leading a busy life at home. "Their house in Alexandria was active with people coming and going," says Carl Smith, who lived with the McCains for four months after McCain had helped him to get the job on the senate committee. "John and Carol were active socially. They probably had people over for dinner three or four nights out of the week, just as they had had in their house in Jacksonville. It was a meaningful procession that came through there too. There were all sorts of interesting people, not just from the navy or the government. It was all sorts of people from the community, and even young people. I remember I was over there one night, and there was a guy in there, a young guy, who had just biked across America. Somehow, John and Carol knew him."

Still, the main focus of McCain's life at present was working with the senators. He was able to get along with senators who fit almost any political description, from left-leaning Democrats like Gary Hart to Southern conservative Republicans like Thad Cochran. "As the senate liaison for the navy, John took some trips with Howard Baker and me and Bill Cohen and a few other senators," Thad Cochran says. "We went to Europe. I got to know him and I developed a very strong feeling of affection for him. I had respect for him as a naval officer, although he was accident-prone. He said it didn't take a genius to get shot down. The real heroes were the great pilots who didn't get shot down. But he had already crashed at least one time before Vietnam. And he had been involved in the *Forrestal* fire. He could have gone overboard or gotten blown up in that explosion too. He had a lot of close calls."

In the spring of 1979, events transpired that would change McCain's life completely. Even though friends saw a rosy picture when they looked at John and Carol McCain's marriage from outside, privately the couple was having difficulty. After years in captivity, McCain was not totally able to return to the life he had led with Carol before he went to Vietnam. As the marriage became rocky, McCain was unfaithful to Carol, or perhaps the marriage became rocky *because* McCain was unfaithful. Later, there would even be reports that he had, as the *Boston Globe* put it, "affairs with subordinate female personnel." The McCains had tried to achieve some semblance of a normal life after McCain's return home—and, to a great extent, they had accomplished this—but the problems continued nonetheless. Years later, Carol would tell a reporter the main trouble was not complicated: McCain may have been 40, but he was acting like he was 25. That, in and of itself, could prove disastrous, and, indeed, the McCains eventually separated. Then, before long, McCain's life took another dramatic turn. The reason: a chance meeting in Hawaii.

McCain was escorting a Senate delegation on a trip that included a stopover in Hawaii. He was now age 42. One night, at a reception for the senators, hosted by the Pacific commander, he met a captivatingly beautiful young woman named Cindy Lou Hensley. She was the age Carol would later say McCain wanted to be at that time: 25. In addition, her demeanor was appropriate for what she was—a school teacher. She was quiet, soft-spoken, perhaps even bashful. She had recently earned her master's degree from the University of Southern California, but she was born and raised in Arizona and was every bit an Arizonan. Dignified and reserved, she had a strength of character and a resolve of will that came from growing up in the shadow of a powerful and successful father. For Cindy Hensley was no ordinary school teacher. Her father, James W. Hensley, owned one of the largest, if not *the* largest, Anheuser-Busch beer franchises in the United States. This made him one of the most prominent businessmen in all of Arizona. He was a father who loved his daughter too; McCain could tell that right away when he met Hensley in Hawaii. Cindy's parents—her mother's name was Marguerite—had accompanied her there for spring break.

McCain became smitten with Cindy that night. They had dinner alone after the reception and agreed to stay in touch. In the coming months, McCain, now separated from Carol, saw Cindy whenever he could. On August 1, 1979, he was promoted to captain as a reward for his excellent work for the navy in the Senate. During the fall of 1979 and into the spring of 1980, it became clear that his marriage to Carol was beyond repair. The couple was divorced on April 2, 1980. In the divorce, which Carol did not contest, McCain agreed to provide generous support for Carol and the three children, an arrangement that helped the couple stay on good terms, even after the divorce.

Some onlookers criticized McCain for divorcing Carol; they claimed that her disfigurement had driven the couple apart. "I think there are some people who have used that improperly in an effort to discredit McCain and make him sound like he was looking for somebody else after he came back and found out Carol had been injured," Carl Smith says. "Carol McCain is an absolutely wonderful person. When John came back, their relationship was still very strong in spite of the accident. He wanted to have another child, as I recall, but unfortunately Carol's doctors told him that could never happen because of what she had been through." In the opinion of Smith and others, McCain desired to create a new life for himself. Having children was the ultimate metaphor for that new life, and his attraction to Cindy offered its fulfillment.

As his separation from Carol was turning into divorce, McCain was seeing Cindy and learning about her family's business, Hensley & Co. It was not a story without history. "James Hensley," the *Arizona Republic* would one day write, "started in the business with his brother, Eugene, before World War II, in the heady days after Prohibition. At United Liquor Co. in Phoenix and United Distribution Co. in Tucson, the Hensleys worked with Kemper Marley Sr., a rancher and political fixer who years later would figure into the infamous car-bomb murder of *Arizona Republic* reporter Don Bolles. Marley died in 1990, but was never legally implicated."

Hensley had served as a bombardier in Europe during World War II and somehow survived when his B-17 was shot down over the English Channel. "Returning to the liquor trade afterward," the *Republic* wrote, "he and his brother were convicted in 1948 of falsifying records to hide the illegal distribution of several hundred cases of liquor. Eugene went to jail for a year. Jim got a six-month suspended sentence. In 1953, Jim Hensley, Marley, and their company again were charged with falsifying records, but they were acquitted. The Hensley brothers soon bought into Ruidoso Downs horseracing track in New Mexico. Eugene stayed to run it. Jim returned to Phoenix, where, in 1955, he landed his Anheuser-Busch distributorship. It was long rumored that Marley had a hand in the deal." Hensley represented many different brands of beer until he was, to quote the *Republic*, "approached by Anheuser-Busch with a deal: He could have the franchise for Maricopa County [in Arizona] if he agreed to sell only its brand." Hensley agreed. From then on, Hensley owned the franchise for the county, which became one of the fastest growing urban areas in the United States. This was the perfect example of Hensley being in the right place at the right time to be offered the right deal. It would make him and his family extremely wealthy.

On May 17, 1980, six weeks after his divorce from Carol, McCain married Cindy Hensley in a ceremony in Phoenix. At the wedding, McCain's best men were two senators, Gary Hart and William Cohen. Throughout the rest of 1980, the year Ronald Reagan defeated Jimmy Carter for the presidency, McCain continued to serve as senate liaison; then, on April 1, 1981, after he had been assigned as a commander of an aircraft carrier, a post he determined he could not hold because of his injuries, McCain made the hard decision to retire from the navy. He had been in the service now for 22 years, but it became obvious that he would never hold the rank that both his father and grandfather had held, so he made the move to retire. The official reason for his discharge was "permanent physical disability."

There was another motivating factor in his decision to leave the navy. On March 22, as he was flying on a military aircraft while traveling in Europe, McCain's father had died of heart failure. He had retired from the navy in 1972, when he gave up his command in the Pacific, and had led a comfortable life with Roberta after that. Part of that life included extensive travel, which Roberta loved. They were on yet another trip when Admiral McCain died suddenly—as his father had, years before. The admiral was 70 years old. As John McCain stood beside his father's grave on the day in March when the admiral was buried in Arlington National Cemetery just as *his* father had been, he realized that there was no immediate reason for his remaining in the navy. Also, he had been gripped by another calling—politics.

Soon after his retirement from the navy, McCain moved to Tempe and was named vice president of public relations for Hensley & Co. McCain worked there through the remainder of 1981 and on into 1982. But early in 1982, he learned that Congressman John Jacob Rhodes, who had enjoyed an illustrious 30-year career in the House of Representatives (it culminated in his serving as minority leader in four sessions of Congress), had decided not to run for re-election. Not too long before this announcement, McCain had gone to Rhodes, then the leader of the Republican Party in the House, to ask his advice about running for public office. Rhodes told him he should go to Arizona and try for either the state legislature or a county board of supervisors; McCain told Rhodes he was not interested in taking either of those political paths. Now, in March, with Rhodes stepping down, McCain announced he was running for *his* seat.

Years later, McCain would focus on just what had motivated him to get into politics. "After Vietnam, I was hospitalized for a period of time," McCain says. "Then I went to the War College; next I was able to go down and be the executive officer and then the commanding officer of an A-7 squadron. But finally I was sent up to Washington to be the navy liaison officer to the Senate, and that's where I first got very interested in politics. I became friends with people like Gary Hart and Bill Cohen. John Tower, I became very close to. When I saw, literally, a senator write an amendment on the back of an envelope that affected the military to a significant degree, I thought: 'Hey, this is something that should interest you.'"

5

THE CONGRESSMAN
FROM ARIZONA

"When John married Cindy," says Senator Thad Cochran, a Republican from Mississippi, "he changed his domicile, from wherever it was, to Arizona. One night, he invited Rose and me over to their house. They lived on one of those W streets in Alexandria. I could sense then he was beginning to think about running for Congress. That night, he mentioned that Barry Goldwater wasn't going to be in the Senate forever. And I figured it out. He had already set his sights on the Senate, not just the House. He would run for the House, but then the Senate. He had it all planned out ahead of time. It was quite amazing. He didn't say anything, by the way, about the White House."

Gary Hart also saw the growth of McCain's interest in politics—particularly in the Senate. "I think something happened in the late 1970s where the navy let him know he wasn't going to get a star," Hart says. "That's when he decided to retire. Also, whenever you get to the Senate, one of the old-timers takes you aside, especially if you're young, and says, 'Young man, you will spend the first six months wondering how you got here, and years wondering how everybody else got here.' So I think McCain's exposure to us made him think, 'If these guys can be senators, *I* can be a senator.' I think that's exactly what happened. He looked around when he got there and realized all these guys put their pants on one leg at a time."

First, however, he had to win a seat in the House of Representatives. At the time McCain heard that John Rhodes was going to retire from Congress, he and Cindy owned a house in a district other than the one Rhodes represented. The McCains quickly bought and moved into a house in Rhodes' district, the Arizona First. As soon as McCain announced he would run, he was greeted with charges of being a carpetbagger. In typical McCain fashion, he ignored the charges—his longest period of domicile in one place, he said at the time, had been in Hanoi—and organized his campaign. Between the time he declared his candidacy in March and the primary election in September, it was his goal to meet as many of the voters in his district as possible. To do so, McCain set out on an unbelievable odyssey: He walked from house to house, knocked on door after door, and talked to as many people as he could meet or greet during the months scheduled for the campaign. By the date of the primary election, he had walked so much he had worn out two pairs of shoes.

"John was a dark, dark horse in that primary," his political consultant, J. Brian Rhodes, later said. "No poll, including our own, had him finishing anywhere higher than third. But the great thing about John is: He can have a 3-in-10 shot and be thrilled." The hard work, motivated by his underdog status, paid off. On September 14, in a four-way primary race among Republicans, McCain got the most votes. The final tally was: McCain 15,363; Ray Russell 12,500; James A. ("Jim") Mack 10,675; and Donna Carlson-West 9,736.

Having become the nominee of the Republican Party, McCain continued his walking tour of the district. From March to Election Day, he knocked on some 20,000 doors. Because McCain's district was heavily Republican, he had less to worry about in the general election than in the primary. The Democrats' candidate, William Hegarty, was able to mount only a less-than-lustrous campaign. On November 2, McCain received 89,116 votes compared to Hegarty's 41,261.

On January 3, 1983, John McCain took the oath of office for the First Congressional District of Arizona and became a member of the 98th Congress. Ronald Reagan had been president for two years, and McCain was more than happy to fall in line behind the man he felt was his party's steadfast and unrelenting leader. For the men who were POWs with him in Hanoi, McCain's entry into the House was especially pleasing. "We were both big fans of Felix the Cat," says Orson Swindle, who would hold a number of posts in the Reagan Administration, among them assistant secretary of commerce, before he became a federal trade commissioner, "the single-dimension, flat, no-depth cartoon character. We laughed about how, when Felix would get into trouble, he would always put his little paws up and rock back and forth with a sheepish grin on his face. When something went wrong among the group when we were prisoners, we would get pissed off at each other and start hollering and screaming. John and I would just look at each other, do the little hand signal, and bob back and forth grinning. I happened to be in Washington right after John was elected to Congress and sworn in. I found a Felix the Cat doll. He was just moving into his first congressional office when I walked in and said, 'I got a friend of yours here.' I gave him the doll and he just grinned. I said, 'I want you to put this somewhere where you can always see it and always remember—when you get too big for your britches—*always* remember where you came from.'"

During his first session as a congressman, McCain was assigned to the Committee on Interior Affairs and the Select Committee on Aging. He also became chairman of the Republican Task Force on Indian Affairs. (Congressional committee assignments are made by the majority party working in consultation with the minority party; among the factors considered is a member's seniority, although all final decisions concerning committee membership and chairmanship are at the discretion of the majority party's leadership.) As he settled into his new office and became familiar with his committee assignments, which were not impressive but were typical of those given to freshman representatives, McCain again attracted the attention of *U.S. News & World Report,* which had been covering him since his return from Vietnam.

In late March 1983, the magazine ran a round-up piece called "A Return Visit With POWs—Ten Years Later." In the article, McCain was quoted as saying: "I spent three and a half years in solitary confinement. During that time, I lost a sense of personal ambition and gained a desire to spend my life serving my country." Later in the interview, he added: "Our role has changed. El Salvador is an example. We obviously have advisers there, but if it had not been for the Vietnam War, we might have had the 82nd Airborne there. I think there is a real reluctance on the part of the government to involve American troops again." McCain, a military hawk, clearly was not happy with the Reagan Administration's caution.

During the 98th Congress, McCain sponsored a number of bills, amendments, and resolutions. His work reflected two main areas of concern: Indian affairs and red-meat conservative issues that were important to his constituents back home. On Indian affairs, he sponsored, to quote from government records describing the proposed legislation, a bill "to add a representative of Indian tribal governments to the membership of the Advisory Commission on Intergovernmental Relations" (the proposal was made on April 13, 1983); a bill "to amend the Act of November 2, 1966 regarding leases and contracts affecting land within the Salt River Pima-Maricopa Indian Reservation" (May 4, 1983); a bill "to amend the Indian Tribal Government Tax Status Act of 1982 with respect to the tax status of Indian tribal governments" (November 18, 1983); and a bill "to provide for the administration and probate of certain estates under laws of the Salt River Pima-Maricopa Indian Community, and for other purposes" (May 22, 1984).

For the most part, the McCain-sponsored bills related to Indian matters got little support, although a few made their way successfully through the Congress and onto the desk of President Reagan. McCain's bill to amend the Act of November 2, 1966, progressed through each step in Congress and was signed into law by Reagan on November 22, 1983. That law, according to its abstract, "[a]uthorizes specified leases of trust or restricted lands on the Salt River Pima-Maricopa Indian Reservation (Arizona) to contain provisions for binding arbitration of disputes. [It also p]rovides that failure to submit to such arbitration or comply with the arbitration ruling shall be deemed a civil action arising under the Constitution, laws, or treaties of the United States."

In addition, McCain sponsored, as quoted from government documents: an amendment "to add that nothing in Title III (Operations and Maintenance) is to be construed to supersede or amend the War Powers Act" (submitted on May 24, 1984); a bill "to amend section 1201 of title 18 of the United States Code to provide a mandatory life sentence in the case of certain kidnappings of persons who have not attained the age of 18 years" (submitted on June 13, 1984)—a bill that, according to a government abstract, "amends the Federal criminal code to provide a mandatory life sentence for any person who kidnaps an individual under the age of 18 and [i]mposes the death penalty in any case where such a victim dies as the result of the kidnapping"; and a bill "to provide for the expansion and improvement of the National Cemetery System to better meet the needs of veterans" (submitted on June 29, 1984)—a bill that, according to a government abstract, "[d]irects the Administrator of Veterans Affairs to report to Congress a plan to expand the national cemetery system in at least ten areas with the greatest need."

By and large, during his first term in the House, McCain supported President Reagan and his agenda. He concurred with Reagan on his hardline stands against the Soviet Union. He voted for Reagan's tax cuts, despite the fact that some critics of Reagan's economic policies, including Vice President George H. W. Bush, who had challenged Reagan for the Republican presidential nomination during the 1980 campaign, had called those policies "voodoo economics." McCain agreed with Reagan that the United States needed to take a firm stand in favor of democracy in Central America, although he noted that, after Vietnam, the United States was much more hesitant to get involved directly in internal military conflicts that take place in other countries.

But, on one issue, McCain dramatically broke ranks with Reagan. In the early 1980s, Reagan had sent American servicemen, mostly marines, into Lebanon to serve as peacekeepers. McCain had been outspoken in his criticism of the decision. He argued: "I do not foresee obtainable objectives in Lebanon; I believe the longer we stay, the more difficult it will be to leave." Instead, he recommended, in no uncertain terms, "as rapid a withdrawal as possible." Reagan did not heed the advice. The marines stayed. Then, on October 23, 1983, a suicide bomber attacked an American military barracks in Beirut and killed 341 U.S. troops, almost all of them marines. In the wake of the horrific attack, Reagan decided to pull the American troops out of Lebanon; some critics, McCain among them, pointed out that the move had come too late. Had Reagan made the decision earlier, the American servicemen could have been saved.

By supporting President Reagan the way he did, McCain showed he was capable of being a team player. By opposing Reagan—and doing it vocally—on issues like sending U.S. troops into Lebanon, McCain signaled he was still his own man, despite the fact that he was now a politician. In his first term in office, when he exhibited a combination of loyalty and independence, McCain became so popular that no other Republican challenged him in the primary when he ran for reelection in September 1984. As if it were an omen of the good things to come, Cindy gave birth, on October 23, to the couple's first child, a daughter they named Meghan. In the general election on November 6, as Reagan crushed Walter Mondale in the presidential race, McCain destroyed *his* Democratic opponent, Harry W. Braun III. McCain got 162,418 votes; Braun drew only 45,609. It was a stunningly lopsided victory, and McCain was happy to celebrate it when he was sworn into office on January 3, 1985. In his second term in the House, he served on the Committee on Foreign Affairs, the Committee on Interior Affairs, and the Select Committee on the Aging. The assignment to the Foreign Affairs committee showed that McCain was building some clout. That assignment also reflected his ongoing interest in geopolitics, a fascination that friends such as John Tower had noticed years earlier.

In the 99th Congress, McCain continued to propose legislation. During the session, as House records show, he offered: a bill "to amend title 38, United States Code, to provide for annual reports to Congress to facilitate the orderly expansion of the National Cemetery System"; a bill that called for the Granite Reef Aqueduct of the Central Arizona Project to be renamed the "Hayden Rhodes Aqueduct"; a bill "to amend title 18, United States Code, with respect to offenses relating to the sexual exploitation of children, and for other purposes"; a bill "to authorize programs for the treatment and prevention of drug and alcohol abuse among Indian juveniles"; a bill "to provide for the settlement of certain claims respecting the San Carlos Apache Tribe of Arizona"; a bill "to recognize the organization known as the Red River Valley Fighter Pilots Association"; a bill "to provide for the proper administration of justice within the boundaries of the Salt River Pima-Maricopa Indian Community"; a bill "to amend the authority of the United States Geological Survey"; an amendment "dealing with the National Endowment for Democracy, making available to the public, upon request, all information regarding its organization, procedures, requirements, and activities, except those exempted by the Freedom of Information provisions of current law"; and an amendment "to set the per diem compensation rate for victims of terrorism at a minimum of $20 a day, adjusted by the Consumer Price Index."

One highlight of his second session in Congress occurred in February 1985. Between February 19 and 22, McCain returned to North Vietnam for the first time since his release from prison in 1973. The U.S. government, through the navy, had asked him to go there a decade before, but McCain had not yet been emotionally ready for the journey. By 1985, time, distance, and his new life gave him a new perspective on his years in the Hanoi Hilton. Specifically, he was traveling to North Vietnam in an effort to obtain information about Americans who were listed as missing in action but were still not accounted for. This effort would dominate much of his time in the coming years. One particularly memorable and emotional moment occurred during the trip. When McCain returned to the spot in Hanoi where he had been shot down in October 1967, he discovered that the North Vietnamese had built a monument there—to him.

"There was one interesting episode at a monument to my capture built by a lake in downtown Hanoi," McCain told U.S. News & World Report. (The magazine published an article about his trip, which was also documented by Walter Cronkite for a CBS-TV special to commemorate the tenth anniversary of the fall of Saigon.) "This was the lake I parachuted into and was pulled out of on October 26, 1967. I still don't understand why they built this monument. They even have the wrong branch of service—air force instead of navy. Anyway, Walter Cronkite and I, and a film crew, went down there one day to the statue. A very large crowd of Vietnamese gathered, all pointing to me and repeating my name—'Mah-cain, Mah-cain.' It was perhaps the first time that someone was more recognized than Walter Cronkite."

Some time after the trip with Cronkite, McCain reflected on his sojourn to his past: "My trip back evoked memories not of my own discomfort but the fact that a lot of my close friends didn't come back and gave their lives in what most Americans describe as a vain effort. My thinking about them again reinforces my opinion that the United States should not send its young men to fight and die in a conflict unless the goal is victory."

To U.S. News & World Report, he also said: "It certainly was an emotional experience for me—and not totally a pleasant one. But it was important to me, as one who did return, to do what I could for those who have not. I wanted to stress to the Vietnamese officials I talked to that the missing-in-action issue is still very large in the minds of millions of Americans. Until the Vietnamese show signs of making much greater efforts at a full accounting of those Americans still missing, there's very little prospect of improved relations with the United States. . . . It's my belief that for ten years Vietnam has used the MIAs in a most cynical fashion. They give back a few bodies every number of months to some visitors. Some of those bodies were of men we know were shot down, captured and photographed. To give their bodies back ten or so years later is the most cynical thing possible."

In particular, McCain wanted more of a good-faith effort from Vietnam, which was still, after all, a client state of the Soviet Union. McCain felt, for instance, that it was necessary for the Vietnamese to allow recovery teams from the United States to come into their country. "The fact," McCain said, "that they recently allowed one of our recovery teams into a plane crash site in Laos, where we think we recovered approximately 13 bodies, indicates that perhaps they're now realizing that their old policy probably wasn't the best way to go."

McCain also believed that the Vietnamese desperately wanted to reestablish a relationship with the United States. "I got the distinct impression," McCain said, "that the Vietnamese do want better relations with the West, largely because their economy is in such terrible shape. I think it is fair to say that they won the war but lost the peace."

In the autumn of 1985, McCain introduced a congressional resolution "condemning the Government of the Soviet Union for the killing of Charles Thornton, an American journalist working in Afghanistan." For this resolution, dated October 10, McCain was joined by 58 cosponsors—among them: Bob Dornan of California, Newt Gingrich of Georgia, Henry Hyde of Illinois, Dan Burton of Indiana, and John Kasich of Ohio from the Republican Party and

Barney Frank of Massachusetts and Morris Udall of Arizona from the Democratic Party. As week after week in the fall passed, most of McCain's time and energy was occupied in probing the rumors that Republican Senator Barry Goldwater might not run for reelection. His seat would then be available if McCain wanted to run for it. McCain had one concern. The Washington gossip was: If Goldwater retired, Bruce Babbitt, Arizona's Democratic governor, might run for the Senate seat. McCain believed he could defeat Babbitt, but he hoped his opponent would *not* be the state's popular and respected governor.

On March 18, shortly after Goldwater had announced he was retiring, Babbitt said he would not seek the Democratic nomination for Goldwater's Senate seat. On March 19, McCain held a news conference at the Hyatt Regency in Phoenix and declared he was a candidate for the Republican nomination for the Senate. Apparently, Babbitt had made up his mind not to run for the Senate because he was convinced McCain *was* running, and he worried that McCain was too strong as a Senate candidate. Instead, Babbitt had decided to run for president.

On May 2, 1986, McCain celebrated the birth of his first son, whom he and Cindy named, in the McCain family tradition, John Sidney McCain IV. Given this boy's name and pedigree, it seemed predetermined that, in 18 years, he would enter the Naval Academy as a preamble to joining the navy, as three generations of McCains had done before him. But John McCain III was not thinking about his son's heritage in 1986; he was busy achieving political successes. On September 9, he won, unopposed, the Republican nomination for the Senate. On October 10, McCain enjoyed a legislative victory when his "Indian Economic Development Act of 1985" was presented to President Reagan, who signed it into law on October 20. The bill had passed the House on June 26, and the Senate on October 3. The law, according to government records, "declares that the Congress finds that the San Carlos Apache Tribe of Arizona has satisfied its obligations to the United States with respect to certain liabilities evidenced in an agreement dated May 15, 1985 [and p]rovides for the per capita distribution of specified judgment funds to members of the Gila River Pima-Maricopa Indian Community."

In the fall campaign, because of McCain's popularity and power, the Democrats had to find a nominal candidate; none of the viable Democrats in the state were willing to challenge him. It didn't hurt McCain that the full force of the Republican Party was behind him. He even had as his campaign manager the man whose job he hoped to fill: Barry Goldwater. "The night before the election," McCain recalled later, "[Barry] got a little nostalgic, and he said, 'You know, John, if I had been elected president in 1964 and had beaten Lyndon Johnson, you would have never spent all those years in a Vietnamese prison camp.' I said, 'You're right, Barry. It would have been a Chinese prison camp.' He was not amused by that."

On November 4, 1986, after an impressive campaign that featured a whistle-stop train trip that took him all across the state, McCain defeated his opponent, Richard Kimball, in the general election. McCain got 521,850 votes to Kimball's 340,965. "It was a cakewalk," says Tim Meyer, the campaign manager for Jon Kyl, a Republican who was running for a seat in the House of Representatives from Arizona in 1986. "It was surprising. McCain had a very weak opponent. When you look back on it, in hindsight, McCain also ran a good campaign, a safe campaign. He ended up winning by a large margin." The race was so easy he had time to help out Kyl. "He made phone calls for us," Meyer says. "He made suggestions on the media. There were a couple of strategy sessions where we sat down and reviewed what our thoughts were, what our message was. I think McCain also helped with some behind-the-scenes introductions. I know I met with his campaign manager constantly, and we actually did a lot of get-out-the-vote efforts together. They allowed us to use their phone banks, and things like that. They were very, very helpful."

On January 3, 1987, McCain was sworn in by Vice President George H. W. Bush as a senator from Arizona serving in the 100th Congress. In the future, McCain would make a name for himself as a senator and would join the ranks of some of the most successful and influential men of his generation. Because of the war injuries he suffered in Vietnam, he was not able to follow in the footsteps of his father and grandfather and achieve the rank of four-star admiral, but, in his own way, during his years in the United States Senate, he attained a comparable level of achievement. He became the best in his field—and *that* was his family's tradition. But John S. McCain III would go down a path that neither his father nor his grandfather could have ever dreamed of. He would run for president.

From the start of his Senate career, politically sophisticated observers studied McCain carefully. He would have a constant admirer in the man who had shaken his hand in 1973 and welcomed him home to the United States after his years in Vietnam. "President Nixon watched McCain operate in the Senate with a sense of bemused admiration," says Monica Crowley, Nixon's final aide. "He relished the fact that McCain was considered a maverick within his own party, a characterization Nixon often applied to himself." Nixon would one day say of McCain's Senate career: "Everything in him told him to fight. It was instinctual. The Senate is a different kind of battlefield, but McCain has it in him to do whatever it takes. He's scrappy. He's a fighter." The same, of course, could have been said about Richard Nixon.

6

ONE HUNDRED KINGS

At the start of 1987, John McCain became a member of the club that many people consider to be the most exclusive in the world: the United States Senate. The Senate's unique political force comes from the fact that each of its members wields immense autonomous power, which is why some observers describe the Senate as being composed of "one hundred kings." A senator does often act as if he or she is running a separate kingdom. Throughout American history, it has not been uncommon for some senators—names like Claiborne Pell, Everett Dirksen, and Jacob Javits come to mind—to use the Senate to develop their own influential power bases. However, those same power bases have produced legislative improvements and social institutions that have had a profound effect on the country as a whole. In recent history, more than a few senators (or former senators) aspired to the presidency, among them John Kennedy, Lyndon Johnson, Edmund Muskie, Robert Kennedy, Hubert Humphrey, George McGovern, Gary Hart, Walter Mondale, and Edward Kennedy. Barry Goldwater, like McCain, was a Republican senator from Arizona when he ran for president against Lyndon Johnson in 1964. Goldwater lost, but his effort was significant. By creating the same kind of base, McCain could launch his own bid for the presidency, should the time ever seem right for him to do so.

In the early days of his tenure as senator, McCain spent some time acclimating himself to his new job, moving offices, shuffling his staff, and familiarizing himself with the power that could be wielded by one of the one hundred kings. He also began getting used to his new committee assignments. He was pleased to be appointed to two committees that were coveted on both sides of the Senate aisle: the Committee on Armed Services and the Committee on Commerce, Science, and Transportation. He was also appointed to the Select Committee on Indian Affairs, generally regarded as an albatross by most Republicans because it dealt with issues that were more important to Democrats.

On April 2, 1987, three months after he was sworn in as a senator, McCain attended the first of two meetings that would fundamentally alter his life and career. On that day, he joined fellow senators John Glenn of Ohio, Alan Cranston of California, and Dennis DeConcini of Arizona—all Democrats—in DeConcini's office for a meeting with Edwin Gray, the chairman of the Federal Home Loan Bank Board (FHLBB). The focus of the meeting was Charles Keating and his Lincoln Savings & Loan (S&L) of Irvine, California, which was owned by American Continental Corporation of Phoenix. In the meeting, DeConcini, Gray later suggested, asked that Lincoln, then under investigation by the board, be given lenient treatment. In return, Lincoln would be willing to limit its high-risk investment, and it would move into the home mortgage business.

A week later, on April 9 at six o'clock, the same four senators, along with Donald Riegle of Michigan, also a Democrat, met again in DeConcini's office to discuss the Lincoln S&L. This time, four officials from the Federal Home Loan Bank of San Francisco were present. The five senators lobbied the officials to go soft with a regulatory action that was about to be imposed on the Lincoln S&L. "We wanted to meet with you because we have determined that potential actions of yours could injure a constituent," DeConcini said to the officials at the start of the discussion, according to a transcript of the meeting that was later released to the *Wall Street Journal*.

To show his willingness to get involved, Glenn said at one point that the Lincoln S&L was an Ohio-based company, even though it wasn't. At another juncture, when one official commented that it was extremely odd to have five senators pressuring them about a case, DeConcini replied, "It's very unusual for us to have a company that could be put out of business by its regulators."

In short, DeConcini argued that the regulators should go easy and allow the Lincoln S&L to make some high-risk loans that could bring in big profits. But the tone of the proceedings changed when the four officials told the senators, in no uncertain terms, that the Lincoln S&L had been managed so badly that its operators could be indicted on criminal charges by the Department of Justice. In later testimony, Glenn, Riegle, and McCain claimed that they departed as soon as they learned of this possibility, and that Cranston and DeConcini were then alone with the examiners. But the damage had been done. It was only a matter of time before these two meetings would become the impetus for what would eventually be known as "the Keating Five scandal," an ordeal that had an acute effect on McCain's life. Much later, he acknowledged: "It will be on my tombstone, something that will always be with me, something that will always be in my biography. And deservedly so."

At the time, McCain could not have estimated the political nightmare that would result from the two meetings he had attended on behalf of Charles Keating. McCain had gone to the meetings for one main reason: For many years, right up until the time of the meetings, the two men had been good friends. They became close not long after they met in 1981. Then, each August, in 1984 through 1986, McCain and his family flew, aboard Keating's company jets, to Keating's home in Cat Cay in the Bahamas for a vacation. In all, McCain, or someone in his family, used Keating's jets for nine corporate or charter flights. In violation of congressional rules, McCain, a member of the House at the time of the flights, didn't disclose the trips. McCain also failed to reimburse Keating's companies for the flights, which cost, as it was later revealed, $13,433. Keating was generous with contributions too. Directly or through associates, he gave McCain some $100,000 over time.

Indeed, by 1986, the McCains' social and political bonds with Keating had become so strong that Cindy and her father invested $359,100 in a shopping center named Fountain Square, which Keating was developing. Later, McCain revealed that he knew about the investment but considered it legitimate because Cindy, a financial force in her own right, was a free agent apart from her husband, and because they filed separate income tax returns. When the McCains married, Cindy had insisted on having a prenuptial agreement that allowed her to continue to have an independent financial status. Filing separate income tax returns was just one way to achieve that.

Apart from their business and political dealings, McCain and Keating simply liked each other. It was not unusual for them to pal around in Arizona, and they spoke on the telephone regularly. But all that changed just before the first meeting in April 1987. Desperate to have the regulators go easy on his struggling savings and loan, Keating had wanted his friends in the Senate—including McCain—to represent him in the offices of Edwin Gray and the bank regulators in San Francisco. McCain had even received a letter in which an accountant at Arthur Young and Company criticized the unusually long examination of the Lincoln S&L. The letter gave some credence to what Keating was asking McCain and others to do. Still, McCain refused to go to the offices of Edwin Gray or of the bank regulators based in San Francisco. When McCain let it be known he wouldn't travel to either office, Keating described him to DeConcini as a "wimp"—a remark that got back to McCain.

Keating met with McCain in McCain's Senate office on March 24, 1987. McCain was direct in telling him what he would and would not do for him and what he thought of the "wimp" remark. "Keating came to my office," McCain later told the *Washington Post*, "and I said to him, a friend of mine, 'I have done all I can. Period.'" That was not good enough; Keating wanted McCain to make additional moves on his behalf. When McCain told Keating he did not believe it would be prudent to take any more actions for him, Keating got mad and called him a "wimp." Now angry himself, McCain gave Keating a "dressing down" in which he said, according to one of McCain's aides, he "had not spent five and a half years in a prisoner-of-war camp to have his courage or integrity questioned." As McCain put it, "[Keating] got angry and left, and we soon heard he called me a wimp"—yet again, when he met with a group of senators. "I," McCain would say, "never had any further dealings with him." As the aide put it: "The relationship clearly had come to a screeching halt."

So why did McCain go to the meetings? Because, as his counsel would later remark, "He also knew that he had a hell of a mess on his hands. He had a letter that stated in no uncertain terms that there was a very difficult problem here with this examination. . . . John McCain's staff determined that there was a legitimate reason to inquire about the length of the examination. . . . [A]t the beginning of the April 2, 1987, meeting, John McCain indicated that he did not want to do anything improper, and that he was only there to inquire. Mr. Gray replied that it was proper to ask questions."

In and around April 1987, McCain no doubt thought his dealings concerning Keating *were* legitimate. He had attended the meetings, which seemed innocent enough, after he had ended his friendship with Keating; now he intended to get on with his job of being the junior senator from Arizona. For the rest of the year, he did just that. In May, he traveled to West Germany to participate in the commemoration of the 750th anniversary of the city of Berlin. In June, he wrote a searing editorial about the Reagan Administration's decision to reflag Kuwaiti tankers so that the United States could provide military protection for them in the event they were attacked by Iran. Iranian officials had threatened to attack the Kuwaiti tankers because they were being used by Iraq, then at war with Iran, to ship Iraqi oil.

"The Reagan Administration plan to reflag and escort Kuwaiti oil tankers can be viewed as a dangerous overreaction in perhaps the most violent and unpredictable region of the world," McCain wrote in the *Arizona Republic* on June 21. "American citizens are again being asked to place themselves between warring Middle East factions, with no tangible allied support and no real plan on how to respond if the situation escalates." The plan's main point seemed to be to guarantee the "unimpeded flow of oil" in this part of the world—a noble but dangerous proposition. "In a real crisis, some of the burden of defending the energy lifeline must fall to our allies, who are much more dependent than the United States on Gulf oil. . . . What would happen if we do undertake the protection of Kuwaiti oil tankers? The United States will be defending the ships of a supposedly neutral nation that, in fact, serves as the conduit for Iraq's oil and most of Baghdad's imported war material. The Iranians have repeatedly stated their intention to attack Gulf tankers, regardless of who is escorting them." This was in mid-1987, when Iraq was an ally of the United States; only a few years later, Iraq, under Saddam Hussein, would become one of America's most notorious enemies.

In August, McCain took a very public position on the Gramm-Rudman bill, a piece of Senate legislation that required the United States government to balance its budget. "There is no doubt in my mind that Gramm-Rudman has motivated Congress for the first time to work seriously toward reducing budget deficits," McCain wrote on August 22 in another editorial in the *Arizona Republic*. "I do not support the approach of raising taxes without making significant spending cuts," he wrote, referring to a recent proposal by the Democrats to balance the budget by increasing taxes in 1988. "Instead, we need to reprioritize our spending needs and cut out unnecessary programs before asking the American taxpayer to send an average of $200 more a year to the Treasury. . . . Clearly, reducing the deficit is the most important and difficult domestic challenge facing this nation. I believe that Congress and the president will need some procedural tools to assist in meeting this challenge. At the top of the list is the Gramm-Rudman effort."

Late in August, at the request of the Republican leadership in the Senate, McCain traveled to Honduras and Costa Rica for a three-day fact-finding trip. Between September 18 and 20, he toured El Salvador and Costa Rica at the request of the Senate majority and minority leadership. In late September, he revealed to the public what he had learned during these two trips to Central America. "Clearly, the United States should give the Central Americas the necessary space and diplomatic support to take the lead in the negotiating process," he wrote on September 27 in still another editorial in the *Arizona Republic*. While few senators publish editorials, even in their home state newspapers, McCain, with these recent editorials, was establishing a practice that he would maintain for years: He would communicate with his constituents—and advance his own political agenda—by frequently running long and well-thought-out editorials in his state's most influential newspaper. As he developed clout as a legislator, these editorials began to affect national opinion, but at first the target was Arizona voters. "To appear, instead, to be mouthing public words of encouragement," he continued, "while privately betting on a Central America failure—or worse, to appear to follow a script whose tragic finale is predictable: negotiations collapse, the United States is blamed—would only serve to isolate the United States in the hemisphere." He was referring, of course, to the debate over whether the United States should continue to fund agents of democracy who were fighting in Central America, particularly the Contras in Nicaragua. "We must not let partisan divisions divert attention from Nicaraguan realities. . . . We must assure that democratization is a fact, not another broken promise. . . . We must not trade our long-term security interests for a short-term political fix."

McCain made one more fact-finding trip to Costa Rica early in November, again at the behest of both the majority and minority leadership in the Senate. His opinions on foreign affairs, at least in this region of the world, had become revered by both parties' leadership in Congress, a not-inconsequential compliment for a first-year junior senator. He also had wonderful news in his personal life: Cindy was now pregnant with their third child. Her due date was in May.

From January 11 to 14, 1988, McCain was back in Costa Rica under orders from the bipartisan Senate leadership. In March, to expand his interest in foreign affairs, McCain began focusing more intently on the country with which his name had become most associated—Vietnam.

Near the end of March, he told the *Washington Post* that it was time for the United States to begin a necessary process, whatever that might be, to "catalyze a resolution of outstanding political and humanitarian issues." In other words, McCain now believed it was incumbent on the United States to find a way to develop, with Vietnam, a relationship that might eventually end the many years of conflict between the two nations. It was a stunning move on McCain's part; he was apparently offering forgiveness to the country that had once brutalized him and held him prisoner. His thinking on the issue of North Vietnam had come a long way, considering that, in the late 1970s, he had refused to go there, and when he *did* go back, in 1985, he called the experience "not totally a pleasant one." Now, he was beginning a long and complicated political connection that would develop with Vietnam during the coming years.

In his personal life, he was thrilled when, on May 21, Cindy gave birth to their second son, whom they named James Hensley McCain, in honor of Cindy's father.

The year 1988 was a presidential year, and in the Republican Party there had been some drama (not enough to upset the expected order of succession, as it turned out) when Senator Robert Dole challenged George H. W. Bush, the sitting vice president, in the primaries. The feud got so heated that, at one point in a debate in New Hampshire, Dole snapped at Bush that he should "stop lying about my record." Dole crushed Bush in the New Hampshire primary, but on Super Tuesday Bush won all 17 contests, many of them in the South, and effectively wrapped up the nomination. From then until the Republican National Convention, which was scheduled to take place in the New Orleans Superdome in August, the speculation associated with the Bush campaign centered around whom he would choose as his running mate. At some stage of the process, McCain's name ended up on Bush's vice-presidential short list. In mid-July, McCain met with Bush at his home in Washington and, as he reported to the *New York Times*, "told him I am not interested in the job."

On Wednesday, July 22, McCain addressed the actions of Jane Fonda, a person toward whom he had harbored deep anger and resentment since her visit to Vietnam years before. Fonda had just made international news during an interview by Barbara Walters in which Fonda apologized for her actions during the Vietnam War. "I'm proud of most of what I did, and I'm sorry for *some* of what I did," Fonda told Walters. The interview was taped in the living room of Fonda's house in Santa Monica and aired on the ABC television network. "I'd like to say something not just to the veterans but to the men in Vietnam who I hurt, or whose pain I caused to deepen because of the things I said or did. I feel I owe them an apology. My intentions were never to hurt them or make their situation worse. It was the contrary. My intention was to help end the killing and the war. But there were times when I was thoughtless and careless about it, and I'm very sorry that I hurt them, and I want to apologize to them and their families." As for the picture in the tank, Fonda admitted: "It was a thoughtless and careless thing to have done. Being in a communications business, and knowing the power of images, it was thoughtless and cruel. I take full responsibility for having gotten on the gun. . . . I should have said no."

McCain could not resist responding to Fonda. "I would call upon Miss Fonda to join with me, with the VFW [Veterans of Foreign Wars], the Disabled American Veterans, the American Legion, the League of Families, and others who have spent these many years trying to resolve these issues," McCain said in a speech on the Senate floor. The issues to which McCain was referring were those involving POWs and men counted as missing in action, and McCain believed that Fonda could prove the sincerity of her apology by helping to resolve the POW/MIA problem. Specifically, McCain was addressing the fact that over 2,000 POWs and MIAs could not be accounted for. "These issues," McCain said, "we know, will only be resolved when we can close this chapter of American history which has caused so much pain, suffering, and division within our country." When Vietnam officials said, soon afterward, that the country would not cooperate with an effort to account for missing United States military personnel—the men who had been the focus of a prolonged debate that had been raging between the countries since 1973— McCain said he would withdraw his support for legislation that would have set up limited diplomatic relations with Vietnam.

For McCain, August was dominated not by the past but by the future. At the Republican National Convention in New Orleans, he delivered a speech that made him a national political star almost overnight. At their convention in Atlanta, the Democrats had nominated Governor Michael Dukakis of Massachusetts, who then selected, as his running mate, a colleague of McCain: Senator Lloyd Bentsen of Texas. McCain may have made a trip to the vice president's house to tell him he was not interested in being *his* vice president, but McCain's name was still on George H. W. Bush's short list. Because Bush did not intend to reveal his choice of a running mate until the convention had started—it was one way to add drama to an otherwise lackluster proceeding—a heightened sense of anticipation surrounded the speech McCain was going to make on Monday, the first night of the convention.

For transportation to the convention, McCain chose a whistle-stop train tour, not unlike the one he used successfully in his Senate campaign in 1986. At seven o'clock on the morning of August 13, the McCains departed from Phoenix by train, en route to Louisiana. McCain was looking forward to resting up on the two-day trip, but, by the time he got to Houston on Sunday, the train was running so far behind that he decided to get off and fly the rest of the way. He arrived in New Orleans on Sunday night, just in time to have dinner with Katherine Graham, whose newspaper, the *Washington Post,* would run a glowing feature article about him the next day. Because his name was on Bush's vice-presidential short list, McCain's profile had elevated. A week before, in a fawning profile in the *New York Times,* he was described as "a young man in a hurry" who had "established himself not only as a key voice in the Senate on defense and foreign policy issues, but also a rising star in the post-Reagan Republican Party." The talk of his being a possible running mate with Bush intensified.

On August 14, the *Arizona Republic* ran an editorial McCain had written in reaction to the Democratic National Convention and Michael Dukakis's acceptance speech. The Democratic candidate had taken shots at the accomplishments of the Reagan Administration and the weaknesses of Bush as a candidate and potential president. "I am proud," McCain wrote, "to be associated as a Republican senator with a Republican administration that has virtually ended inflation (that was double-digit when the administration took office) and slashed unemployment to its lowest level in many years. I am proud to be associated with an administration that has restored U.S. military strength while working diligently and successfully with the Soviet Union on agreements to reduce nuclear weapons. . . . To win in November, [Bush] needs to present not only a vision of the future but also how he plans to implement that vision." To underscore the fact that Bush was more qualified to be president, McCain then compared the resumes of Bush and Dukakis on foreign policy, child care, the economy, and other issues.

When the day finally arrived for McCain to give his speech at *his* convention, he spent the morning rehearsing, and the rest of the day making the rounds of luncheons, receptions, and caucus appearances. He did a series of radio talk-show interviews as well. On Monday night, he headed for the Superdome. The evening's lineup was impressive. There would be a five-minute video tribute to Barry

Goldwater, who would watch from the VIP section. There would be a tribute to First Lady Nancy Reagan and then a farewell address by President Reagan. But before those main events, three speeches would be delivered, addressing the topics of the economy, jobs, and national defense. The economy and jobs would be covered by Congressman Jack Kemp of New York and Elizabeth Dole, who had been the secretary of transportation in the Reagan Administration. For the convention's 2,277 delegates, the speakers would put the best spin possible on what the Reagan Administration had done on those key topics, and would then describe what a Bush Administration would hope to do. Next on the program was a short video introduction that featured McCain's military service. His speech, which he had written himself, would deal with national defense and foreign policy.

At first, McCain's speech—12 minutes long and centered around the themes of "Duty, Honor, Country"—sounded as if it would be purely political. When he proclaimed that Bush would continue the legacy of a strong defense policy, a hallmark of the Reagan presidency, McCain took a swipe at the Democratic nominee. "Michael Dukakis," McCain said, as he stood at the podium, a mere spec in the cavernous Superdome, "like Jimmy Carter before him, clearly doesn't understand [what it means to have a strong national defense]. . . . Michael Dukakis seems to believe that the Trident is a chewing gum, that the B-1 is a vitamin, and that the Midgetman is anyone shorter than he is." It was a political cheap shot not worthy of the rest of the speech, for, soon after he made the remark, the speech turned personal. Leaving behind the hyperbole that any midrange political-speech-writing hack could have produced, McCain told a story only he could tell. He described an incident, during his years as a POW in Vietnam, that he would never forget.

He told the audience about Mike Christian of Selma, Alabama, one of his fellow POWs in the Hanoi Hilton. Using white and red cloth, McCain told his audience, Christian had sewn, with a bamboo needle, a replica of the American flag inside his blue shirt. The

POWs, as McCain recalled, would hang Christian's shirt on the wall and pledge their allegiance to the flag. "I know that saying the Pledge of Allegiance may not seem the most important or meaningful part of our day now," McCain told the silent audience, "but I can assure you that, for those men in that stark prison cell, it was indeed the most important and meaningful event of our day." Then, one afternoon, the Vietnamese guards discovered the shirt. Livid, they confiscated it, dragged Christian from the cell, and, out of sight from the other POWs but close enough for all of them to hear what was happening, they beat him severely.

When Christian was returned to the cell, "He was not in good shape," McCain told the crowd, now fully enraptured by the story he was telling. Moments later, McCain said, in the faint light of the cell, Christian had retrieved his bamboo needle and gotten a piece of red cloth, a piece of white cloth, and a shirt. When McCain looked over at him, "With his eyes almost shut from his beating," McCain said, his voice steady but full of emotion, the pain of the many-years-old event now defining his every word, "he was making another flag."

Throughout the hall, delegates were openly weeping. Off in the wings, waiting to come on stage to make his much-anticipated farewell address, Ronald Reagan could be seen with tears welling up in his eyes. When McCain finished, he was given a sustained, impassioned standing ovation by the delegates. It was that rare thing one hopes to see at contemporary political conventions: an honest moment full of personal pathos and social and political meaning.

If that was what McCain thought he needed to do to impress Bush enough to become his running mate—from all accounts, McCain was on the short list until the very last moment—it didn't work. The next day—the second day of the convention—Bush announced at a press conference held away from the convention hall that he had chosen as his running mate Senator Dan Quayle of Indiana. The short list itself was leaked only 20 minutes before Bush made his choice, and McCain's name was on it, despite the fact that no one from the Bush campaign had ever contacted McCain about a background check. On Tuesday, instead of being named as the party's vice-presidential candidate, McCain got the job of national chairman of an organization called Veterans for Bush, a political group that had been invented to help get Bush elected.

No sooner had the name "Dan Quayle" come out of Bush's mouth than the choice looked like a disaster. The whole ordeal of Quayle's introduction to a national audience had an unsettling, awful feel to it. As Bush announced his name and brought him up before an audience at a staged event on the Mississippi River in New Orleans, the two men looked like cheerleaders at a high school pep rally, except that Bush was old enough to be Quayle's father. Then, because the nation had no idea who he was, Quayle got to make his first impression. It was unforgettable. Wearing white shirtsleeves and with a goofy expression plastered on his face, Quayle delivered a speech so silly, so startlingly inappropriate and amateurish, he reminded onlookers of a giddy schoolboy running for a student-body presidency—not the American vice presidency. Party officials were horrified; so were others elsewhere who were watching the episode as it was being broadcast live on national television. By the time Quayle finished with his spectacle, only sturdy Barbara Bush would have the stomach to refuse to admit that her husband had jeopardized his career, not to mention his chances of winning the presidency, by picking this mindless caricature of a politician.

Immediately, so much criticism of Quayle began that rumors started to circulate that he might not survive as a member of the ticket. Also, as soon as Bush named him, a controversy emerged involving Quayle's service in the National Guard. Apparently, Quayle's family had pulled strings to get him into the National Guard, a way of avoiding the unpleasantness of going to Vietnam as McCain and others had. The media made it a headline issue, but the Democrats didn't. Lloyd Bentsen, the Democrats' vice-presidential nominee, had exerted the same influence to get his son into an exclusive unit of the Texas Air National Guard. Although there were few if any reports about it at the time, Bush had made phone calls to get his son, George W., into the same unit Bentsen's son was in. Annoyed that Bush had selected a chicken hawk over McCain, a legitimate war hero, many delegates were calling for Bush to rethink his choice of Quayle. McCain himself called the choice "a mistake." He also told the *Arizona Republic*: "Once you're burned like this, I think you're going to look at somebody like Dole or Simpson or one of those who clearly have been heavily screened. My God, it's one thing to make a mistake once." Still, McCain said he was unaware of any attempt to try to get him on the ticket to replace Quayle.

Bush refused to budge; an inability to admit mistakes was one of his character traits. Bush aides insisted there was no plan to remove Quayle from the ticket, and, sure enough, on Thursday night he was nominated. When McCain was asked if Quayle was now acceptable simply because he had received the nomination, he said, "Oh, no, the issue has got to be resolved." Specifically, he was bothered by the flap over Quayle's National Guard service. "I think it's clearly serious," McCain said. "One of the reasons why it's serious is because it's already beginning to overshadow [Bush]. Here we are talking about how important the [acceptance] speech is, and I think that most of the reporters are going to the . . . floor tonight asking questions about Dan Quayle rather than focusing on [Bush's] speech. And, by the way, that's entirely normal. I don't criticize that. That's their job."

Quayle was not replaced, and when Bush, Quayle, and the Republicans left the Superdome, they were damaged by the controversy but ready to take on the Democrats. Luckily for Bush, he had a political genius working for him: Lee Atwater. Vicious, ruthless, and blindly ambitious, Atwater would do whatever it took—no matter how ugly, ethically questionable, or hurtful to other people—to get his candidate elected. He would do all of that for Bush.

When McCain returned to Phoenix after his appearance at the Republican National Convention, he could tell right away that he was being treated differently. To anyone who had watched him at the Superdome, especially the Arizonans he represented, it was apparent that he was a rising star on the national political stage. Because all politics are local, McCain had accepted an invitation to be a keynote speaker at a meeting of the Phoenix Union High School District on the Tuesday after he returned from New Orleans. The venue for this speech was much different from the one he had experienced at the convention—2,000 teachers were assembled at the South Mountain High School—but McCain hit his marks just the same. He denounced the epidemic use of cocaine in the country. He blamed the crisis in the Arizona governor's office (in February, Evan Mecham had been impeached for concealing an illegal campaign contribution, misuse of state funds, and obstruction of justice, and in April he had been removed from office, having been found guilty of high crimes and misdemeanors) on voter apathy, saying, "One reason we went through the turmoil of the past year and a half is voter apathy. That's a chapter in our state's history we never want to see repeated." Most notably, he attacked Proposition 106, a statewide referendum that was being advanced by the so-called English-only movement. "I don't understand why," McCain told the teachers, "we would want to pass some kind of initiative that a significant portion of our population considers an assault on their heritage and our culture."

In early October, because of his position on the English-only initiative and his willingness to fight for a pluralistic American culture, McCain was one of 10 members of Congress who were honored by the National Council of La Raza, a nationwide coalition of Hispanic organizations. In a speech at a ceremony in Washington, before an audience of 500, McCain again attacked English-only initiatives. "The building of our great nation is not the work of immigrants from one or two countries," McCain said at the event, which took place on Wednesday, October 5. "It is the work of many cultures." As for Arizona's Proposition 106, McCain said: "It makes us a smaller country. I prefer to live in a bigger place. I prefer to live in a growing America, as proud of its diversity as it is of the ideas that unite us. . . . Our nation and the English language have done quite well with Chinese spoken in California, German in Pennsylvania, Italian in New York, Swedish in Minnesota, and Spanish throughout the Southwest. I fail to see the cause for alarm now."

Because this was the political season, McCain immersed himself in the local and national politics that led up to the November election. He was an honorary cochairman of the campaign of Keith DeGreen, the Republican candidate who was running against the Democratic incumbent, Senator Dennis DeConcini. An unwritten rule in the Senate forbids a sitting senator to campaign actively against another sitting senator; that practice is seen as demeaning the carefully maintained dignified tone of the Senate as a government body. Under that rule, McCain should have sat out the campaign DeGreen was running against DeConcini, but, as would later be revealed, there was more than a little bad blood between McCain and DeConcini, so McCain decided not to remain as removed from the campaign as he could have been.

One gesture McCain made involved the Republican Senatorial Campaign Committee. As DeGreen surged in the polls toward the end of the campaign, the senatorial trust decided to give DeGreen $212,000, which DeGreen spent on a barrage of negative television ads attacking DeConcini. Furious, DeConcini accused McCain of being behind the effort to get the senatorial trust to give DeGreen the money; on that issue, DeConcini pointed out that he had refused to do the same in the previous election, when McCain was running for the Senate. McCain denied that he had anything to do with the commercials and challenged DeConcini to provide documentation that he had been involved—which, of course, DeConcini could not do. However, McCain could not deny that, toward the end of the campaign, he, along with other prominent Republican senators like Bob Dole, had become visible in their support of DeGreen over DeConcini—a tactic that also irked DeConcini.

On Election Night, McCain watched with pleasure—and, to be honest, with some surprise—as George H. W. Bush defeated Michael Dukakis in a landslide victory. Somehow, the choice of Dan Quayle had not torpedoed the campaign, although the effort was helped considerably by the brilliance of Lee Atwater. Using techniques like an ad campaign that featured Willie Horton, a felon who committed murder while on early release in Massachusetts during Dukakis's watch as governor, Atwater successfully painted Dukakis as an out-of-touch egghead Massachusetts liberal who was bent on destroying the national pride and patriotism that had become the earmarks of the Reagan years. It did not hurt that Bush had been Reagan's vice president. Many Reaganites felt compelled to continue the Reagan legacy by voting for the man the retiring president wanted as his successor.

On the local front, by the end of Election Night, it was clear that DeConcini had won reelection to the Senate by a wide margin. In the final count, he got 57 percent of the vote, compared to DeGreen's measly 41 percent. On the day after the election, DeConcini held a press conference in which he criticized McCain and charged him with helping DeGreen get the money needed to pay for all of the negative ads that had attacked him. "In politics," DeConcini said, "you find out who your friends are and who you can rely on, and you deal with a lot of people. I have no quarrel with Mr. McCain. I'm going to deal with him because it's good for Arizona, and we have had successes together in the past, and I see no reason we can't continue. Am I disappointed? You bet I am." Specifically, DeConcini held McCain responsible for the negative ads, since, if he had not actually gotten the money for them, he could have tried to get DeGreen not to run the ads, at the very least. "[McCain] knows and I know that he could have done something about it," DeConcini said, "but that's his judgment."

McCain ended the year with another major trip. He and Cindy traveled to Pretoria (the capital of South Africa) and Johannesburg, as well as other places in a country that had begun a historic political and social transformation. The journey did not involve official government business, so the McCains paid for the trip themselves.

In January 1989, McCain again left the United States on a fact-finding mission. On January 4, he departed for the Middle East, on a trip for which he paid the $2,403 airfare himself, where he and Senator Nancy Kassebaum of Kansas, among others, would spend 10 days meeting with officials in the region and visiting the Israeli-occupied territories, as well as Israel, Jordan, and Syria. In the middle of the trip, while he was visiting Damascus, McCain gave a telephone interview to the *Arizona Republic* in which he said of the situation in Palestine, "I think that there's very little doubt that the Palestinian people believe that at this time Yassar Arafat and the PLO [Palestinian Liberation Organization] speak for them." McCain, who would meet that day (Thursday, January 12) with Egyptian president Muhammad Hosni Mubarak before returning to the United States on Friday, was questioned carefully by the reporter about Arafat. Did McCain believe Arafat's recent peace initiatives were genuine? "I remain skeptical," McCain said flatly. "I hope . . . that he is sincere."

McCain returned to Washington in time for the inauguration of the new president. Then, during the first days of the Bush Administration, McCain became embroiled in one of the ugliest fights of his political career. For the post of secretary of defense, Bush had nominated John Tower, the former Texas senator and a longtime friend of McCain. (Elected to the Senate from Texas in 1960 to fill the seat being vacated by Lyndon Johnson who had just been voted vice president, Tower had resigned from the Senate in January 1985.) In conducting its background search on Tower, the FBI had unearthed myriad stories, many of which directly addressed the issue of character. In the 1970s, Tower apparently drank heavily, and, as a result of what could have been called his borderline alcoholism, he had, at times, engaged in questionable behavior such as womanizing—or so some reports implied. The Senate had to confirm Tower for the cabinet post, and many senators had had memorable experiences with him when he was drinking excessively. More than a handful of the senators were concerned that, though Tower said he now controlled his drinking and, on any given day, never had more than a couple of glasses of wine with dinner, he still might have an addiction to alcohol. This could pose a severe problem, considering the cabinet post for which he had been nominated.

On Tuesday, February 21, it became apparent that rumors of Tower's drinking and womanizing were going to delay the Senate's confirmation hearings. Bush, fearful that this episode could turn into a debacle that would mar the early days of his administration, held a press conference in which he claimed that the extensive FBI investigation had "gunned down" any negative information on Tower, especially the stories that depicted him as an out-of-control drunk and a would-be seducer. "What I got from [the report]," Bush said, "was that there has been a very unfair treatment of this man by rumor and innuendo, over and over again, rumors surfacing with no facts to back them up. I saw this [report] as a reaffirmation of what I've felt all along, and that is that John Tower is qualified to be secretary of defense. . . . The allegations against him, hanging over this, simply have been gunned down in terms of facts."

But because the controversy would not go away, the Senate postponed its vote on Tower's confirmation. Then, on Thursday, March 2, the *Washington Post* ran a story alleging that Tower, between 1976 and 1978 on two trips to Bergstrom Air Force Base in Texas, was drunk and had sexually harassed two women. These stunning charges, if true, would have fatally damaged not only his nomination as secretary of defense but also his standing in the Washington community as a power broker. Furious about the character assassination of someone who had been a friend for over a decade, McCain went to the floor of the Senate on Thursday to attack a man named Robert Jackson, a retired air force sergeant, who was a key source for the *Post* article.

Armed with a letter written by a Pentagon official who quoted from Jackson's medical records (which McCain released to the press), McCain charged that Jackson, who had accused Tower of this inappropriate behavior at the air force base, had been placed on temporary disability in 1977 because he "exhibited symptoms of a mixed personality disorder with antisocial themes and hysterical features." What's more, McCain went on, Jackson was not even present at Bergstrom in 1976 when Tower conducted his visit. Besides unequivocally questioning the mental capacity of Jackson, McCain offered to produce a list of people who had witnessed Tower at Bergstrom and would swear that he was not drunk and did not sexually harass any women.

To confuse the situation even more, Senator John Glenn was recognized to speak on the Senate floor and began to read from a confidential FBI report that contained damaging information about Tower. McCain shouted Glenn down and, in doing so, showed his willingness to get into a public squabble over the dual reports. Finally, Senator Sam Nunn, who was leading the effort to undermine the Tower confirmation process, suggested that the material should be discussed in a closed session. "I personally believe he had a serious drinking problem in the 1970s and the 1980s, including recent years," Nunn said. "We're not talking about the secretary of the interior; we're talking about someone next to the president at the very top of the nuclear chain of command. The example we set here is going to work its way down." Next, Senator Phil Gramm spoke up for Tower and offered a weird, if accurate, defense: Great men like Ulysses S. Grant and Winston Churchill drank. As it happened, McCain's confrontation with Glenn was suggestive. Around this time, he had become so angered by what his colleagues were doing to a man he admired that he participated in a shouting match in an elevator with one senator and had a heated argument in a hearing room with another. McCain's temper, often written about but rarely witnessed by the writers, was clearly evident during the Tower confirmation hearings.

On Friday, the *Washington Post* printed a front-page story about McCain's spirited defense of Tower. That same day, Senators Nunn and Warner released more of Robert Jackson's medical records. One report said Jackson had been found to have a "personality trait disorder." The record, signed by Colonel Kenneth G. B. Joyce, ended with these comments: "A review of available medical records fails to substantiate the presence of any neurosis or psychosis. There is evidence of a personality disorder marked by uncooperative behavior. Reliability may be a problem. My review of the member's personnel records reflects an average NCO [noncommissioned officer] who was generally well thought of, but overly idealistic. He also seems to have consistently fallen short in the area of bearing and behavior, in the judgment of his superiors." On Saturday, the *New York Times* published an article in which the accusations made against Tower by Jackson were described as "apparently false ones"; on Sunday, McCain appeared on *Meet the Press* to continue his defense of Tower.

Ultimately, the efforts of McCain and others fell short. The allegations, whether false or otherwise, had done their damage. So when Dennis DeConcini spoke from the Senate floor and said that he had witnessed Tower in the Senate chamber under the influence of alcohol, any hope of saving Tower vanished. On March 9, admitting defeat, Bush withdrew the nomination of John Tower to be secretary of defense. Bush substituted the name of Richard ("Dick") Cheney, the former congressman from Wyoming.

However, the way Tower was treated left a bad feeling with many in Washington. "Here were people pointing fingers at Tower who were living the life of high society themselves," Senator Alan Simpson says. "Then they were using anonymous sources and FBI reports. I finally called one guy in, and I said, 'Who the hell is Witness P-1?' He said, 'That's anonymous. We can't tell you who that is.' So I said, 'But that guy, you know, maybe Tower married his ex-wife. How the hell do we know who he is? What are the reasons for this secrecy?' I mean, they were anonymous witnesses. We couldn't find out who they were.

"One of these anonymous sources had Tower watching a ballerina dancing on a piano at the Jefferson Hotel. Later we found out it was all absolutely false. Then some congressman—he wasn't then but he is now—reported that Tower was so drunk one night he had to remove his cuff links, because he couldn't even get them off. And later that was repudiated and found not to be true. It was a series of very bad things. But that's the savagery of Washington. And McCain is a guy who hates to see that kind of savagery because he had it inflicted upon himself."

The internal squabbling had faded by April, and Congress got back to the workings of government. On Monday, April 17, McCain made a speech in the Senate in which he asked for the president to have what he called a super line-item veto. In introducing the "Anti-pork" Bill of 1989, a subject that was dear to him, McCain said: "The problem is that our current budget process doesn't require us to be thrifty and conscientious with money that is entrusted to us. We pick the taxpayer's pocket to play pork-barrel politics."

Two days later, when mass killings in Nicaragua and El Salvador were reported, McCain announced that in his capacity as cochairman of the Senate Central American Observer Group, he would be traveling to Honduras, El Salvador, and Nicaragua within the week. On his final stop, he said, he would meet with the Contras—who were being backed by the United States government—and with the Sandinista government. McCain headed a congressional delegation that included senators Bob Graham of Florida, Chuck Robb of Virginia, and Connie Mack of Florida. They met with the contras in Nicaragua and determined that the civil war in El Salvador was growing because the Soviets were supplying the leftists with arms. They also predicted massive fraud in the May 7 election in Panama because Manuel Noriega had done everything within his power to ensure his reelection as that country's leader. When the four senators returned to Miami on Monday, April 24, they held a news conference during which McCain, the group leader, declared: "I believe the United States of America and all Latin American countries have an obligation to prevent this tragedy from being inflicted on the Panamanian people."

In April, while McCain was concentrating on foreign affairs within the hemisphere, another plot point in the Keating drama unfolded: The government took over the Lincoln Savings & Loan, a move with a potential cost to the taxpayers of as much as $3 billion—or more. But McCain tried to move ahead and not focus on the potential Keating disaster. After all, he was part of a 13-member delegation the Bush Administration had chosen to observe the election in Panama.

On May 6, the group arrived at Howard Air Force Base in the Panama Canal Zone, McCain's birthplace. On the previous day, the Senate had passed a resolution condemning Noriega's blatant attempts to fix the election. On the election day itself—Sunday, May 7—McCain witnessed, in his words, "a colossal fraud" in the form of gross voting irregularities. By Tuesday, May 9, the government, which had gathered all of the ballots cast in the country, had still not counted them. "Every objective observer from the church to the polls indicated the government would have lost by two to one," McCain said upon his return to Washington. He and the others in the delegation met with Bush and told him what they had seen. If McCain had been undecided about such an issue in the past, he was now convinced that Bush should use military force to overthrow the government in Panama and remove Noriega from power.

One night in early June 1989, McCain created a hassle over an issue important to Arizonans. In 1988, Congress had enacted the Medicare Catastrophic Coverage Act, which allowed senior citizens to get catastrophic health care coverage if they paid an income tax surcharge. Many senior citizens, concerned about living on a shoestring budget, opposed the program because, they argued, they could not afford to pay the surcharge. In his office in Arizona, a state known for its large senior citizen population, McCain had received more than his share of telephone calls. Many senior citizens felt they simply couldn't afford the program. So, on the night of Wednesday, June 7, McCain attached an amendment to a supplemental appropriations bill and submitted it to the Senate. The legislation, if passed, would essentially kill the new catastrophic benefits—and the prohibitive surcharge. Determined to keep the law in place, the Senate voted 51 to 49 not to eliminate the program, which prompted Lloyd Bentsen to say that the Senate would have to reexamine the program in the fall session.

The ordeal could not wait. The debate continued and, on Sunday, July 9, the *Arizona Republic* ran an editorial by McCain about catastrophic health care coverage and the mandatory participation in the program that cost some senior citizens as much as $800 a year for coverage. "As the Senate returns from the Fourth of July recess," McCain wrote, "a whole new kind of fireworks begins. The Senate Finance Committee will reexamine whether Congress made a mistake in passing the Medicare Catastrophic Coverage Act of 1988. The committee undertakes this effort under duress, reluctantly doing so only because of the protests by millions of the nation's seniors. . . . On July 7, the Senate concluded two days of contentious and often stormy debate over the Catastrophic Coverage Act. The issue was whether to delay the act's surtax and reexamine its benefits and financing mechanism, a proposal I put forth with the endorsement of 44 organizations nationwide representing some 19 million seniors."

By the end of July, the Senate was ready to vote one more time on McCain's proposed legislation, which would kill the catastrophic health care coverage. On Thursday, July 27, the Senate voted again on the McCain bill, which would have either done away with the law previously passed or delayed it for a year. This time, the vote was overwhelmingly against McCain: 58 to 40. For the second time in two months, the legislation had been shot down in the Senate, but now it was not even close.

In early August, McCain was again working on an issue that was vital to him: the line-item veto. In a meeting at the White House on Friday, August 4, McCain, along with three other Republican senators—Dan Coats of Indiana, Gordon Humphrey of New Hampshire, and William Armstrong of Colorado—presented Bush with a bill proposing that a Congressional majority vote would be required to overrule any line-item veto used by the president. This was the latest proposal in an ongoing attempt by some members of Congress to provide the president with a method whereby he could limit Congress's tendency to engage in pork-barrel spending. Bush liked this version of the bill. After his meeting with the Republican senators, he commented that the bill would allow him to "do what the American people want . . . control spending."

On Sunday, October 8, a story broke that took a slow-burning but potentially dangerous scandal involving Charles Keating and his Lincoln Savings & Loan and, at least as far as McCain was concerned, placed it right on the front page. On that day, the *Arizona Republic* reported that McCain had failed to pay for the trips he and his family had taken in Keating's corporate jets, a bill that totaled $13,433. Nine separate flights were involved, and McCain had not paid for any of them—or so it was charged. McCain had first learned in March that he had not paid for the flights, he said, when Keating's office had contacted him to say the IRS was going to force Keating to pay for the flights if McCain didn't. In May and June, McCain made payments, from his personal funds, totaling $13,433. In his mind, the matter had been resolved.

In an interview on October 11 for an article that appeared in the *Washington Post* the next day, McCain admitted that his failure to pay for the flights "was a serious error," but he added that "it doesn't mean I did anything improper for Charles Keating." What he had done for Keating, and when, had now become exceedingly important. For American Continental Corporation, Keating's company, had filed for bankruptcy in April, when the federal government took over his Lincoln Savings & Loan. The government was suing Keating for $1.1 billion; he was charged with illegally transferring assets from his bank to his personal account and then making huge contributions to politicians.

The public disclosure of McCain's failure to pay for the flights came at a time when he was making a concerted effort to distance himself from what was turning into a full-scale scandal concerning Keating and his savings and loan. But, on September 14, a senate staffer, according to an article in the *Arizona Republic,* charged that McCain had invited Donald Riegle to the second meeting. Since Riegle sat on the Senate Banking, Housing, and Urban Affairs Committee, this allegation implied that McCain may have been more involved in trying to help his friend, Charles Keating, than he wanted reporters and members of Congress to believe.

For the record, McCain denied that he had invited Riegle to the second meeting. Indeed, McCain said Riegle had invited *him* to come to his office and give him a briefing on what was going on with Keating and Lincoln Savings & Loan. However, Kevin Gottlieb, a Riegle aide, as the *Arizona Republic* reported, claimed that McCain just showed up at Riegle's office without an appointment and invited Riegle to a meeting that was going to take place in DeConcini's office. "Riegle said McCain came to Riegle's door . . . and said something about that he'd like to have Riegle come to the meeting," Gottlieb told the Arizona paper. But McCain denied it happened that way. "[Riegle] said he wanted to discuss the Keating issue with me," McCain said. "I came to his office, we . . . discussed it."

All of this was important because the Senate Ethics Committee had launched an investigation into Keating's involvement with his friends in the Senate. The committee wanted to determine what role, if any, the senators played in the failure of Lincoln Savings & Loan, the largest bank default in American history. Through meetings held on Keating's behalf, had the senators prevented federal bank officials from taking over Lincoln earlier, a move that would have saved the government—and American taxpayers—hundreds of millions, or maybe billions, of dollars?

In an effort to minimize his role in the meetings, McCain wrote a letter to Edwin Gray, the chairman of the Federal Home Loan Bank Board, requesting Gray to go on record as to whether McCain had done anything illegal or improper. Writing back to McCain, Gray said McCain had done nothing wrong, but Gray did take the opportunity to criticize DeConcini. Indeed, an all-out war had broken out between DeConcini and McCain over the Keating matter. The two men had certainly handled the situation differently. McCain had ended his relationship with Keating—perhaps out of anger but the separation had occurred nonetheless. DeConcini, who had stayed friendly with Keating, continued to fight for him even after the situation looked as if it could become problematic. Then, once DeConcini realized he was in the middle of a controversy from which McCain had managed to distance himself, DeConcini insisted, "[McCain's] in it like I am," when, in fact, McCain was not. DeConcini's entanglement with Keating was deep and disturbing, as evidenced by the revelation that DeConcini's campaign aides had reportedly gotten a whopping $50 million in loans from Lincoln Savings & Loan. That figure explained why DeConcini, more than any of the other senators, fought hard for Keating.

DeConcini had made a token gesture: He was willing to return the $48,000 in campaign contributions he had received from Keating over the years. But that still left a lot unexplained, and the way DeConcini was being viewed in the Keating mess was not helped by another fact. In the past, he had been charged with investing heavily in land that was due to be bought by the federal government—an act that, if true, tended to show his willingness to push the boundaries of business arrangements. In fact, DeConcini had never stopped trying to help Keating. He continued to pressure regulators to allow Keating to go through with a potential sale he had lined up for Lincoln Savings & Loan, even though the bank was in deep financial trouble. Knowing this, regulators refused to approve the sale and took over the institution on April 14. Lincoln's $3.4 billion default was the biggest ever, making it nothing short of a symbol of the savings and loan excesses of the 1980s. That's one reason why, on October 13, 1989, Common Cause, a political watchdog group based in Washington, filed a complaint—another development the Senate Ethics Committee would have to deal with.

In the middle of this emerging scandal, McCain resolutely plowed ahead. On the political front, in early October, he announced that he would champion efforts to keep as many airlines up and running as possible, hoping to prevent a situation where a handful of major airlines would buy up smaller ones and reduce competition in the industry. McCain argued that a lack of competition would require the federal government to reimpose regulation. McCain-Danforth, the bill McCain was proposing with John Danforth of Missouri, would keep the industry from killing competition and would protect Southwest Airlines and America West, two airlines vital to Arizona.

In late December, he published an editorial rebuttal in the *Arizona Republic*. The paper, on December 14, had described McCain as having "misled the public" and "exaggerated the impact" of the repeal of the Medicare Catastrophic Coverage. "I criticized the final outcome . . . because I believe Congress went too far when it also repealed the $4.80 flat premium and the benefits it paid for— catastrophic hospitalization, hospice care, respite care, mammography screening and immunosuppressive and home IV drugs," McCain wrote. "It's for our seniors to decide whether they would be better off under the original Catastrophic Act, the Senate version that kept the core catastrophic protection benefits but repealed the surtax, or the final version which repealed all premiums and all benefits."

In his personal life, in 1989, McCain saw Cindy enter the hospital to have surgery performed on her back. The resulting operation, instead of correcting her back problem, would leave her in chronic pain for years.

In early 1990, a recall effort was organized by an Arizona resident named Ed Buch who wanted to recall his two senators, apparently, for their involvement in the Keating Five scandal. To recall a senator in Arizona, Buch needed to gather at least 291,135 valid signatures within four months—an almost impossible task. As the year went on, the recall effort fizzled, but it revealed the growing concern surrounding a scandal that McCain hoped would go away.

Meanwhile, historic events were developing around the world. In November 1989, the Berlin Wall had come down, reuniting East and West Germany and signaling the end to communism as the world had come to understand it. In early December 1989, President Bush met with Mikhail Gorbachev at a summit in Malta; in March 1990, Gorbachev was elected president of Russia, the country that emerged after the Soviet Union had disintegrated. In June, Gorbachev traveled to Washington to meet with Bush. The two world powers had clearly reached a new milestone in their shared history. After 40 years, the Cold War, the standoff that had produced conflicts such as the one in Vietnam, had ended.

By September 1990, Robert Bennett, who had been named special counsel for the Senate Ethics Committee, had studied the Keating case and had met with the Senate committee on at least three occasions. The committee was made up of three Republicans—Trent Lott, Jesse Helms, and Warren Rudman (vice chairman)—and three Democrats—David Pryor, Terry Sanford, and Howell Heflin (chairman). Bennett advised the committee to drop any investigation of Glenn and McCain, but to continue pursuing Riegle, Cranston, and DeConcini. Bennett filed a formal recommendation with the committee on September 10, but Heflin, a senator from Alabama, was not sure Glenn and McCain should be dismissed so quickly. Heflin wanted the committee to study the matter fully before it exonerated anyone. After all, Keating, under indictment for fraud for the sale of $200 million in junk bonds, was in a Los Angeles jail trying—so far, unsuccessfully—to come up with $5 million in bail.

All of the controversy surrounding Keating and his failed savings and loan overshadowed an invitation McCain received in late October. The Vietnamese government wanted him to return to Hanoi. "They look on me as some kind of folk hero," McCain said on November 1. "It's weird. I don't understand it. The transition"—to the status of folk hero—"seems to have taken place about the middle-to-late 1970s, about the time the monument was built." (McCain was referring to the stone marker built at the lake where he was shot down.)

Through the fall, the Keating controversy dragged on. In October, McCain, in an interview with the Ethics Committee, described his relationship with Keating: "He was a supporter. I vacationed at his home in the Bahamas. He was one of the wealthiest men in the state of Arizona. He involved himself politically heavily in Arizona. That was the extent of my knowledge of his financial involvement in the state. And I was grateful for his support and his involvement in my political career. I had a friend. That friend wanted me to do something that was wrong. I refused to do so. That ended the friendship."

On Monday, October 22, McCain addressed the Senate. "I cannot accept a deliberate effort to withhold the truth and continued suspicion of a cover-up," he said in an effort to force the Ethics Committee to be more forthcoming with the public over what it was doing. "I myself have served this nation for 35 years, always with honor and integrity. I do not deserve to be strung out week after week." He admitted he had been warned "that the remarks I am about to make may upset the very powerful Ethics Committee and could, in turn, cause me some political damage." But he made the speech anyway. "My concern is about my honor," he concluded, "my integrity, my reputation. There comes a time when you can no longer hold your tongue in the face of things that are wrong."

In November, the Ethics Committee began interviewing the senators and members of their staffs. During the first three days of hearings, the senators claimed, as a group, that by attending the meetings they had broken no Senate rules nor violated any laws. In other words, they had done nothing wrong. On Friday, November 16, John Dowd, counsel for McCain, defended McCain to the committee. His long prepared statement read in part: "Mr. Chairman, when you opened this hearing and this proceeding, you stated that many of our fellow citizens apparently believe that the services of these senators were bought. I tell you that there is no evidence that John McCain's services were bought. . . . John McCain placed integrity above friendship, and principle above political support. There is no mystery about the standards of conduct in this case. Senator McCain knew where to draw the line, and he drew the line. . . . In short, when John McCain was requested to go to Ed Gray's office, he said 'No.' . . . When John McCain was asked by Charles Keating to negotiate with the Bank Board for Lincoln Savings & Loan, he said 'No' to his longtime political friend and supporter. . . . When John McCain was invited to meet with Ed Gray, the Chairman of the Bank Board, he made it very clear that he was only going to inquire about two specific legitimate subjects."

By November 20, the day on which the committee interviewed two of McCain's aides, the proceedings had been reduced to squabbles over who asked whom to what meeting and—as strange as it may have seemed—who had been called a "wimp" by Keating: McCain alone or McCain and DeConcini. Specifically, McCain's side contended that DeConcini had lured McCain to the meetings because he wanted the proceedings to have a bipartisan image. DeConcini's lawyer, James Hamilton, responded that McCain had engaged in "pure speculation" and had been leaking negative stories about DeConcini to the press. Next, the McCain and DeConcini forces squared off over whether Keating had called *both* senators wimps. Aides for both sides seemed to agree that Keating had indeed called McCain a wimp. DeConcini's side claimed that Keating had also called DeConcini a wimp, although there was no record or evidence he had ever done so. Why was all, or any, of this important? "What it shows is," said Chris Koch, an assistant to McCain, "that John McCain had shown an unwillingness to do something that Charlie Keating wanted."

The day also featured an appearance by Gwendolyn Van Paasschen, the aide who dealt with McCain's banking issues. She argued that DeConcini wanted McCain in the meetings because "Senator McCain was a Republican and that would ensure that it was a bipartisan effort." Keating had raised money for both senators, so "if the press were to ever get a hold of it," Van Paasschen said, "it would be more embarrassing for Senator McCain than for Senator DeConcini." In fact, according to Van Paasschen, in mid-March, DeConcini tried to persuade McCain to go with him to Ed Gray's office or to the office of the California bank regulators, located in San Francisco. McCain wouldn't do it. "It was my view," Van Paasschen said to the committee, "and I told Senator McCain . . . that it was my view that what Senator DeConcini had suggested was inappropriate." Finally, McCain agreed to go to the meetings if they were held on Capitol Hill. When DeConcini's lawyer tried to get Van Paasschen to provide evidence that what she was saying was true, she offered none. That prompted him to charge that she was making up what she said. "DeConcini's demeanor was very persuasive," she responded. "He was coming to Senator McCain instead of Mr. Keating himself. He was a Democrat. We were Republicans. And as I said before, Keating had raised more for Senator McCain than he had for Senator DeConcini at that time."

At the end of 1990, McCain continued to present the impression that he was conducting business as usual. In another editorial published in the *Arizona Republic,* he projected a self-image: He was continuing to attend to the business of his constituents, even in the face of the Keating scandal. Specifically, he addressed the vital issue of Saddam Hussein and his recent aggression in the Persian Gulf. "As America and the world face Saddam Hussein's aggression," McCain wrote on December 9, "the Senate Armed Services Committee just completed a week of hearings that raised important questions about several dimensions of the Persian Gulf Crisis. Chief among these concerns were questions about the efficacy of economic sanctions, the timing and the use of force, Hussein's control of mass destruction weapons and whether to convene a special session of Congress to address these and other issues raised in the hearings. . . . What is ultimately at stake in the Persian Gulf is much more than the settling of yet another Middle East regional dispute. Saddam Hussein—the unwanted child of the Cold War—is a precursor of future challenges to global stability. . . . I enthusiastically support the president's decision to send Secretary of State James A. Baker III to Iraq. We must thoroughly explore every opportunity to resolve this crisis short of war. . . . Congress should pass a resolution authorizing the use of force if peaceful alternatives to such force fail. . . . The peace and security of the world for future generations [demand] that the world community act decisively to end the Gulf Crisis now, and to reduce the threat of new crises in years to come. The single most important aspect of this challenge is to limit or stop the proliferation of modern weapons technologies."

McCain may have tried to present a picture in which he was conducting the business of his office as usual, but, at times, the pressure of what was happening to him showed. In November, McCain became mired in a debate over 92 slots, at Washington National Airport, that were owned by Trump Shuttle, an airline owned by Donald Trump. The slots had become the focus of attention of America West. Trump had paid more than $70 million for the slots when he started his New York-to-Washington shuttle service. Now, America West wanted the slots. Trump had gone on record as saying that he ordered his people to do anything necessary to protect the value of the slots, which were being held as collateral against loans.

With this as backdrop, now came an episode involving Roger Stone, the hard-hitting Republican strategist who also advised Donald Trump on business matters. "I was lobbying for the Trump Shuttle," Stone says, "and the Trump Shuttle and America West were vying over landing slots at LaGuardia. With his position on the Commerce Committee, McCain had enormous say about the regulations of airlines. So I went in to McCain's office to meet with him about the airlines. I opened the meeting by saying, 'Senator, you know I represent the Trump Shuttle and I wanted to talk to you about the landing rights issue at LaGuardia. I understand that America West is an Arizona-based company. . . .' And that's all I had to say. He went crazy. Crazy! Like a madman. Seething, drooling, his face turned beet-red. 'Get out of my office. How dare you talk to me like that! No one talks to me like that! Not even United States senators!' So I walked out and haven't seen him since. I had considered him a friend. I gave money to each one of his House campaigns, even the very first one. But that day in his office he just became unglued. He was seething." It was an issue—which became known as the "temper" factor—that would be used against McCain in the future.

On January 4, 1991, the Keating Five senators began their closing remarks before the Ethics Committee. In his comments, McCain admitted that the senators had created "an appearance that something was improper" by attending two meetings almost four years earlier, but he also noted that each of the senators had good reasons for being at the meetings. McCain claimed that, at the time, he had been worried by the fact that no aides were included in the meetings. Most members of Congress are accompanied by an aide, who serves as a witness for what is said or done in the presence of another member of Congress. However, McCain said, he had attended both meetings because they involved a constituent who employed a number of people in his home state.

The chairman, Howell Heflin (a Democrat), then asked McCain why it took so long for him to pay Keating for the trips he and his family had taken to Keating's home in the Bahamas. McCain responded that he had been unaware that Keating had not been fully paid and when Keating's office told him about the problem, he promptly paid the money he owed. McCain acknowledged that failure to pay for the flights in a timely fashion had been "a mistake." Then Heflin proceeded to add up the expenses for the purpose of suggesting that McCain had underpaid Keating. When Heflin added the numbers up for the third time, McCain said bluntly: "I've watched you go through this before. If you can find some flight that I didn't pay for that should have been paid for . . . I'd like to write you a check. You can fill it out for whatever you want to, Mr. Chairman, because . . . we have attempted to pay and double pay everything."

The detail McCain noted was meaningful: He now believed that he *had* paid for the trips, although there was no record of those payments being made, so he had actually paid for the trips twice. This claim addressed a part of the story that was more important to Cindy than it was to the Senate. Cindy was often responsible for paying for expenses related to the McCains' private life—even their family vacations. It was her recollection that monies had been paid to Keating, but, even though she had searched repeatedly over the years, she had not been able to find any documentation of those payments. She was sure the documentation existed; she was just unable to locate it. That failure produced an untold amount of stress in her life, which only exasperated her emotional and physical states that were often bad because of her chronic back pain.

During his testimony, McCain also spoke to the larger issue of his friendship with Keating. He said he ended his relationship with Keating in March 1987 because his former friend had asked him to cut a deal with federal regulators that would keep Lincoln Savings & Loan open if it issued home loans. McCain said he attended the two meetings to see what kind of investigation was being conducted—Lincoln Savings & Loan was, after all, a major employer in his state. McCain had been concerned because the investigation had, at that time, gone on for over a year. When he went to the two meetings, he testified, he realized that the probe was taking so long because the Lincoln officials were not cooperating. "I am fully satisfied that my conduct at all times was . . . in keeping with the standards of my office," McCain said. Other senators seemed to agree. When McCain was finished, Trent Lott chimed in to defend him, saying, "You have shown repeatedly and clearly that you did nothing improper. In fact, when asked to do so, you refused."

Following McCain, on that day of testimony before the Select Ethics Committee—a panel that had been holding hearings on the Keating scandal now since November—John Glenn restated what McCain had just argued: Their actual behavior was what was important, not their appearances. So, despite all that had happened, McCain and Glenn maintained they had never done anything wrong.

On January 15, John Dowd, McCain's attorney, told the Ethics Committee in his closing remarks that McCain had "conducted his public office with honesty, courage, and fidelity." He added: "The past fourteen months have been very painful and very difficult for

John McCain, for he has been judged not by his conduct, but by his association with the conduct of others."

Finally, on the last day of February 1991, nearly four years after the two meetings that initiated the Keating Five scandal, the Senate Ethics Committee handed down its ruling. For his role in the mess, McCain was found guilty of exhibiting "poor judgment" in attending the meetings. According to the report generated by Heflin's committee, only Cranston had been guilty of actual ethics rules violations. McCain, Glenn, DeConcini, and Riegle had not committed any violations. The committee did criticize McCain and Glenn for their judgment, and it said that DeConcini and Riegle had conducted themselves in ways that "gave the appearance of being improper." The actions of the senators, though not "improper" (except in the case of Cranston), *had*, the panel found, intimidated the regulators, who waited another two years before taking over the failing Lincoln Savings & Loan, a delay that cost the government $1 billion. For this, the committee gave DeConcini and Riegle a rebuke. Cranston received a formal reprimand.

For all intents and purposes, the panel absolved McCain of any improper or unethical behavior. At a press conference in Phoenix on March 1, McCain said he would return to the United States Treasury the $112,000 Keating had given to his campaigns between 1982 and 1986. Saying he hoped the committee's decision would "close the book" on the whole Keating nightmare, McCain vowed never to meet with another federal regulator. "Ever. Period." Then he said: "I have chosen to return this money now, rather than at some earlier time, for one simple reason: Returning those funds before the committee rendered its judgment could have been interpreted as admitting wrongdoing." On the issue of money, McCain had already reimbursed Keating for the trips to the Bahamas; he reiterated that he had thought the trips had previously been paid for. Finally, he said he intended to run for reelection in 1992 and, in doing so, he underlined his new signature issue: campaign finance reform. Now, because of what had just happened to him, he said he was absolutely determined to pass campaign finance reform. "Rightly or wrongly, the American people and the people of Arizona feel that the system has been corrupted," he said.

While the final stage of the Keating Five drama was playing itself out, Saddam Hussein was taking actions in the Persian Gulf that were having a direct effect on American politics. On August 2, 1990, Hussein had invaded the small, oil-rich, and strategically vital country of Kuwait. Iraq had then positioned troops on the border with Saudi Arabia, a development that indicated Hussein's willingness to invade that country, which would have been unthinkable to the West. During the fall, President Bush rallied world opinion against Hussein. He also sent 425,000 U.S. troops to the region, where they joined with 118,000 troops that had been sent by other countries. On November 29, the United Nations Security Council gave the allied forces permission "to use all necessary means" to get Iraq out of Kuwait if Iraq had not withdrawn by January 15, 1991.

Four days before the cutoff date, McCain went to the floor of the Senate to argue that sanctions would not keep Hussein from carrying out "naked aggression of the most heinous and disgraceful kind." McCain said: "Who are the ones who would suffer as a result of sanctions? In my view, it is the innocent civilians, children and others that Saddam Hussein would view as nonessentials in his war efforts. Clearly, the American people do not seek a replay of that tragic chapter in our nation's history. I think you can make an argument: If we drag out this crisis and we don't at some time bring it to a successful resolution, we face a prospect of another Vietnam War."

The cutoff date came and went. Hussein did not pull his troops out of Kuwait. On Thursday, January 17, President Bush requested Congress's permission to conduct military operations in the Persian Gulf. The Senate voted 99–0 to approve the president's request. Not only did McCain vote in favor of the request, but before the vote, he had proposed that the Congress should adopt a declaration of war—

a move much more severe than simply committing troops to the region, as the president had requested. That very day, January 17, the Allied forces started bombing Baghdad. The air campaign, it was hoped, would make Hussein withdraw his troops from Kuwait.

On Sunday, January 27, McCain met at the Arizona Army National Guard headquarters with about 40 relatives of Arizonan service personnel fighting in the Persian Gulf. The war "will be over in a matter of weeks," McCain said, adding, "I would like to see Saddam Hussein dead. I don't know anyone who wouldn't." Noting that, under American law, Hussein could not be targeted, McCain said, "If he just happens to suffer death, it will not be to anyone's sorrow."

In the middle of the country's preoccupation with the Gulf War, there was a political news item that affected McCain. On January 25, the *Arizona Republic* reported that the Democratic Senatorial Campaign Committee was encouraging Bruce Babbitt, the former governor of Arizona who had run unsuccessfully for president in 1988, to run against McCain when he stood for reelection in 1992. This was an indication of how much damage the Keating Five scandal had done to McCain: He was now considered vulnerable as a viable political figure.

On Wednesday, February 13, McCain appeared at Phoenix College where he addressed the student body. "The world economy," McCain said, "is dependent on a free and unfettered flow of oil" from the Persian Gulf. "There is no doubt in my mind," he added, "that there are significant signs that the Iraqi morale is cracking, and that many of their troops, particularly the 17-year-old draftees and the over-50-year-olds that have been drafted by Saddam Hussein, are not happy where they are." Nine days later, on February 22, speaking before 2,000 employees at McDonnell Douglas, McCain revealed that the first shots of the Persian Gulf War were fired by eight Apache helicopters that attacked, among other targets, the early-warning radar facilities in Iraq. "The Iraqis [at the radar sites] did not know how they were being attacked," McCain said. He was speaking in the building where the Apaches were actually built, so when he showed a video of Hellfire missiles and 70-millimeter rockets hitting their targets, the audience erupted in wild applause.

In late February, after five weeks of bombing that had not forced Hussein to remove his troops, the Allied forces began a ground attack. The 100-hour land battle, called "Desert Storm," ended on February 28 and resulted in the total destruction of Iraq's so-called million-man army.

In March, McCain and other senators—among them, Dennis DeConcini and John Kerry, the junior senator from Massachusetts—traveled to the Persian Gulf to survey the aftermath of the war. Much of Kuwait had been destroyed at the hands of the Iraqis. When Hussein realized that he was going to be defeated by the Allied forces, he ordered his men to set the oil wells in Kuwait on fire and caused one of the worst acts of devastation the region had ever endured. On March 18, McCain had just returned from Kuwait, and the firsthand events he had seen prompted him to say he supported the anti-Hussein forces in the region. A party of some 20 senators had met with Crown Prince Saad Abdullah Sabah of Kuwait. The prince promised the senators that his country would do more to promote democracy in Kuwait. "The carnage is unbelievable," McCain said. "You feel sorry for anyone who was caught in that sort of holocaust, but at the same time your sympathy is tempered by what you saw in Kuwait."

In 1991, McCain was able to advance his legislative agenda without the threat of the Keating scandal hovering over him. He introduced two bills concerning health care: The Private Long-Term Care Insurance and Accelerated Death Benefit Incentive Act of 1991, which would expand private long-term care, and The Long-Term Care Protection Act, which would, according to a McCain editorial in the *Arizona Republic* on November 10, "provide federal consumer protection in the long-term care insurance market."

As it happened, McCain had direct experience with the health care system in America at that very moment. In 1991, while she was on a mission to Bangladesh, Cindy had visited an orphanage in Dhaka that was run by Mother Teresa. At the clinic, Cindy found an infant girl born with a severe cleft palate. The child's mother had abandoned her; the child's father had either been killed or had abandoned her as well. The cleft palate was so bad that, had the condition been left untreated, the child would have died. Cindy carried the baby home to Phoenix for surgery and for adoption. The child, who would be named Bridget, was three months old when Cindy brought her to America. McCain went to the airport to meet Cindy, who presented the baby to her husband and said, "Meet your new daughter." Almost as soon as Cindy got her back to Arizona, Bridget would begin a total of a dozen operations.

During 1991, McCain also ended up at the center of a controversy that would have a profound effect on his political life. In early April, he returned to Vietnam at the request of the communist government; once again, he was there to help in the accounting of MIAs. In 1985, he had been in the country for the tenth anniversary of the fall of Saigon. On that trip, he had gone to the Hanoi Hilton and jokingly asked his tour guides not to close the door behind him. His 1991 visit would be much broader in scope. McCain left Washington en route to Bangkok and then to Hanoi for a two-day visit. Saying he was "struck by the amazing differences" in the country, compared to six years ago, McCain reported: "There are shops, stalls and little restaurants, and the people are profiting from this free-market economy." McCain had gotten guarantees from Nguyen Co Thach, the foreign minister, that the government would allow the United States to set up an office in Hanoi to help determine the fate of the 2,282 men still listed as missing in action. Of those, 1,665 were missing in Vietnam. The rest were missing in Laos, Cambodia, and China, which was why, following his stop in Vietnam, McCain proceeded on to Phnom Penh, the capital of Cambodia, and to Laos. On this trip, he had one goal: find out as much as he could about the fate of the MIAs.

In July, only weeks after his return to the United States, the mystery of the MIAs gained national attention. A *Newsweek* cover story featured a picture of three men, purported to be American POWs who were still being held against their will in Southeast Asia. The trio was given a nickname—"The Three Amigos"—and the picture was reprinted throughout the American media. There was only one problem. The picture was a hoax generated by people who wanted to perpetuate the myth that Americans were still being held captive in Southeast Asia—a notion the *Rambo* movies had popularized. This image was important because, in numerous schemes concocted at the time, grieving American families were paying large sums of money to private investigators who promised to go to the region and make every effort to retrieve their loved ones—who surely were being held against their will.

The *Newsweek* cover story brought to a head an issue that had been alive in America, in one way or another, since U.S. troops had left Vietnam in the mid-1970s. Senator Bob Smith of New Hampshire now asked for a formal congressional investigation into the matter of MIAs and POWs, and John Kerry, himself a decorated navy veteran who had returned from Vietnam to help lead the protest against the war, was asked to chair the select committee. McCain joined the committee as well. For many years, McCain had held Kerry's actions against him because, while McCain was a POW in the Hanoi Hilton, Kerry was organizing veterans back home in the United States to protest the war. But, only weeks before, as the two senators flew to Kuwait to witness the aftermath of the Persian Gulf War, they sat next to each other on the airplane and, after a long—and, at times, emotional—conversation about Vietnam, they had finally put the past behind them.

"Our differences occurred when we were kids, or at least close to being kids," Kerry says. "It was a long time ago, and we both came back and realized that there were a lot of difficulties in the prosecution of that war for a lot of different people and a lot of different places in their lives. What's important is: John and I both volunteered, both wanted to go to Vietnam, both wanted to win, and both were disappointed, though we came to the disappointment in different ways—and I played out that disappointment in different ways than John did.

"I played it out by actively opposing it, believing I was going to save lives in the process, and I believe to this day that I did. John McCain today would tell you he believes huge mistakes were made in the prosecution of that war—the lies that were told. And I think we would both agree there were big mistakes and we were two of the people caught in the middle of all of that."

"It is hard to overstate how profoundly our historic victory in the Cold War will affect the world," McCain wrote in the *Arizona Republic* on March 8, 1992. "However, whether Americans will be the principal beneficiaries of our formidable adversary's decline will depend in large part on whether our reduction of Cold War defense-spending levels promotes, rather than retards, economic growth. . . . Arizona must acknowledge that defense cuts will be an annual reality for years to come. . . . Threats to American security have diminished, but they certainly have not vanished. Arizona can still contribute significantly to the defense of our national interests in a changing yet still dangerous world." There were plans for base closings, starting in 1993. "Arizona, as much as any state, deserves credit for its contributions to our successful defense of American principles. All we ask is that the costs of peace do not exceed the price of victory."

McCain was still a hawk on military affairs, but he had been drifting toward the middle on other issues. Looking at the stands he now held on a number of political, social, and economic topics, McCain was not nearly as conservative as he had been when he arrived in Washington a decade earlier. On social issues, some observers might have considered him a moderate. He favored sanctions against South Africa, for instance, and he argued that the federal government should expand its telecommunications system to help those citizens who were hearing-impaired. On abortion, he voted in favor of fetal tissue research, probably because his friend, Morris Udall, the former congressman from Arizona, had developed Parkinson's disease, and a cure was being sought through fetal tissue research. When he had come out in support of fetal tissue research, the antiabortion lobby, a group that in the past had supported McCain, now began to attack him.

On fiscal issues, McCain remained a staunch conservative. He was in favor of Gramm-Rudman, which required the federal government to balance its budget, and he supported most, if not all, of the tax cuts that had been advanced by President Reagan. However, in his campaign for reelection (the primary was scheduled for September 8), McCain decided his key issues were the environment, the elderly, and Hispanic and American Indian affairs—and on those issues he had come to take moderate stands. If he had been a red-meat Reaganite when he arrived in Washington, he had repositioned himself on some issues as he continued to look for ways to take his politics more toward the mainstream. Some of his colleagues identified his willingness to change his mind. "I have huge affection and respect for John McCain," John Kerry says. "He's just a very special human being who has tons of courage and an open mind and a willingness to change as he goes along. He seeks input that comes to him and opens his mind and his eyes to things he might not have been aware of. He isn't afraid to change."

Having positioned himself in the middle—politically speaking—and having survived the potentially career-ending debacle of the Keating scandal with little more than a slap on the wrist by the Ethics Committee, McCain was ready to run for reelection in 1992. On the Democratic ticket, he would be opposed by Claire Sargeant, a civil rights activist who had no statewide political presence and no chance of winning. (Babbitt decided not to run.) Evan Mecham was running as an Independent. A former car dealer from Glendale, Mecham had won the governorship in a three-way race in 1986. He was impeached and forced from office when the Arizona Senate found him guilty of obstructing justice. He allegedly tried to stop a state investigation into a threat said to have been made against a grand jury witness. He lent $80,000 from a protocol fund to his car dealership, which was illegal. In 1990, he tried to mount a comeback in a five-way race for governor, but Fife Symington won. McCain didn't support Mecham during the impeachment proceedings, and that angered Mecham.

In his reelection campaign, McCain was endorsed by Colin Powell, chairman of the Joint Chiefs of Staff. Speaking at an event called "A Salute to Arizona's Veterans," held at the Camelback Inn, Powell said: "I don't do politics, but I do friendship." McCain, to Powell, was "a great senator" and "a steadfast buddy." McCain received some unexpected criticism from his opponents, who accused him of grandstanding during the fall campaign because he flew to Vietnam one weekend as part of his work on the select committee on the issue of MIAs and POWs. Immediately, Kerry organized a letter, signed by Democrats and Republicans, defending McCain. McCain's efforts, as exemplified by the Powell endorsement and the Kerry defense, worked. The Keating Five scandal did not sink him as a politician. On the first Tuesday in November, in the general election, McCain got 55 percent of the vote as compared to 31 percent for Sargeant and 10 percent for Mecham.

Perhaps because he was up for reelection so soon after the Keating scandal, McCain had distanced himself from the presidential race. George H. W. Bush and Dan Quayle ran for reelection against Bill Clinton and Al Gore. So, on Election Night, as he rejoiced in his own victory, McCain watched as the national Republican ticket was defeated. Perhaps voters now viewed Bush as someone who was completely disconnected from the common people. (His surprise at how a supermarket scanner works was matched only by his having glanced at his watch to check the time during one of the debates, as if he had to be somewhere more important.) Or, perhaps it really was because the American economy had gone bad and Bush was blamed for it. (The Clinton motto, "It's the economy, stupid," had become a mantra for a reason.) The majority of voters decided Clinton would do a better job than Bush. The Bush loss was even more surprising because, a year or so before his defeat, Bush had enjoyed unprecedented approval ratings for his handling of the Persian Gulf War. That scenario, however, belonged to the distant past. The United States had a new Democrat as its president. Now that he was a member of the opposition party, McCain would suddenly become presidential timber himself, if—and it was a big if—he could only cleanse himself of the taint put on him by the Keating Five scandal.

On January 13, 1993, just as Bill Clinton was becoming the new president, the select committee chaired by Kerry and featuring the work of McCain issued a 1,223-page report, the product of numerous trips to Vietnam by committee members (Kerry alone made eight trips), the examination of countless photographs and documents, and the declassification, by the Department of Defense, of over a million pages of documents. The report concluded that "while the Committee has some evidence suggesting the possibility a POW may have survived to the present, and while some information remains yet to be investigated, there is, at this time, no compelling evidence that proves that any American remains alive in captivity in Southeast Asia."

The work of the committee that unfolded during 1991 and 1992 had not been without controversy. One battle concerned whether the Kerry committee would call Richard Nixon himself to testify concerning what he knew about the issue of MIAs and POWs. Some felt the testimony Henry Kissinger had provided the committee was not complete enough. "By the end of 1992, Kerry had suggested publicly that he still might summon Nixon to testify," Monica Crowley later wrote, "and Nixon remained defiant: 'What the hell. I can't believe that after all this they're still at it. I'll just say that Kissinger testified and that I have nothing to add. I don't have anything to add. What are they going to do? They can't force me to say things I don't know. If I sit there with nothing to say, that will put an end to their questioning of me. That whole committee, with a few exceptions, are jackasses. And I know I've said this before, but very few of our people are any good. [Senators] John McCain and Hank Brown are okay: they're smart and tough, but I don't think they grasp what this means historically for Kissinger and me. Well, McCain probably does because he suffered through the goddamned war.'"

Eventually Kerry decided not to call Nixon as a witness. The committee reached its conclusions without the former president's direct input, and those conclusions were ultimately unanimously agreed upon by the entire committee. Even people like Bob Smith, who repeatedly voiced skepticism about the motives and actions of the Vietnamese, signed on. In the end, though, all committee members had to acknowledge the findings of the committee, which, in time, proved to be historic.

"In the late 1980s and early 1990s," John McCain says, "there were a lot of things that came out of Vietnam that appeared to be hard evidence that Americans were still alive. There was the picture on the cover of *Newsweek* of three people, supposedly POWs alive in Southeast Asia, who turned out later to be Soviet farmers. There were these manufactured pictures, dog tags, et cetera. Many Americans, understandably, were absolutely convinced that we left Americans alive in Vietnam. So I came out on many occasions and said, 'Look, we don't have the evidence. I'm not saying they aren't there, but we've got to have the evidence.' When I did this, people were very disappointed in me, and then angered, because, obviously, I had been one of them. People felt that I betrayed those who I 'left behind.'

"Well, the select committee chaired by John Kerry met for over a year, and our conclusion—*unanimous* conclusion—was that there

was no compelling evidence that Americans were alive in Vietnam.
I've spent thousands of hours—on many trips to Vietnam—trying to
get any evidence. I must say I think John Kerry and I and some others did play a role in getting the Vietnamese to agree to this full access to the records. But I also understand the feelings of someone
who is the son or the wife or the brother of a man who's been listed
as missing in Vietnam."

7

THE SENATOR
FROM ARIZONA

I n January 1993, McCain began his second term in Barry
Goldwater's former senate seat, knowing Goldwater had been
too conservative to be elected to national office. So, while he
admired Goldwater, while he was honored to hold his seat,
while he was proud to call himself a conservative, McCain knew
that he needed to continue his move toward the middle. During the
Memorial Day holiday, McCain and John Kerry made yet another
trip to Vietnam. The select committee had finished its work, but the
two senators were still pursuing any avenue that might resolve the
issue of MIA/POWs. In June, two weeks after their trip to Vietnam,
McCain and Kerry met with Bill Clinton, at the White House, to
lobby for an end to the economic embargo the United States still
maintained against Vietnam. This topic was not popular with a large
segment of McCain's party, especially the right wing.

Later that summer, McCain continued to redefine his political
positions; this time, he focused on gay rights. The way he made his
case was typical of McCain. He would go to an organization known
for its antigay politics and make a speech about tolerance. He may
suffer the wrath of gay groups for agreeing to speak to an antigay

organization, but the larger victory would be more important: He would challenge the thinking of the antigay organization, and he would do it in person. This had become McCain's mode of operation: create controversy while advancing an agenda.

The group he chose was the Oregon Citizens Alliance, an association known for its antigay politics. (It had been linked to a failed statewide ballot initiative that described homosexuality as "perverse.") McCain addressed the Alliance on August 30. The event was a fund-raiser, and McCain had been invited to speak. His agreement to help the Alliance raise money angered some gay groups. A senator of McCain's stature, they argued, should not raise money for such an antigay organization; simply by being there—regardless of what he said—McCain would generate revenue. McCain, of course, had planned how he would use the occasion in his favor.

Early in the speech, he quoted Abraham Lincoln's reminder, in an address to Union soldiers, that Americans have "this inestimable jewel," our birthright. "The 'inestimable jewel' to which Lincoln referred," McCain told his audience, "was the promise contained in our Declaration of Independence, in its sparse but eloquent affirmation of the rights of man: 'that all men are created equal; that they are endowed by their Creator with certain unalienable rights; that among these are life, liberty, and the pursuit of happiness.'"

In his own way, McCain was being subversive. He was telling his audience that, in America, each person has the right to liberty and the right to pursue happiness—by implication, that included the right to realize one's sexual orientation—and he quoted Lincoln to make his point. "In the exercise of these rights," McCain went on, "some Americans will live their lives in ways that I would not choose for myself. They may pursue happiness in ways very different from my own pursuit of happiness. I may not approve of every way an individual chooses to exercise his or her rights as an American. . . . But I will not oppose them. . . . That, my friends, is the essence of tolerance." This point was not lost on his audience, whether or not it was well received.

"As you may know, some of my fellow Americans objected to my decision to join you tonight," McCain said, referring to gay groups that considered it inappropriate for McCain to dignify organizations like the Oregon Citizens Alliance. "They are free to do so. But they are not free to prevent me from addressing you, despite their objections." The argument was subtle but important: By opposing McCain's guest appearance, the gay groups were showing an intolerance as dangerous as that displayed by antigay groups. The gay organizations also missed this vital fact: The only way groups like the Oregon Citizens Alliance could be disproved was to have thinkers like McCain show up to challenge their opinions. On this night, that was exactly what he did. "The Republican Party," McCain concluded, "is big enough to support a variety of interests, so long as they are united in our pursuit of the fundamental interests of the nation. . . . It is generous enough to include different voices in honorable disputes about specific approaches to the questions of our time."

During the fall, a controversy erupted on Capitol Hill concerning the universal health care plan being advanced by the Clinton Administration under the direction of First Lady Hillary Rodham Clinton. McCain was opposed to the Clinton plan, although, in a break with many members of his party, he did believe all Americans should have access to the health care system. His concern with the Clinton plan was simple: He felt that socializing medicine, which was what the plan actually did, would destroy America's health care system as it had come to be known—the best in the world. McCain was also worried about the Clinton plan's distribution of money. "All Americans deserve the opportunity to obtain the health care coverage of their choice," McCain wrote in the *Arizona Republic* on October 13. "I hope that we will never see the day in which the government tells us which health care plan we may enroll in or who will provide the care. To socialize our health care system, as the Clinton reform plan would, will be to ruin it. . . . The Clinton plan will cost this country hundreds of billions of dollars and will substantially worsen our deficit crisis. Even more troubling, history has taught us that social programs tend to cost much more over time than policymakers originally project."

By the end of 1993, McCain himself had to depend on the excellence of the American health care system he defended when on December 3 he underwent outpatient surgery to remove a malignant melanoma on his shoulder. Early periods of intense exposure to the sun are known to contribute to fair-skinned people's tendency to develop skin cancer in later years. McCain, certainly fair-skinned, had often gotten sunburns during his youth from being outdoors. His personal doctor, Thomas Hudak, performed the procedure in his office—an indication that the melanoma, although malignant, did not require removal of a large section of the surrounding tissue. After the procedure was finished, McCain's office released a statement indicating that he would be "monitored occasionally in the future" to protect against any recurrence of the skin cancer.

Later in December, McCain headed for Russia to help monitor the country's first elections since the fall of the Soviet Union. The Russians voted on Sunday, December 12, to elect two houses of parliament and to ratify a new constitution. Boris Yeltsin had called for the elections back in September, and, for help in monitoring the event, he approached the United States Agency for International Development and the International Republican Institute, of which McCain was chairman. Along with McCain, a bipartisan delegation of 25 American politicians, including Vice President Al Gore, went to Russia. They used Moscow as a base from which to visit 12 other Russian cities during the elections.

When he returned from Russia, McCain addressed a subject that had become important to him: the escalating violence among American youth. It was not clear to him exactly what should be done about it, but, in mid-December, he decided it was time for him to weigh in. One of McCain's suggestions was obvious: Parents had to be held accountable for the actions of their children. "Every day in Arizona," he wrote in the *Arizona Republic*, "we hear about young people out of control. Violent behavior among young people is on the rise. Television violence is influencing our children. Our kids are playing video games that depict graphic events, including decapitation and the draining of people's blood. What can we do? That answer is simple: Parents must be accountable for properly raising their children. Parents must take a greater role in their children's lives, and greater responsibility for their children's actions."

Three weeks later, McCain confronted, again in the *Arizona Republic*, a foreign policy issue on which he took a hawkish stand. "The greatest challenge to U.S. security and world stability today," McCain wrote on January 9, 1994, "is the proliferation of weapons of mass destruction. The most dangerous and immediate expression of that global threat now stares at American forces across the frozen landscape of the Korean DMZ [demilitarized zone]. There can be no serious doubt that our vital national interests are imperiled by North Korea's nuclear program and the war they may wage to protect it." McCain's focus on North Korea's growing nuclear threat was in keeping with his overall hard-line positions on military matters and national security: North Korea should be isolated economically on a global scale until it ended its nuclear program.

Later in January, McCain took a much more dovish position on the issue of the U.S. trade embargo against Vietnam. He and Kerry offered a Senate resolution asking the president to end the embargo. In early February, Clinton dropped the 19-year embargo, setting up the possibility that the United States could normalize its diplomatic relations with Vietnam. That was the subject on which McCain and Kerry were going to work next.

In April, when the debate over the country's health care system was again a hot-button issue, McCain underscored his apprehension about a federal government takeover of the medical establishment nationwide. He stressed that he was not being an obstructionist on this topic simply to be an obstructionist. "There are some who have characterized opponents of the Clinton health reform bill as political obstructionists who are not concerned with finding meaningful solutions," McCain wrote on April 21 in the *Arizona Republic*. (By writing a series of editorials that were published in his state's largest newspaper, a practice he had used successfully in the past to communicate with his constituents, McCain was making an orchestrated effort to rebuild his image after the Keating scandal.) "They suggest that if you are not in favor of the Clinton plan, or some other government-run takeover of the health care system, you are against constructive health reform. Such claims are erroneous, simplistic and do not help resolve the real national debate that we are having on health reform. . . . There are many of us in Congress who want health care reform, but are extremely concerned about a system that is run by the government or in which there is undue government intrusion in private decision."

McCain was not willing to reform the health care system to fit the Clintons' model, but he *was* working to reform parts of government. Since he had become a member of Congress, McCain had been annoyed by a practice he witnessed at each of Washington's two airports. For some reason, each airport provided free reserved parking for members of Congress, Supreme Court justices, and diplomats. There were 175 reserved spaces altogether, and they often remained empty. Other passengers had to park much farther away, then trek across the empty parking lot to the terminal. McCain had become upset one day as he watched a woman struggling to roll her suitcase across that extra distance. She could have parked her car much closer to the terminal if the spaces, almost all of them empty, had not been reserved.

McCain wrote a so-called Sense of the Senate amendment, which proposed to do away with the free reserved parking lots at the two area airports. (A Sense of the Senate resolution is a nonbinding proclamation that is used to show the will of the body as a whole; it normally reflects the Senate's strong support for or outrage about a subject.) The gesture of reform was in keeping with the recent actions that had been taken to end the practice of providing free health care for members of Congress—not to mention a free gym and discounts on haircuts. When debate about the bill began, McCain took to the Senate floor to explain that the free reserved parking was yet another example of how Congress was out of touch with reality. "Is it that members are underpaid and cannot afford to pay for parking at these two airports as every other man and woman in America must do?" McCain argued. "Obviously not. . . . We have unfortunately awarded ourselves a salary that dwarfs the incomes of over 99 percent of all families in America." But the majority of the Senate did not agree. "When is this Congress-bashing going to stop?" pleaded Carol Moseley-Braun, the Democratic senator from Illinois. Her colleagues *did* agree with her. When the Senate voted on McCain's Sense of the Senate amendment on April 21, 1994, the final tally was not really close: 53 members voted to reject the bill and only 44 supported it. (For the record, Moseley-Braun, the first African-American woman elected to the Senate, was eventually roundly voted out of office and left under a cloud of scandal; she went on to be ambassador to New Zealand in the Clinton Administration.)

That summer, McCain experienced an honor that reminded others of the McCain family's rich tradition. On Saturday, July 2, McCain attended a ceremony at the Bath Iron Works on the North Pier in Bath, Maine, to witness former president George H. W. Bush, who had driven up from Kennebunkport, commission a new 8,300-ton Burke class destroyer: the *USS John S. McCain.* It was the second ship to have that name, the first having been part of the fleet from 1953 until 1978. Before an audience of 1,000 civilians and sailors, McCain summed up his feelings about the day, declaring, "The navy is the world I know best and love most." Then he introduced Bush, himself a former naval aviator, who drew thunderous applause from the audience when he defended the navy. "I don't like to see the navy under constant attack from its antimilitary critics," he said, adding that the "talking heads" with their "outrageous" attacks based on the Tailhook scandal were "an embarrassment to the country." Using Tailhook as an example of distortion was certainly an odd way to defend the military, since much of the navy brass would say that the sexual harassment in the Las Vegas hotel was certainly not the American military's finest hour, but that's what Bush wanted to do. On the other hand, all he had to say was that, although it was a scandal, Tailhook was an aberration for a military that rarely had incidents like Tailhook. Still, Bush, being the strange public speaker he had become, made the remarks he did before he performed the official duty of commissioning the ship that would sail at once from Maine to Pearl Harbor, its future home port.

On August 22, 1994, Cindy McCain issued a prepared statement about a problem she had been dealing with for years. From 1989 until 1992, she had used Percocet and Vicodin, two prescription pain killers. At the height of her addiction she was taking between 15 and 20 pills a day. She was getting the drugs, she said, "from several physicians, none of whom knew that I was being treated by others. I occasionally supplemented my supply by taking extra prescription drugs which were obtained by the American Voluntary Medical Team [AVMT], a charitable organization of which I am president. Although my conduct did not result in compromising any missions of AVMT, my actions were wrong, and I regret them." Around the date of the release of the statement, Cindy did a series of interviews with selected broadcast and print outlets to discuss her drug problem. In these interviews, the *Arizona Republic* reported, Cindy McCain often became emotional and cried at times.

Her problem had begun in 1989 when she had back surgery twice for ruptured discs. While she was in the hospital recovering, the story of the Keating Five scandal broke. Cindy had been the family bookkeeper during the time the McCains vacationed at the Keating home in the Bahamas, but she could not locate any records to show that she had paid Keating's company for the flights involved in those trips. During 1989, 1990, and 1991, as she dealt with the excruciating and ever-present back pain and as she coped with the stress she and McCain were living under because of the

Keating scandal, she became more and more addicted to prescription drugs. Finally, she began to use her charity, AVMT, as a way to augment the drugs prescribed by her personal doctors.

Cindy McCain had founded AVMT in 1988. Fulfilling its concept, AVMT sent doctors around the world to provide emergency medical care where it was needed. In its first years, teams of doctors, which she often accompanied, had traveled to Vietnam, Micronesia, Bangladesh, Nicaragua, El Salvador, and Kuwait, among other countries. Naturally, as a medical organization, AVMT had access to prescription drugs. AVMT only had to file a requisition order in triplicate and send one copy to the Drug Enforcement Agency (DEA). When Cindy McCain began to use her charity as a way to get prescription drugs, she turned to the company's chief physician, John ("Max") Johnson. Later, Johnson claimed Cindy McCain had him write prescriptions in the names of other company employees. Johnson wrote eight prescriptions under the names of three employees—Kathy Walker, Tracy Orrick, and Thomas Gosinski (the director of governmental and international affairs). The employees didn't know their names were being used. Six prescriptions were for 100 pills each; two were for either 400 or 500 pills each. Johnson also wrote three prescriptions to Cindy McCain, for her back pain and for a broken toe.

Gosinski had other dealings with Cindy McCain, or so he would claim. Specifically, he would charge that, at the time the McCains were trying to adopt Bridget, Cindy called him and asked whether he would be willing to testify that the baby's father had been killed in a rickshaw accident. Walker later told investigators that after Gosinski got off the phone with Cindy McCain that day, he looked at Walker and said, "I can't believe she asked me to lie." Then Gosinski threatened, in Walker's presence, "I'm going to get her! I'm going to blackmail her if she ever fires me."

Apparently, the nuns from whom Cindy McCain got Bridget in Bangladesh had told her that Bridget's father had been killed in a rickshaw accident, but there were no records to prove it. The adoption process would be easier for the McCains if Bridget had no parents, so Cindy McCain needed some testimony that would confirm the absence of parents. According to Gosinski, that's why she approached him. In point of fact, in 1992, the McCains' adoption lawyer, Donald Gilbert, had told the court that Bridget's mother was dead and her father, who could not be found, was presumed dead as well.

Events turned ugly when Gosinski was fired from AVMT in January 1993—because of cutbacks, the company said. In April, Gosinski's lawyer, Stanley Lubin, wrote a letter to the McCains' lawyer, John Dowd, threatening to go public with damaging material about Cindy McCain by filing a law suit if his client was not paid $250,000. The suit did not use the word "drugs," but Lubin's letter offering a settlement did. "It is clear that you made it appear that Mr. Gosinski was ordering the drugs," Lubin wrote to Cindy McCain through her attorney, "many of which were controlled narcotics, in an effort to hide your personal use of them." Gosinski "has done what he could to keep the sensitive matters from exposure." Dowd refused Lubin's request. In a letter to the Maricopa County Attorney's office, he charged that Gosinski's actions amounted to "a shakedown" and asked to have Gosinski investigated for alleged extortion of the McCains. Gosinski retaliated by tipping off the DEA to Cindy McCain's scheme involving AVMT and prescription drugs, about which he seemed to have firsthand knowledge. He then went forward with his lawsuit for wrongful termination. Gosinski had been asked "on numerous occasions," the suit said, to "engage in acts that were improper." The suit stated that Gosinski "was responsible for the maintenance of certain sensitive records and the overall operation and integrity of the organization." Gosinski also sued for libel and slander because Cindy McCain, the suit charged, had bad-mouthed Gosinski when he tried to get another job.

Once the outside government agencies became involved, Cindy McCain more or less lost control of the story. Before long, AVMT was being investigated by the DEA and the U.S. Attorney's Office for the illegal prescriptions written by Johnson. By then, Cindy McCain no longer had a drug problem. In 1992, when she was confronted by her parents because her behavior was sometimes clearly influenced by drugs, she confessed to the problem and went "cold turkey." She simply stopped and somehow found a way to live with what had caused her to take the drugs in the first place—severe back pain. Then, in January 1993, her obstetrician discovered a medical problem that required her to undergo a hysterectomy. As soon as she had the operation, the pain she had been suffering for years suddenly ended. Now, she had a new problem: the various investigations into AVMT and her activities related to that company. She had never told her husband about the drug problem. In January 1994, given the possibility that the story was going public, she told him about her problem and the ongoing investigations.

Eventually, the DEA agreed not to prosecute Cindy McCain. She cut a deal that required her to do community service and join Narcotics Anonymous. She also agreed to pay for the cost of the various investigations into AVMT. In January 1995, John Johnson became the target of an investigation by the Arizona Board of Medical Examiners; eventually, Johnson, who admitted to writing fraudulent prescriptions, was forced to relinquish his medical license. A general surgeon for 30 years, Johnson was now prohibited from practicing medicine anywhere.

For a while, Cindy McCain's reputation within the state was damaged. In September 1994, the Variety Club of Arizona had to cancel a fund-raiser for which she was to have served as chair. Too few of the $125 tickets had been sold. Then again, the event was to have occurred during the media frenzy that resulted from Cindy McCain's going public about her past prescription drug problem and the deal she had worked out with the federal authorities.

Ultimately, the scandal was put into the context of Cindy McCain's life. She had no greater defender than her husband. "For anyone to imply that Cindy acted improperly in this matter is as despicable a falsehood as I have ever had the misfortune to observe,"

John McCain wrote on August 26, 1994, in response to a recent article in the *Phoenix Gazette*. "Cindy never asked Mr. Gosinski to lie about Bridget's adoption. The adoption was proper in every respect. The adoption court ruled that Bridget was an abandoned infant. There are no more relevant circumstances to this story than the facts which I have just provided—except this: The *Phoenix Gazette* decided to run a story without evidence to remotely prove its accuracy that has attempted to tarnish a story of kindness with the brush of scandal. I will accept a great deal in public life, but I cannot accept this."

As this painful drama was unfolding for Cindy, McCain did his best to get on with his political life. At one point during the summer, while he was campaigning in Oklahoma for James Inhofe, a Republican senate candidate, McCain was attacked for his role in the Keating scandal. Dave McCurdy, Inhofe's Democratic opponent, issued a press release in which he called McCain "a tainted Washington insider" who had "a lot of experience with failed financial institutions." It was a cheap shot, but it indicated that, even though he had been reelected in his own state after the scandal, the Keating mess was not completely behind him. Perhaps it never would be. Maybe McCain had been right when he said that the incident would be mentioned on his gravestone. If the political residue of the scandal did not go away, McCain would have a hard time mounting a serious presidential campaign.

In June 1994, McCain continued to define himself on the issue of gay rights. In the wake of going before the antigay Oregon Citizens Alliance to make a speech about tolerance, McCain joined a movement in the Senate that evolved into a public gesture: As employers, senators would not discriminate on the basis of sexual orientation. Specifically, 71 senators, McCain among them, signed a statement that pertained to hiring practices on Capitol Hill. Sexual orientation, to quote from an announcement made by the Human Rights

Campaign, a gay lobbying organization, "is not a consideration in the hiring, promoting, or terminating of employees in their offices."

McCain also continued to focus on foreign affairs. One country that had concerned him for much of 1994 was North Korea. "Late in the year, McCain and I appeared together on Jim Lehrer's *News Hour* to discuss North Korea," says Congressman Gary Ackerman, a Democrat from New York. "My position was, we had to be very careful and walk them back from the nuclear precipice that they were in. We needed to do that through every available diplomatic means, including an international consortium. But McCain's position was pretty tough, which surprised me, because he was so reasonable as a Vietnam POW. He was so reasonable on Vietnam that he helped establish relations with the country. His position on North Korea was: 'Well, if they don't do what we want, we should basically blow them up.' It was a hardline position that surprised me. Still, he's a very smart guy, and I respect him tremendously."

At one point in 1994, McCain did something that would have an enormous effect on his life. One day, he picked up the phone and called Russell Feingold, the Democratic senator from Wisconsin who had been elected to the Senate in 1992 at the age of 39. Feingold had the reputation of being a squeaky-clean politician. During his campaign for the Senate in 1991, he ran a television ad that featured him giving a tour of his ranch house. In one sequence, he stopped at a closet, opened the door, and said to the camera, "No skeletons." When he arrived in Washington, some people thought of him as a Boy Scout, perhaps because he wore his hair in a crew cut. So McCain knew what he was doing when he approached Feingold about working together to develop legislation that would bring true campaign finance reform to the American political system. After McCain had seen what could happen to a politician in a scandal like the Keating debacle, he was determined to reform the system. The first step, McCain believed, was to clean up the way campaigns were financed. Feingold jumped at the chance to work on the issue. The resulting McCain-Feingold bill became one of the most famous pieces of federal legislation in modern American political history. It also served to erase the stain left on McCain's political career, and to open up the chance that he could still run for president and have a legitimate shot at winning.

In the first half of 1995, McCain turned his attention to an issue that continued to dominate his thinking: normalization of relations between the United States and Vietnam. The effort had grown out of the work Kerry and McCain had done on the select committee and the end of the trade embargo, championed by McCain and Kerry, that Clinton had facilitated in February 1994. In April 1995, during an appearance at a symposium sponsored by the Discovery Channel, McCain said that the United States had to move beyond the Vietnam War and that the president should normalize relations with Vietnam. McCain also revealed that he and Kerry were prepared to cosponsor a Sense of the Senate resolution suggesting just that. McCain recognized that there were MIAs "who were lost at sea or in other circumstances which offer no hope of survival and little hope of recovery." Still, because of the lack of hope of recovering any more bodies, he felt it was time to resolve the issue of the MIAs once and for all. Normalizing relations with Vietnam would help accomplish that goal.

On May 23, McCain and Kerry met with Clinton in the White House and lobbied for normalization. Five days later, in the *Washington Post*, McCain stated his position in an editorial titled "Time to Open an Embassy in Vietnam." McCain wrote: "The issue involved in our relations of greatest importance to the American people is the accounting for our missing servicemen. Vietnam's cooperation with the United States on this issue is extensive and has increased since we lifted our trade embargo against Vietnam last year. . . . There remain only 55 cases that offer even the slightest hope that the servicemen in question did not die at the moment of their initial loss and that we think might be resolved through joint investigation with Vietnam or possibly through unilateral action on the part of the Vietnamese. . . . It is . . . absolutely to our national security interests to have an economically viable Vietnam strong enough to resist, in concert with its neighbors, the heavy-handed tactics of its great-power neighbor [China]. That reason, more than any other, urges the normalization of our relations and makes Vietnam's membership in the Association of Southeast Asian Nations, and the increasingly responsible role Hanoi is playing in regional affairs, a very welcome development."

The public campaign McCain had launched was working. In mid-June, the Vietnamese allowed an American recovery team to go into a Vietnamese military cemetery to look for remains of any U.S. POW or MIA. That gesture provided political clout for McCain to push for a treaty that would establish ties between the countries. His had been an odd and telling journey on the subject of Vietnam. He had been shot down over Hanoi in October 1967, and remained a POW there until March 1973. For years after, he privately railed against the "gooks" who had tortured him and his friends. When the government had asked him to go to North Vietnam in the late 1970s, he was offended by the request. But slowly, throughout the 1980s, as he made trips back to the region and allowed the ugliness of the past to fade into memory, McCain came to view Vietnam differently. To resolve what had happened in Vietnam, the United States had to find a way to deal with its former enemy. Only then would there be a kind of healing.

Many of McCain's colleagues disagreed. When McCain was asked how he could break ranks with Phil Gramm, whom he had chosen to support in the upcoming 1996 presidential campaign, McCain said that Gramm "did not serve in Vietnam." When an NBC reporter confronted McCain and told him that Bob Dole opposed normalizing relations with Vietnam, McCain responded that Dole had "served in another war which has ended, and I would like for Senator Dole to let us end this one." (Dole earned a Purple Heart during his service in World War II.) On Tuesday, July 11, McCain joined up with an unlikely political ally, Bill Clinton, to endorse a normalization of relations. In a ceremony in the East Room of the White House, with McCain, John Kerry, Bob Kerrey, Chuck Robb, and others present, Clinton granted formal recognition to the Vietnamese government. "Today, I am announcing the normalization of diplomatic relationships with Vietnam," Clinton said. Those diplomatic relations had ended on a fateful day in April 1975, when Ambassador Graham Martin, carrying a folded American flag tucked under his arm, had left the U.S. embassy in Saigon by helicopter. Clinton had now reopened America's dealings with the country Martin had left 20 years before.

In his office in the Russell Senate Office Building on the morning before the ceremony, a reporter from the *Arizona Republic* had asked McCain how he felt about the historic development. "This is a time to heal," McCain said. "I experienced closure a long time ago—the day I left Vietnam in 1973. But others, they still need to heal." Following the ceremony, a reporter from another news outlet asked McCain if he believed he was being used by the Clinton Administration. "Maybe," McCain said, "but I'm just trying to do what's in the best interest of the country. . . . Do I trust them [the Vietnamese]? No, but I trust the history. They are meeting their commitments, and we should meet ours. It's a way of ending the war. It's time to move on."

There were, however, other Americans who couldn't move on. In July, the *U.S. Veteran Dispatch*, an underground publication circulated among a segment of the veteran population in the United States, called McCain "a fraud, a 'rhinestone hero' and a national security risk." The publication spoke for the portion of the veteran community that was angry at McCain because he would not accept their notion that a large number of POWs and MIAs were being held in Southeast Asia, particularly in Vietnam. The veterans were livid because McCain, whom they had considered to be one of their own, had modified the positions he had held in the past and now advocated—indeed, endorsed—resuming relations with Vietnam. "John McCain is no hero," the *Dispatch* said in its July edition. "He was never brutally tortured and, by his own admission, he collaborated with the communists." Without even attempting to justify how it could make such outrageous statements, the publication further undercut its credibility by claiming McCain was given "his own private affection nurse." The charges were not even worth answering, so McCain ignored the material and dismissed the source. Attacks like these had started during the years when he and Kerry worked on the select committee; now, given his advocacy of normalized relations, they had become even worse.

In July, decidedly more favorable press came to McCain in the form of Robert Timberg's highly praised book on the U.S. Naval Academy called *The Nightingale's Song*. Timberg had used Oliver North, James Webb, Robert McFarland, John Poindexter, and McCain as subjects for his examination of life before, during, and after Annapolis. Writing in the *New York Times Book Review*, Nicholas Proffitt had called the book "a significant contribution to our understanding of recent political and military history" and "a fascinating chronicle of the human element behind all history." Mark Shields declared in the *Washington Post*: "[The book] will help you understand why the unhealed wounds of the Vietnam War still pain and divide this American nation and shadow American politics. . . . Robert Timberg explains brilliantly the price paid by those who went, by those who didn't, and by the nation's leadership that failed them." *The Nightingale's Song* was the first serious attempt to document the facts and meaning of the life of John McCain, or at least a part of it.

Autumn in 1995 was a season of disappointment and triumph. On a personal note, McCain was saddened by the spectacular fall from grace of a friend in the Senate, Robert Packwood of Oregon. Packwood had been the object of an Ethics Committee investigation based on allegations that he had made unwanted sexual advances toward 17 women. Through the long and painful ordeal, Packwood defiantly made every legal and ethical move possible to keep himself in the Senate. But on Wednesday, September 6, the Ethics Committee unanimously voted to have Packwood expelled for sexual misconduct. Ultimately, too much evidence suggested that the women were right, or so the committee concluded.

On Thursday morning, September 7, McCain and Alan Simpson, a Republican from Wyoming, met with Packwood in Bob Dole's Senate hideaway. "John and I sat there," Simpson remembers, "and said: 'What are we going to do for our friend?' He was getting torn to bits. It was going to be tough. He had no chance. Nobody was listening. The Ethics Committee was cutting him to ribbons, both parties. So we said, 'Bob, it may be time to go.' And he was heartbroken. He said, 'But I didn't do these things. I mean, I'm being crucified.' And, of course, the statute of limitations had expired on every one of them, in any other court."

Finally, McCain summed up the situation. "It's over," McCain said to Packwood. "You gotta go. I envision no scenario where the Senate would overrule a unanimous recommendation of the Ethics Committee." Packwood sat quietly, the weight of the moment bearing down on him. When Dole joined the meeting, the discussion shifted from *whether* Packwood should resign to *how* he would resign. "You should talk about how much you've achieved as a senator," McCain said, "and how much you love the Senate, and go out with grace." Later that day, on the Senate floor, McCain addressed the point at which the Senate had arrived: Packwood had no choice but to resign or face being expelled from his office by his colleagues. "I resent assumptions that all men in this institution require an object lesson made of Bob Packwood so that we might learn to treat half of humanity with dignity," McCain said, referring to a circulating argument that said Packwood should be set up as an example of misogyny run amuck. "I grieve for [Bob Packwood] today, I regret this moment's arrival, I wish him good fortune, and I say without reservation, I am proud to call Bob Packwood my friend."

In December, Dole and McCain teamed up to sponsor a resolution on Bosnia called Dole-McCain, a piece of legislation that would allow the president to commit U.S. troops to help the Bosnian Muslims in their ongoing struggle with Serbia. The resolution passed easily (77 to 22) but, within the process, which had far-reaching implications, a highly personal piece of information was revealed by Dole to McCain—a detail of history that brought the two good friends even closer.

"There was a debate in the Senate," McCain says, "and Bob Dole and I had joined together, against a lot of Republicans, in favor of sending troops into Bosnia. I had already spoken. Bob was to give the last speech before the vote, which is traditional for the majority leader. I was very interested in what he had to say because, on this issue, he had taken on the right wing. So I went down and sat in this little chair next to the podium, where the president of the Senate sits, so I could see him from that part of the Senate and watch him speak. To make a long story short, he gave the speech, and in it he mentioned the fact that he'd worn my bracelet while I was in prison. He had never told me that he wore a bracelet with my name on it— until that speech.

"I was floored when he talked about it. After the speech, I went up to him and said, 'Bob, how come you never told me?' And he said something like, 'Well, I didn't think about it.' Something like that. And that was the way I found out that he wore a bracelet with my name on it while I was in prison in Vietnam."

It was a touching, emotional moment; its pathos would stay with McCain for years. Then again, the autumn had been full of emotion. In late October, McCain had had another cancer scare. When a spot on his face had become discolored, he went to a doctor and learned that, as a precaution, the splotch needed to be operated on. Near month's end, McCain had surgery to remove precancerous skin cells from his forehead.

For the presidential election of 1996, McCain chose to support Senator Phil Gramm of Texas in the Republican primaries. Gramm, a staunch conservative, was much farther to the right than

McCain on a number of issues. Even so, McCain was such a strong supporter, Gramm made him the national chairman of his presidential campaign. During the fall, McCain had worked hard for Gramm; he lobbied to get a number of elected officials in Arizona to support Gramm. But in the second week of February 1996, in the wake of a dismal showing in the New Hampshire primary, Gramm saw his campaign fall apart. The frontrunner in the party was McCain's friend Bob Dole, whom McCain endorsed on February 16, as soon as it was clear that the Gramm candidacy was finished. This was hardly a risky move. As the primary season proceeded, it became more and more apparent that Dole would be the nominee of the Republican Party and would go up against Bill Clinton in the November general election.

In the late spring, after Dole had the nomination locked up, he decided to resign from the Senate so he could devote all of his energy to his campaign. One person who pushed strongly for him *not* to resign was McCain. In the end, Dole did not take McCain's advice. On June 11, 1996, he delivered a speech and formally resigned from the body he had come to cherish. Of the many senators who offered testimonials to Dole, McCain gave one that was especially poignant.

"Before I close, I would like to offer a personal expression of gratitude to my leader," McCain said at the end of his address from the Senate floor. "A long time ago, in another walk of life, I lived for a period of time without liberty. I and a great many men whose courage and honor enabled me to endure that experience wanted nothing more than to keep faith with our country and for our country to keep faith with us. When well-intentioned members of this institution unwittingly attempted to break faith with us by denying support for the war necessary to ensure our eventual liberation, Bob Dole led the opposition to that effort. For seven weeks, he forcefully debated a cutoff of funding while so many of America's sons remained the prisoners of our enemies. All the while he waged that debate, Bob Dole wore a bracelet that bore my name. I have never properly thanked him for the great honor he did me. I wish to do so now. For myself, for my comrades who came home with me, and for the many thousands who did not, thank you, Bob, for the honor of your concern and support for us. We fought in different wars, but we kept the same faith."

This was not the only time in the spring of 1996 McCain was willing to show his emotions. "I went to the funeral of David Ifshin," says Congressman Eliot Engel, a Democrat from New York, "a friend of mine who had been active in Clinton's first election. President Clinton came to the funeral and delivered one of the eulogies. The other person who delivered a eulogy was John McCain. I remember feeling very surprised, because Dave had been a radical left-winger on the Vietnam War, a real student activist who was even featured in magazines as a leader of the anti-war movement. And when John spoke he made a reference to it. Apparently, they first met each other almost as adversaries—John said he initially had disdain for him—but somehow they became acquaintances and then very close friends. When he got up and spoke, it was the first time I ever saw a side of John McCain that was more than what I thought he was: a right-wing reactionary Republican. That day, I saw the other side of McCain and I realized you can't put a mold on him. He spoke of David in glowing terms, this former adversary. He spoke with empathy, sensitivity, and heartfeltness."

On Wednesday night, March 27, 1996, the Senate voted for the line-item veto, a concept McCain had been fighting for for 10 years. He believed pork-barrel spending could be contained, at least in part, if the president was allowed to veto specific lines on the federal budget. Apparently, this idea's time had finally come: The vote in the Senate was not even close. The bill establishing the line-item veto passed 69 to 31. To erase any doubt that Congress was ready to pass the bill into law, the House waited only 18 hours after the Senate vote and then passed the bill with a vote of 232 to 177.

After this legislative success, McCain saw his name floated around as a possible running mate for Dole, but the convention in San Diego was still four months or more away. As the gossip was circulating through the usual channels in Washington, William Safire wrote a stunning editorial in the *New York Times* in which he identified McCain not as a vice-presidential candidate but as a *presidential* candidate. The nomination for the year 1996 was all wrapped up, but Safire was pondering the future national elections, in either 2000 or 2004. Because the piece was so unrelated to what was going on at the time, most readers did not know how to interpret it. McCain knew what to do. On Monday, April 22, he made it clear to Dole that he did not want to be considered as a running mate. Instead, he happily accepted the position of national security adviser to the Dole for President campaign.

McCain had gone out of his way to take himself off Dole's vice-presidential short list because, as of early May, one name seemed to dominate that list more and more: Colin Powell, the former chairman of the Joint Chiefs of Staff who, along with General H. Norman Schwarzkopf, had achieved hero status during the Persian Gulf War. As of Sunday, May 5, Powell was at the top of the short list, and, while there was also talk of putting a woman on the ticket, McCain's name was still on the list too, even though he had made a great effort to have it taken off. By May 17, the *New York Times* had decided that McCain was serving Dole as "a factotum," "a shadow adviser, surrogate, articulator, and filial booster." McCain chose to downplay his involvement in the burgeoning campaign, saying he was "sort of like the family dog."

As a part of this McCain-as-vice-president scenario, in early June, *Foreign Policy* published an article in which McCain described the Clinton Administration's foreign policy as "[f]eckless, inattentive and uncertain"—a denunciation that convinced some observers that McCain was trying to ensure his place on a list he said publicly he didn't want to be on. McCain's deep involvement in one of the Clinton Administration's foreign policy successes—the normalization of relations with Vietnam—only made the criticism more relevant.

On June 24, McCain took an action that, while personally important to him, further elevated his national profile. That day, on the Senate floor, he introduced the product of his and Russell Feingold's efforts toward campaign finance reform. The 1996 version of the reform banned political action committees and ended soft money—moves that had caused Senator Mitch McConnell of Kentucky to call the proposed legislation "an unconstitutional, undemocratic, bureaucratic boondoggle." McCain saw the reform differently. "This bill will not cure public cynicism for politics," McCain said on the Senate floor, "but we believe it will prevent cynicism from becoming contempt and contempt from becoming alienation. . . . We know the consequences of failing to act are far more frightening than the consequences of involuntary retirement." Apparently, the Senate didn't agree. The next day, Tuesday, the Senate killed campaign finance reform on a procedural vote. McCain saw the defeat coming when he said to the body before the vote, "The people's will cannot be forever denied, no matter how well inoculated we are by the financial advantages we claim as incumbents. . . . The people will have this reform, if not by our work, then by the work of our replacements."

While some legislative work got done during the summer of 1996, most of the time and energy of McCain and others were taken up with politics, for the Republican National Convention was looming in August. From the looks of things, President Clinton was going to be a difficult candidate for Bob Dole to defeat. Through July and on into August, a political soap opera developed around whom Dole would pick to be his running mate. This drama only heightened when Kenneth Duberstein, a well-placed Washington insider and kingmaker, had set up a luncheon at his home and invited Dole and Powell for the express purpose of Powell's being offered the vice-presidential spot on the ticket. The meeting did not go well. Powell made it clear that he was not interested in being vice president, mostly because his wife, Alma, was strongly opposed to the idea.

The soap opera continued into August. On August 1, the name of John McCain was formally added to the list, and the FBI began a background check of McCain and his family. By August 8, other names had been leaked to the press, among them Governor John Engler of Michigan, Senator Connie Mack of Florida, and a former governor, Carroll Campbell of South Carolina. Some of Dole's aides believed he might pick someone whose name was not even on the list. A rumored phantom list included names like James Baker III, the former secretary of state under Bush; William Bennett, the former drug czar; Donald Rumsfeld, the former secretary of defense under Ford; and Dick Cheney, the former secretary of defense under Bush. Then, because Dole had decided to make, as the centerpiece of his campaign, a proposed across-the-board 15 percent tax cut, Jack Kemp, the former football quarterback and congressman from New York, was seen by some as an unusually appropriate pick, a more-or-less walking advertisement of the Dole tax cut. The plan that was finally put into place required Dole to make the announcement in his hometown of Russell, Kansas, on the Saturday before the start of the Republican National Convention.

"Ultimately, the short list was down to Connie Mack and Jack Kemp," says Joyce Campbell, the deputy press secretary of the Dole for President campaign. "Dole was literally sitting in a campaign trailer in Russell, Kansas, trying to make his decision whether it would be Mack or Kemp. Finally, Senator Dole got on the phone with Jack Kemp for one last conversation, and that was when he made up his mind. Kemp was down in Texas, I believe, at the time, so Sheila Burke and Rod D'Arment were dispatched down to Texas on a private plane to pick him up."

Observers should have known the campaign was going to have problems when Dole arrived in San Diego and, as he made his opening informal remarks while standing near the city's beautiful picturesque bay, told the audience how happy he was to be in San Francisco. McCain was featured at the convention. It was he who actually delivered the nomination of Dole on August 14. At one point, he said about himself, "A long time ago, in another walk of life, I was deprived of my liberty." But the convention was stolen by the candidate's wife, Elizabeth Dole, who gave a dramatic and poignant talk about her husband as she wandered about, Oprah-style, on the floor of the convention. Microphone in hand, she stopped along the way to interview important people in Dole's life who had been preselected for the performance. Elizabeth Dole even upstaged her husband, whose schizophrenic acceptance speech—the sweeping, elegant passages were written by novelist and *Wall Street Journal* columnist Mark Helprin; the clunky info-speak parts were put together by a bevy of run-of-the-mill, work-for-hire speech writers—served as a preamble to a campaign that was, at best, disjointed.

"Before long, Dole was getting to the point where he was, while not going off message, having a hard time focusing on his stump speeches on the road," Joyce Campbell says. "So McCain was kind of called in to become a cheerleader." As they went from stop to stop on the campaign trail, McCain simply hung around Dole. He sat with him in Dole's private area on the plane and he milled around with him backstage at events. "Sometimes McCain would stand in the audience of some of the stump speeches or sit in the front row and prompt Dole to smile. I remember one or two occasions on which McCain drew a happy face on a legal pad and sort of flashed it at Dole—he'd hold it up so Dole could see it—to get Dole to smile at different moments during the speech."

Not long after Labor Day, more problems developed within the campaign. "Dole was getting really frustrated with Kemp," Campbell says, "and thought he was not pulling his weight. Kemp had a hard time keeping a coherent message or articulating anything about the campaign's main platform. As this was happening, McCain became someone Dole could confide in. McCain was always very openly and physically kind toward Dole. He would pat him on the back, put his arm around him. It was kind of, like, here were two guys who had been through hell and back. I thought McCain was an extremely likable guy."

Maybe, but some campaign staffers saw what many people in Washington knew McCain had—a temper. "McCain was loyal to Dole, and we liked him for that," says someone who worked on the Dole campaign. "We all liked him because we thought he was honest and tough—and a very warm person. But he had a really bad temper. When he got mad, he'd use every expletive in the book. He had the mouth of a sailor, which should not have been surprising, since he *was* a sailor. He just had, I guess you'd say, a very feisty personality."

In November, on the night of the election, McCain watched as Dole lost to Clinton in a race that was never really close. Still, during the campaign, the two men had become close. "The common bond of their friendship," Campbell says, "was that they had been war veterans whose experiences in war had molded and defined their world views and their view of public service. They had both overcome enormous adversities. Dole was almost killed; McCain was almost killed. They had this near-death experience in combat that they shared. They also both felt that they were American success stories—kind of up-by-your-boot-straps personalities. Finally, because McCain was of a different generation, he held Dole in enormously high esteem. He saw Dole as having leadership qualities, which was why he considered Dole a role model."

A few days after the election, McCain made another trip to Southeast Asia. On November 12, in Phnom Penh, Cambodia, McCain unveiled a plaque honoring American troops who were killed on the coast of Cambodia 21 years earlier in the final action of the Indochina War. Eighteen men from the marines, the air force, and the navy were killed by the Khmer Rouge as they attempted to rescue the crew of the *Mayaguez* on May 15, 1975. During this trip, McCain met, for the first time, Mai Van On, the man who had saved him years before, when he parachuted into the lake in Hanoi. On, who still lived in Hanoi, was happy to meet the man he had saved. "We shook hands and hugged each other," On would one day tell the *Los Angeles Times*. "He sat next to me and asked me, 'I was your ad-versary; why did you rescue me?' I told him, 'You were about to die. Based on the humanitarian nature of the Vietnamese people, I res-cued you.'"

When he returned to Arizona, McCain addressed an issue in which he was becoming more and more interested—the environ-ment. "As Republicans prepare to begin a second term in control of Congress," McCain wrote in the *Arizona Republic* on November 27, "a deep skepticism exists in the electorate about the party's com-mitment to protecting the environment. . . . Have Republicans abandoned their roots as the party of Theodore Roosevelt, who maintained that government's most important task, with the excep-tion of national security, is to leave posterity a land in better con-dition than they received it? The answer must be 'No.' . . . The estimable Morris Udall, the former Democrat representative from Arizona and a nationally recognized environmental leader, once taught me a valuable lesson. He reached across the aisle to enlist my help in his efforts to address the environmental problems of our state. We were able to place more than 3.5 billion acres of land into wilderness protection, increase the preservation of public lands and tackle complex environmental threats to the Grand Canyon."

McCain was obviously making a political statement with the new—and increasingly tough—stand he was taking on the environ-ment, but, some time before the fall election, he had had to deal with a personal matter that also could have had political implica-tions. In 1984, he had campaigned for Jim Kolbe in his successful ef-fort to win a House seat as an Arizona congressman. This year, as Kolbe was preparing to run for reelection once again, word began to spread through political circles that he was gay. The information had become so well known that Kolbe decided to go public with it, but, before he did, he wanted to tell his friends and supporters. One of the first people he called was McCain. "Before I got two words out," Kolbe later told a reporter, "John said, 'I know what this is about, and it doesn't matter.' He wasn't shocked or offended." What McCain did was remain Kolbe's friend. In the end, Arizona voters didn't care either. Kolbe won.

In 1996, McCain had also made known his stand on the conflict between Great Britain and Northern Ireland. "I was at the British Embassy when the new British ambassador invited a bunch of us to a formal dinner to discuss the Northern Irish situation," says Congressman Peter King of New York. "It was very elaborate, as only the British can do it. Among those attending were Chris Dodd, John McCain, Joe Kennedy, and some people from the White House. Well, I was convinced it was sort of a setup, because the ambassador had McCain sitting right opposite me. I didn't really know McCain at all, except that he was very pro-British on the whole Irish issue. During the course of the evening, McCain made some very pro-British statements, at which point I started to disagree with him. Within 30 or 40 seconds, we were going at each other across the table. Dodd said, 'Will you guys knock it off?' Then Kennedy said, 'No wonder nobody wants to invite the Irish anywhere.' We calmed down, but during the rest of the night I would see him occasionally looking over at me."

By the fall of 1997, McCain was ready to fight the next battle in what had become a war over campaign finance reform. In a speech at American University, Clinton had said he expected Majority Leader Trent Lott to prevent campaign finance reform from coming up in this session of Congress. "Every year I have seen the bill blocked by a filibuster in the United States Senate—every single year," Clinton said. On September 10, Russell Feingold announced that he and McCain were willing to force a fight in the Senate over campaign finance reform, if that's what it would take to get the issue discussed. So, whatever the reason—Clinton's taunting remarks or Feingold's threats—Lott proclaimed, on September 25, that the Senate would—that very day—begin debate on the subject of campaign finance reform.

The debate would last for two weeks, Lott said. After that, the Senate could vote, depending on what happened during the debate. Lott's move was so unexpected that even McCain was shocked; in fact, Lott's quick move forced McCain to reveal that the final draft of the bill was not ready. "All I asked was that [Lott] bring it up and he did," McCain said. "Would I prefer a couple of more weeks? Sure, because the pressure is mounting." But he was more than willing to proceed, since Lott seemed ready. As written, McCain-Feingold banned unregulated soft money given to the political parties by either individuals or groups; it also regulated issue ads. Naturally, the forces opposed to McCain-Feingold, headed most notably by Mitch McConnell, were prepared for a fight. On the day of Lott's announcement, McConnell restated his willingness to filibuster the bill, declaring: "We're ready."

Regardless of whether the bill passed during this session, McCain-Feingold was having a profound effect on McCain's career in ways he had never imagined. Conservative advocacy groups, angered by McCain's attempt to push campaign finance reform through Congress, targeted McCain as a politician who needed to be eliminated from the national political scene. These groups, it seemed, believed campaign finance reform would affect their ability to be successful because it would limit the ways money could be raised and how it could be spent on issue-advertising. To get rid of McCain, one group, the National Right to Life Committee, decided to air a radio campaign attacking McCain in the key states of Arizona, New Hampshire, and Iowa. Discrediting him in his home state made sense, if the goal was to try to make him vulnerable in his next Senate race. But the idea of running negative ads in Iowa and New Hampshire meant that, even in 1997, some groups had identified McCain as a possible—or maybe even a probable—presidential candidate in 2000. The presidential rumors were so widespread that as recently as August McCain had been asked if he ever wanted to be president. His answer was flip but telling—pure McCain: "I prefer to be emperor."

McCain-Feingold died on February 26, 1998, when the Senate voted 51 to 48 to end a filibuster on the bill. In effect, the bill was nine votes shy of becoming law because to pass in the Senate, a bill actually needs 60 votes—the number required to end a filibuster. (From the Senate, a bill is then combined with a similar bill passed in the House. If the bills are the same, the combined bill is sent to the president for his signature. If the House and Senate versions are different, a conference is called to merge the two bills and produce a compromise bill. If the conference fails, the two versions are sent back to their respective bodies.) McCain-Feingold remained far short of the votes needed to end a filibuster. As it happened, the House version of the bill—called Shays-Meehan for its sponsors (Christopher Shays of Connecticut and Martin Meehan of Massachusetts)—was scheduled to be debated during the coming month. Many Washington insiders felt that, of the two bills, the House version of campaign finance reform had a much better chance of passing.

Lott officially tabled McCain-Feingold on the morning of Thursday, February 28, 1998, when two procedural votes failed. After McCain-Feingold died, Lott commented on the proceedings, which technically ended with a filibuster, by saying McCain didn't have the votes to halt it. "We had a fair discussion," Lott said. "It's obvious we don't have consensus here yet. We've got a lot of very important business to do, domestically and in foreign policy."

Soon after the Senate had killed campaign finance reform, McCain launched another crusade that was destined to generate controversy. On April 1, the Commerce Committee, which McCain chaired, passed a bill that, according to McCain, was designed to reduce the number of teenage smokers in the United States. The bill would raise the tax on a pack of cigarettes so high that teenagers would find smoking unaffordable. Much to the surprise of some political observers, the bill, which amounted to a hefty tax increase, albeit on an activity that was now generally considered to be harmful, had been passed, out of committee, by the overwhelming margin of 19 to 1. As soon as the committee passed the bill, the chairman of

R. J. Reynolds, Steven Holdstone, who had been working closely with Washington until now, severed all relationships with both the White House and Congress.

On Friday, April 10, McCain clearly identified his new enemy: Big Tobacco. In Florence, South Carolina, at a town hall meeting, he told a group of 500 tobacco farmers that he was proposing a bill that, if passed, would protect farmers—both those who wanted to get out of the tobacco business and those who wanted to stay. The bill, McCain told his audience, was designed especially to reduce the number of teenagers who smoke. "More than 3,000 children start smoking every day in this country," McCain said. "Of that number 1,000 will die prematurely because of smoking-related illnesses. Our entire thrust is to reduce tobacco consumption, which will inevitably reduce the number of tobacco farmers. We're trying to shape a fair program that will compensate any farmer who wants to get out, as well as any farmer who wants to stay in."

While McCain was getting ready to fight the good fight against the tobacco industry, perhaps one of the most powerful business groups in America, the tobacco executives were preparing their response. They planned to spend $50 million on an ad campaign designed to take on McCain's bill. Addressing this plan, McCain told the tobacco farmers: "These are the same people who in [an] agreement last June didn't say one word about taking care of the tobacco farmer, but who now are running full-page ads suggesting that this bill is going to put them out of business and talking about the plight of the tobacco farmers. Since they lied to the American people and lied to Congress about the effects of smoking and their efforts to target kids, I think they're going to have a real credibility problem. It wasn't you who marketed tobacco products to kids. The American people know that you've done nothing wrong, that you grow a legal crop, and that you're entitled to make a living."

By mid-May, McCain and the White House had reached an agreement on the amendments to McCain's tobacco bill. Most of the amendments dealt with civil lawsuit liabilities and the cigarette tax itself, which, if McCain and the White House got their way, would total $65 billion over five years. The Senate debate over the tobacco bill could now begin—as soon as possible. That debate raged throughout the rest of May and June. As it did, McCain's name showed up in the national press in another way as well.

On June 6, 1998, a Saturday, the *Los Angeles Times* ran a story about Mai Van On, the man who had saved McCain's life by pulling him from the lake in Hanoi. The article seemed to focus on the fact that On and his family (his wife and two sons) were not employed and were living on a modest government pension of $18 a month. On seemed more than a little bitter about his situation. He had saved a man who later became an important national figure not only in America but also in Vietnam. "There is a reason for everything," On said to the reporter. "Consider: I save an unknown pilot. He becomes a famous man and leads the way for America and Vietnam to become friends. If I had let him die, would this have happened?" It was a question that had no answer, or, rather, a question that answered itself. "What's done is done. I never hated Americans, only the American government and I never regretted what I did that day, even though a lot of people wanted to kill your pilot, Mr. McCain."

Later in June, there was a showdown over the tobacco bill. The Republican senators, most of whom opposed McCain's bill, had met for a luncheon during which the bill's opponents criticized the legislation. A flow chart was produced to show the cumbersome bureaucracy the bill would create, should it ever become law. McCain was incensed over the flow chart. "That's a chicken-shit chart!" he snapped, much to the chagrin of the stately senators who had been badmouthing his bill. In the end, his pleas did no good. On June 17, after a four-week debate and much support from the White House and from numerous public health groups, the bill—which would have called for a $1.10 tax on a pack of cigarettes to be phased in over five years as well as other restrictions on the tobacco industry—was killed when it failed to receive 60 votes (the number needed to overcome a filibuster) on two separate roll-call votes. The first time, the bill was three votes shy; the second time, seven votes. It was a terrible defeat for McCain—especially since the bill had come out of committee with almost unanimous support—and an unqualified victory for the tobacco companies. Their eight-week national television and radio ad campaign had achieved its goal: Many senators didn't have enough nerve to vote for the bill. McCain had taken on another Goliath-size issue, one equally as sweeping as campaign finance reform, and he had lost. He had also taken on the leadership of his party, and the leadership had won.

Coming off the defeat, McCain moved on to his next battle: re-election in Arizona. To run against him, the Democrats had found someone named Ed Ranger, a motorcycle enthusiast who owned a Harley-Davidson that was painted to look like the Arizona flag. The election in November was not close; McCain got almost 70 percent of the vote. He then decided to go forward with an idea he had been considering for a while: He set up a presidential exploratory committee. Officially, the committee was established on Wednesday, December 30, 1998, when aides went to the Federal Election Commission in Washington and filed papers that made him the first Republican to declare his intention of running for president in 2000. McCain could not have been more unavailable for comment on the filing of his papers; he and his family were on a vacation in Fiji. He made no formal statements on the matter for several weeks. McCain's reticence was odd, since he was known to be one of the most media-friendly members of Congress. Eventually, it would become apparent that the media loved McCain just as much as McCain loved the media. When his presidential campaign was fully under way and biographical material about McCain was flooding the airwaves and the national magazines, a joke made the rounds in Washington that summed up the mutual love affair. Question: "How do you know the media loves John McCain?" Answer: "The Keating Four!"

In the first weeks of 1999, McCain cast one of his most important votes as a senator when he voted to convict President Bill Clinton in the impeachment trial that had come before the Senate. In August 1998, Clinton admitted, in a highly charged and disturbing appearance on national television, that he had lied about having an affair with Monica Lewinsky while she was a White House intern. Clinton had lied about that affair at various points in the past as well. Because one of those occasions was a deposition he was required to give as a result of a law suit brought against him by Paula Jones, Clinton was now guilty of lying under oath. For that, the House of Representatives impeached him in late 1998. But unless the Senate voted to convict him, Clinton would not be removed from office. It didn't. Needing 60 votes to convict, the Senate finally weighed in with a vote of 56 to 43, a number well short of the minimum. (One senator, Arlen Specter, a Republican from Pennsylvania, voted "not proved.") After the ordeal, which left a profound scar on the national psyche, McCain sounded conciliatory. "It's time to move on," he was quoted as saying in the press. As evidence of that thinking, McCain urged Kenneth Starr, the special prosecutor who had investigated Clinton, not to indict the president.

In January, in his office on Capitol Hill, McCain held a meeting with his advisers, one of whom was a new addition to his staff. Having recently made overtures to McCain, who agreed to see him, Michael Murphy arrived in McCain's office with a plan for how McCain could win the Republican presidential nomination. Murphy's scheme was simple: Skip Iowa. Election after election, the tradition within both national parties required starting one's presidential campaign by running in the Iowa caucus and the New Hampshire primary. The latter event presented a potential political land mine, since the New Hampshire voters were stridently independent and often did not foreshadow how people in other parts of the country would vote. But the Iowa caucus had its own—different—problem. Voters had to show up physically at various locations across the state on caucus night—places like public schools, civic centers, and town halls—where they sat in rooms and, when asked, voted for their candidates as a group. To do well in a caucus, a candidate had to have an extensive network of volunteer supporters, which meant that the candidate favored by the party usually performed well.

That day, in McCain's office, Murphy told McCain he would not have the support of the vast majority of his party. Most Republicans would line up behind Governor George W. Bush of Texas, who was widely rumored to be thinking about running for president. Therefore, McCain should skip Iowa, make an issue out of the fact that he was skipping Iowa, and focus all of his early effort on the New Hampshire primary. McCain had a good chance of winning New Hampshire because the independent voters in the state would respond well to his maverick streak and because the voters there had never really liked Bush's father—an aversion that might be passed down to the son.

McCain listened carefully because Murphy had extensive experience with high-profile campaigns, though his candidates did not always win. In 1992, he had worked on the George H. W. Bush campaign that lost to Bill Clinton. He had served on the Dole presidential campaign in 1996, but he fought so much with Dole's staff that he quit before the election. He had also worked on the failed senate campaign of Oliver North. But Murphy chalked up some successes too—most notably, the gubernatorial races of Christine Todd Whitman in New Jersey and Jeb Bush (George W.'s younger brother) in Florida. The presentation in McCain's office was not extensive. It took 25 minutes, and 40 slides were projected. McCain was impressed. In 1999, from January until the Iowa Straw Poll in August, Murphy advised both McCain and Lamar Alexander, the former governor of Tennessee who was also running for the Republican presidential nomination and had already retained Murphy as a consultant.

In the early months of 1999, as McCain was preparing to make his first moves on a national level to show he would run for president, the situation in Bosnia, Serbia, and Kosovo became more complicated and violent. Slobodan Milosevic had conducted a kind of holocaust against the ethnic Albanians through massacres, gang rapes, and forced marches. McCain was extremely vocal in his criticism of the way the Clinton Administration was handling the problem, by getting the United States more deeply involved in the internal strife in Kosovo, but, even now, he did not believe the United States should remain neutral in a conflict that was being played out in the middle of Europe.

Throughout March, the conflict in central Europe worsened. McCain had planned to announce in April that he was running for president, and to follow the announcement with a tour that included stops in New Hampshire, South Carolina, and Arizona. The rally in Phoenix would feature marching bands, thousands of balloons, and 3,000 people in attendance. But the conflict in Yugoslavia became so serious that McCain decided to postpone the tour, though he did make the formal announcement by releasing a statement from his Washington office. The statement read: "While now is not the time for the celebratory tour I had planned, I am a candidate for president and I will formally kick off my campaign at a more appropriate time." His presidency, the statement continued, would offer Americans "the kind of leadership Americans expect in crises like this one." A McCain presidency would "reform our institutions of government to make us proud again"—a line he would use throughout the upcoming campaign. The date of his declaration that he intended to run for president was April 14, 1999.

Because he was about to mount a presidential campaign, McCain became an even bigger political target than he was before. In late March, as rumors about his plans to run for the White House spread, a story in the *Phoenix New Times* had included a line of attack that would be used repeatedly against McCain by his enemies, particularly those who had come to dislike him because of the position he had taken on the normalization of relations with Vietnam. On March 25, the publication ran an article that contained allegations made by two air force colonels—Ted Guy and Gordon Larson, both former POWs—who said they doubted McCain was physically harmed while he was a POW being held in solitary confinement in The Plantation. "Between the two of us," Larson said, "it's our belief, and to the best of our knowledge, that no prisoner was beaten or harmed physically in that camp [The Plantation]. My only contention with the McCain deal is that while he was at The Plantation, to the best of my knowledge and Ted's knowledge, he was not physically abused in any way. No one was in that camp. It was the camp that people were released from." Their allegations seemed to be disproved by countless eyewitnesses who were prisoners in Hanoi at the same time McCain was there, and by men who were tortured, but that did not keep the article from being published.

On Monday, April 19, as McCain made a luncheon appearance at the Cobb Galleria Centre in Atlanta, Georgia, for the Georgia Public Policy Foundation, a conservative group, the war in Yugoslavia was very much on his mind. But first he reflected on his own military experience. "I would like to point out that it doesn't take a lot of talent to get shot down," McCain said. "I was able to intercept a surface-to-air missile with my own airplane, which was Robert Strange McNamara's way of winning the Vietnam War." Then, McCain introduced two people in the audience who were important to him. The first was Colonel "Bud" Day, whom McCain identified as his first prison roommate after he was released from the hospital in Hanoi. The second was Everett Alvarez, the first American pilot shot down over Vietnam. The more personal part of the speech behind him, McCain proceeded into his topic for the occasion, the unfolding unrest in Kosovo.

"Avoiding casualties—theirs and ours—is not our primary objective," McCain told the audience of 200. "Winning is. The sooner the better." He was not opposed, he said, to putting ground troops in Kosovo. "To that end, we should commence today to mobilize infantry and armor divisions for a possible—I emphasize *possible*—ground war in Kosovo." McCain had recently criticized Clinton for limiting the air strikes carried out by NATO and for refusing the use of ground troops. McCain had come to believe that the United States had to use military power against Milosevic. "The best [outcome] for us, NATO, Kosovo, Russia—and even Serbia—is," McCain said, "to begin fighting this war as if it were a war . . . instead of some strange interlude between peace initiatives."

In May, McCain started to make campaign appearances. On May 27, as he gave the commencement address at Johns Hopkins University, in Baltimore, Maryland, McCain, sounding like a man running for president, said politicians have "squandered the public trust" through "our poll-driven policies, our phony posturing, the lies we call 'spin,' and the damage control we substitute for progress." On Monday, July 26, McCain said he had no intention of leaving the Republican Party to join the Reform Party. The day before, Jesse Ventura had said McCain would make a good Reform Party candidate, and McCain rushed to release this statement: "Although I am flattered by his kind words, I would instead ask him and his supporters to consider pursuing our shared reform agenda through the party to which I am a proud and loyal member—the Republican Party." At an appearance in Houston, Texas, at the conference of the National Council of La Raza—the Latino civil rights group—McCain said: "I intend to reach out to Reform Party members and reform-minded voters everywhere to support my candidacy for president because our cause is greater than partisan politics. . . . The influence of money is corrupting our ability to address the problems that directly affect the lives of every American."

Then, on Friday, July 30, while McCain was back in Washington voting on a $792 billion Republican tax-cut bill, Cindy stood in for him at a stop in South Carolina. "I'm a full-time mother," she told a crowd of veterans and she hoped she would "raise decent children" who wanted to serve in the military. She also commented on the role of a presidential candidate's wife, telling an Associated Press reporter, "I've always taken a more traditional role in the campaign." As for the Clintons, who never had a problem allowing Hillary Rodham Clinton to play an integral role in the campaign, Cindy McCain said, "That's their choice."

On August 14, in keeping with his intention of skipping Iowa, McCain did not participate in the straw poll. Instead, he called it a sham. In the poll, Dan Quayle and Lamar Alexander did so poorly that they dropped out of the race before it had even begun. Still, the presidential field was becoming more crowded than observers had originally predicted. In addition to McCain, George W. Bush had announced he was a candidate for president. With Bush as the front-runner and McCain as the dark horse, the rest of the Republican field included Elizabeth Dole (wife of Bob Dole), a former secretary of both labor and transportation; Steve Forbes, the publisher of *Forbes*; Pat Buchanan, a conservative political commentator and former Nixon speech writer; Gary Bauer, a conservative political and religious activist; Orrin Hatch, the senator from Utah; and Alan Keyes, an ultraconservative firebrand and former ambassador to the United Nations. During the coming months, Buchanan would leave the Republican Party to join the Reform Party, and Dole would drop out of the race, citing an inability to raise money. Six candidates held on for the Republican presidential primary season: Bush, McCain, Forbes, Bauer, Hatch, and Keyes.

The candidate to beat was Bush. In 1994, he had ended a long and lackluster business career that saw him drift from one failing oil-related venture to another, all the while drinking heavily (the record would never be clear on his cocaine use) until his 40th birthday when his wife threatened to leave him if he didn't straighten up. He ended this earlier chapter of his life by running for governor of Texas against Ann Richards—and winning. How he defeated the popular sitting governor was never apparent—the day she lost, Richards enjoyed an approval rating of 60 percent—but he did. Many political observers chalked up the win to a trio of advisers who came to be known as "the iron triangle": Joe Albaugh, a longtime friend of Bush whose loyalty to the Bush family was unquestioned; Karen Hughes, a former television reporter who had joined the Bush campaign as communications director and helped shape the image Bush projected to the voting public; and Karl Rove, a former protégée of Lee Atwater, the political wunderkind who had gotten Bush's father elected president and who was ruthless in his willingness to advance the political fortunes of his clients. If there was one person opponents feared in the Bush inner circle, it was Rove, who guided Bush's first term as governor so brilliantly that some prominent Texas Democrats ended up supporting him in his landslide reelection bid in 1998. Bush would have the same "iron triangle" around him as he ran for president—a team that would appear daunting to any opponent.

In August, McCain went on a 10-day bus trip through California, a state that would be vital to him if he was going to win the nomination. He interrupted the trip to make an appearance in Kansas City at the annual convention of the Veterans of Foreign Wars. Then, back in California, on Friday, August 23, he spoke to the *San Francisco Chronicle* on the issue of abortion. After making two points—he had a 17-year congressional voting record that was decidedly antiabortion, and in 1998 he had written a letter to the Roman Catholic bishops in which he had proclaimed he was a "lifelong, ardent supporter of unborn children's right to life"—he delivered a remark that gave pause to some antiabortion activists: "I'd love to see a point where it is irrelevant and could be replaced, because abortion is no longer necessary. But certainly in the short term, or even the long term, I would not support repeal of *Roe v. Wade*, which would then force X number of women in America to [undergo] illegal and dangerous operations."

In late August, Random House published *Faith of My Fathers*, the memoir McCain had written, with his chief-of-staff Mark Salter, about the life and career of both his grandfather and father; his own early life, especially his years as a POW; and his return to the United States. As a two-book advance, Random House had paid McCain $500,000, half of which went to Salter and half to McCain, who donated his portion to charity. In September, McCain set out on a 15-city book tour that coincided more or less with the planned stops along the campaign trail. McCain could certainly take pride in the book; reviews of it were almost exclusively positive. Calling the work "[a] fascinating history of a remarkable military family," the *Christian Science Monitor* said McCain "gets to the core of those ineffable qualities of wartime brotherhood and self-sacrifice that are so far beyond common notions of 'patriotism,'" and *Newsweek* said this: "McCain's character has withstood tests the average politician can only imagine. . . . He may be the last of his kind."

September 1999 was a busy month. On September 1, McCain was in the midst of a five-day bus tour through New Hampshire, which began in Dixville Notch. That morning, in Concord, before he headed on to Plymouth, McCain made the kind of comment that riled his political handlers but earned him the status of maverick. He said: "The Democrats are controlled by the trial lawyers and the Republicans are controlled by the big money of the insurance companies." This, according to McCain, was why the country needed campaign finance reform. On September 15, McCain and Feingold announced that they would focus their bill and ban only soft money, in an effort to get some version of campaign finance reform through Congress. The House had just voted 252 to 177 to pass the bill. But McCain and Feingold were worried that they might not get the 60 votes needed in the Senate, so they modified the legislation as much as they could—just to get it passed. Given this new push to get the bill through Congress, McCain had to prepare for the inevitable: In the presidential campaign, he would be assailed by the National Rifle Association, the National Right to Life Committee, the American Conservative Union, the Christian Coalition, and others.

On Friday, September 24, even as he advocated overhauling the military for a post-Cold War world, McCain attacked Bush's plan to increase military spending. On the previous day, at the Citadel in South Carolina, Bush had made a speech on military spending. McCain, when he wasn't signing copies of *Faith of My Fathers* at bookstores, spoke candidly as a member of the Armed Services Committee. "I believe that Governor Bush's speech left out an important part of the equation," McCain said. "That is that we have to restructure the military. We have to close bases. We have to contract out maintenance and other repair work to civilian contractors to save money, and we've got to stop the pork-barrel spending." One thing McCain favored was better pay for military personnel. But the military had problems besides low pay. "It took two months to get 24 Apache helicopters from Germany to Albania," McCain said; "they trained, crashed two and never used them in combat. That is an apt metaphor for the severe problems that the military has."

That weekend, in the Sunday press, McCain focused on Pat Buchanan but included his other rivals in his attack. In a newly published book, *A Republic, Not an Empire,* Buchanan argued that the United States was not justified in entering World War II because Germany did not pose a threat to this country. Because Bush had refused to attack Buchanan, McCain made the following statement: "Like Governor Bush, I want to see a united Republican Party. But no political campaign is worth sacrificing our principles." It was not all that long before Buchanan broke away from the Republican Party and joined the Reform Party.

8

PRESIDENTIAL POLITICS

On Monday, September 27, 1999, a cloudy but warm fall day, John McCain greeted a crowd of 1,000 people packed into Greeley Park in Nashua, New Hampshire, and announced his candidacy for president of the United States. In his 25-minute speech, McCain said he would "renew pride in public service" by getting the "corrupting influence" of money out of politics. America was facing a "new patriotic challenge," McCain said, "a fight to take our government back from the power brokers and special interests and return it to the people. I run for president . . . so that Americans can believe once again that public service is a summons to duty and not a lifetime of privilege." Besides government reform, McCain also hit on the importance of a president's being prepared to command the military. "When it comes time to make the decision to send our young men and women into harm's way," he said, "that decision should be made by a leader who knows that such decisions have profound consequences. There comes a time when our nation's leader can no longer rely on briefing books and talking points, when the experts and the advisers have all weighed in. . . . For no matter how many others are involved in the decision, the president is a lonely man . . . when the casualty reports come in. I am not afraid of the burden."

On the general issue of the military, McCain said: "Both parties in Congress have wasted scarce defense dollars on unneeded weapons systems and other pork projects while 12,000 enlisted personnel, proud young men and women, subsist on food stamps. That's a disgrace." On other issues, McCain wanted to institute nationwide school vouchers by ending subsidies for sugar, ethanol, and oil and gas drilling. But mostly he concentrated on his love of country. Being a prisoner had taught him "both the blessing and the price of freedom." Describing himself as "the son and grandson of navy admirals" and someone "born into America's service," McCain said: "It is because I owe America more than she has ever owed me that I am a candidate for president."

For the campaign, McCain assembled a team that would be with him for the many months to come. Rick Davis was the campaign manager, the staff member in charge of the day-to-day operation of the campaign. Greg Stevens—a moody, mercurial professional who worked well with McCain—was the media adviser. Mike Murphy, one of his political consultants, was the main force behind the overall strategy McCain was now formulating. John Weaver, his chief political adviser, was a savvy, hard-working devotee of McCain and wanted nothing more in his career than to see McCain win the White House. Mark Salter, who had long been his chief-of-staff, wrote many of his speeches. Howard Opinsky was his press officer.

In general, the team saw that they had one asset beyond question: John McCain. Because McCain was barely showing up in the opinion polls, the team made an early decision: To get the media coverage McCain now desperately needed, they would make him completely available to the press. So, the campaign featured a bus called the Straight Talk Express. Reporters could pile in, sit in the back with McCain as he held court in a red overstuffed captain's chair, and listen to McCain talk about any subject thrown at him. This level of access to a candidate had never before been seen in politics. Any reporter from anywhere—if there was enough room in the bus—could get on board and ask McCain questions. Even more amazing, he would answer them in a direct, unvarnished, unscripted manner—using, that is to say, straight talk. Ultimately, the Straight Talk Express became one of the brilliant aspects of the McCain for President campaign.

As McCain proceeded on a presidential announcement tour, he traveled to Simi Valley, California, which hosts the Ronald Reagan Presidential Library and Museum. At the library, McCain had a private meeting with Nancy Reagan; the former president, now deeply debilitated by Alzheimer's disease, had retired from public life. While there, McCain delivered a speech about a man—Reagan—whose presidency would no doubt influence his own, should he ever be elected to that office. As he spoke in the museum, McCain invoked the memorable speech Reagan delivered on Omaha Beach on the 40th anniversary of D-Day. Then McCain made a political point. "I read these words," McCain told the audience, his voice clear and unwavering, "as a lesson to anyone who would question the courage of those brave men, or who question the necessity of the cause for which they fought."

With a subtlety he often did not employ, McCain was attacking both Buchanan and Bush: Buchanan because he questioned the decision by Franklin Roosevelt and the 1941 Congress to wage war in Europe, as well as the Pacific, when, according to Buchanan, Hitler did not pose a threat to the West; and Bush because he did not have the nerve to criticize Buchanan for his comments. "Ronald Reagan's words stand, too, as a challenge," McCain continued. "For not only must Americans be prepared to defend the honor and glory of our country but to speak out forcefully against those who would urge us to abandon our world leadership."

McCain started the month of October with some political inoculation. Any keen political adviser could have told him that he had two major liabilities as a national candidate: his involvement in the Keating Five scandal, and his wife's episode with prescription drug addiction in the early 1990s. Because the Keating scandal had been examined and reexamined so much over the years, most critics had agreed that McCain's role in it was just what the Ethics Committee said it was—a case of "poor judgment." But because Cindy's prescription drug problem had played itself out more in the local press in Arizona than in the national media, that drama was ripe for exploiting, should one of McCain's opponents in the upcoming campaign decide to use it. So McCain and Cindy made the logical move: They appeared together on an edition of NBC-TV's *Dateline* and addressed Cindy's past drug problem head-on.

In mid-October, McCain went to the Senate to wage another fight for campaign finance reform. It had become his signature issue and it would prove to be the foundation on which he would base his bid for the presidency. As chairman of the Senate Commerce Committee and, now, a presidential candidate, he had some clout, but, year after year, McCain and Feingold had met with defeat, and this session did not promise any different result. The House of Representatives had passed the legislation in September. The debate began in the Senate on October 14. The system "is nothing less than an elaborate influence-peddling scheme in which both parties conspire to stay in office by selling the country to the highest bidder," McCain said in his opening statement. "Who is corrupted by this system? All of us are corrupted." Just as McCain had fought a long and arduous battle to pass reform, Mitch McConnell, the hard-charging Republican from Kentucky, had mounted an equally long effort to defeat it. In 1998, he had led the forces that shot it down on two different votes. "The question is," McConnell said in the debate, picking up on McCain's provocative question, "who is corrupted? How can there be corruption unless someone is corrupted? You can't say 'the gang is corrupt but none of the gangsters are.'"

On Friday, October 15, the debate continued as the Democrats, led by McCain and Feingold, tried to force two test votes on the legislation for the following week. One vote would concern the version of campaign finance reform recently passed in the House; the second would be a scaled-down version of the original McCain-Feingold. The floor votes on the two measures were scheduled for Tuesday, October 19. On Monday, October 18, Guy Molinari, a former congressman from Staten Island in New York City, held a press conference to announce his endorsement of McCain—a significant development because Molinari had supported Bush's father in the 1988 presidential election. In return, McCain named Molinari chairman of his campaign in New York State.

McCain may have been thrilled with the Molinari endorsement on Monday, but he met with defeat—one more time—on Tuesday, when the Senate killed campaign finance reform not once but twice. The two procedural votes were 53 to 47 and 52 to 48. To that point, there had been 19 votes on campaign finance reform, and reform proponents were still significantly shy of the 60 votes needed to avoid the filibuster McConnell had been promising for some time. For the second year in a row, the Senate had rejected campaign finance reform after the House had passed some version of it by a huge margin. McCain was undeterred. "We will not give up," he told reporters after the defeat. "Eventually, we will prevail." McConnell was just as determined. "There is no momentum whatsoever for this kind of measure," he said. Trent Lott echoed McConnell's sentiments by saying curtly, "It's dead for the year."

On Wednesday, October 20, just to prove he had no intention of disappearing in the face of defeat, McCain generated headlines when he spoke at the International Republican Institute Freedom Award Dinner in Washington. That night, he presented the International Republican Freedom Award for 1999 to Aung San Suu Kyi, a woman who had devoted her life to fighting for freedom in Burma. Suu Kyi, a 1991 Nobel prize winner, was unable to attend because, as McCain noted in his speech, "the generals [of Burma] continue to persecute her." Of Suu Kyi and the people of Burma, McCain said, "Her people suffer terribly for their democratic faith in Burma's gruesome prisons. Across the country, insecurity and fear are palpable among the people; the influence of the police state is pervasive. A dark shadow has fallen over their homeland. Against all odds, one woman's moral courage in the face of evil shines through the dark as a lantern, lighting the way for all those in her country who love liberty. Her faith touches millions." Whatever charges McCain's critics might level against him, his love for and devotion to democratic principles were clearly evidenced that night.

When McCain had announced his presidential campaign at the end of September, most political observers felt he had little or no chance of doing any damage to the Bush campaign, which seemed to have associated with it an air of inevitability, even fate. But as the month of October unfolded and as McCain waged and then lost his latest battle for campaign finance reform, something odd happened. More than one poll of New Hampshire voters seemed to indicate that they were open-minded about McCain's insurgency campaign. A state long known for its political independence, New Hampshire, come February, could prove to be a launching ground for a McCain campaign that could ultimately have viability on a national level. So it became clear to the Bush campaign, as well as to some elements of the Republican Party, that McCain needed to be stopped in New Hampshire. That way, he could never pose a serious threat to Bush. In politics, one does not always have to advance one's own effort; sometimes it's just as effective to tear down the campaign of one's opponent—or better yet, one's opponent.

On Monday, November 1, the *Arizona Republic*, which had been at odds with McCain for some time, ran an editorial that said, in short: McCain was not fit to be president. Describing his temper as "volcanic," the paper claimed that McCain, who could be "sarcastic and condescending," "often insults people and flies off the handle." The paper did not disclose that it had developed a strained relationship with McCain in 1994, when it ran a cartoon in which Cindy was caricatured holding a black child upside down and shaking him to get drugs. McCain felt the paper had gone too far with its senseless personal attack against his wife, so he gave the paper few interviews after that. But the *Republic* mentioned none of this as it hypothesized that there is "reason to seriously question whether McCain has the temperament, and the political approach and skills, we want in the next President of the United States."

On November 3, the story about McCain's temper had spread so widely through the media that Howard Kurtz documented its development in a piece in the *Washington Post*. Soon after, an article in the *New York Times* quoted Governor John Engler of Michigan, an ardent supporter of Bush, as saying that McCain had a problem with his temper. At a campaign stop in San Francisco, McCain responded by saying that the allegations were unfounded.

On Thursday, November 11—Veterans' Day—McCain tried to put behind him what he considered to be the nonsense about his temper. As he barnstormed New Hampshire on the campaign trail, he focused on an important topic that was dear to him: the meaning of the holiday. Starting out his day with a visit to a VFW hall in Laconia, McCain then stopped by a veterans' home in Tilton. At noon, he marched in a parade in Nashua, where he was joined by other Vietnam veterans. On days like this one, McCain's personal history carried him above the fray. Bush, in the previous week, had sent out a press release announcing that various veterans' groups in New Hampshire had endorsed him, but, on this day, even he praised McCain as "a war hero" and affirmed that "people respect him and so do I." McCain repaid the compliment to Bush, who was also campaigning in New Hampshire. "I think he's a very fine and decent person who's been a good governor," McCain said. The pleasant, cordial exchange was not indicative of what was to come.

That evening, McCain concluded Veterans' Day by holding a rally in a tent next to a VFW hall in Hudson. To a crowd of 500 veterans, McCain told a story about a fellow Arizonan, Morris Udall, who had run for president in 1976 but lost the nomination to Jimmy Carter. In a small town in New Hampshire, Udall bounded into a barber shop and announced: "I'm Morris Udall of Arizona and I'm running for President of the United States." Without missing a beat, one of the locals looked up and said, "Yeah, we were just laughing about that this morning." McCain then launched into a piece of rhetoric that showed just how much the polls had changed in recent weeks. "That's the way we began this campaign, my dear friends," McCain said. "A lot of people were laughing about it and said this thing was a done deal. Thanks to you, dear friends and comrades in arms, it ain't any done deal." As the applause started, McCain added, "We're having a great time and we're on a roll!" Finally, concluding his speech, which naturally focused on military and veterans' issues, McCain made a direct play to his audience. "I'd like for you to do me a favor," he said, "probably a favor that will make me forever in your debt. I would like for you to join me in one more mission and help me get to the White House."

The evening's proceedings had the feel of a USO show. Among the entourage traveling with McCain was entertainer Connie Stevens, who spoke on McCain's behalf to both his audience and the media. "He has the qualities I've always admired in my father, in my brothers," Stevens said that night. "Strength of character. Funny. Fun. Protective. He can't be bought and he can't be bullied."

On November 16, McCain made official his decision to use New Hampshire as the launching point of his national campaign. In a letter to Kayne Robinson of the Iowa Republican Party, he formally declared that he did not intend to campaign in Iowa. "I will not conduct any organized campaign effort," McCain wrote. "Nor will my campaign be spending money on advertisements, staff, or organizational activities." He agreed to participate in debates to be held in Iowa on December 13 and January 15 (before the January 24 caucus), but McCain would make no other commitments. "My decision not to establish a campaign organization in Iowa," McCain said, "is based solely on the compressed nature of the primary schedule and the increasing influence of big money on the nominating process."

Another factor now came into play. The New Hampshire race, which at first appeared as if it were going to be a blowout for Bush, was tightening significantly. As this happened, some Washington observers began to sense that an organized whisper campaign had been started to smear McCain. Using "temper" as a code word, a group of Republican senators began to imply that McCain was unstable. The line of reasoning went like this: The five and a half years McCain spent as a POW had damaged him mentally, and his outbursts of anger were evidence of emotional unsteadiness. On November 19, Elizabeth Drew, a journalist who had written about American politics for many years, published an editorial in the *Washington Post* in which she claimed that the whisper campaign against McCain was being conducted by Trent Lott, Don Nickles, Paul Coverdale, and Robert Bennett (the senator from Utah, not to be confused with the former lawyer for the Senate Ethics Committee).

The whisper campaign was a stroke of genius for McCain's opponents. It took one of McCain's strongest assets as a candidate (not to mention as a person)—his years of military service, as represented so dramatically and emotionally by his confinement in a prisoner-of-war camp—and turned that asset against him. It was a move worthy of Lee Atwater, perhaps one of the most heartless, if successful, operatives in the history of American politics. Atwater routinely identified his candidate's opponent's best feature and then viciously attacked that feature straight on. Candidate McCain was most proud of his military service. To negate that advantage, one had to single it out and imply that, because it contained lengthy periods of psychological torture that would have left almost anyone emotionally scarred, it disqualified him for the very office for which he was running. Had Atwater not died of a brain tumor in 1991, he would surely have suggested that line of attack to his friend, Karl Rove.

Near the start of the whisper campaign, someone close to the Bush camp called James Stockdale, a retired navy admiral and a friend of McCain from the time they were both POWs in Vietnam. Stockdale had been Ross Perot's vice-presidential running mate in 1992. The caller, a friend of Stockdale, had approached him, to quote from a piece Stockdale published in the *New York Times* on Friday, November 26, "soliciting comments on Mr. McCain's weaknesses." The caller implied that one of McCain's weaknesses was a mental instability brought on by his imprisonment. "I think John McCain is solid as a rock," Stockdale told the caller. "And I consider it blasphemy to smudge [McCain's] straight-arrow prisoner-of-war record." On reflection, Stockdale decided to become even bolder in his defense of McCain. "The military psychiatrists who periodically examine former prisoners-of-war have found that the more resistant a man was to harsh treatment," Stockdale wrote in the *Times*, "the more emotionally stable he is likely to become later in life."

Stockdale adds: "His experience in Vietnam actually made McCain *more* balanced than he had ever been. It was a building block. He had been brought up in a family of very high principles. He is a guy who can handle a crisis and not feel sorry for himself. He can keep his balance and not go off half-cocked." Others dismissed the entire issue of his temper as false. "There's a difference between anger and irritation," Senator Alan Simpson says. "And just because he's pretty feisty doesn't mean he's angry. He doesn't seethe; he's not a seether. He might say, 'Oh, that's just BS! That's nuts!' and steel his jaw. And then they see his jaw steeled and think he's angry. Well, there's a difference. With me, people say: 'Now what are you doing? Are you ranting?' I say: 'Ranting is a good thing.' It doesn't mean you want to stab anybody or spit at them. It just means you are saying: 'God, I'm tired of this crap! Tired of it!'"

In Washington, on Wednesday, December 1, McCain addressed 250 members of the Republican Jewish Coalition and outlined his foreign policy platform, which was decidedly hawkish. The Clinton Administration's foreign policy, he said, could be best described as suffering from "strategic incoherence and self-doubt."

On the evening of December 2, the Republican primary season achieved a milestone of sorts. For the first time, all six candidates for the nomination debated on the same stage in New Hampshire. Until then, Bush had skipped two debates in New Hampshire and one in Arizona, but because both his detractors and his supporters had started to criticize him for ducking the debates—and because McCain was making a race out of the primary season—Bush decided to join the fray in a nationally televised 90-minute debate in Manchester. In answer to a question about foreign policy, McCain referred to Israel and declared that he would "never ask Israel to sign onto any peace agreement that endangers the lives of Israelis for a false promise of peace." He drew laughs when he said that he was such an admirer of Alan Greenspan in his role as chairman of the Federal Reserve that, should Greenspan be so unfortunate as to die during a McCain presidency, "I'd prop him up and put dark glasses on him"—an allusion to the motion picture *Weekend at Bernie's*. During discussion of the Middle East, Bush said he would "take out" weapons of mass destruction in Iraq. "He"—meaning Saddam Hussein—"just needs to know, I'm going to take them out."

As McCain worked hard heading for the primaries, the whisper campaign that suggested he was unfit to serve as president continued to sweep through political gossip channels. Elizabeth Drew's article may have exposed the whisper campaign, but little had been done to slow its spread. McCain and his handlers then made a decision. McCain would deal with this controversy in the same way he had dealt with similar controversies in the past—he would address it publicly. On Saturday, December 4, McCain gave the Associated Press three three-inch-thick binders containing hundreds of pages of his medical records. Their release to the general public came on Monday. The full and accurate account of McCain's medical history was an impressive presentation. The file contained general information—for example, the fact that McCain had twice taken an intelligence quotient test; his IQ was established as 128 the first time and 133 at a later time. McCain also had a slightly enlarged prostate gland—not unusual for a sixty-year-old man—and he was on a daily aspirin therapy.

But most impressive was the mental chronology established by the documents. Starting in 1973, McCain had taken a series of physical and mental tests at the Robert E. Mitchell Center for Prisoner of

War Studies. There was this note written just 10 days after McCain's release from prison in 1973: "Patient's mental status has not been influenced by recent situational stress." That same year, when he was asked how he had withstood the ordeal of being a POW, McCain said, according to a note in the records, "Faith in country, United States Navy, family, and God." Indeed, one examiner wrote that the years McCain had spent as a POW taught him "to control his temper better, to not become angry over insignificant things." Three years later, another examiner drew an equally benign conclusion when he wrote: "There is no sign of emotional difficulty." In short, McCain's medical records proved that he suffered no apparent psychological wounds from being a POW for five and a half years. The experience had left McCain with degenerative arthritis in his shoulders and right knee, which indicated that he might need joint replacements some day, but, psychologically, he was fine. "He had a very healthy way of dealing with his experiences," concluded Dr. Michael Ambrose, the director of the Center for Prisoner of War Studies. "There was never any mental illness." John Eckstein, McCain's personal physician, summed up McCain's general condition. Declaring him to be in "good physical and mental health," Eckstein wrote, in a letter addressed to McCain: "I found you to be in excellent health."

There was only one disconcerting detail in the documents. The records in the three binders included information about the skin cancer episode from six years before. In December 1993, McCain had had a cancerous mole removed. Since then, there had been no recurrence of malignant cancer.

On Sunday, December 5, McCain made a visit to his past. At the Ritz-Carlton hotel, in Pentagon City, Virginia, McCain attended a fund-raiser organized by his classmates from Episcopal High School. In all, 60 classmates and faculty members showed up for a brunch, and paid between $250 and $1,000 to attend. Jonathan Bryan of Alexandria, Virginia, served as a host; Dick Thomsen,

John Sidney McCain III, in the arms of his grandfather in 1936. His father, John S. McCain Jr., is at left. (*Photo credit:* Corbis Sygma.)

Vice Admiral John S. McCain and Admiral William F. Halsey (*right*) on board the *USS New Jersey* en route to the Philippines in 1944. (*Photo credit:* Corbis.)

A commemorative plaque identifies McCain Field, the U.S. Navy training base named for McCain's grandfather, Admiral John S. McCain. Photographed here, on July 14, 1961, are Lt. John S. McCain III and his parents, Roberta Wright McCain and Rear Admiral John S. McCain Jr. (*Photo credit:* AP/Wide World Photos.)

Aboard the carrier *USS Forrestal*, Lt. Commander Robert Browning, Lt. Commander Kenneth McMillen, and Lt. Commander John S. McCain III survey the damage on July 30, 1967. Browning and McMillen, who were in their aircraft, were injured when the fire broke out. (*Photo credit:* Bettmann/Corbis.)

Freed from his years of captivity in Hanoi, Lt. Commander John S. McCain III smiles as he limps down the ramp and is welcomed at Clark Air Force Base in the Philippines, on March 14, 1973. (*Photo credit:* AP/Wide World Photos.)

Lt. Commander John S. McCain III and his family, on March 18, 1973. Awaiting his arrival at Jacksonville Naval Air Station in Florida were his wife, Carol, and his son, Doug, who had broken his leg in a soccer game. (*Photo credit:* AP/Wide World Photos.)

Ronald Reagan (then former governor of California), Nancy Reagan, and actor Michael Landon posed with McCain at a POW reunion party in Los Angeles on May 28, 1978. The party featured entertainers from film and television. At left are U.S. Navy Captain Howard Rutledge and his wife, Phyllis. (*Photo credit:* AP/Wide World Photos.)

Cindy and John S. McCain III were married on May 17, 1980. (*Photo credit:* Corbis Sygma.)

McCain revisited Vietnam with Walter Cronkite in the summer of 1985. (*Photo credit:* Corbis Sygma.)

Senators John Glenn (D-OH), Dennis DeConcini (D-AZ), and John McCain (R-AZ) arrive at the Senate Ethics Committee hearing room on November 15, 1990. (*Photo credit:* AP/Wide World Photos.)

McCain stayed close to the 1996 Republican presidential candidate Robert ("Bob") Dole. Here, Dole is shaking hands with Dr. Alice Kelikian, daughter of the doctor who treated Dole's World War II injuries. Dole later spoke to supporters at a hotel in Washington, DC, but by the end of that day, November 5, 1996, Bill Clinton had won reelection. (*Photo credit:* AP/Wide World Photos.)

McCain and Ben Davol, a political consultant in Connecticut, campaigned for Kevin O'Connor, a Republican who was running for the House of Representatives in 1998. Davol later was chairman of the McCain for President campaign in Connecticut, a state that McCain won during his 2000 effort to gain delegates for the Republican convention. (*Photo credit:* Ben Davol.)

The McCains on vacation in Zebra Falls, Arizona, on August 1, 1999. Their children's ages were then: Meghan, 14; Bridget, 8; Jimmy, 11; and Jack, 13. Bridget was adopted from an orphanage in Bangladesh. (*Photo credit:* McGoon James/Corbis Sygma.)

Admiral ("Chuck") Larson, USN, CINCPAC, and Superintendent at the U.S. Naval Academy (Annapolis); Federal Trade Commissioner Orson Swindle, Lt. Colonel USMC; Colonel George E. ("Bud") Day, a Congressional Medal of Honor recipient; and John and Cindy McCain on day two of the Presidential Candidacy Announcement Tour, September 1999. (*Photo credit:* Angie Williams.)

McCain spoke with Norman Mailer, among many other attendees, at his *Faith of My Fathers* book party in New York City. Bloomberg LLP hosted the event in September 1999. (*Photo credit:* Marina Garnier.)

John and Cindy McCain with Henry Kissinger at the book party hosted by Bloomberg LLP in September 1999. (*Photo credit:* Marina Garnier.)

The Election 2000 Republican presidential hopefuls. From left to right: Steve Forbes, Alan Keyes, Texas Governor George W. Bush, Senator Orrin Hatch of Utah, Senator John McCain of Arizona, and Gary Bauer, prior to the GOP debate on December 13, 1999, in Des Moines, Iowa. (*Photo credit:* AP/Wide World Photos.)

McCain and Democratic presidential candidate Bill Bradley at the Earl Bourdon Senior Centre in Claremont, New Hampshire, on December 16, 1999. They pledged their support for campaign finance reform. (*Photo credit:* AP/Wide World Photos.)

McCain traveling on the Straight Talk Express, with reporters, December 20, 1999. "Mr. Anonymous," *Primary Colors* author Joe Klein, sits in the foreground. (*Photo credit:* Bergsaker Tore/Corbis Sygma.)

The Straight Talk Express (well, one of them). (*Photo credit:* Ben Davol.)

McCain and his son, Jack, watched the election results in their hotel room on February 1, 2000. (*Photo credit:* Kennerly David Hume/Corbis Sygma.)

On January 20, 2000, outside the Russian Consulate in New York City, McCain
pointed out the need to get his name on the ballot in *all* New York districts.
(*Photo credit*: AP/Wide World Photos.)

On January 31, 2000,
McCain was doing what
every politician has to
do: kissing babies. (*Photo
credit*: Wyman Ira/
Corbis Sygma.)

A sampling of South Carolina primary
propaganda, February 17, 2000. (*Photo
credit*: Stone Les/Corbis Sygma.)

The Sacred Heart University, Fairfield, Connecticut, campaign event, March 3, 2000. (*Photo credit:* Ben Davol.)

Cindy McCain at the Sacred Heart University campaign event, March 3, 2000. (*Photo credit:* Ben Davol.)

In Sedona, Arizona, on March 9, 2000, with Cindy at his side, McCain announced that he was suspending his bid for the Republican presidential nomination. (*Photo credit*: AP/Wide World Photos.)

A camera caught a McCain reaction at a joint press conference with George W. Bush on May 9, 2000, in Pittsburgh, Pennsylvania. McCain had to be prompted to use the "e" word—endorse. (*Photo credit:* AP/Wide World Photos.)

This awkward pose, with Cindy and George W. and Laura Bush, was captured at Red Rock Crossing in Sedona, Arizona, on August 13, 2000. (*Photo credit:* AFP Photo/Files/Paul J. Richards.)

At the Bush Inauguration brunch, hosted by NBC, the McCains chat with Katherine Graham at the Willard Hotel in Washington, DC, in January 2001. (*Photo credit: Marina Garnier.*)

McCain with Bob Wright, Alan Greenspan, and Cindy. (*Photo credit: Marina Garnier.*)

Commander Everett Alvarez, USN (POW Aug. 5, 1964–Feb. 12, 1973); Lt. Colonel Orson Swindle, USMC (POW Nov. 11, 1966–Mar. 4, 1973); Senator John S. McCain, Captain, USN (POW Oct. 26, 1967–Mar. 14, 1973); Captain Frank Gamboa, USN (ret.), Annapolis classmate and roommate of McCain; and Justin Oppman (campaign worker), at a mini-reunion of McCain 2000 campaign workers on July 19, 2001. (*Photo credit*: Angie Williams.)

McCain, in his office on Capitol Hill, during the Senate debate of the McCain-Feingold campaign finance reform bill, March 23, 2001. (*Photo credit*: AP/Wide World Photos.)

McCain and Massachusetts Senator John Kerry (D) walk by the Ohio Clock in the U.S. Capitol, September 25, 2001. (*Photo credit:* Tom Williams, Roll Call photos.)

Episcopal's principal during McCain's high school years, also attended. Some classmates flew in from out-of-state—Randolph Washburn of Sonoma County, California, and George Bruce of Houston, to name two. With Cindy at his side, McCain talked about his years at Episcopal. "I'm a victim of Episcopal High School," he said. "The principles embodied in the school and especially in its honor code are those I've tried to embody in my own life. I haven't always succeeded . . . but I've tried." Inevitably, McCain's recollections turned to the example set by William B. Ravenel, who, McCain pointed out, had fought in Europe with General George Patton's Third Army during World War II. One of the people McCain wanted to see when he returned from Vietnam was Ravenel, he told his classmates, but Ravenel had died while McCain was in prison. "I still want to talk to him," McCain said with emotion. "I would like to ask him what quality he detected in me that remained unrevealed to others."

McCain focused on personal events and recollections during the brunch, but earlier that morning, during an appearance on *Meet the Press*, he made news by saying that "under no circumstances" would he consider the vice-presidential slot on a Bush ticket. "I'm closing it down completely," McCain declared. What about a Cabinet post? Tim Russert wanted to know. "Those would have some attraction," McCain said, "but my first preference, obviously, would be to remain in the United States Senate."

On the evening of December 6, the six Republican candidates appeared in a 75-minute debate aired on CNN from Phoenix. McCain participated via satellite from Boston. At one point, McCain could not resist taking a dig at Bush's recently released tax plan, which proposed a whopping $483 billion tax cut. "I do not envision surpluses forever," McCain said. "I don't know that we're going to have surpluses forever."

The next day, December 7, McCain observed the 58th anniversary of the Japanese attack on Pearl Harbor and, in Concord, New Hampshire, gave a major address on the military. Calling the United

States Army "The Food Stamp Army," McCain said that the current treatment of the military was "a stain on our national honor." He also touched on a subject that would be sadly relevant in the far-too-close future. "Rogue states," McCain said, "are the main threat to peace and freedom and they require a strong, comprehensive policy response . . . a rogue state rollback. We must be prepared to back up [diplomatic] measures with American military force when the continued existence of rogue states threatens America's interests and values." That night, on board the *Intrepid* (the Vietman-era aircraft carrier is permanently docked in the Hudson River in New York City and has been turned into a military museum), McCain was awarded the 1999 *Intrepid* Freedom Award at a gala dinner. It was an especially happy occasion for McCain. He had served on board the *Intrepid* on two different tours before he was shot down over Hanoi.

On Wednesday, December 8, McCain went out of his way to challenge the Bush campaign by appearing at an institution that should have been off limits to McCain—Yale University. Bush's grandfather, Prescott Bush, had been a United States senator from Connecticut, and three generations of Bushes—Prescott, George H. W., and George W.—had attended Yale. Both George W. and his father had been elected into Yale's secret society, Skull and Bones. George W. had even been born in New Haven when his father was a student at Yale in the 1940s. The state of Connecticut in general, and New Haven in particular, should have been all wrapped up for Bush. After all, not far south of New Haven, the birthplace of George H. W. Bush had become a landmark—a presidential landmark, to be precise.

So, that day in December, when he strode across the Yale campus with his traveling entourage in tow, McCain was rather surprised to meet only a handful of Bush supporters standing outside Silliman College, the building in which he was about to speak. One newspaper would place the number of Bush supporters—all students—at four. They held two signs. One read "Bulldogs for Bush" (a bulldog is the Yale mascot); the other claimed that "Yale is Bush Territory." Maybe it was, but when McCain was led into the common room where he was to give his talk, Yale didn't look like Bush territory. Hundreds of students had jammed into the room, and another 100 or more had been turned away.

Delivering his first public speech in Connecticut, McCain stood before the overflow crowd with neither a podium nor notes, and he spoke off-the-cuff. The event, a "master's tea," had previously hosted guests such as author Kurt Vonnegut and Supreme Court Justice Sandra Day O'Connor, but, to McCain, it was simply another stop on the campaign trail. He talked about social issues such as health insurance and prescription drugs, saying, "We have to address the fact that 11 million children are still without health insurance and many senior citizens can't afford prescription drugs." He touched on his signature issue when he noted: "Those lobbyists in Washington are scared to death; they know the status quo will not prevail if I'm president." On foreign affairs, he made comments that would prove to be prophetic. "Unless something changes," he told the Yale students, "it's likely one of those [rogue states] will acquire one of those weapons [of mass destruction] and a way to use it. I'd hate to see an American president held hostage." Finally, he turned to a subject he often included in his public addresses: patriotism. "During my time in prison I had the opportunity to fall in love with America," he said. "When I was deprived of her, I realized what a wonderful and noble experiment America is."

After his talk, McCain took questions from the audience; eagerly, the students shot him question after question. One student asked him about the "whisper campaign" that suggested he had a temper. "Do I get angry?" McCain fired back in jest. "Yes. I'll have a temper tantrum here for you if you want." Another student asked about Vietnam. "The shadow of Vietnam doesn't fall over everything I do or say," McCain offered, his tone as studied and even as always, before he moved on to a sentiment he frequently delivered when asked to describe his time as a POW in Vietnam. "I was not a hero. My privilege was to serve in the company of heroes." Another student asked him to identify the biggest challenge he faced in the presidential race. "The biggest challenge I face?" McCain paused; then he became mischievous. "One, while we're having this meeting, Governor Bush is probably raising another $2 million or $3 million"—a reference to the painful reality that, so far, McCain had raised only $14 million compared to $65 million pulled in by the Bush campaign. "The biggest challenge I face is: going against the Republican establishment." And how worried was he about lagging behind in the fund-raising process? McCain could not resist an ironic response. Quoting Chinese Chairman Mao Tse-tung, he said dryly, "It's always darkest before it's totally black."

On Thursday, McCain and New Jersey Senator Bill Bradley, a Democrat, announced that, on the following Thursday morning, they would meet in Claremont, New Hampshire, to sign a mutual pledge that neither man would accept soft money from his party if he received his party's nomination. They chose to meet in Claremont because, in June 1995, President Bill Clinton and Speaker of the House Newt Gingrich had met there to shake hands on a vow to reform the campaign finance system. In retrospect, Claremont may have been a bad choice on the part of McCain and Bradley. The Clinton-Gingrich effort had died in Congress, and the two men ended up blaming each other for the failure. "They basically shook hands and talked about it," says Congressman Christopher Shays, a Republican from Connecticut who coauthored Shays-Meehan, "but Newt unfortunately agreed to something his conference didn't agree to. The Republicans saw him on TV, they saw what he agreed to, and they wouldn't go along. Newt realized all Dick Gephardt had to do was bring a few Democrats on and it was not going to happen. So Newt backed off because he didn't want to take on the Republican Conference."

On the night of Monday, December 13, the six Republican candidates met again—this time in Des Moines, Iowa—for a 90-minute debate sponsored by WHO-TV and aired nationally on MSNBC. McCain had decided to skip the Iowa caucus, he had said, because of the compressed primary schedule; however, longtime observers argued he was avoiding the state because of his outspoken effort to end the ethanol subsidies that had been historically important to the Iowa economy. Early in the debate, McCain went out of his way to point out the differences—namely his stand on ethanol—that separated him from the general voting population of the state. "I'm going to tell you the things that you don't want to hear as well as the things that you want to hear," McCain said. "Ethanol is not worth it." The other candidates present that night would agree, McCain added, "if it weren't for the fact that Iowa is the first caucus state."

Bush answered by saying haughtily, "I'd have supported ethanol whether I was in Iowa or not."

But this exchange was minor, compared to Bush's attempt to go after McCain on campaign finance reform. "Here's my worry with your plan. It's going to hurt the Republican Party, John, and I'm worried for this reason." Specifically, Bush and others were concerned that campaign finance reform would ban soft money but would not limit unions from deducting money from members' paychecks and contributing that money to political candidates. Because of this, Republicans wanted "paycheck protection." Without it, "Our Republican Party and our conservative values don't have a shot," Bush said.

On this point, Orrin Hatch joined in, adding, "Have any of you ever wondered why basically all the Democrats support it and hardly any of the Republicans [do]?"

But, of all the night's answers, perhaps the one most remembered was the reply Bush gave to the question, Which philosopher changed you the most? "Christ," Bush said without hesitation, "because he changed my heart."

On December 14, McCain began a two-day campaign swing through South Carolina. (The South Carolina primary would be held 19 days after the New Hampshire primary, so McCain had to start making some appearances in the state.) At a lunch in the Charleston Rotary Club, in what was billed as a major address on health issues, he pledged to support a "responsible" patient's bill of rights and he said he favored tort reform that would "tame legal predators and address the problems of runaway punitive damages." Championing a plan that called for a pharmaceutical assistance program for seniors and the right of patients to sue their HMOs, McCain said: "The nation remains woefully unprepared for the long-term health care needs of the baby boom generation. Too many Americans go to sleep at night desperately fearing illness or injury to themselves or a family member because they are without health insurance to pay the bills. Too many Americans feel held hostage by HMOs. Eleven million children go without health care coverage. My friends, we are a better country and a better people than that."

Lately, McCain had been thinking a lot about campaign finance reform. On Wednesday, December 15, as he spoke to a group of supporters in an auditorium at Converse College in Spartanburg, South Carolina, he broached the topic directly. "The reality is," McCain said, "that passing these reforms won't occur until we take on the entrenched power of the special interests. As conservatives, our priority must be to give the government back to the people. But in Washington, success is no longer defined by the passage of either party's agenda but by the size of our campaign committee war chests."

One event about which McCain was especially excited was the joint appearance he would make the next morning, in New Hampshire, where he and Bill Bradley would sign a pledge promising that neither man would take soft money if he won his party's nomination. For some time, the two senators' staffs had been working out the details and protocols of the pledge, and it looked as if all the particulars had now been agreed to.

On Thursday, December 16, as a morning frost coated the ground in the mill town of Claremont, New Hampshire, McCain and Bradley made their way to a worn wooden table on a hilltop near a senior citizens' home. Bundled up in overcoats and wearing gloves, the two men hunched over the table to put their signatures to this carefully worded pledge: "We pledge that as nominees for the Office of President of the United States we will not allow our political parties to spend soft money for our presidential campaigns, and we commit to working together toward genuine campaign finance reform." (Bradley agreed to ban the use of soft money only if his Republican opponent did as well; McCain agreed to the soft-money ban outright.)

Near where the two men met, a limestone bench bore the inscription, "Site of historic summit between President William Jefferson Clinton and House Speaker Newt Gingrich." Since the only thing that had come out of that summit was a photo opportunity for Clinton and Gingrich, Bradley and McCain, as they spoke to reporters at their pledge-signing, were careful to avoid discussing the previous ceremony that had taken place on this hilltop. But McCain couldn't help taking a swipe at Vice President Al Gore's fund-raising shenanigans. "The vice president of the United States asked monks and nuns to pay thousands of dollars to violate their vows of poverty so they could spiritually commune with him," McCain said, referring to a fund-raiser Gore had attended at the Hsi Lai Buddhist temple in Hacienda Heights, California, in April 1996. It had been one of the incidents that, later that year, forced Gore to claim he had "no controlling legal authority" to stop questionable fund-raising activities in the Clinton-Gore campaign. "If I'm elected president," McCain said, "I will be the controlling legal authority."

For his part, Bush tried to advance his position on this issue. In a written statement released to respond to the pledge-signing carried out by McCain and Bradley, Bush said: "We cannot afford a version of campaign finance reform that unilaterally disarms our Republican Party and our conservative principles." But the drama of the event did not involve Bush; it centered around the coming together of these two senators. As McCain said at that time, "Bill Bradley is a liberal Democrat; I am a proud conservative Republican. We disagree on almost everything. But one issue on which we do agree . . . is that politics is broken." Voters seemed to agree. At a one-hour town hall meeting featuring McCain and Bradley, which had aired on ABC's *Nightline* before the pledge-signing, the audience appeared to understand what McCain meant when he talked about a broken political system. Then again, maybe the audience was responding to the respect these two men had for one another, as evidenced by the inscriptions they wrote when they exchanged books after the town hall meeting. "To Bill," McCain wrote in *Faith of My Fathers*, "With admiration and appreciation." Bradley wrote, in *Values of the Game:* "To John McCain, with respect for your life and your commitment to campaign finance reform."

McCain and Bradley scheduled their joint appearance to coincide roughly with the release of each party's fund-raising numbers for the year. As of December 17, 1999, according to a memo by Carla Eudy, who was in charge of McCain's fund-raising efforts, the numbers were as follows: December deposit: $1,175,000 (through 12/13/99); Fourth Quarter deposits: $4,745,000 (10/1/99–12/13/99); Year-to-Date deposits: $12,091,000 (1/1/99–12/13/99). "Our quarterly income will be in excess of $5.2 million," Eudy wrote, "which will be an increase of over $2 million from the third quarter." At the end of 1999, McCain had on hand, in cash, only $1.5 million; he was expecting another $6.2 million in federal matching funds. In contrast, Bush, to date, had brought in $67 million, without the help of federal matching funds; a good portion of that money was in the bank as a reserve for the primary season.

On Sunday, December 19, in a telephone interview with Reuters, McCain said that, one day, an openly gay person could be elected president, although he still opposed allowing openly gay people to serve in the military. "People make judgments based on a candidate's qualifications," McCain said about the issue of a president's sexual orientation. "I don't think that [sexual orientation] would rule anybody out." If McCain offended the right wing of his party with his comments about a gay president, he didn't make matters any better the next day, when he gave a major address on environmental issues in Bethlehem, New Hampshire. Speaking at a town hall meeting not far from the White Mountains, McCain focused on the topic of oil-drilling leases on federally controlled lands on the California coast. "The idea that Washington knows best and that local residents cannot be trusted to do what's right in their own backyard is the epitome of federal arrogance," McCain told an audience of 60 people. "If land is governed by decree absent genuine public participation, we will only widen the chasm of distrust between the people and the government."

With the new year—2000—came heightened tension between the Bush and McCain camps. Before, civility had defined the way the two candidates talked about each other. Clearly, neither of them thought McCain really had a chance to be president. Bush had set every record imaginable for fund-raising, he had gotten all of the important endorsements within his party (and a vast number of endorsements that were not important, but he took them anyway), and, at least early on, it looked as if Bush would sail smoothly through the primary process and into the national convention in August. Then, McCain hit the campaign trail in New Hampshire, began his seemingly endless string of town hall meetings, and started to eat away at Bush's lead in the opinion polls—if not nationally, at least in New Hampshire. Because the New Hampshire primary, now less than one month away, was shaping up to be competitive after all, Bush had to treat McCain less like a war hero mounting a novelty act and calling it a presidential campaign, and more like a viable opponent who could actually beat him.

The first truly edgy exchange of words between the two campaigns occurred on January 4, the day Elizabeth Dole, who had dropped out of the race, endorsed Bush. In Bedford, New Hampshire, before an audience at the C. R. Sparks Center, she compared Bush to Reagan, in whose Cabinet she had served. "Today," she said, "we rally to another Western governor, just as bold in challenging the status quo, just as resolved to restore pride in our institutions, just as determined to be himself." In his speech, Bush took aim at McCain for gypping the middle class with the tax cut he was about to propose.

Responding on the campaign trail, McCain argued that Bush's tax cut, which totaled $483 billion, would kill Social Security and help the rich. "Sixty percent of the benefits from Bush's tax cut go to the wealthiest 10 percent of Americans," McCain said, "and that's not the kind of tax relief that Americans need. . . . I'm not giving tax cuts to the rich."

The Dole endorsement—by implication, Elizabeth Dole was speaking for her husband as well—was not without its history. "Senator Dole had actually sent McCain a $1,000 check while Mrs. Dole was still a candidate," Joyce Campbell says. "After the press found out about the contribution, Dole kept saying, 'Elizabeth sent me to the doghouse.' But Dole saw McCain as having great potential. Some of Dole's past jealousy and animosity and all those tenuous feelings he had about Bush Senior were resurfacing a little bit too. Ultimately, though, Dole is a party man. There was a flirtation with McCain at the beginning"—maybe fueled by his former unpleasant encounters with George H. W. Bush—"but then the party won out. McCain had to know that the Doles had no choice but to do what was right for the party, especially since Mrs. Dole had been a candidate."

On January 5, McCain had to deal with another dilemma. The *Boston Globe* ran an article that said that McCain, in his capacity as chairman of the Commerce Committee, had lobbied federal regulators to vote on a television license that had been applied for by Paxson Communications, a company that had been a major contributor to McCain's presidential campaign and had allowed him the use of its corporate jets. That was the story in a nut shell; over the next few days, as the story was picked up in the media, a fuller picture emerged. In the past few months, McCain had flown on Paxson corporate jets four times, and company executives had given his campaign $20,000. On December 9, as the *Washington Post* would report, McCain had flown on a Paxson company plane to West Palm Beach, Florida, where he attended a fund-raiser on a yacht. The very next day—supposedly at the request of Paxson's Washington lobbying firm, Alcalde & Fay—McCain sent a letter to the Federal Communications Commission (FCC), a government agency mindful of the influence of the Commerce Committee, to encourage a quick vote on Paxson's request to buy a television station in Pittsburgh. One week later, the FCC approved the sale. However, William Kennard, the FCC chairman, criticized McCain in a letter; McCain's request, he said, was "highly unusual." McCain had often fought with the FCC through the years because he believed the agency was slow and ineffectual. McCain had even told the *Globe*, when the paper first ran its story on the Paxson case, that he felt the FCC was "the least efficient, most bureaucratic, least responsive bureaucracy" in Washington.

Faced with the prospect that the Paxson matter could blow up into a full-scale scandal, McCain made the cautious move of canceling a fund-raiser that Lowell ("Bud") Paxson had scheduled for the coming weekend at his home. Sure enough, at a debate in Durham on Thursday night—an hour-long affair again featuring all six Republican candidates and sponsored by New Hampshire Public Television, New England Cable Television, and the *Manchester Union Leader*—the first question from Tim Russert, the debate's moderator, concerned Paxson. Was the Paxson case an example of hypocrisy or of bad judgment? Neither, according to McCain. "People deserve to know the answer," McCain said, meaning that companies with business before the Federal Communications Commission deserve to get prompt rulings. "I think that's appropriate in my role as chairman," McCain added, setting up the line of defense he would soon use. It centered around the notion that, as commerce chairman, he felt he had an obligation to prod regulators for action—not suggest decisions, only prod—regardless of whether the company involved was a contributor. McCain added that he had now spent two days defending himself on this issue, and he had canceled a fund-raiser to be held at Paxson's home because "I knew that if I didn't we'd be talking about *that* most of the time."

When given the opportunity, Bush didn't pursue the Paxson case. In political circles, there was more than passing gossip that a source close to Bush had brought the relationship between McCain and Paxson to the attention of the media. "I trust your integrity," Bush said to McCain on this subject during the debate. "I trust your judgment." Campaign finance reform was another matter, however. On that topic, McCain and Bush sparred. "It's bad for Republicans and it's going to hurt the conservative cause," Bush said.

"I don't think you have an idea of how important campaign finance reform is to restore the confidence of young Americans in their government," McCain answered.

"What you don't need to do is tell me what I have no idea about," Bush said. His syntax was garbled but his meaning came through nonetheless.

The two also fought over taxes. When Bush was asked if he would pledge to impose "no new taxes"—a reference to the famous promise his father made at the Republican National Convention in 1988 ("Read my lips: no new taxes," George H. W. Bush had said) and then proceeded to break when he was elected president—Bush boasted, "This is not only 'no new taxes,' this is 'tax cuts, so help me God.'" McCain countered that Bush's massive tax cut would squander the surplus without protecting Social Security. McCain proposed a more reasonable approach: put 63 percent of the surplus aside to build up Social Security and pay down the debt; the rest could be used for a tax cut. "Here's my problem with that kind of Washington mind-set," Bush answered. "It is a large leap of faith to assume that Congress will not spend the money."

If McCain thought the Paxson affair had gone away after his answer in Durham on Thursday, he was wrong. When the candidates assembled in South Carolina the next night for a debate to be moderated by Brian Williams of NBC-TV, the first question addressed to McCain involved another McCain contributor—Ameritech—for which McCain had also lobbied the FCC.

By the end of the first week in January, more problems were brewing for McCain. Specifically, in New York, Guy Molinari was having trouble getting McCain's name on the ballot in all of the state's 31 districts. This was not a problem unique to the McCain campaign; historically, New York's balloting system is so complex that only the nominees for the major parties can get on the ballot without difficulty. A candidate must secure a certain number of valid signatures in a district before his or her name can be placed on the ballot in that district. In other words, a candidate has to treat the process of running in New York as if he or she is waging 31 separate races. Because Bush was the candidate favored by the Republican Party, his name easily appeared on the ballot in all of the state's districts, and the party made sure it had the required number of signatures in each district. McCain had lined up enough signatures to qualify in 25 or 26 of the state's districts, but he was having difficulty in the remaining five or six, and he had received word that his own party might mount challenges to the signatures in some of the districts he had already secured. To remedy the situation, McCain filed a lawsuit, in federal court, against the New York State Republican Party. The suit argued that, because of needlessly complicated rules, only the party's handpicked candidate would appear on the ballot in all districts.

By Saturday of that first week of 2000, the Paxson matter had not gone away, so McCain made the decision to do what he had done to stop the whisper campaign: release a mountain of information to make the unwanted story disappear. With this goal in mind, McCain took the unusual step of having his staff release to the media some 500 letters he had written to various government agencies on behalf of companies and individuals, some of whom were contributors to his political efforts. The strategy was simple: prove that the Paxson example was not suspect by showing that this approach to lobbying was not out of the ordinary. On Sunday, McCain returned to New Hampshire. At a press conference in Goffstown, he was asked by a reporter if he believed the Bush campaign was behind the original leak of the letter he had written on behalf of Paxson. "It doesn't matter," McCain said. "This campaign is very tough and it's getting more intense. The worst thing you can do is to get diverted by something like this, which causes you to get off your game."

As McCain was making these comments, newspapers, armed with this new batch of material, were preparing articles about McCain and Paxson. The *Hartford Courant,* for example, published a story that restated the facts but added some new information. As chairman of the Commerce Committee, which oversees the Federal Communications Commission, McCain had written not one but two letters during the fall—at the very time he was running for president—to the FCC commissioner. Each letter asked for a decision on a television license application made by Paxson Communications. For the record, McCain had reimbursed the company for the flights he had taken on its corporate jets, and when he had written to the FCC commissioner, he had not lobbied for any particular decision in either case. He had just implored the commissioner to reach a decision because the applications had been before the FCC for months. But the letters were to the point, as if McCain were demanding that the FCC must make a move right away.

All in all, the mass release of documents had the effect the McCain camp intended. After the new spate of stories based on the document dump came out, the controversy, such as it was, went away. McCain had clearly written similarly prodding letters on behalf of companies and individuals who had not given him any money. Here was the bottom line: McCain wrote the letters, in large part, because he was unhappy with the incompetency of the Federal Communications Commission, an organization over which he had some, but not complete, managing authority.

On January 10, for the third time in five days, Bush, McCain, and the other Republican candidates participated in a debate. This one lasted for 90 minutes and took place on the campus of Calvin College in Grand Rapids, Michigan. A noteworthy exchange occurred when a student in the audience asked the candidates if they would agree not to run negative ads during the campaign. Forbes refused, but McCain leaped at the prospect, saying, "I'd like to shake hands right now. We will not run negative ads." As he gestured toward Bush, Bush agreed, and extended his hand so the two of them could shake. Prior to the debate, McCain had his staff release to the press the details of his new tax plan, which featured a $237 billion cut over five years. "There is a fundamental difference here," McCain said during the debate, referring to his tax cut as compared to Bush's. "I believe we must save Social Security, we must pay down the debt, we have to make an investment in Medicare. For us to put all of the surplus in tax cuts is not a conservative effort. I think it's a mistake."

The next day, in his first major address on the economy, McCain unveiled his tax reform plan to the public. Countering the Bush plan, McCain proposed to save Social Security and provide a $237 billion tax cut over five years. "We can afford a tax cut, and American taxpayers deserve one," McCain said at a luncheon held by the Chamber of Commerce in Concord, New Hampshire. "But it must be a tax-cut promise a leader can keep." McCain, who made references to his being a conservative, quoted Reagan: "[E]mpowering free markets and free people is the path to prosperity." He also told a story about Harry Truman, who liked to say he only listened to one-armed economists so he could avoid the vast majority of economists who would say, "On the one hand *this*, but on the other hand *that*." In the end, McCain emphasized that he was in favor of the concept of a tax cut. Campaigning in Charleston, South Carolina, Bush quipped: "Maybe the man recognizes a good idea when he sees one." The implication was apparent: McCain had borrowed the idea of a tax cut from Bush.

As the campaign proceeded, another controversy emerged. Recently, the National Association for the Advancement of Colored People (NAACP) had voted to boycott South Carolina because the state continued to fly the Confederate flag above the statehouse. (David Beasley, the former governor, had suggested taking the flag down from the statehouse. This so angered the state's conservatives that they refused to vote for him and he was defeated.) In the previous week, McCain had wandered into the controversy when he said the Confederate flag was a symbol "of racism and slavery," and he found its presence "offensive." But as the days passed and as his staff studied the way the issue tracked in South Carolina, McCain decided to moderate his position. He had to play up the fact there were two sides to this debate, but, even though Bush refused to take a position, he concluded he had to, and it wasn't necessarily the one he had initially stated off-the-cuff.

So, on Thursday, January 13, while campaigning in Dublin, New Hampshire, McCain read a statement he hoped would clarify his past comments. Taking a piece of paper from his inside coat pocket, he unfolded it and read his revised stand. "I understand both sides," he said, setting up the parameters of the dispute. "Some view it [the Confederate flag] as a symbol of slavery; others view it as a symbol of heritage." Then McCain took a position contrary to the one he had chosen the previous week. "Personally, I see the battle flag as a symbol of heritage," he said. "I have ancestors who fought for the Confederacy, none of whom owned slaves. I believe they fought honorably." The fate of the flag, McCain said, "should be left up to the people of South Carolina." (A reporter would later point out to McCain, after a check of public records in Mississippi, that his family *had* owned slaves, a revelation that surprised McCain.)

The day before, Bush had gotten agitated at a press conference in Wilmington, Delaware, when the issue of the Confederate flag was mentioned. "People have strong feelings about that," Bush said, refusing to take a stand. "Some people feel one way about it, some people feel the other way. The people of South Carolina can make up their own minds."

On that same Thursday, McCain spoke before the New Hampshire state legislature, which was controlled by the Republicans. With 400 members, it was the third largest legislative body in the world. Naturally, McCain couldn't resist advocating government reform. As he talked to the massive legislative body, he announced that, should he be elected president, he would create a cabinet-level position he would call "reform czar." Such a position would, McCain said, "help me implement the changes in the institutions of government we must make if we are to restore a government of, by, and for the American people as intended by our Founding Fathers." Standing before a portrait of George Washington, McCain compared his reform czar post to that of the chairman of the Joint Chiefs of Staff. But he could not help underscoring a theme he had advanced for years. The country needed to get rid of "the cynical and corrupting influence of special-interest money," McCain said. "You are the victims of pork-barrel politics. And it must stop." As they had when he delivered various lines throughout the speech, the legislators applauded loudly at McCain's bold declaration. In a political world often defined by misdirection and compromise, McCain was unwaveringly clear on the issue of government reform. Even the world's third largest legislative body agreed with the argument he was making.

While he was going about his campaign schedule in New Hampshire, McCain had unleashed a new ad comparing Bush's tax plan to his own. The $483 billion Bush tax cut, McCain believed, was most helpful to the rich. In his ad, McCain said, "There are big differences between me and the others—I won't take every last dime of the surplus and spend it on tax cuts that mostly benefit the wealthy. I'll use the bulk of the surplus to secure Social Security far into the future to keep our promise to the Greatest Generation." At an impromptu news conference at the Des Moines airport, Bush responded: "The two voices criticizing my plan are Al Gore and John McCain"—a not-so-subtle attempt to put McCain in the Democrats' camp, and thus chip away at Republican support.

Bush was in Iowa for a debate sponsored by the *Des Moines Register* on that Saturday night, January 15. Moderated by the paper's editor, Dennis Ryerson, it would be the last debate before the Iowa caucus (now nine days away), and, even though McCain was not running an active campaign in Iowa, he attended and sat on the stage with the other candidates. Because of the recent squabble over taxes, Bush hit McCain hard by saying that what McCain really wanted to do was put in for a $40 billion tax *increase* because McCain had proposed taxing the fringe benefits paid to corporation employees.

McCain didn't take the bait. "The first thing I'd say to a single mom," McCain responded, "is that I've got a tax cut for you, and George W. Bush doesn't."

"That's not true," Bush snapped.

"Yes, it is," McCain said.

The matter was left unresolved, but McCain had made his point: Bush's tax plan had been invented to help Bush's rich friends, not working mothers. (Unintentionally, McCain helped put himself in the liberal camp by appearing to attack rich people—a mistake Democrats regularly make. The one Democrat who had been careful *not* to make that technical error was Bill Clinton, who fundamentally understood that middle-class people, while not actually rich, like to think of themselves as comfortable and therefore more rich than not.)

Bush also had to defend himself because of his association with Arthur Ravenel, a South Carolina state senator who had called the NAACP "the National Association of Retarded People." When confronted, Ravenel had offered an apology—to retarded people! Until now, Bush had avoided the controversy surrounding Ravenel, who was one of his supporters. When he was asked about Ravenel during the previous week, Bush said only that the remark was "unfortunate." But when Alan Keyes challenged Bush about "that kind of racial slur," Bush could no longer dodge the issue. "I agree with you, Alan," Bush said. "His comments are out of line and we should repudiate them."

Eventually, the conversation got back to taxes. "Governor Bush's plan," McCain charged, "has not one penny for Social Security, not one penny for Medicare, and not one penny for paying down the national debt. And when you run ads saying you are going to take care of Social Security, my friend, that's all hat and no cattle."

Sitting near McCain on the stage, Bush was stunned. "That's cute but. . . ." Bush trailed off, as if unsure what to say next.

"They're always cutest when they're true," McCain said.

"That's not true," Bush offered.

"That certainly is," McCain said.

And it went on like that. If Bush and McCain had gone out of their way to be cordial to one another in the past, they were backing off that approach now. McCain was doing better in the polls—at least in New Hampshire, if not in Iowa.

The weirdest part of the evening unfolded just before the exchange about Ravenel. Alan Keyes attacked Bush for allowing El Cenizo, a small town in Texas, to pass a town ordinance that said all town business had to be done in Spanish. As Texas governor, Bush should have tried to stop such an edict.

"No es la verdad," Bush said, meaning Keyes' charge was not true.

"Es la verdad, señor," Keyes interrupted.

"Un momento!" Bush exclaimed.

McCain couldn't stand it any longer. Trying to shut them both up, he declared, "Vamonos!"

When McCain appeared on *Meet the Press* on Sunday, January 16, Tim Russert asked him about new charges coming from the Bush camp—namely, that McCain was trying to incite class warfare. "I always thought that class warfare was to take away from the rich," McCain said, and then added that a widening gap in America, between "the haves and the have-nots," was apparent to him.

On Monday, while all of the other candidates were campaigning in Iowa in anticipation of the upcoming caucus, McCain was alone in New Hampshire, fighting the gusty winds, the ever-present snow, and the subzero temperatures. While he rode on the Straight Talk Express that day, McCain, seated in the big red captain's chair and surrounded by the pack of reporters who studied his every word, could not help but state the obvious. "It's a very high-risk campaign we're running," he said. "I feel sometimes like the Wallendas" (the world-famous family of high-wire acrobats). To hedge those odds, he had a secret weapon for winning New Hampshire: He would campaign in the state more intensely than any other candidate. To that end, he had held town meeting after town meeting. On this day, as he wound his way through the state, McCain held town meetings numbers 93, 94, and 95. His approach—knocking on doors and talking to as many people as possible—had worked all those years ago in Arizona, at the beginning of his political career. He believed he would win this race only if he used the same dogged approach.

There was a downside to what McCain was doing. By continually holding so many events that allowed him to interact with the public, and by making himself so available to the press, McCain knew there was a possibility, or even a probability, that he would misspeak—perhaps the worst mistake a politician can make. In the middle of his blur of campaigning on that Monday, McCain committed just such a blunder. At one point, on the bus, McCain was talking about how he had served with gay men in the navy. Later, the bus stopped along the side of the road at Calef's Country Store. As McCain was walking through the store, a reporter asked him how he knew the navy men he had served with were gay. "Well," McCain said, "I think we knew by behavior and attitudes. I think it's clear to some of us when some people have that lifestyle. But I didn't pursue it, and I wouldn't pursue it, and I wouldn't pursue it today." McCain stopped, then added, "But, look, that to me was something—and still is something—that is private. It's very different from a manifestation of that behavior in the line of duty."

In fact, what McCain was describing was "Don't ask, don't tell"—a policy he endorsed. When he had met on November 8 with the Log Cabin Republicans, the gay activist group that gave $40,000 to his campaign, he told them he supported "Don't ask, don't tell." He also voted for the antigay Defense of Marriage bill, but, in general, McCain held moderate positions on gay issues. He believed that one's sexuality is a private matter. On Monday night, January 17, at a town hall meeting in Stratham, McCain commented on "Don't ask, don't tell" when he said, "I think the policy works, but I'm opposed to discrimination of any kind in America." That last concept—being against discrimination of any kind—seemed to indicate that he was not in favor of discrimination based on sexual orientation. Thus, his earlier comment to the reporter on the bus, about "behavior and attitudes," was startling; it implied that he might judge someone on his or her appearance. When the story hit the papers on Tuesday, gay groups were up in arms.

That Tuesday, in New York, as he dealt with the fallout from Monday's comment about gay mannerisms, McCain found himself among the "haves" attending fund-raisers so he could keep advancing his message about reaching out to the "have-nots." In the late afternoon, he went to a reception at The Luncheon Club on Broad Street, in the heart of the Wall Street community. Attendees ponied up $1,000 each to McCain's hosts—Peter Henderson, Jim McGuire, and Joe Cangemi—for the chance to meet the guest of honor. Then, starting at six o'clock, McCain was hosted at a reception given by Edgar Bronfman Jr. of Seagram's; the price tag for this fund-raiser, held in the Seagram's Building on Park Avenue, was, again, $1,000 per person. Later, Michael Bloomberg hosted a $1,000-a-plate dinner for McCain at his home on the Upper East Side of Manhattan.

A little over a month had passed since McCain had made an official campaign stop at the Yale campus, in Connecticut. On Wednesday, January 19, he was scheduled to speak at a noontime luncheon given by the Hartford Chamber of Commerce. He arrived before noon at Brainard Airport and took a campaign bus to Trumbull Street in downtown Hartford. Because the weather was frigid—the day's high was expected to be 10 degrees—McCain was impressed as he made his way into the Hartford Hilton and saw a group of 20 or more veterans, many wearing their military caps and holding copies of *Faith of My Fathers*, who were willing to brave the cold to greet him. "John Wayne McCain!" they chanted in unison. "John Wayne McCain!" McCain shook hands with each member of the group before he proceeded into the hotel and headed for the ballroom.

There, he gave a 40-minute speech before a standing-room-only crowd of 200 people who had paid a remarkably reasonable tab of

$25 a person to attend. Because most tickets to fund-raisers of this sort are usually much higher, it was no wonder that, for the year 1999, McCain had raised only $19 million (including federal matching funds) for his presidential campaign, compared to the $67 million the Bush campaign had collected. At the luncheon, McCain hit on many of his standard issues—among them, Social Security. "More young Americans believe Elvis is alive," he quipped, "than believe they'll ever receive a Social Security check."

On January 20, 2000, McCain had no choice but to take his campaign to New York. Guy Molinari had not been able to guarantee that McCain's name would appear on the ballot in all of the districts in the state. McCain decided to use the one ally he knew he could rely on: the media. If the New York State Republican Party was going to try to block any chance he had for winning New York—a state in which he could do well because Republicans there tended to be moderate, and McCain was certainly more moderate, on a host of issues, than Bush—then he would draw that fact to the attention of the media and unleash a flood of attacks on the party.

With this in mind, McCain called a press conference across the street from the Russian embassy, on the Upper East Side of Manhattan. He charged that the tactics carried out by Bush and the New York State Republican Party were antidemocratic. "My message today is: 'Mr. Powers, open up those ballots,'" McCain said, singling out the state party chairman, William Powers. Then he made a comparison between the state party officials and the bosses of the Communist Party in the Soviet Union. "There's an interesting kind of coincidence here as we stand by the Russian consulate. In March, there will be an election here in New York to determine the Republican and Democratic nominees. And in Russia there will be a presidential election. In Russia, there will be more than one name on the ballot. In New York, unless something happens, there will be only one name on the ballot. It seems to me that history has been turned on its head." Then, with the Russian embassy hovering in the background, McCain added, for the benefit of the crush of television cameramen and newspaper photographers, that he intended to "fight in the courts, fight in public opinion, and I will fight at the Republican National Convention if necessary"—for access to the ballot. As McCain was walking back to the bus, a reporter asked him why he had chosen to pose in front of the Russian embassy, and, as if to confirm that he had decided to unleash the media on Bush and the New York State Party, he said, "Because I think it makes a good photo op." Sure enough, the next day, when the story appeared in papers across the country, McCain had made his message clear: Bush was trying to control the election as if he were a communist dictator.

On Thursday night, as he waited for the full effect of his media appearance that day, McCain attended a fund-raiser at the home of John Billock, the president of Home Box Office, and his wife, Elizabeth, in Greenwich, Connecticut. The house on Rock Maple Road was jammed with people who had paid $1,000 each to mingle with McCain and hear his 10-minute fund-raiser stump speech. After the speech, he took questions. "A woman there asked him about abortion and he answered her so well," says Ben Davol, who would be the chairman of the McCain campaign in Connecticut. "He said, 'I'm pro-life. But what you need to understand about the abortion issue is the same thing you need to understand about so many issues in Washington. People have turned causes into businesses, and I'm about not having abortions at all. We need to understand this subject and come together and get away from the business of making it a business and let's talk about it and move forward.' The woman said, 'I'm 72 years old. I have fought for the right for women to have abortions, I'm a lifetime member of Planned Parenthood, and you are the first person to answer the question in a way in which I think we can talk.'"

On Friday, January 21, McCain began another campaign swing through South Carolina. Among his stops was a town hall meeting with several hundred supporters at the Greenville County Library in Greenville. McCain delivered an impassioned speech on

Internet pornography, an issue about which he felt enormous concern, but, in the question-and-answer session that followed, someone stood up and asked him about his stand on abortion. McCain had often said that he was staunchly pro-life, but he always seemed to have a list of exceptions to his pro-life position. On this occasion, he made sure to note that he supported exceptions in the cases of rape, incest, and danger to the life of the mother. He also favored the use of fetal tissue in research—a practice most pro-life proponents opposed—because he felt it could be useful in curing diseases such as Parkinson's disease. Overall, on this occasion, he said he supported overturning *Roe v. Wade*—a position that was different from the one he had taken in the past.

Also on Friday, McCain focused on a new television ad that the Bush campaign had started to run. The ad argued that McCain's tax plan would actually impose a $40 billion tax increase on workers because McCain was proposing a tax on fringe benefits. McCain argued that the ad broke the promise that Bush had made two weeks before, when he and McCain shook hands and agreed not to run any negative ads. Bush, McCain said, knew this ad was a distortion of the truth—McCain did not see his plan as a new tax but more as an effort to view fringe benefits as income—and ran it anyway. McCain then unveiled an ad that challenged Bush's. "I guess it was bound to happen," McCain said in his ad. "Now my opponent has started the political attacks after promising he wouldn't. Mr. Bush's attacks are wrong. . . . There is no tax increase." Finally, McCain added: "I'm keeping my pledge"—not to run attack ads.

At a press conference in Greenville, a reporter asked McCain about his new ad. Was it an attack ad? "Of course not," McCain said. "It is a direct response to an ad he's been running saying that I'm trying to raise taxes by $40 billion." McCain went on: "If he'll take down his ad, our ad will come down just as soon as we can. But I have to respond. . . . In American politics, it is incumbent on you to respond when there is paid advertising that is totally false on an important issue." Maybe, but that's not the way Bush saw it. Campaigning in Iowa, Bush said there was just one problem: His ad wasn't negative.

On Saturday morning, at a campaign stop in Aiken, South Carolina, McCain was greeted by a group of retired marines in dress uniform. They saluted him when he got off his bus. Later, in Orangeburg, McCain was introduced by Congressman Mark Sanford who, in an obvious effort to take a dig at Bush, told the crowd at the Orangeburg Fine Arts Center, "If you are going to be the commander-in-chief of the armed services and put your men and women in harm's way, you yourself should have been in harm's way." That theme—the one that said McCain was ready to be commander-in-chief and Bush was not—was carried by McCain and his surrogates into the early part of the next week.

Not at all subtle, McCain's theme of the day on Monday was: "I am fully prepared to be the President of the United States." The line was meant to tie into a new ad that had just been launched. Called "Commander," the ad focused on national defense and foreign policy. In it, the narrator said: "There's only one man running for president who knows the military and understands the world: John McCain." Then the ad noted McCain's navy pilot experience and his years as a POW. The point was obvious. McCain was a war hero with extensive military experience; Bush was not. Nowhere did anyone in the McCain campaign mention publicly that, in 1968, at the height of the Vietnam War, Bush had allowed his father to pull strings to get him into a unit of the Texas Air National Guard so Bush could avoid active military duty and the more-than-remote possibility he would be sent to Vietnam. The McCain campaign could have made that point, too; the facts were apparent. While McCain was being held in the Hanoi Hilton, Bush was living in an upscale "singles" apartment complex in the Galleria area in Houston, driving around in a sports car, and serving his country by flying practice runs as a member of the Texas Air National Guard. The prospects that Bush would have ever seen any active combat were nil.

As expected, Bush won the Iowa caucus on Monday night, but he beat Steve Forbes by only 11 points—a much slimmer margin than most political observers had expected. When the final numbers came in, McCain finished fifth in a field of six, proof that the Iowa voters had punished him for refusing to campaign there. Orrin Hatch finished last, which spelled the end to his campaign. Because McCain had made his strategy of skipping Iowa so clear, he could use his poor showing to his advantage in New Hampshire. At the very time the Iowa caucus was being held on Monday night, McCain was holding a "First-in-the-Nation Primary" rally at Dartmouth College where he told the cheering crowd, "The eyes of the nation will be on the main event"—the primary in New Hampshire. "Iowa is the preliminary."

Bush did not echo that sentiment when he arrived in New Hampshire on Tuesday, fresh from his victory in the Iowa caucus the night before. However, he could see from the internal tracking polls that he was in trouble in New Hampshire. The Bush campaign was not yet ready to admit there was any way he could lose the state, but, just in case, Bush went out of his way to hedge his bets. "I'm in it for the long run," Bush said in an interview in New Hampshire on Tuesday afternoon. "I will be the last man standing."

On Wednesday morning, as he was sitting in the captain's chair in the back of the Straight Talk Express, a reporter asked McCain one of those questions that, if answered too quickly, can get a candidate into trouble. What would he do, the reporter wanted to know, if his teenage daughter, Meghan, told him she was pregnant and didn't want to have the baby? The question may have been triggered by remarks McCain made earlier in the week; he said he believed the Republican Party should add to its platform language that made abortion acceptable in cases of rape, incest, and danger to the life of the mother. "It would be a private discussion that we would share within the family and not with anyone else," McCain said to the reporter about Meghan's hypothetical pregnancy. "I would discuss the issue with Cindy and Meghan and this would be a private discussion. Obviously, I would encourage her to know that the baby would be brought up in a warm and loving family. The final decision would be Meghan's, with our advice and counsel."

The answer did not sound as if it were coming from someone who had espoused a career-long belief in the right of the unborn to be born. McCain's statements implied clearly that he believed in a woman's right to choose, or at least in his daughter's right to choose. When the bus got to Manchester and McCain and the press pool separated, McCain had an aide search out the reporter so he could clarify his comments. The aide got McCain on his cell phone; then the reporter listened as McCain said that he had misspoken on the bus. The discussion over Meghan's unwanted pregnancy, should that unfortunate development ever happen, would be a private family decision. End of story.

That Wednesday night, the five remaining Republican candidates met in Manchester in a 90-minute debate sponsored by CNN and WMUR, the state's major television station. This last debate before the primary was moderated by Bernard Shaw of CNN and Karen Brown of WMUR. With Forbes, Bauer, and Keyes looking on, Bush and McCain fought, now more sharply than ever, over taxes, school vouchers, campaign finance reform, and government spending. At one point, Bush accused McCain of writing a tax proposal worthy of the Clinton-Gore Administration. Later, when Bush again compared a McCain position to that of the Clinton Administration, McCain turned to Bush and said, "George, if you're saying that I'm like Al Gore, then you're spinning like Bill Clinton."

Bush did not seem unduly insulted by the zinger. Nor did he later when McCain made yet another attempt to compare Bush to Clinton and Gore by saying, "When I'm in the debate with Al Gore, I'm going to turn to Al Gore and I'm going to say, 'You and Bill Clinton debased the institutions of government in 1996. . . . And, George, when you're in that debate, you're going to stand there and you'll have nothing to say because you're defending the system."

"John," Bush said in return, "I don't appreciate the way you've characterized my position. I'm for reform. I sure am."

"The people of this country are suffering from Clinton fatigue," McCain said, "and it's because they want someone who will look them in the eye and tell them the truth."

As if to reaffirm his belief that many Americans were longing for someone who would be direct with them, McCain launched another verbal assault on Bush when he refused to name one corporate loophole he would close as president. "You," McCain said to Bush, "seem to depict the role of president as some kind of hapless bystander."

But perhaps the night's most heated line of disagreement occurred between McCain and Keyes, not McCain and Bush. Keyes went after McCain on the issue of abortion. If McCain were truly pro-life, he would not be as wishy-washy as he was on the subject. "I am proud of [my] pro-life record and I will continue to maintain it," McCain said. "I will not draw my children into this discussion." McCain hoped this would prevent Keyes—or anyone else, for that matter—from revisiting the blunder he had made earlier in his dialogue with the reporter about Meghan. It didn't. Keyes brought it up again and charged McCain with being weak on abortion. This prompted McCain to snap back. "I've seen enough killing in my life," McCain said to Keyes. "I know how precious human life is and I don't need a lecture from you."

"I didn't lecture you," Keyes said.

"Next time, use decaf," McCain shot back.

On Thursday, Jack Kemp, the former New York congressman and vice-presidential candidate on the Republican ticket with Bob Dole in 1996, endorsed Bush at the Lockheed Sanders plant in Nashua. But, amazingly, just four days before Primary Day in New Hampshire, at a time when most candidates would be campaigning around the clock, Bush decided to take a day off. His decision was not missed by McCain, who told reporters, "He took the whole day off today. I was surprised he took the day off today."

The last thought on McCain's mind was to take a day off. Indeed, he kept a full schedule. That morning, he held a photo opportunity at a factory in Newington. Later, in Hampton, a town on the seacoast, McCain sympathized with the plight of the American Indian, an issue he had often dealt with in his congressional career. At a town meeting, an audience member asked a question about the American Indian. McCain said the treatment of Indians in this country was "one of the darker chapters of the American people." He talked about a Lakota (Sioux) reservation located in South Dakota "where people live in the worst conditions of grinding poverty." Afterward, on his bus, reporters asked him to continue to discuss the issue of Native Americans. In 1983, he said, when he was a freshman congressman, he was put on an Indian affairs subcommittee by Morris Udall, who was chairman of the House Interior Committee. "The only way I got it," McCain said about his appointment, "was that nobody else wanted it. When I talked to a lot of Republicans, they said, 'They don't vote and when they vote, they vote for Democrats. Don't get involved.'" McCain, as it happened, was instrumental in helping the Pequot tribe get its casino in Connecticut.

On Thursday night, McCain held a rally at Timberlane Regional High School in Plaistow. There, he voiced what had now become a running theme in the campaign—his willingness to expand his conservatism to include more moderate votes. "My friends," McCain told the excited crowd, "I am a proud conservative Republican. I have a 17-year record as a conservative Republican. But Jack Kennedy and Ronald Reagan had something in common: They would inspire a crowd to causes greater than their own self-interest." The reaction McCain received on this night was much like the reaction he was now getting at event after event. These days, the crowds were cheering for him as if he were a famous actor or rock star. The response was much more visceral and highly charged than run-of-the-mill politicians got, even if they were running for president. The audiences and the opinion polls let McCain know that he was making headway in New Hampshire. With Primary Day looming, some

McCain insiders thought he might actually be able to win, a development that would certainly change the political landscape as it was then defined. McCain knew what this meant too. While he sat in his captain's chair on the Straight Talk Express that Thursday night, he answered a question that the reporters sitting around him had not asked. "My question is," McCain said—prophetically, as it turned out—"will the Bush campaign go negative?" The question was rhetorical, for McCain knew the answer. He just wanted to lay down a marker with the reporters who were covering him. If he won New Hampshire, he knew what was going to happen to him next.

On Friday, at a town hall meeting in Rochester, McCain made a speech in which he stressed the need for federal tort reform, an issue that Bush, as governor, had championed in Texas, and, historically, a wedge issue between the Democratic and Republican parties. Simply put, Republicans favor tort reform and Democrats do not, because it is generally believed that tort reform benefits business while a strong legal system helps the middle and lower classes. On the issue of tort reform, McCain was a good Republican. In Rochester, McCain appeared on stage with "Sharkman," a prop (a man dressed in a shark outfit) supplied by Citizens for a Sound Economy. That same day, McCain appeared in the high school gym in the town of Exeter before an enthusiastic crowd of 1,000 students, teachers, and local supporters. "We're having a great and uplifting experience," McCain said. "We've had wonderful progress."

But in these days before the New Hampshire primary, it was not always campaigning as usual. The Christian Coalition and the National Right to Life Committee had started to run radio ads attacking McCain. In the past, the National Right to Life Committee had charged that McCain-Feingold would limit its ability to sponsor political advertising; this, the organization said, would profoundly hamper its ability to advance its pro-life agenda. The groups were particularly distressed over the provision in McCain-Feingold that would impose restrictions on issue advertising 60 days before an election. Groups like these two had been able to raise unlimited amounts of money at will, without ever revealing the names of contributors, and to run advertising right up until an election. To help protect their ability to raise money and run ads at their will, the Christian Coalition and the National Right to Life Committee implored the voters of New Hampshire, by way of their radio ads, not to vote for McCain. If passed, McCain-Feingold would address the use of these very kinds of ads.

By Friday, it had become clear that McCain's media attack on Bush and the New York State Republican Party was not going to be as successful as he had hoped. The McCain campaign then started a legal battle in New York to make sure he would be on the ballot on March 7. On the day before, a state judge had removed McCain's name from eight congressional districts, and election officials took his name off the ballot in two more. McCain had filed petitions in only 26 of the state's 31 districts, so he now stood the chance of being on the ballot in only 16 of 31 districts. Campaigning in New Hampshire on Friday, McCain told reporters, "I'm very disappointed in Governor Bush. He could've exercised some leadership and told [the state party officials] to let me on the ballot. Everybody knows he has control."

On Saturday, with just two days left before Primary Day, McCain once again addressed Bush's charge that his tax-cut proposal "mimicked" Clinton's budget plan. "Everybody knows I'm the anti-Clinton," McCain said at a town meeting in a high school in Raymond, before a crowd of several hundred. Then he set his sights on Bush. "And maybe some people are saying [Bush] is not ready for prime time with that kind of charge." After the town meeting, he talked to reporters and specifically addressed the fact that, the day before, Bush had received the endorsement of John Sununu, the former governor of New Hampshire who had served on the White House staff of his father (and who, it was rumored at the time, had been fired from that job by George W., not George H. W.). "The establishment is obviously in a state of extreme distress, if not panic," McCain said of the Sununu endorsement, "because they know I will break the iron triangle of money, lobbyists, and legislation." Later that day, McCain had another town meeting, this one in Windham, where people packed the room to see him. "Governor Bush is out there raising money," McCain said. "I'm going to be out there raising hell, because we're going to stop these special interests."

That day, Bush had *not* been out there raising money. He was busy hosting a good portion of the Bush clan at what was supposed to be a spectacular rally that would put Bush over the top in New Hampshire. At the afternoon gathering, which took place outside a health club in Milford, 1,500 supporters, many of them wearing straw hats and cowboy boots, showed up for the Bush family's mini-reunion. As a pop country band, the Bellamy Brothers, played songs like "Let Your Love Flow" and "Redneck Girl," the Bushes assembled to wish George W. well. Present were George H. W., Barbara, two brothers (Marvin and Neil) and their wives, one sister (Dorothy Koch) and her husband, a bunch of nieces and nephews, and, naturally, Laura. "We were just sitting in Washington," Barbara Bush offered from the podium, "and said, 'We got to go up.' So we just want you to know that we are so excited to see you all here. . . . Thank you for all you're doing for my boy." Picking up on the boy motif, George H. W. added, using language that would make headlines in newspapers across the country: "To say that Barbara and I are thrilled to be here is the understatement of the year. I'm proud of our son. And this boy, this son of ours, is not going to let you down. He's going to go all the way and serve you with great honor, all the way." There was something disconcerting about a presidential candidate being referred to as "this boy," and the media coverage of the event reflected the oddity. For much of the presidential campaign so far, Bush had gone out of his way to separate himself from his father and his father's legacy. Now, in a single appearance with George W. on the eve of the New Hampshire primary, George H. W. had seriously damaged much of his son's effort to distance himself from the failures of the first Bush presidency. On stage that Saturday afternoon, Bush made the best he could of the situation. "My family gives me strength," he said. "My family gives me love."

Coming down the home stretch of the campaign, McCain appeared on *Meet the Press* on Sunday. When Russert brought up the issue of abortion, which McCain had been asked about repeatedly during the campaign, especially at the town hall meetings, McCain reiterated that he had "come to the conclusion that the exceptions of rape, incest, and the life of the mother are legit exceptions" to any ban on abortion. "I don't claim to be a theologian," he added, "but I have my moral beliefs." And what would happen if *Roe v. Wade* were overturned, as he had once advocated in the campaign? "I would not prosecute a woman" who got an abortion, McCain said flatly. With this statement, McCain's position on abortion was now even more cloudy.

McCain proudly said, over and over during the campaign, that he was pro-life. However, he had added exceptions: instances of rape, incest, and danger to the life of the mother. What's more, he might be in favor of the Supreme Court's overturning *Roe v. Wade*, but he was not in favor of prosecuting a woman if she got an abortion. Finally, judging from the remarks he had made regarding Meghan's hypothetical pregnancy, he actually believed, in the example of his daughter, *she* should have the right to choose what to do about an unwanted pregnancy. If this was a pro-life stand, it was not one most pro-lifers would have endorsed.

On *Meet the Press*, McCain also underscored an issue he had often advanced during the campaign: He was more prepared to be president than Bush. "There's only one man who is fully prepared," McCain told Russert. "I am fully prepared and do not need on-the-job training, particularly in fulfilling the job of commander-in-chief." Bush responded, in a manner of speaking, when he appeared on Sunday morning on *Face the Nation*. Playing up his experience as governor of a large state, he said: "I am the one person in this race who has been elected to an executive position. I have been in the position of setting agendas, of making decisions."

With the *Meet the Press* appearance behind him, McCain went on to hold his 114th—and final—town hall meeting in New Hampshire. In Peterborough, 1,000 supporters showed up to cheer McCain on. "Whether we prevail or not," McCain told the excited crowd, "this has been one of the greatest experiences of my life." At the end of his appearance, confetti rained down on McCain and Cindy and music blared over the public address system as a band launched into the song "Play That Funky Music, White Boy."

This was where he had held the first town meeting back in July. How far he had come since then! Six months earlier, McCain had been a little-known senator from Arizona, someone perhaps best identified as being a POW in Vietnam or one of the senators involved in the Keating Five scandal. Now, he was a widely acknowledged challenger to Bush's lock on the Republican presidential nomination. He had done it with style, tenacity, and what had become his trademark sense of humor, as exemplified by the time a reporter asked him what he thought about a Bush ad that attacked McCain's tax-cut proposal. In an obvious attempt to poke fun at the image Bush surrogates had painted of him as having an out-of-control temper, McCain said, "That makes me want to punch him in the face." Then, deadpanning to the press corps, he told them to describe him when he made that remark as "quivering with rage."

As they always did for important elections, the residents of two famous tiny New Hampshire towns, Dixville Notch and Hart's Location, voted on Monday night at midnight, during the first moments of Election Day. On the Democratic side, their votes would not predict the way the rest of the state would vote the following day. Bradley received 13 votes; Gore, 5. But on the Republican side, the vote did predict who would win, if not by how much. Bush got 17 votes; McCain pulled in 19. If that vote was any indication of what was to come, McCain would win on Tuesday in a relative squeaker. As it turned out, it was not a squeaker at all.

By midafternoon on February 1, McCain had been told that, in all likelihood, he was going to win the New Hampshire primary.

Superstitious as ever—he always carried a lucky eagle feather and a lucky compass; he also carried a lucky penny and, occasionally, a lucky rock; an aide always carried his lucky ink pen (a Zebra Jimnie Gel Rollerball, medium blue); he wore lucky shoes (L.L.Bean rubber-sole dress shoes); he ate barbecue on the day of each debate and on an election day; and he always made a point of going to a movie while the polls were open—he said he would wait until that evening, when the returns came in, before he became hopeful. He was superstitious about being too confident as well.

So he waited upstairs in his suite at the Crown Plaza Hotel in Nashua, the town where he had started his campaign in September 1999. Since then, McCain had traveled all over the state of New Hampshire; in all, by the time he had finished campaigning, observers would estimate he had shaken the hands of some 60,000 people in New Hampshire, roughly five percent of the state's population. As the hours went by, the mood in the hotel suite became more and more charged. "I went up to the suite," says Peter Rinfret, one of McCain's national finance cochairs. "He had a private function in his suite—for the senior campaign staff, senior campaign volunteers, the finance committee, and his family. Everybody was standing there. He was coming in and out of the living room, and they're letting certain press people in. And then came the official announcement—I think MSNBC broke it—that he had won by 21 points, some huge number. Brian Williams broke it. The place just turned into pandemonium. McCain threw his arms around Cindy and hugged her, and then he started hugging everybody. Everybody was hugging everybody. Everybody was screaming, yelling. Then all the networks started announcing. CNN. ABC. NBC. After that, it just sort of became a roller coaster."

As the night went on, McCain waited for Bush to make his concession speech so he could go downstairs and make his acceptance speech. For days, Bush had been saying he was going to win the primary, and he seemed to mean it. Now it was clear that not only did he not win, he was crushed. In a college auditorium, at what was supposed to be his victory celebration, Bush, appearing on stage with

Laura and his two daughters, tried to put the best face on this disas-trous loss. Saying McCain had run "a really good race," Bush added: "He spent more time in this great state than any of the other candi-dates, and it paid off. Tonight is his night and the night of his supporters. And we all congratulate him." Then he went on, "New Hampshire has long been known as a bump in the road for front-runners. And this year is no exception. The road to the Republican nomination and the White House is a long road. Mine will go through all 50 states, and I intend it to end at 1600 Pennsylvania Avenue."

Not long after Bush finished, McCain headed downstairs to make his speech. In the descending elevator, McCain was surrounded by his top staff and advisers. At one point, he looked over at Peter Rinfret and said in a calm, stoic voice, "Well, now the toughest part is to come." Still, he was thrilled. "He was very pumped in the elevator," Ben Davol says. "He had that big grin on his face and he was very pumped, very determined. There was never a tinge of, 'God, I won this thing.' It was always, 'I'm glad we won. We were right to win. We need to win.' There is a difference there. Sometimes you go into a game and you think, 'I don't know if I am going to win.' It wasn't a matter of the senator winning because he wanted to win. He wanted to win because he felt it was right for him to win for the country. That he had the ideas, the thoughts, the background and the enthusi-asm to really change Washington and change the culture."

When McCain arrived downstairs and stopped at the doorway to the ballroom, he looked into the room and couldn't believe what he saw. "When I tell you the ballroom was beyond packed, I mean beyond packed," Rinfret says. "It was obscene. Then McCain came in and it was insanity. Sheer insanity. The place went absolutely bonkers. Sheer unmitigated pandemonium. I am not sure there were that many dry eyes in the whole place. It was a feeling like none of us had ever had. It was a moment I will never forget as long as I live. Here you had Bush—a guy who had raised $75 million and was backed by the entire party. And little old John McCain doesn't beat him by two or three points—he blows him out!"

Others in the room were just as overwhelmed. "It was just very electric," says Phil Pulizzi, who worked with the campaign as an advance man. "The feeling in the air, and the feeling among those people, was electric. The idea McCain could beat the leader—all the work for a year and a half, two years, coming together and winning New Hampshire that night—that was just very electric. To be in his presence on a night like that was very special. I will never forget that night for the rest of my life."

Nor would Orson Swindle, the man who had slept next to McCain for 18 months in the Hanoi Hilton. "I am on that door where John is to come in on the right side," Swindle says. "Bud Day is there with several other former POWs. We are the first people John sees when he walks in, and he just has this stunned look on his face. We all got choked up. It was an emotional moment, an incredible moment. To think where we had been and the unlikely probability that we would ever be where we were. Just the leap—from the bad days in Hanoi to that moment. . . ."

McCain started his acceptance speech by saying, "Thank you. Thank you. Thank you. Thank you." The victory was by 18 percentage points, which represented a 40,000-vote advantage in a race that brought out 225,000 voters. McCain got 49 percent of the vote to Bush's 31 percent. (Forbes received 13 percent; Keyes, 6 percent; and Bauer, 1 percent.) "We have sent a powerful message to Washington that change is coming," McCain said. "This is a good thing. And it is the beginning of the end of the truth-twisting politics of Bill Clinton and Al Gore."

As McCain made his speech, many in the crowd still had trouble absorbing the moment. For McCain's family, the whole night had a surreal, fantasy-like quality. The McCains simply could not believe what was happening. "I was standing, looking at the TV," Ben Davol says. "McCain's brother Joe was next to me looking the other way. His sister was on my other side. And then they flash across the screen 'McCain Wins!' I turned and I said, 'Mr. McCain, it looks like your brother is going to be President of the United States. Look at that.' Now the brother is really hyper. He's wild. He goes at, like, a million miles an hour. He looked at me and he said—I'll never forget, these were his exact words—'This, this is better than sex!' I said to him, 'Better than sex?' He said, 'Absolutely!'"

Following his victory speech and the myriad media appearances, McCain made his way to the airport where he, Cindy, his family, and his entourage boarded an airplane to fly to South Carolina. The battle there was going to be so intense that he decided to skip the upcoming Delaware primary, which was going to be held a week after the New Hampshire primary. But if he won in South Carolina, that victory would set him up to win the next two primaries, in Michigan and Arizona. Should he then do well in the primaries in Virginia and Washington state, he would be a formidable power on the first real day of reckoning—politically speaking, that is: March 7, Super Tuesday. But he had to win South Carolina. If he didn't, he could continue, but he would lack the red-hot momentum he needed to challenge the campaign of George W. Bush, not to mention the Republican Party establishment. So McCain felt hopeful when, at three o'clock in the morning, he landed in Greer, South Carolina, to discover that the hangar where a rally had been planned was jam-packed with supporters, many of them students happily partying to the ear-splitting rock music pounding through the cavernous room.

"We just came down from making history in the state of New Hampshire tonight," McCain told the cheering crowd, one not unlike the mob he encountered later that morning when he arrived for a rally in a gymnasium at the Presbyterian College in Clinton. "Cindy and I are feeling wonderfully refreshed after both hours of sleep," he said. Cindy was standing by his side as she often did now at rallies like this one. Later that day, McCain would also be happy about his newly energized fund-raising capabilities. In the first 24 hours after he was declared a winner at seven o'clock on Tuesday night, his campaign received $450,000 from the public.

9

"THE DIRTIEST RACE I'VE EVER SEEN"

McCain may or may not have known it at the time, but the next 18 days of his life would determine his political future. His lopsided victory in the New Hampshire primary had stunned the Republican Party and confounded the Bush campaign. If he could pull off a victory—even a squeaker—in South Carolina, the damage to the Bush effort would be enormous, perhaps lethal. That was exactly what Mike Murphy had said, all those months ago, when he met with McCain in his Capitol Hill office. So, as McCain prepared to spend 12 or 13 of the next 18 days in South Carolina, he felt hopeful that he could take the message that had played so well in New Hampshire and sell it to the South. If he could do that—appeal to Southern voters—there was no stopping him.

Not surprisingly, McCain was as excited about politics as he had ever been. In New Hampshire, he had gone up against the considerable forces of the Bush campaign and the Republican Party apparatus, and he had won *big!* The unqualified joy he felt on primary night propelled him on as he got ready for the battle in South Carolina. He knew it would be a battle too. He was not naive. To underestimate the determination of Bush and the party would have been foolish. So McCain did not buy, on face value, the comments Karl Rove made to the *New York Times* on February 2, the day after the most humiliating defeat through which Bush had ever lived. "There will be no change in the governor's message," the *Times* said in paraphrasing Rove's remarks in the immediate wake of the Bush loss, "but much more of the personal campaigning and question-and-answer sessions that worked so well for McCain in [New Hampshire]." No change in message; just a change in style—that's what Rove was saying the campaign needed. Nowhere in his comments did Rove say what the Bush campaign was really about to do: go ugly.

But first, even though he had built his campaign on the idea that he was a "compassionate conservative," Bush felt the need to play up the fact that, truth be told, he was a lot more conservative than he was compassionate—a concept that would go over well in South Carolina. Rove's remarks were just hitting the papers on Wednesday morning when Bush made a campaign stop that would set the tone for the fight for South Carolina. Knowing how important it was for voters to view him as being conservative in a state where its senior senator had been the ultraconservative Strom Thurmond for as long as anyone could remember, and where locals proudly pointed out that the first shot of the Civil War was fired in South Carolina, Bush started his two and a half weeks of campaigning in the state by making a speech at Bob Jones University, an institution in which the faculty and student body come from the far-right Christian movement. There was a family precedent for this particular campaign stop: Bush's father had appeared at Bob Jones in 1988 to shore up *his* credentials as a conservative.

Before an audience of 5,000 students and faculty—attendance at the speech was required by the school—Bush seemed undeterred by his crushing loss in New Hampshire. "My spirits are high, I feel great," he told his audience. "I feel good about my life, about my chances of becoming president." Then he did what he had come to do: He identified himself as the real conservative in his race with McCain. Calling himself "the conservative candidate," Bush all but labeled McCain a closet Democrat for daring to question Bush's proposed tax cut. "It's bad enough when Democrats make these arguments against meaningful tax cuts," Bush said, only slightly off-message—or so it seemed—for a religious group. "It's worse when Republicans, like my chief rival in this state, use them. It's worse because our party ought not to be reflecting these arguments; it ought to be rejecting them."

Bush then zeroed in on his target: McCain. "We have a different approach to government," Bush said. "Our goal is to spread opportunity, not resentment; our goal is to unite Americans in prosperity, not divide them with distrust." To make his point—that he, not McCain, was the conservative—Bush, according to the *Washington Post*, used the word "conservative" six times in 32 seconds, in one particular passage of the speech. Giving a speech at Bob Jones University about conservative values certainly made sense; few schools in America were more conservative. All of Bush's talk about uniting America and fostering trust was out of place there. The values of Bob Jones were founded on two notions: An important division existed between races, and the Protestant religion, especially the far-right-wing version of that religion, was superior to any other.

Underscoring the school's conservative Christian tenets, the Bob Jones administrators had, for some time now, banned interracial dating on campus and endorsed the teachings of previous school officials who had called the Catholic Church a "satanic cult." Because the university embraced the religious radical-right, many politicians refused to appear there. But Bush, who spoke to the faculty and students in a friendly if slightly dull-witted manner, didn't seem to mind being at Bob Jones at all. He apparently didn't care that a school official once referred to the Pope as "the greatest danger we face today," or that, in the 1970s, the school had lost federal funding because it refused to admit African-American students. Bush's agenda was to portray himself as a conservative in a state that was decidedly

conservative—a state he desperately needed to win to get his fledgling presidential campaign back on track. Making a speech at Bob
Jones more than filled that bill. After all, Bush's father had had to do
the same, which was why George H. W. Bush was willing to ignore
the fact that someone associated with the school had once called
him "a devil." At a news conference after the speech, George W. Bush
reiterated the day's theme of endorsing conservatism when he said, "I
am the right. I am the conservative candidate." Then, as if to hit that
note one more time, Bush accepted an endorsement, on Wednesday
afternoon, from Dan Quayle.

On one level, Bush's plan in South Carolina was simple: win by
appealing to the religious conservatives. In some polls, 45 percent of
the state's likely voters described themselves as religious conservatives. It had worked for Bush's father in 1988. He won the national
election because he got support from the religious conservatives
who viewed as repugnant the prospect of voting for Michael
Dukakis, a bonafide Massachusetts liberal. Because he knew that, at
some point, he would have to reach out to the religious right, Bush
had selected, as one of his first hires, Ralph Reed, whose standing in
the religious conservative community was beyond reproach.

Bush had roughed up McCain on Wednesday, but things really
got ugly on Thursday, when a new poll conducted by John Zogby revealed that Bush was trailing McCain in South Carolina by five percentage points: 44 to 39. At a rally at the town courthouse in Sumter,
Bush took his place on the steps beside a man who had one of the
most controversial reputations of anyone in the military. The chairman of the National Vietnam and Gulf War Veterans Coalition,
J. Thomas Burch had made a name for himself by criticizing politicians from Ronald Reagan to George H. W. Bush to John McCain.
On that day, as he stood surrounded by other veterans, some of them
retired generals and Medal of Honor winners, Burch took aim
squarely at McCain. In presenting what he considered an analysis of
McCain's record on military issues, Burch told the crowd of 350 that
McCain did not favor assistance for veterans who suffered from

Agent Orange and Gulf War Syndrome, and that McCain was "the leading opponent" of efforts to help veterans' families learn about MIAs in Vietnam. Saying that McCain "had the power to help the veterans," Burch summed up by uttering a line that would infuriate McCain, his friends, and his supporters. "Senator McCain has abandoned the veterans," Burch said as Bush stood silently beside him, a smile frozen on his face. "He came home from Vietnam and forgot us."

When Bush spoke that day, he didn't let up. He actually told the audience he—not McCain—would make the better commander-in-chief. He did not mention a detail from his youth—how he avoided active military duty in 1968, the year he graduated from Yale, by allowing his father to get him into the Texas Air National Guard. "We must have a commander-in-chief who understands the role of the military," Bush said. The audience and the traveling press corps were stunned by the display. Here Bush was coming to a state where 400,000 veterans lived—more veterans per capita than in any other state in the country—and he was challenging McCain, a man who had built the very basis of his campaign on his military record, on McCain's history on military issues. It was a stunning example of what is so hard to pull off in politics: damaging one's opponent by attacking his strength. To make sure this was what Bush was up to, reporters peppered him with questions at a press conference following the rally. Did Bush endorse Burch's comments? one journalist asked. "These men have their opinion," Bush said, referring to Burch and the other veterans; "they have stated their opinion. The thing I respect is, they have chosen me to be their candidate." Then Bush added, almost as an aside, "John McCain served our country very well; he was a warrior on behalf of America."

That afternoon, the McCain campaign answered Burch's charges by distributing to reporters a document detailing some of McCain's accomplishments on veterans' issues. In 1991, he had cosponsored the Agent Orange Act, which provided disability benefits for veterans afflicted with the debilitating medical condition—a fact that tended to dispute Burch's contention that McCain had waffled on the subject of Agent Orange. In Arizona, McCain had helped found a Gulf War Syndrome support group—further proof that McCain was sensitive to the medical needs of veterans. In 1997, McCain had sponsored a law that provided medical and dental care for retired and active military personnel suffering from Gulf War Syndrome. Later, the McCain camp, still furious, called Burch "a discredited trial lawyer" and demanded an apology. It never came.

The McCain campaign may have had the facts on its side, but politics is often more about impressions than about facts. As if following Burch's lead, individual veterans and veterans' groups took to the Internet to attack McCain, frequently without supporting facts, on the part of his life that was vitally important to him—his participation in the military. On February 4, on a Web site called "The Manchurian Candidate," someone claiming to have the name William Cooper posted a piece in which he argued that McCain *was* the Manchurian candidate, an allusion to a 1950s Frank Sinatra film in which a politician is brainwashed to take certain actions based on cues to which he has been programmed to respond. "I knew Senator John McCain's father when Admiral John S. McCain Jr. was the Commander-in-Chief of the Pacific (CINCPAC)," Cooper wrote, as a way of establishing his credentials on the subject of John McCain. "I sincerely believe that Admiral McCain, if he were alive, would tell you exactly what I am about to tell you. Admiral McCain always put his country first and foremost above all other issues.

"The fact that Senator McCain was shot down and captured over North Vietnam does not make him a hero. The goal of any pilot is to not get shot down. The fact that he was a Prisoner of War does not make him a hero. The goal of all military personnel is to not become a POW. . . . However, Senator John McCain was tortured and brainwashed by the communists for over five years. Regardless of what you may have been told, or what you may believe, no one, not anyone on this earth can withstand torture and brainwashing without breaking down, giving up information, and permanent damage to the mind. . . . Many brainwashing victims become fractured personalities programmed to perform some task or tasks in the future. Their programming can be activated by audio, visual, or other types of stimulation. These are facts, not conjecture. . . . I doubt that Senator McCain knows the extent of the damage done to his mind . . . but Senator John McCain is, without any doubt, the real Manchurian Candidate. When I look at his voting record in the United States Senate, I do not see a conservative Republican. I see a record that reveals a closet socialist, a proponent of the New World Order."

Cooper's attack may have sounded extreme, but it was representative of a type of character assassination that was being directed toward McCain. In its own way, the Burch appearance reflected the same drastic negative bias as Cooper's posting. Burch's feelings were given legitimacy because Bush took the stage with him. As it happened, the reaction to the Burch episode was quick and, in certain cases, emotional. Furious at what he saw as baseless criticism of McCain, carried out by a surrogate as Bush stood and watched, John Kerry organized the other Vietnam combat veterans in the Senate to write a letter of protest to Bush.

On February 4, Kerry, Max Cleland of Georgia, Bob Kerrey of Nebraska, and Chuck Robb of Virginia (all Democrats) and Chuck Hagel of Nebraska (a Republican) signed a letter written on United States Senate stationery in which they said, "[W]e are writing to express our dismay at the misinformed accusations leveled by your surrogate, J. Thomas Burch Jr., regarding our colleague John McCain's commitment to our nation's veterans. These allegations are absolutely false. . . . Indeed, Mr. Burch was a leading critic of President Reagan's and your father's policies on POW/MIA." As for McCain, the five senators declared, "From his courageous efforts on POW/MIA affairs, to his most recent advocacy of decent living standards and adequate compensation for men and women serving in the military today, Senator McCain has earned recognition from his colleagues on both sides of the aisle as a real leader on veterans' issues in the United States Senate. . . . We are familiar with the intensity of political campaigns, but we believe it is inappropriate to associate yourself with those who would impugn John McCain's character and so maliciously distort his record on these critical issues. We hope you will publicly disassociate yourself from these efforts, and apologize to Senator McCain for Mr. Burch's misguided statement made on your behalf."

Fellow POWs who had served with McCain in prison in Vietnam were also offended by the Burch incident. "The first indication we got that things were about to get ugly came," Orson Swindle says, "when a guy I happen to know, Tom Burch—who, as Al Hunt says, claimed to be some titular head of some organization representing veterans—got up there with Bush. I heard what Burch said with his little Green Beret hat on. I think if you looked into his Green Beret experience you might be shocked. When he got up and said in front of God and everybody, with George Bush standing beside him, that John McCain abandoned veterans, I just went berserk. It was just a blatant damn lie. He said McCain abandoned the Vietnam veterans, he abandoned the POWs and the guys left behind. That just infuriated me because I didn't know anybody left behind. None of us knew anybody left behind." Other POWs were just as angered. "What a farce Burch was," Everett Alvarez says. (Only Jim Thompson served longer than Alvarez as an American POW in Vietnam.) "I couldn't believe this guy was out there saying what he said. He was such an opportunist . . . and what a farce. It was all lies, what he was saying about John. I mean, I was there."

On February 4, the same day the senators sent Bush their letter, the Bush campaign began airing a commercial that said a McCain ad attacking the Bush tax plan "isn't true, and McCain knows it." Another new ad was being run by the National Smokers Alliance. The ad questioned McCain's recent claims that he had never voted for a tax increase. The ad said McCain had proposed a huge tax increase, but, because it wasn't passed, he could claim he had never voted for one. He had fought hard for the increase, the ad implied, but Congress had the good sense to shoot it down. "Saying one thing and doing another, that's the real John McCain," the ad said. But what the ad failed to note was that McCain's proposed tax increase was the tax on cigarettes designed to make them so expensive that teenagers would not be able to afford them. Nor did the National Smokers Alliance mention that McCain had waged a crusade against the tobacco industry for years, and that was the real reason tobacco groups opposed him and supported Bush. McCain took the public stand of being amused by the ad. "I'm honored by the attacks by the people who addicted our children and lied to Congress," McCain said at a press conference in Seabrook, South Carolina. "I hope that they will spend more money because that authenticates this crusade of ours to get the influence of special interests out of politics."

That Friday, McCain was scheduled to appear on *The Tonight Show with Jay Leno.* As he drove from the airport to the NBC studios in Burbank, California, accompanied in the limousine by his entourage, McCain, still livid over the Burch appearance and the willingness of the Bush campaign and its surrogates to question McCain's integrity, resolved himself to the reality that it was time to strike back. The New Hampshire primary victory was quickly fading into memory; such was the nature of politics. If he did not hit Bush back, he would look weak and defenseless, the way Bill Bradley did during much of the primary season because he refused to respond to the negative ads run by Al Gore. Therefore, McCain gave Mike Murphy a go-ahead to write a new commercial script—one that would get the Bush campaign's attention. His message to the Bush camp was this: John McCain was no Bill Bradley. Attack McCain and McCain will hit back—with a vengeance.

That night, in a hotel room in San Francisco, Murphy worked on a new script for a McCain commercial that was meant to draw blood. McCain already had a commercial ready to go; it included the line, "Do we really want another president in the White House America can't trust?" That question was meant to compare Bush to

Clinton in the most divisive way possible. Still, asking a question was not as powerful as naming a name. As Murphy sat alone in the hotel room, hunched over his laptop computer, he decided he had no choice but to stop pulling punches. In an hour or so, he had finished a new script, this one with a tag line no one would forget any time soon. Murphy knew McCain was angry enough to name names and accuse Bush of "twisting the truth like Clinton."

On Saturday, McCain had another problem to worry about. For some time, the *Arizona Republic* had been developing an article that might prove to be potentially damaging to McCain. A journalist named Ron Bianchi had been peddling a story that said that McCain was having an affair with actress and singer Connie Stevens, and that, according to Bianchi, "they had met through mobsters." Naturally, the story had a kind of Frank Sinatra/Jack Kennedy/Judith Exner Campbell feel to it, as if McCain had stepped back in time to the days when the Rat Pack ruled Las Vegas and when it was not that unusual, though it was rarely reported in the papers, to see mobsters and politicians socializing in the casinos, their girlfriends in tow.

The McCain story had some problems. First, Bianchi had no evidence that McCain and Stevens were having an affair; only four meetings between the two could be documented, and all of them were public. Second, the story was too sexy for McCain at this stage of his life; in the past, he had certainly been guilty of chasing women, but now, with his commitments and his travel schedule, he didn't have the time or the energy. Still, the *Arizona Republic* had been trying to get the article into print for some weeks, mostly because the story of Bianchi trying to sell his article had become newsworthy. Bianchi, for reasons that were not clear, had ended up dead.

When publication of the article was imminent, the McCain camp felt strongly enough about stopping it to send Rick Davis to Arizona. On that Saturday night, as it became obvious that the paper's editor, Pam Johnson, was going to give the article the green light, Davis arrived at the *Republic's* offices. Standing on a desk in the newsroom, he threatened to sue the paper if Johnson went ahead with the article. But, after Sunday's first two editions had been printed, Johnson gave the go-ahead to run the article. "What you are about to read is a true story fraught with lies," the article began. "It is the factual account of a murder, how it became snarled with presidential politics, Major League Baseball, con games, Hollywood celebrities, Mafia fantasies, media ethics, and a bloody torso." There it was—on the front page of the Sunday *Arizona Republic.* All the McCain camp could do was wait and see what impact, if any, the article about the dead journalist would have on the campaign unfolding in South Carolina.

On Sunday, February 6, as news of the *Arizona Republic* article spread through political gossip channels, Bush sent out his surrogates to pound away at McCain on television. On *Face the Nation* on CBS, Rove described McCain as a "17-year Washington insider whose accomplishments are few and far between" because he "cannot lead people and persuade them to back his agenda." Bush, on the other hand, was "a successful governor of a big state." As for campaign finance reform, Rove said, "Senator McCain portrays himself as an advocate of campaign finance reform, as somebody who is cleaner than anyone else around the table, and yet he has accepted contributions and sought contributions from people with legislation pending before his committee." Meanwhile, Carroll Campbell, the former South Carolina governor who had endorsed Bush, attacked McCain on *Fox News Sunday,* saying, "The fact is that people parade before John McCain's committee and they give him money. He's been flying on some of their jets in the past. . . . [W]hat I see is a man that is talking literally out of both sides of his mouth." (Naturally, Campbell didn't note that Bush had taken twice as many flights on corporate jets as McCain and that some of those jets were owned by corporations that regularly did business with the state of Texas.) Finally, another Bush surrogate, Ralph Reed, hit the airwaves on a different Sunday morning show to say that McCain was "one of the most powerful men in Washington and he has little or nothing to show for it." His point was that McCain was not even successful at being a Washington insider.

With the television appearances of Rove, Campbell, and Reed, the Bush campaign was showing just how affective the use of surrogates could be. Bush himself did not make any of the attacks; he sent out others to carry out the attacks for him. Successful campaigns often use surrogates; that way, a campaign can attack its opponent, while its own candidate appears to remain above the fray.

On Sunday, when McCain made a stop in his home state on his way to Michigan, he mentioned neither the *Republic* article nor the orchestrated assault by the Bush surrogates. At a rally at the Sky Harbor International Airport in Phoenix, McCain told an audience of 250 that he was ready to fight. "We're still the underdog," McCain said. "We're still running an insurgency campaign. But I can't tell you how excited I am." He had reason to be, too. That day, another article in the *Arizona Republic* said early polls indicated McCain had a slight lead in South Carolina. Now, almost a full week into the South Carolina campaign, McCain was doing better than he thought he would. But the early polls did not reflect the full effect of the Bush campaign's new assault on McCain.

Some of the Bush surrogates had appeared on television from Austin, Texas, because the Bush campaign had returned home for the weekend to regroup. From the campaign's point of view, it had been a good week after the disaster of Tuesday, even if the opinion polls did not yet reflect that fact. On Wednesday, Bush had staked out his credentials as a conservative. At the same time, he appealed to the religious-right vote without which he would not win the state. Then, on Thursday, he hit McCain where he lived—on his military service. All the while, Bush seemed like a new candidate. Gone was the unfocused, petulant whiner who openly longed for the comforts of the governor's mansion in Austin while he stumped on a cold and often exhausting campaign trail in New Hampshire, a state he didn't particularly like in the first place. Now, he was upbeat, centered, energized, and motivated; he had a clear and identifiable target: John McCain.

In their strategy sessions over the weekend, Karl Rove and the rest of the Bush staff—Karen Hughes, Joe Albaugh, and others—had come up with another plan of attack. They unveiled it on Monday, February 7, as Bush made appearances in Delaware on the day before the primary in that state. (Bush had no intention of skipping Delaware, regardless of McCain's plans.) In Dover, as he stood before a big blue-and-white banner emblazoned with his new motto, "REFORMER WITH RESULTS," Bush proudly declared he was just what his new motto said he was—a "reformer with results." The slogan was a calculated rip-off of the reform role in which McCain had cast himself from the start of his presidential campaign, but that did not seem to faze Bush one bit.

In fact, Bush had been flirting with the concept during the past few days. On Friday, as he campaigned in Michigan, Bush had begun toying with this new idea: He, not McCain, was the reformer. "I'm the person who has been a reformer," Bush said at one point on the trail. "It's hard to be a reformer if you have spent your entire career in Washington, D.C., which [McCain] has done." Over the weekend, the Bush handlers completed the thought Bush had started to form on Friday. When they met, they decided Bush was not just a reformer, he was a reformer *with results!* But they weren't happy merely stealing McCain's message; they also felt a need to discredit McCain's ability to *claim* he was a reformer. They came up with this: McCain was not a reformer; instead, he was a typical Washington politician who was willing to say anything to get elected. The reformer mantle he embraced was nothing more than a guise to make himself electable, a message he could sell to the public. The evidence they used against McCain was his willingness to accept campaign contributions from corporations that had business before the Commerce Committee, which he chaired. If he had been a *real* reformer, their line of reasoning went, he would not have taken money from companies like Paxson Communications. All during the day on Monday, as if he had been programmed over the weekend in coaching sessions, Bush repeatedly delivered his prepared line about McCain: "He says one thing and does another."

When a reporter asked Bush if he was calling McCain a hypocrite, Bush replied, again as if he had been anticipating the fairly obvious question, "That's your word." Then what word would Bush use? the reporter wanted to know. "Washington," Bush said.

When pressed about why he should be considered a "reformer with results," Bush insisted he had brought to Texas, among other things, tort reform and tax cuts. "I'm going to remind people that of the two of us running," Bush said, "I'm the reformer with results." In his own way, Bush addressed the reason why his camp had to come up with this new campaign strategy, which portrayed him as a reformer. At an American Legion post in Dover, Delaware, Bush said he lost New Hampshire because he allowed McCain to "define me"—a mistake he was not going to make in South Carolina. "I'm gonna take it to him," Bush told his audience; "I'm not going to let that happen again." After that appearance, Bush seemed to underscore his new resolve when he met with a group of reporters and quipped, "Ya'll haven't seen the Barbara Bush in me yet." Part of his allowing the "Barbara Bush" in him to come out meant this: In defining himself, he would also undercut his opponent's strength. Specifically, he did this by saying he was exactly like McCain, only better.

After hearing that Bush was calling himself a "reformer with results," McCain could not help responding to Bush's over-the-weekend conversion. "I understand Governor Bush is now a reformer," McCain told the reporters who were traveling with him in Michigan. "If so, it's his first day on the job. He should join me in going to the heart of what's wrong with the system today, and that's campaign finance reform." McCain had challenged Bush on this issue because he knew Bush had used the current fund-raising system to amass more money for his campaign than any politician in the history of the United States. Campaign finance reform would be among the last topics Bush would ever take up as a cause for which to fight.

On Tuesday, McCain warned that he would hit Bush hard if Bush didn't stop his "character assassination" of him—that is, his determination to question McCain's honesty and integrity. "We're going to respond harder than we're hit," McCain said as he talked to reporters on the Straight Talk Express on a day when a new poll showed that the race in South Carolina was a dead heat. "That's an old tactic that we used in warfare." When the Bush campaign unleashed a new attack ad that charged that "McCain solicits money from lobbyists with interests before his committee and pressures agencies on behalf of contributors," McCain, true to his warning, answered with two TV ads. The first one slammed Bush. "This is George Bush's ad promising America he'd run a positive campaign," the ad's narrator said as Bush's own voice came on to say, "A campaign that is hopeful and optimistic and very positive." Then the ad showed "The Handshake" in New Hampshire, when Bush and McCain agreed not to engage in negative campaigning. "This is George Bush shaking hands with John McCain," the narrator said, "promising not to run a negative campaign." Next the ad showed another clip, which the narrator explained by saying, "This is George Bush's new negative ad, attacking John McCain and distorting his position." Then came the tag line: "Do we really want another politician in the White House America can't trust?"

The allusion to Clinton was obvious. But on that Tuesday the McCain campaign wasn't finished. The second ad hit Bush even harder than the first. McCain was now willing to run Murphy's ad in which he named names. The allusions to Clinton were gone; instead, McCain directly compared his opponent to the one man, Clinton, currently most loathed by Republicans. "I guess it was bound to happen," McCain said in an ad that became notorious almost instantly. "Governor Bush's campaign is getting desperate with a negative ad campaign against me." Finally, McCain spoke directly into the camera as he made the charge that Bush "twists the truth like Clinton. We're all pretty tired of that." It was a move that changed the direction of that year's Republican primary process. After McCain had made his accusation against Bush, everything was different.

On February 8, as the contest in South Carolina became even uglier, Bush got a much-needed boost: He won the Delaware primary. There was, however, good news for McCain as well. He had not campaigned in Delaware at all, but he still got 25 percent of the vote. Steve Forbes, who campaigned heavily in a state where he had won the primary in 1996, mustered 20 percent of the vote—a showing that, only hours after the polls had closed, made him realize he had to rethink whether he should remain in the race. Bush got 51 percent of the vote—not an overwhelming result, but good enough to win. Still, because McCain had not challenged him, the win somehow didn't count as much. South Carolina's Primary Day, February 19, became even more important.

On Wednesday, the day after the Delaware primary, Forbes dropped out of the race, as many expected he would, but he refused to endorse either Bush or McCain. He had spent $76 million of his own money—$34 million in 1999 alone—and he had been able to place no better than third in a primary he had won four years before. With Forbes gone, Bush and McCain focused on trying to woo any former Forbes supporters in South Carolina. The Bush campaign's inner circle, after deciding that this could be done best by tearing down McCain, released a new ad with a message not unlike McCain's "do we want someone in the White House we can't trust" ad. The new ad said that McCain "promised a clean campaign, then attacked Governor Bush with misleading ads. McCain says he's the only candidate who can beat Gore on campaign finance, but news investigations reveal McCain solicits money from lobbyists with interests before his committee and pressures agencies on behalf of contributors. He attacks special interests, but the *Wall Street Journal* reports, 'McCain's campaign is crawling with lobbyists.'"

This was not the only new attack ad directed at McCain that aired during the second week of the campaign in South Carolina. An antiabortion lobby launched an ad that began by asking, "Who is Warren Rudman?" Most of the mainstream population of South

Carolina didn't know that Rudman was a distinguished former senator from New Hampshire who was a cochair of the McCain presidential effort. That, of course, would have been one way to identify him. Instead, the ad said Rudman was someone in favor of abortion rights whom McCain wanted to name attorney general. "Don't vote for John McCain," the ad concluded with a directness that seemed harsh and brutal. After all, political advertising, even when it is negative, usually tries to end on a positive note. It is rare for an ad to conclude with an admonition that the listener or viewer should *not* do something. But that was just how ugly the battle in South Carolina was becoming.

On Wednesday, the National Right to Life Committee endorsed Bush even as another antiabortion group, South Carolina Citizens for Life, which had endorsed Bush some time before, put up an ad that said, "If you want a strong pro-life president, then don't vote for John McCain." This support was in keeping with what the Bush campaign believed it needed to win, for, in the second week of the campaign in South Carolina, the Bush organization, trying to appeal to the religious far-right the way it did when Bush spoke at Bob Jones University in the previous week, produced, as surrogates, Ralph Reed, Roberta Combs, and Pat Robertson, all past and present principals of the Christian Coalition. The surrogates asked voters, especially those who might have supported Forbes, not to vote for McCain. In one automated call, Robertson, the founder of the Christian Coalition, warned voters that they could "protect babies and restore religious freedom" by not supporting McCain. Robertson could have just as easily praised Bush; oddly he went out of his way to attack McCain. This ad was merely one example of a barrage of negative campaigning directed—sometimes personally, it seemed—at McCain. At McCain rallies, plants in the audience would walk up to supporters of McCain and whisper that McCain was no hero. Phone banks put out calls charging that McCain was a traitor because he had wanted to normalize relations with Vietnam. Then there were the e-mails. One group even suggested that McCain had fathered illegitimate children.

"It was a black child," a McCain insider says. "They actually used the word *nigger*. The calls said McCain had a nigger baby. There were other push-calls that said McCain had given his wife venereal disease, which caused her to have to have a hysterectomy."

"In South Carolina," Frank Rich wrote in the *New York Times*, "Bush supporters—none of them affiliated with his campaign, we're told—circulated fliers calling Mr. McCain the 'fag candidate' even as Mr. Bush subtly reinforced that message by indicating he wouldn't hire openly gay people for his administration. A professor at Bob Jones University distributed email accusing Mr. McCain of choosing 'to sire children without marriage.' (The McCains have an adopted daughter from Bangladesh—from a Mother Teresa orphanage, no less.) Bob Jones IV wrote a cover story for a rag called *World* magazine slapping around the McCain family. Mr. Bush had nothing to do with this 'religio-political sleaze,' as William Safire described it, either, though *World* is edited by Marvin Olasky, the sometime Bush adviser who invented, if you please, 'compassionate conservatism.'"

On February 10, when a reporter asked Bush why he couldn't "state his positions . . . and just forget about McCain," Bush shot back, "Remember what happened in the past"—meaning New Hampshire. "I was defined as the insider. I learned my lesson."

It was Thursday morning, February 10, and the town hall meeting was proceeding like so many others McCain had had during his presidential campaign. This one was being held in the Fine Arts Center at the University of South Carolina in the modest town of Spartanburg. McCain had given a 20-minute talk on education before opening up the event to a question-and-answer period. Microphone in hand, he was answering questions when a woman, later identified as Donna Duren, stood up and told McCain what had happened to her 14-year-old son, a Boy Scout named Chris, the night before. "My son has found himself a hero," Duren said, meaning McCain. "But yesterday, [he] was push-polled. He was so upset. I don't know who called him. I don't know who's responsible. But he was so upset when he came upstairs and he said, 'Mom, someone told me that Senator McCain is a cheat and a liar and a fraud.' And he was almost in tears. I was so livid last night I couldn't sleep."

As the woman began to cry, McCain became furious. At first, his anger took over and he couldn't speak. Then he muttered, in a low, hushed voice, "The disillusionment of a young boy is something I think any of them, even as crass and as base as some of the people can get in this business, would be ashamed of." After a moment, he was able to regain his composure enough to complete the town hall meeting, but his heart wasn't in it. He had been shaken by what Duren had said. As soon as he thanked the audience, McCain went over to talk to Duren personally and, embracing her, promised to phone her son that afternoon.

Outside, McCain called an impromptu news conference. He started by saying he was so rattled by what had happened he could not answer questions about education, which was supposed to have been the focus of the town meeting. Instead, he wanted to discuss negative campaigning and what he was going to do about it. "I'm calling on my good friend George Bush to stop this now," McCain said, clearly furious. "Stop this now! He comes from a good family. He knows better than this. He should stop it. I'll pull down every negative ad that I have. . . . Let's treat voters of South Carolina with some respect." He paused, then continued. "What's being done to the people of South Carolina is being done with disrespect. I've made my position clear. I'm making it very clear. Take down these ads. But most importantly as well, stop this sort of thing. We're not in the business of harming young people."

When the press conference ended, McCain boarded the Straight Talk Express and headed for the next campaign stop. Thirty minutes later, he spoke by telephone with a reporter for the

Washington Post. "Frankly, it's the first time in the campaign I've been a little rattled," McCain said about the Duren episode, "because of the way the woman spoke about it and the harm it did to her son. That's not what political campaigns are supposed to be about."

As the day wore on into evening and McCain continued with his campaign stops, he thought about what he should do. He had many options, but the one with which he felt most comfortable was the one that was most risky. He would pull all of his negative ads, just as he had offered to, and would challenge Bush to do the same. If Bush refused and kept running his negative ads, the damage done to McCain could be enormous. On the other hand, McCain could get an unexpected boost by making an unconventional move and running only positive ads when he was being attacked by a barrage of negative ones. By the end of the day, McCain had made up his mind. He would announce his decision that next day, in New York City, following the fund-raiser that Herb Allison, his national finance chairman, had scheduled at the Grand Hyatt adjacent to Grand Central Station.

As McCain looked out onto the huge gathering of reporters in a meeting room next to the ballroom in the Grand Hyatt, where his fund-raiser had just been held, he was still shaken by the scene Duren had made at the town meeting. Today had been a spectacular day, so far, for McCain. When he arrived at a $1,000-per-person VIP reception before the fund-raiser, he was greeted with a hero's welcome. The crowd, jammed into the meeting room where he now stood, had pushed in on him. In the crush of people, he could see, over here, the actor Rip Torn; over there, Peter King, the Long Island congressman who was thinking about breaking ranks with the Republican Party and shifting his allegiance from Bush to McCain. After the VIP reception, he had attended the luncheon, a barbecue hoedown in honor of the upcoming primary—it was called the South Carolina BBQ Lunch—where he was surrounded by people like Peter Rinfret, Georgette Mosbacher, and his daughter Sidney, who, in her job at Capitol Records, had become a celebrity of sorts now that her father was so famous.

But the upbeat tenor of the day faded when McCain started talking to the reporters about his decision to pull his negative ads, no matter what the ramifications might be. "I called a meeting last night and told my staff we can't be involved in this kind of thing," he said soberly. "I urge George Bush to do the same thing. I hope he will be able to recognize the damage this kind of thing does to the electorate." McCain admitted his move "defies a lot of conventional wisdom and I know that some may view this as not an intelligent approach to winning the primary. But the most important thing to me at the end of the campaign is that my kids, my children, would be proud of me." Finally, McCain unveiled the new ad he *would* be running in South Carolina. Entitled "Courage," it equated the struggle he endured while he was a POW with the battle he had waged in Washington to pass campaign finance reform. Courage, the ad implied, was what motivated him in both instances.

Bush responded right away. "My reaction is," he told reporters in Charleston, "his ads trying to link me to Bill Clinton didn't work. The people of this state don't appreciate it and neither do I." His answer to McCain's challenge for him to pull his negative ads? "It's an old Washington trick. It's a bait-and-switch trick." In other words, no, Bush would not be pulling his attack ads. Just to prove it, he unveiled another one that day in South Carolina. In it, Bush looked straight into the camera and said in an unhappy but controlled voice, "When John McCain compared me to Bill Clinton and said I was untrustworthy, that was over the line. Disagree with me, fine, but do not challenge my integrity."

Across the country, in Arizona, McCain got another message from the Bush campaign. Jane Hull, the Arizona governor and a Bush surrogate (her son was chairman of the Bush state campaign), went out of her way to give a quote to the press about what was starting to look like a distinct possibility: a primary victory for

McCain in his home state on February 22. As a way of downplaying the win long before it happened, Hull said McCain had to win Arizona by 30 points or the victory should be disregarded. "There is a track record that says you ought to be winning your home state by a huge, huge margin," Hull said. "And I don't think there is anyone who is claiming that that margin is going to be huge in Arizona."

Message to McCain from the Bush campaign: Even Arizona isn't safe for you.

At a campaign stop on February 12, a quick exchange, caught on camera when Bush thought he was not being watched by the press, revealed much about what was going on in the South Carolina race. Unaware that a C-SPAN camera was rolling, Bush began joking candidly with a state senator attending his rally. "You all haven't even hit [McCain's] soft spots," the state senator, Mike Fair, said to Bush, who then quipped, "I'm going to, I'm going to. . . . I'm not going to do it on TV."

In the coming days, when the short unscripted bit of dialogue was analyzed, the media determined that Bush was admitting that his campaign was behind calls like the one Duren had received. The origin of a push-poll call is impossible to trace; unless the caller records it, there is no proof that the call even existed. Should someone record a call, how could it be shown that the Bush campaign was behind the call in the first place? For Bush, the damage done to McCain could be substantial, yet McCain's ability to establish, beyond a shadow of a doubt, that Bush was behind the calls was remote. McCain knew the power of negative campaigning. On the day Bush made his off-the-cuff remark to Mike Fair, McCain addressed his decision to pull his negative ads as he spoke to the ever-present gaggle of reporters on the Straight Talk Express. "We're rolling the dice," he said. "I have no illusion about the impact of the ceaseless barrage of negative ads." It was a gamble, apparently, that Bush was not willing to take.

On Sunday, February 13, after the paper had been flooded with complaints about the article it published about the murder of Ron Bianchi, the *Arizona Republic* tried to justify the decision to print the piece when one of its columnists reasoned, "[The] editor ran the story because it was a compelling, highly readable tale of a Valley man's life and brutal death [and] because a presidential aspirant from Arizona was interviewed by Gila County sheriff's investigators about a murder." That Sunday, 1,000 miles away in Atlanta, McCain was not focused on the fallout from the *Republic*'s article about Bianchi. He was dealing with the fact that, at a book-signing for *Faith of My Fathers* at Peachtree Battle Shopping Center, 1,000 people had shown up and turned the occasion into a campaign rally. After the book-signing, McCain went to a fund-raiser hosted by Lewis Jordan, one of the founders of ValuJet Airlines, at the Grand Hyatt. Supporters paid $250 each for a seat.

The next day, February 14, McCain accused Bush of "savagery" for claiming that McCain was inconsistent in his voting record in the Senate; specifically, that McCain now said he was not in favor of public financing of congressional races but had voted for it five times in the past. "Five times, he voted to use your taxes to pay for political campaigns," the ad said. "That's not real reform." Bush saw this as an example of McCain's hypocrisy, though he was careful never to use that particular word. Bush returned to South Carolina late on Monday morning after spending part of the weekend in Austin, where he rested before the final week of campaigning in South Carolina. The state was quickly becoming a must-win for both candidates. At a press conference in Saluda, Bush responded to McCain's charge by saying, "How can he call it savagery if the man made five votes, legitimate votes, on the floor of the Senate? It's not savagery. It's what we call full exposure, full disclosure."

And so began the last week of the South Carolina contest, a week that saw the anti-McCain forces in full swing. In the final days of campaigning in South Carolina, ugly ads continued to appear on radio and television. Bush spent $6 million on his media buy in South Carolina—a staggering sum of money for a state primary. In one radio commercial, former governor Carroll Campbell implied that McCain, to quote the *New York Times'* description of what he said, "is the tool of a Democratic plot." The former governor said: "Send the Clinton-Gore Democrats a message Saturday. Vote for the man they're desperately trying to stop: George W. Bush." In another ad paid for by an antiabortion group, McCain, it was implied, secretly supported abortion rights. The tag line: "So if you want a strong pro-life president, don't vote for John McCain."

The push-poll calls and mass mailings continued as well. The National Right to Life Committee sent out a mass mailing that claimed McCain "voted repeatedly to use tax dollars for experiments that use body parts from aborted babies." Beginning on February 14, the Bush campaign unveiled a phone call with a message taped by Congressman Henry Hyde of Illinois, a figure made popular on the national political stage by his involvement in the Clinton impeachment. Saying that Bush had "a strong pro-life record in Texas," a state that now, thanks to Bush, had "a parental notification bill that is a model for the nation," Hyde declared, "It has been suggested that changes be made to the party platform on the life issue"—a shot at McCain, who had made just such a recommendation. Hyde concluded, "As president, [Bush] will be a defender of the unborn. He has my full support." Hyde's recorded message was also used by the Bush campaign in a 60-second radio commercial.

But what was impressive was the sheer volume of the ads being played on radio and television. In the last week of the campaign, it was all but impossible to turn on the radio or television and *not* hear an anti-McCain ad. Local call-in radio programs were also flooded with callers. Many of them were believed to be coordinated by the Bush campaign in the same way that whisperers at McCain rallies subtly suggested he was no hero. Even Rush Limbaugh, with his massive national audience, got into the act; day after day in the weeks of the South Carolina primary campaign, Limbaugh pounded away on McCain and used talking points that were unusually similar to those of the Bush campaign.

The rancor between the two camps was evident on Tuesday, February 15, just four days before Primary Day, when Bush and McCain, along with Alan Keyes, the only other candidate left in the race, appeared live on a 90-minute nationally televised debate moderated by Larry King. With all four men sitting elbow to elbow around a table in a television studio, the feel of the debate was much more casual and informal than previous debates had been. King asked questions about a variety of topics—religion, taxes, foreign policy, national security—but the most lively exchange concerned the negative campaigning that had come to define the primary race.

"He ran an ad that equated me to Bill Clinton," Bush said about McCain at one point. "He questioned my trustworthiness. . . . That's about as low a blow as you can give in a Republican primary."

"I was beat up very badly by all of his surrogates," McCain hit back. "Turn on the radio, turn on the television—unfortunately now, pick up the telephone—and you will hear a negative attack on John McCain. But let me tell you what really went over the line. Governor Bush had an event, and he paid for it, and stood next to a spokesman for a fringe veterans group. That fringe veteran said that John McCain had abandoned the veterans. I don't know if you can understand this, George, but that really hurt. That really hurt."

"Yeah," Bush said softly, as if under his breath.

Then McCain glared at Bush and said, "You should be ashamed of sponsoring an event with that man." He was referring to Burch.

"Don't compare me to Bill Clinton," Bush said, and then added, "That man was not speaking for me. . . . If you want to know my opinion about you, John, you served our country strongly and admirably. But if you're going to hold me responsible for what people for me say, I'm going to do the same for you. And let me give you one example. Warren Rudman said about the Christian Coalition that they're bigots. I know you don't believe that."

"He's entitled to his opinion," McCain answered.

"So is this man," Bush said, meaning Burch.

When McCain said he had taken down all of his negative ads, Bush, reaching inside his suit coat, suddenly produced a printed flier from his inside pocket and started to wave it in the air.

"That is not my campaign," McCain said.

"It says, 'Paid for by McCain Committee,'" Bush replied.

Then Keyes, who seemed to be the odd man out during much of the evening, chimed in. "Is this kind of pointless squabbling what we want them [the viewers] to see?" he said, to the surprise of both Bush and McCain. "We have a lot more important things to discuss. We are talking about electing the President of the United States. All I'm sitting here listening to is these two guys going on about ads."

On Wednesday, part of the flap over who won the debate—there was really no clear winner—was thwarted by Gary Bauer's decision to endorse McCain. Standing alongside McCain at a rally at Furman University in Greenville two weeks after he had dropped out of the race, Bauer, whose conservative credentials—former adviser to Ronald Reagan and former head of the Family Research Council—made him extremely valuable to McCain in a state as conservative as South Carolina, said he had chosen to support McCain because "he is our best shot." Bauer may have said publicly that he would work for McCain because he felt McCain, not Bush, could most easily win the White House in the fall, but his friend William Kristol, another authentic conservative, would tell the *Washington Post* that Bauer had decided to go for McCain because he had been offended when Ralph Reed and Pat Robertson had joined Bush's negative campaign against McCain. That, Bauer believed, sullied the reputation of the conservative religious movement.

The campaign to tarnish McCain's character had not stopped. At the very rally at Furman University where Bauer endorsed McCain because he couldn't abide the smear campaign directed at McCain, a man approached a woman in the crowd and told her that McCain was "no hero" and that "there are questions as to what he did in that POW camp." His words were overheard by Scotty Morgan, a retired naval aviator who had spent six months with McCain in "that POW camp." "I straightened that out in a hurry," Morgan said. He countered the anonymous man's unsubstantiated claims by telling a correspondent for the *Washington Post* about the incident. The woman who had been approached by the whisperer, according to the *Post,* "was upset."

On Thursday, at a rally in Spartanburg, McCain said, "We can lose here and still go on. But I'll tell you what. If we win here, I don't really see how we can be stopped." On that same day, at a press conference at Ebenezer Baptist Church in Florence, Bush got testy when he was asked by reporters about his appearance at Bob Jones University and his unwillingness to criticize the state's decision to continue flying the Confederate battle flag over the capitol building. "Do not," Bush said to the reporters pointedly, "judge my heart on issues that this state ought to resolve."

On Friday, the candidates' last day for campaigning, the polls showed that Bush was finally beginning to open up a lead on McCain—the apparent result of McCain's decision to pull his negative ads and Bush's resolve *not* to pull his. An old rule in politics says that negative campaigning, when done right, works more than it doesn't. Given the Bush campaign's attack on McCain, that seemed to be true. On the other hand, one could argue that McCain's ad, claiming that Bush "twists the truth like Clinton," may have backfired because many voters in the state agreed the ad had gone too far. Still, it was hard to understand the impact of the ad since McCain had decided to pull it after only three days. Strangely, knowledge of the existence of the ad reached a much larger audience than the ad itself did. For that achievement, the "twists the truth like Clinton" ad would take its place alongside ads like the famous "mushroom cloud" ad of 1964, which showed a young girl playing with a daisy while, in the background, an atomic bomb explodes to create a mushroom cloud that is about to obscure the young girl. The ad was pro-Lyndon Johnson; it implied that his opponent, Barry Goldwater, would be too trigger-happy to be president in a nuclear age. The ad ran only once, but it became one of the most notorious ads in political history.

On the last day of the South Carolina campaign, McCain appeared at a noontime rally in an old gymnasium at the College of Charleston. With rock music pounding, McCain entered the event along a roped-off wooden walkway that wound through a sea of people standing on the gym floor. On stage before the overflow crowd, McCain delivered his message as Cindy stood behind him. "We win tomorrow—and we will win—there is no way that we can be stopped," McCain said to the roar of the mob. Then he reiterated, one more time, that he could win because of his appeal to voters who were not Republicans. "I say to Independents, Democrats, Libertarians, vegetarians," McCain said to more cheers, "come on over. Vote for me." Later that day, at a retirement home in Hilton Head, he sounded the theme again. "Remember the Reagan Democrats?" he said to an audience of 800, many of whom were senior citizens. "Remember them? Remember those who helped us govern? Welcome back. Come back. Come back, Reagan Democrats." Throughout the campaign in South Carolina, a state where voters did not have to adhere to party affiliation, McCain had not been subtle about appealing to Democrats and Independents. Outside many of his events, workers had posted signs that read "Democrats and Independents: Vote for McCain February 19."

Bush began his last day of campaigning by doing two network television interviews before 7:00 in the morning—one with ABC, the other with CBS. During the day, he appeared at four rallies and conducted a constant stream of interviews with local media. "Tomorrow's a big day in American politics," Bush told a crowd at Presbyterian College in Clinton. "Tomorrow, South Carolina can send a strong message about what our party stands for." During the day,

Bush continued to slam McCain, a tactic he had all but perfected over the past three weeks. At a campaign stop in Florence, Bush told reporters at a church, "This is a man"—McCain—"who says he's going to do one thing and does another. You can't have it both ways in the political process. You can't take the high horse and then claim the low road." As Bush waved a McCain flier he claimed was "an attack piece," a reporter asked Bush exactly what the flier said. The headline read: "When it comes to keeping Social Security secure, George Bush's figures simply do not add up!" This, to Bush, was an example of negative campaigning.

McCain might have quibbled with just what constituted a negative ad. If that was negative, witness what one Bush supporter, someone named John Carney, who was identified as "a third-year law student at the University of Pennsylvania," posted on a Web site called LewRockwell.com. Entitled "McCain's Savagery," the piece said: "Something ugly is going on in South Carolina. Struggling to deflect criticism and win public sympathy, Senator John McCain has taken to decrying his Republican primary opponent's supposed negative campaigning. What McCain doesn't mention is that three months ago he helped lead the brutal smear campaign that sought to paint Pat Buchanan as a Hitler-sympathizer. . . . After Buchanan left the GOP behind last October, McCain launched [an] on air war to demonize Buchanan. . . . Now under attack from George W. Bush and his allies in the GOP establishment, McCain whines that 'this kind of savagery is not necessary in an American political campaign.' This attempt to turn public resentment against negative campaigning to his advantage reeks of hypocrisy. . . . McCain's hypocrisy on negative campaigning borders on pathological. It's as if part of him never really left the Hanoi Hilton, where he was a prisoner of war for five years. Still looking through the lens of his imprisonment, he sees his opponent's criticism as cruel torture and is utterly without remorse for his own savage smears and assaults."

By the end of the South Carolina primary campaign, McCain had seen it all—a flood of negative television and radio ads, push-poll phone calls, automated phone calls, a church flier describing him as the "fag candidate," a Bob Jones University professor's e-mail accusing him of fathering children out of wedlock, and on and on. Conservative religious leaders criticized him for his first marriage, his alleged affairs, his use of profane language, his willingness to meet with the Log Cabin Republicans, "his softness on gays."

"One of the entertaining vignettes from South Carolina," McCain says, "involved a professor at Bob Jones University who was blasting out mass e-mails saying that John McCain had fathered illegitimate children. Well, CNN tracked him down. It was Jonathan Karl, if I remember it right, and he finds this guy and he says, 'You've been saying that John McCain's fathered illegitimate children. Do you have any proof of that?' And this professor says, 'No.' So Karl says, 'Why are you doing it?' And he says, 'Well, it's up to John McCain to prove that he didn't.' And this was on CNN!"

In his entire political career, McCain had never seen anything like it. But of all the ugliness, of all the blows both legitimate and below the belt, one hurt more than any other. Months later, McCain would still be reeling from what he considered to be a piece of campaigning that simply went beyond the pale. The one detail that angered him more than any other was a flier that emerged in the final days of the primary campaign and was followed by a flurry of calls placed by a phone bank. In the most unflattering terms, this attack said that Cindy McCain was a drug addict.

On February 19, the polls would be open throughout the state from 7:00 in the morning until 7:00 at night—or at least they were supposed to be. From the start, polling irregularities developed. Specifically, a number of polling places didn't open in areas of the state where there was a large concentration of Independent or Democratic voters, particularly in African-American neighborhoods. Naturally, these were areas where McCain would have been expected to do well. When the morning dragged on and it became clear that these polling places were not going to open at all, J. Sam Daniels, the executive director of the Republican Party in South Carolina, was questioned about a development that hardly could be called coincidental. Daniels explained the situation by saying the polls had not opened because workers could not be hired to man the stations—a gross deficiency that should have been anticipated well before Primary Day. But Daniels had an excuse ready. Claiming voters were being sent from the closed polling places to those that were open, he reasoned, "Voters are just inconvenienced a little bit." Of the state's 1,752 polling places that opened in a general election, only 1,429 opened on February 19.

While this drama unfolded, McCain fulfilled the one campaign commitment he had scheduled for the day—a morning meeting with a veterans' group. As the day wore on, it became clear that 20 or more polling places in Greenville County alone—mostly in areas where the residents were black and Democratic—were going to remain closed or, as election officials called it, "consolidated" with other polling places. Kweisi Mfume actually got complaints at the NAACP on Saturday morning from people in South Carolina who said black polling places were closed. This meant confused voters had to go to alternative polling places, all the while being "inconvenienced a little bit." What's more, party officials revealed they knew on Friday that polling places would be unmanned, but they did nothing about the problem. Other irregularities also occurred across the state. Poll watchers were not being allowed into some polling places, and ballots with Bush's name already marked were being handed out at others. Matters were made worse by the fact that, on this day, a record number of people went to the polls and voted in the primary election in South Carolina. In all, over half a million people voted, compared to 276,000 four years before. That fact tended to undercut the notion that negative campaigning suppresses voter turnout.

As he had in New Hampshire, Tim Russert called the McCain camp by early afternoon with the results of the exit polling. By the time McCain returned from the meeting with the veterans and was getting off his bus in the parking lot of his hotel in North Charleston, he knew the odds of his winning South Carolina were against him. "He got off the bus that day at the hotel and walked over to Cindy, who was standing there," Peter Rinfret says. "He gave her a big hug and a kiss. Then he leaned over and whispered into her ear, 'It's really bad. It's much worse than I ever believed it could be.'"

At first, McCain thought the voting irregularities in the state might cause him to lose, but, soon after he had made his way upstairs to his suite, he realized that the numbers were going to break against him much more than he had imagined—and much more than the final polls had predicted. By early evening, when it was clear that he was not going to win, McCain took each of his children individually into a bedroom of the suite and told them he was going to lose. As she wandered about the suite, Cindy could not keep from crying.

After the polls closed, the early numbers looked grim. At about 7:10, McCain called Bush to congratulate him. It was a brief conversation. As he made his way down to the convention center next to the hotel, McCain realized what the final numbers would approach: Bush, 53 percent; McCain, 42 percent; Keyes, 5 percent. The 11-point spread meant the results were not even going to be close. It also meant that the negative campaign against McCain—"the dirtiest race I've ever seen," as a McCain insider later put it—had worked. Karl Rove, other Bush strategists, and the Bush surrogates had determined, after New Hampshire, that the only sure way Bush was going to win South Carolina, a state that he had privately referred to as his "firewall," was by attacking McCain. The resulting assault was one of the most brutal in modern presidential politics.

As McCain, Murphy, Weaver, Salter, and Davis had huddled upstairs in McCain's suite to decide the content of what would be called his "nonconcession concession speech," they had kept this fact in mind. So, while McCain stood in front of the cheering crowd, with Cindy and his family standing behind him on the stage, he delivered a speech, mostly written by Salter, that was anger-filled, defiant, and provocative. Tonight, he had a target—Bush—just as Bush had had one now for three weeks—him.

"My friends," he began, "you don't have to win every skirmish to win a war or a crusade, and although we fell a little short tonight our crusade goes stronger." McCain then continued, moving into the heart of the speech. "I'm going to fight with every ounce of strength I have," he said, "but I'm going to keep fighting clean, I'm going to keep fighting fair, and I'm going to keep fighting the battle of ideas. And my friends, we are going to win. I will not take the low road to the highest office in this land. I want the presidency in the best way, not the worst way. The American people deserve to be treated with respect by those who seek to lead the nation. And I promise you, you will have my respect until my last day on earth. The greatest blessing of my life was to have been born an American, and I will never dishonor the nation I love by letting ambition overcome principle. Never. Never. Never."

The crowd erupted into loud applause. "My friends," McCain went on when the audience quieted down, "I say to you I am a uniter, not a divider. I don't just say it, I live it. I'm a real reformer. I'm a real reformer. I don't just say it, I live it. And I'm a fighter for this country, and I don't just say it, I live it. As this campaign moves forward, a clear choice will be offered, a choice between my optimistic and welcoming conservatism and the negative message of fear. Between Ronald Reagan's vision of inclusion and the defeatist tactics of exclusion so cherished by those who would shut the doors to our party and surrender America's future to Speaker Gephardt and President Al Gore. A choice between a record of reform and an empty slogan of reform. A choice between experience and pretense."

When McCain finished, amid the loud music and the cheering crowd, he made his way out of the auditorium and back to his hotel. Upstairs, he and Cindy got ready for bed, aware that they would need to be rested, after this horrific defeat, for the coming battle that next awaited them in Michigan and Arizona. McCain could not help feeling that he had been ambushed unfairly by Bush and his cronies.

On the night of the defeat, John Weaver summed up the whole experience in South Carolina for reporters, at least as far as the McCain campaign was concerned. "Ralph Reed, Pat Robertson, and Jerry Falwell are to be congratulated," he said flatly.

M uch later, McCain would name the person he believed to be the real victim in South Carolina—his wife. "Cindy had always been with me during my previous campaigns for the House and the Senate," McCain says. "In the presidential campaign, she became a bit of a star. On a number of occasions, particularly near the end, she went out and did individual campaigning.

"But she did it in an interesting way. She didn't say, 'Here's why I'm for Medicare reform, and why we need it, et cetera.' She did it in a way where she sort of talked about me and our vision for the future, rather than as a policy wonk. It seemed to be very well received. In fact, some people said, 'Why isn't she the candidate?'

"On a very subjective basis, she's a good person. She's a good mother. She doesn't try to be something she isn't. She really believes that what I do is good for America. Therefore, when she talks about me, she can say it with a certain degree of confidence. But she has never subordinated her duties as a mother to her duties as a politician's wife. I think that's a very important aspect of her character. People, when they see her, appreciate that.

"The rumors about her, spread in South Carolina, made me angry. They made me feel terrible for her because she didn't deserve it. Whatever they wanted to say about me was okay, but to attack her was unkind and cruel. Yet I knew if I let it upset me and affect me, that would accrue to the benefit of the opposition. So I kept my game face on, but, deep down, I was very unhappy about it.

"Let's face it. There were phone calls that said, 'Do you know that Cindy McCain's a drug addict?' Or phone calls that said, 'Do you know the McCains have a black baby?'

"Hundreds of thousands of those calls went out. That's really the ugly underside of politics."

10

THE BEST MAN

T he day after he won the South Carolina primary, George W. Bush made a startling confession—one that may or may not have affected the vote, had he made it earlier. In short, Bush said he regretted going to Bob Jones University. Arguably, it was the one move that turned around a campaign that had been decimated in New Hampshire; now he was saying it had been a mistake to go there. Obviously, in the days after South Carolina, Bush didn't dwell on whether or not he should have gone to Bob Jones but continued to attack McCain, an approach that had proven successful for him. In a media briefing in Pasco, a town in rural eastern Washington state, Bush said, "He"—McCain—"claims he's a Reagan Republican. Ronald Reagan didn't run those kinds of campaigns."

McCain started off the day after his defeat in South Carolina by appearing on *Meet the Press.* He boasted, "I am a proud conservative Republican with a 17-year voting record. In fact, I'm far more conservative in many respects than Governor Bush." Mostly, McCain spent the day trying not to look like a loser. At Michigan State University in East Lansing, before an enthusiastic crowd of several hundred, McCain sounded a theme he hoped would resonate. "My friends," he said, "I lived in a hotel once where there were no mints on the pillow. I know how to take a punch, and I know how to fight back." Specifically, "fighting back" meant slamming Bush. Over and over that day, McCain mocked Bush by repeating the line "If he's a reformer, I'm an astronaut." On the Straight Talk Express early in the day, McCain's monologue was even tougher: "We're not letting you get away with that, pal. You're not a reformer. Anybody who believes you're a reformer believes in the tooth fairy." In the Michigan State speech, McCain got down to specifics. "In five and a half years," he charged, "as governor of the state of Texas, he did not propose a single campaign finance reform proposal in a state where anything goes." According to McCain, Bush was lying "when he says I'm not a reformer, when he says that I'm a hypocrite, when he says that I'm in the pockets of lobbyists."

Later, at a campaign stop in a Detroit suburb, McCain continued to play up the fact that he knew how to recover from hardship. "If you want the government back that's been stolen from you by the special interests and big money people and a system that George Bush wants to perpetuate," he said, after arriving on stage as the theme from *Star Wars*—his favorite, these days—blared over the public address system, "then you're going to vote for me and you're going to get our vote out."

There was *some* good news on the day after the South Carolina defeat: McCain got a key endorsement from Congressman Peter King of New York, who had been supporting Bush but, after Bush's appearance at Bob Jones, changed his mind. "I endorsed McCain the day after he lost South Carolina," Peter King says. "What struck me the most was you could tell the McCain campaign was facing a battle. For a guy who just weeks before was getting ready to be anointed president, the whole thing was coming undone very quickly. He was just being outspent and outmanned. In comparison to the Bush operation, this was like a small family business. I endorsed him because I really felt that the Republican Party was becoming an isolationist party. McCain struck me as being the only adult when it came to foreign policy. He reminded me of the Eisenhower era when there really were people who had a global view."

By the time the two candidates arrived in Michigan for the primary on Tuesday, the battle between the camps in the media was well under way. Although the McCain campaign would not admit it at the time, it was telling voters, through automated calls, that Bush had stood beside Bob Jones administrators who had openly attacked the Pope and the Catholic Church. These "Catholic Voter Alert" calls charged that a past president of Bob Jones had described the Catholic Church as "a satanic cult" and implied that Bush supported such stands. "This is a Catholic voter alert," the voice on the phone said. "Governor George Bush has campaigned against Senator John McCain by seeking the support of Southern fundamentalists who have expressed anti-Catholic views. . . . Bob Jones has made strong anti-Catholic statements, including calling the Pope the anti-Christ and the Catholic Church a satanic cult. John McCain, a pro-life senator, has strongly condemned this anti-Catholic bigotry, while Governor Bush has stayed silent." The calls were designed to incite a state where one-fourth of the electorate was Catholic, but when Howard Opinsky, a campaign spokesman, was asked whether the McCain campaign was behind the calls, he said the campaign "is not making any such calls." (Only later, on Tuesday night, did the campaign admit it was behind the phone calls; McCain himself would not make the admission until Wednesday.) Bush countered that his brother was Catholic, as was his strong supporter in Michigan, Governor John Engler. But the Bush campaign didn't just defend itself; it decided, as it had in South Carolina, to launch an assault.

So they had Pat Robertson record a telephone message that would be made by automated dialing to homes throughout the state on Monday, the day before the primary. "Protect unborn babies and restore religious freedoms once again in America," Robertson said. "Tomorrow's Republican primary may determine whether our dream becomes reality or whether the Republican Party will nominate a man who wants to take First Amendment freedoms from citizens' groups while he gives unrestricted power to labor unions." In the message, Robertson suggested Warren Rudman, a national cochair of the McCain campaign and former senator from New Hampshire, was a "vicious bigot who wrote that conservative Christians in politics are antiabortion zealots, homophobes and would-be censors." McCain was distressed when he first learned of the Robertson phone calls. "It's outrageous," he told reporters. "It's disgraceful. Pat Robertson should go back to wherever he came from."

On Monday, Bush complained about McCain's charges that he was anti-Catholic. "Mr. McCain's making phone calls in this state accusing me of being an anti-Catholic bigot," he said, "and I don't appreciate it." As for the Robertson message that actually *did* call Warren Rudman a bigot, Bush claimed, "We have nothing to do with that. Mr. Robertson made these calls on his own mind." But McCain spokesman Howard Opinsky wasn't buying it. It was another example, Opinsky told reporters, of the Bush campaign's use of surrogates to make "totally false allegations against John McCain. It's the same tactics they used in South Carolina." McCain himself was even tougher. At a town hall meeting in Traverse City, he said the citizens of Michigan "deserve better than the trash that's on your television set and over your radio." He implored voters to "reject this negative campaigning, reject this character assassination, reject the low road to the presidency and support the high road." This said, McCain then flew from Michigan to Arizona where he would vote for himself in the primary the next day.

On Tuesday, as the exit polls began to come in, McCain realized he was going to win not only in Arizona, where he was expected to sweep Bush away in a landslide, but also in Michigan—by eight points, not even a close margin. McCain had not been sure he could win Michigan, and if he lost there, his continuing on to Super Tuesday would have been difficult to justify. But he had won big in Michigan. When he appeared at a rally in Phoenix that night, McCain could barely control his elation. With two solid victories, he had new momentum.

"What a difference a couple of days make!" he said, amid thunderous cheers. "Today, Michigan sent a powerful message across America. A message that our party wants real reform from the real reformer. We are creating a new majority, my friends, a McCain majority. And we are Al Gore's worst nightmare." To the delight of the audience, McCain continued: "Don't fear this campaign, my fellow Republicans. Join it! Join it! This is where you belong, in the spirit of Teddy Roosevelt and Ronald Reagan—Republicans who practiced the politics of addition over the politics of division."

The next day, Bush tried to rationalize why he had lost Michigan. Arizona had not been a surprise, but even the Bush camp was startled by McCain's margin of victory in Michigan. Much of the momentum Bush had gained by winning South Carolina had vanished, and, as often happens in politics, the seeds for the McCain win in Michigan had been planted by Bush himself in South Carolina. The phone calls accusing Bush of being anti-Catholic because of his appearance at Bob Jones—or at least insensitive in the face of raw political ambition—worked more successfully than even the McCain campaign had imagined. If Michigan was a portent of things to come, Bush could have serious problems on Super Tuesday—the day when Republican primaries would be held in California, New York, Ohio, Maine, Connecticut, Rhode Island, Georgia, Massachusetts, Missouri, American Samoa, Maryland, Minnesota, and Vermont. (The Democrats would hold 16 primaries that day.)

To help explain what happened, Bush held a news conference following a campaign stop at the Dream Center in Los Angeles, a privately funded inner-city community center. Bush said of McCain, "I was amazed last night to hear my opponent is reaching out to Republicans. It's an amazing admission to make." Bush was referring to one reason for McCain's convincing win in Michigan: He had attracted a large number of Democratic and independent voters in a state where the primary was open (voters could pick either party when they went into the voting booth). A new type of voter was emerging in the race: the McCain Democrat—Democrats who wanted to vote for McCain because of his biography, his independence, and what they perceived as being his overall middle-of-the-road political philosophy.

So many McCain Democrats were ready to support him that, at times, as in his victory speech on Tuesday night, McCain had to remind *Republicans* that they should vote for him too. This fact was not missed by the Bush campaign, but Bush and his handlers realized the need to accept the reality that Democrats and Independents liked McCain, reinterpret it, and use it against him in the same way that Bush had used McCain's war record against him in South Carolina. At the press conference in Los Angeles, Bush said he had lost Michigan by eight points because "the liberal Democratic vote[rs]" wanted to "hijack the primary to help Al Gore." It was a stunning ploy, but, who knows, it just might work. To play it safe, Bush went after McCain on the Catholic Voter Alert calls, which the McCain campaign had finally acknowledged making. Angry, Bush said, "They admitted they were making those calls. I don't accept that kind of campaign. And I don't appreciate it one bit."

McCain ignored Bush's complaints and flew to Washington state on Wednesday. His first stop was Spokane, where, at the Gonzaga student union building, an overflow crowd turned out to see him. Then, at a campaign stop at the Rotary Club in Seattle before a packed house of 800, McCain played up his Republican credentials while still underscoring his ability to appeal to non-Republicans— the formula for his success. "I am a proud conservative Republican," he said. "I am a Reagan Republican. Have no doubt about that. I have to convince and tell our Republican Party establishment: 'It's great over here. Come on in. Join us. Join us in this effort to be an inclusive party. Join us in this effort to reach out.'"

That night, in Bremerton, a small town that is home to the Puget Sound Naval Base, 5,000 people stood in a cold rain along the waterfront for up to three hours, awaiting McCain's final campaign stop of the day. After he gave his stump speech and received an enthusiastic response from an audience made up heavily of naval personnel, McCain boarded his campaign plane to head for Sacramento. But as the plane was taxiing on the runway, the pilot cut short on a left turn and the left rear wheels got stuck in a muddy island. For two hours, with the wheels buried in mud, the pilot tried to maneuver the 727 free. McCain and Cindy napped during this two-hour wait. Workers dug out landing lights and used wooden planks to try and get the jet out of the mud. Finally, to lighten the load, all of the passengers were asked to get off the plane; then, as the passengers waited in buses, the pilot fired up the engine and floored the accelerator, and the plane lunged free. At 10:40, the plane was ready for the passengers to reboard for takeoff. If McCain was a superstitious man—and he was—somewhere in the back of his mind he had to wonder just what sort of omen this episode might have been.

On Thursday, February 24, in a 1,300-seat auditorium overflowing with students, faculty, and supporters at Sacramento State University, McCain, who had gotten only two hours of sleep because of the previous night's episode with the plane, used the university setting to continue his attack on Bush for appearing at a school much different from Sacramento State—Bob Jones University. "It's clear," McCain said, "that campus bans interracial dating, and that [the university's] president's been anti-Catholic and anti-Pope. That's racism. That's racism. That's out-and-out racism." At the same time, McCain went out of his way to play up his conservatism; he opposed gay marriage, abortion, and the general political slant of the Clinton Administration.

On Friday, McCain spent part of the day resting in his cabin in Sedona, Arizona, a lull in the around-the-clock campaigning. Late in the day, he held a rally at Balboa Park in San Diego. Three thousand people showed up—another massive crowd. That afternoon,

McCain said, "I'll tell you what's going to determine who the nominee of the Republican Party is and who the next president of the United States is: It's the state of California."

Maybe that was true but, on Saturday, McCain spent the day campaigning across the state of Ohio. On his first stop at the West Side Market in downtown Cleveland, he walked through the crowd shaking hands and signing copies of *Faith of My Fathers* as butchers rushed around and shoppers went about making their purchases. From Czuchraj's market, he bought smoked kielbasa and beef jerky. Someone held up a sign: "Vegetarians for McCain"—a reference to the line he often used in his stump speech that said he hoped to attract the support of Democrats, Independents, Libertarians, and vegetarians. McCain was barely able to hold a press conference at the market because a nearby crowd started chanting loudly, "Ohio for McCain!" Later, at a town hall meeting at Ohio State University in Columbus before an audience of 2,000, McCain described himself as "a proud fiscal conservative" but noted the many differences between his tax plan and Bush's. Saying his hero was Ronald Reagan, he proclaimed he was "the real fiscal conservative in the race." At the university, McCain was interrupted more than once by hecklers yelling, "Give us a living wage!" As if to prove his conservative credentials, McCain answered bluntly: "I'd be glad to. Go to work."

For several days now, there had been some talk within the campaign about taking a calculated risk that, if successful, might propel McCain ahead in the neck-and-neck race that was shaping up for Super Tuesday. The next round of voting—primaries in Virginia and Washington state, and a caucus in North Dakota—would be held on Tuesday, February 29. To be realistic, McCain was having to close ground in all three races. "In Virginia, we had no organization, and we weren't getting any help from the Republican Party," says Paul Galanti, who had been a POW in Vietnam with McCain and who now served as the state campaign chairman for McCain in Virginia. "We were running everything off my little Macintosh laptop computer. We had no organization at all, really. We had retired military guys. The Bush campaign had seven full-time employees plus the overt cooperation of the Republican Party of Virginia."

The scope of the campaigns may have been different, with the Bush campaign being run by party professionals and the McCain campaign being run for the most part by volunteers, but the tones of the campaigns were different, as well. McCain town hall meetings often felt like church services, as the true believers gathered to groove with their political guru. McCain rallies sometimes resembled rock concerts, complete with the theme from *Star Wars* as entrance music (à la Elvis taking the stage to the theme from 2001), worshipful fans surging for their idol, and a speech that occasionally resembled performance art more than a political diatribe. In contrast, Bush events routinely felt like company picnics where attendees were there because they were required to be, not because they wanted to be. In this sense, the Bush election was not so much a coronation, as critics often claimed it was, as the rightful succession of the chosen company man to the presidency.

If, against the odds, McCain could do well on February 29, he would certainly help his chances for Super Tuesday. So, after much discussion, McCain decided to take the chance he and his handlers felt he needed to take. He would make a speech on Monday, February 28, that would alter the direction of the presidential campaign as it had been defined so far.

The setting for the speech had been chosen carefully: a high school in Virginia Beach, Virginia, the quiet Southern town that was home to Pat Robertson's Christian Coalition. The timing of the speech had been considered too: the day before Tuesday's primaries and caucus. McCain's traveling companion on that day would also be relevant: Gary Bauer, a former candidate in this presidential race and a man whose conservative Christian credentials were excellent. After he delivered the speech, McCain said that, since the South Carolina primary, he had been thinking about making a speech that his aides would describe as "a call to the grass roots," but he had decided to go through with it only recently. In fact, as late as Sunday, if he had backed out of the speech, no one within the McCain inner circle would have been surprised.

The speech was, simply, a no-holds-barred hit on the religious right and the Republican Party. Most of the speech was about, to quote McCain, "the fine members of the religious conservative community." In the speech, McCain said he was "proud to help build a bigger Republican Party, a party that can claim a governing majority for a generation or more by attracting new people to our cause with an appeal to the patriotism that unites us and the promise of a government we can be proud of again—and for that I have been accused of consorting with the wrong kind of people."

But McCain knew that the media covering the speech would focus on one passage that was unquestionably electric—and a shocking political gamble. "I am a Reagan Republican who will defeat Al Gore," McCain said at the start of the passage. "Unfortunately, Governor Bush is a Pat Robertson Republican who will lose to Al Gore. Neither party should be defined by pandering to the outer reaches of American politics and the agents of intolerance, whether they be Louis Farrakhan or Al Sharpton on the left, or Pat Robertson or Jerry Falwell on the right. We are the party of Ronald Reagan, not Pat Robertson."

As if this language was not inflammatory enough, McCain went on to say: "[W]e reject the practices of a few self-appointed leaders [who primarily hope] to preserve their own political power at all costs." Robertson and Falwell "distort my pro-life positions and smear the reputations of my supporters. Why? Because I don't pander to them, because I don't ascribe to their failed philosophy that money is our message. The union bosses who have subordinated the interests of the working families to their own ambitions, to their desire to pervert their own political power at all costs, are mirror images of Pat Robertson."

The media did indeed cover the speech, and the debate over whether McCain's rebuke of the religious right was a smart move started at once. Was it a stroke of genius that would, as his handlers hoped, motivate the grass roots, or was it a stupid political blunder that would end up costing him any chance of winning the nomination? Some campaign staffers in Virginia had no doubt that it was a mistake. "They sent out a press release about the speech beforehand," Paul Galanti says, "and as soon as I saw it I said, 'Oh, my God! No, no, no, no, no, no, no! Don't do it.' And not because I particularly like Pat Robertson or Jerry Falwell, but it really wasn't appropriate for John to make the speech there. John had gotten hammered bad down in South Carolina—yes. Still, to come back and attack those guys was just not smart. I mean, nobody attacks Pat Robertson. That's like attacking Santa Claus. It cost John votes in Virginia."

Late on Monday, following a campaign stop in Bellevue, Washington, Bush told reporters how he felt. McCain "obviously wants to divide people into camps," Bush said. "It sounds like Senator McCain has taken to name-calling, needless name-calling. Ronald Reagan didn't point fingers. He never played to people's religious fears like Senator McCain has shamelessly done."

As the Tuesday papers featured front-page stories about McCain's sojourn into the land of the religious right, McCain made comments that only pushed his attack on Robertson and Falwell further. On the Straight Talk Express on Tuesday, McCain said Robertson and Falwell were "an evil influence . . . over the Republican Party. . . . To stand up and take on the forces of evil—that's my job, and I can't steer the Republican Party if these two individuals have the influence that they have on the party today."

If McCain expected the speech to give him a bump in the voting on Tuesday, it didn't. Bush won the primaries in both Virginia and Washington. In Washington, the vote was too close to call on Tuesday night, so the Bush victory was not declared until Wednesday. But in Virginia, the state where McCain had made his controversial speech, it was not close at all. Bush won by nine percentage points, 53 to 44. (Keyes got three percent of the vote.) To make matters worse for McCain, Bush won the North Dakota caucus by a huge margin, 76 to 19. (Keyes got five percent of the vote there.) At a rally in Cincinnati (Ohio was a state he hoped to win on Super Tuesday), Bush celebrated his victory: "Tonight, in an open primary by a solid margin . . . the voters of Virginia rejected the politics of pitting one religion against another. This campaign is winning, and we are doing it the right way. Tonight, we are one step closer to victory."

On Wednesday, March 1, Bush and McCain appeared opposite one another on late-night television programs. Bush showed up as a guest of David Letterman on *The Late Show*, and McCain was welcomed by Jay Leno for yet another appearance on *The Tonight Show*. That same day, while McCain was in Los Angeles, the *Los Angeles Times* ran a story about how Hollywood had fallen in love with McCain. Not only had Barry Diller bought the film rights to *Faith of My Fathers* for USA Films, but some of Hollywood's heaviest hitters had pumped money into McCain's campaign. Among them were: Harrison Ford, Bob Newhart, Tom Selleck, Milos Forman, Rip Torn, Sydney Pollack, Brian Grazer, William Friedkin, Norman Lear, Ahmet Ertegun, Berry Gordy, Richard Zanuck, Brad Grey, Burt Bacharach, David Geffen, Ron Meyer, Lew Wasserman, Edgar M. Bronfman, Sumner Redstone, Bob Daly, and Frank Mancuso. The last week of February, at a $1,000-a-ticket fund-raiser in the Beverly Hilton Hotel, a number of stars came, including Morgan Fairchild, Connie Stevens, Shirley Jones, Lainie Kazan, and Diane Ladd—most if not all of whom were Democrats. "His is a voice that needs to be heard," Morgan Fairchild told the *Los Angeles Times* that night. "People in the industry, even hard-nosed Democrats, all know star quality when we see it."

Later that night, after he had finished taping *The Tonight Show* in the afternoon, McCain made a campaign appearance in Little Saigon, a community started by South Vietnamese who had fled their country at the time of the fall of Saigon. A crowd of 3,000 filled a public space outside the Asian Gardens Mall where McCain talked for 20 minutes while a group of South Vietnamese veterans, some of whom McCain had helped to free, stood on the stage beside him. In his speech, McCain thanked the Vietnamese people in the audience for fighting communism. His sacrifice was nothing, he said, compared to that of the Vietnamese soldiers. "These," McCain said, referring to the veterans standing there with him, "are our enduring examples of the human spirit in surviving the most challenging circumstances. In their company I am humbled." But of all the remarks he made that got a reaction from the audience, this line received the biggest cheer: "My experiences with you were the defining period of my life." At the end of the speech, streamers filled the air and music blared. The colors of the streamers—yellow and red—were the colors of the South Vietnamese flag.

On Wednesday, McCain had to do some backpedaling. His remark about Robertson and Falwell being "evil" had taken on a life of its own. If members of the religious right were unhappy with McCain's speech in Virginia Beach, they were livid when he called the two leaders "evil." No better barometer was Gary Bauer, who had accompanied McCain to Virginia Beach on Monday so he could be there as McCain criticized the religious right. When reporters had asked him about his presence in Virginia Beach, Bauer defended McCain, saying, "If this were an attack on Christian conservative voters, I wouldn't be here." But after McCain's "evil" remark on Tuesday, Bauer released this prepared statement: "I must in the strongest possible terms repudiate Senator McCain's unwarranted, ill-advised, and divisive attacks on certain religious leaders. Senator McCain must not allow his personal differences with any individual to cloud his judgment." Bauer specifically asked for an apology from McCain. So, on Wednesday, realizing that he *had* gone too far, McCain released a statement as well. In it, he apologized for saying Robertson and Falwell were "forces of evil." The statement read: "I do not consider them evil, and I regret that my flip remark may have mistakenly created that impression. . . . In my campaign, I often joke about Luke Skywalker, evil empires, and death stars. It was in that vein that I used the phrase yesterday."

On Thursday night, Bush, Keyes, and McCain participated in a debate. Bush and Keyes were at the headquarters of the *Los Angeles Times*, which, along with CNN, sponsored the debate. McCain participated via a satellite hookup from St. Louis. For a while, the sponsors wondered whether McCain would even show up for the debate. Earlier, Bush could not decide whether he should accept the invitation to debate, though McCain had already consented. Then McCain decided *not* to accept because Bush couldn't make up his mind. Next, Bush accepted but McCain was not willing to change the plans he had made after he had turned down the invitation. Changing his schedule yet again would make him appear to be placating Bush. On Tuesday, after an internal upheaval in his campaign staff—communications director Dan Schnur threatened to quit—McCain agreed to debate, although he would not concede to flying back to California for the event. Not surprisingly, one line of discussion in the debate centered around McCain's recent assault on the religious right. McCain defended what he had to say about Robertson and Falwell; he believed the two ministers had hurt the Republican Party through "intolerance and wrongheadedness." McCain said: "Ours is a message of inclusion."

Ironically, McCain had been in California that day before he went to Missouri. In fact, he had given a press conference in East Los Angeles in which he acknowledged that the campaign had flaws. "We've made a lot of mistakes in this campaign," McCain said, "primarily because we haven't got the most brilliant candidate. But one of the things we are going to try to do is keep it on the issues. I am going to try to keep it on the issues and not get bogged down in a tit-for-tat kind of thing."

Still, the verdict was out on the Virginia Beach speech. "I think," Gary Hart says, "that John, given his refusal to kowtow to the religious right and their dominance in the party—and [given] his native independence—I think he had no choice but to challenge the party. Did he make a mistake in Virginia, giving a speech attacking the religious right? It depends on whether your view is pragmatic or cosmic. Pragmatically, yes; cosmically, no. I mean, his popularity had to do with his independence and his willingness to say things that nobody else would say."

One fact was certain. The dirty tricks in the race had not stopped after the South Carolina primary. In the days before Super Tuesday, another barrage of negative campaigning started up. Some of it duplicated what had been seen in South Carolina. For example, an organization called the National Right to Life PAC (political action committee) in Washington paid for a new spate of automated-message phone calls. One state targeted for the calls was Connecticut. The message there said that McCain "has made conflicting statements about abortion" and would not support reversing *Roe v. Wade.* In contrast, the message said, Bush "has maintained a strong and consistent pro-life position both as governor and throughout this campaign." The message did not point out that in 1978, when he was asked about the issue of abortion during his failed attempt to win a seat in the House of Representatives, Bush did not sound as equivocal, using language that was consistent with supporters of abortion rights. Instead, the automated message simply endorsed Bush and then concluded: "For the children's sake, please vote George Bush for president."

Around the same time, in early March, another ad began running in the New York media market. It would become one of the most talked-about—and, for McCain, one of the most personally hurtful—ads in the campaign. The ad featured the voice of a woman named Geri Barish, who was the head of an organization called One in Nine, which was based in Baldwin, Long Island. The name One in Nine was a reference to the fact that, in some medical surveys, one in nine women on Long Island suffers from breast cancer—one of the highest per capita rates in the country. In the ad, Barish attacked McCain for not supporting federal funding for breast cancer research. "[I] had thought of supporting John McCain in next week's presidential primary," Barish said in the ad. "So I looked into his record. What I discovered was shocking. McCain opposes funding for vital breast cancer programs right here in New York." At the end of the ad, Barish said: "Next Tuesday, John McCain won't have my vote. We deserve a candidate with a record on women's issues we can trust." Then a voice-over said the ad was paid for by the Bush campaign.

The ad was stunning. It charged that McCain had a bad record on women's issues and was specifically opposed to breast cancer research when, in fact, McCain's record did not bear out those accusations at all. In 1991, McCain voted for increased funding for women's issues—breast cancer and osteoporosis—and $25 million was awarded to the National Cancer Institute. He also supported the general issue of breast cancer research, and he had voted, on various occasions in the past, for federal funding of such research and of other health programs that benefited women. He did vote against legislation that would have earmarked millions of dollars for breast cancer research, but he did so because the funding for the programs—there were two of them—was contained in other spending proposals that McCain opposed. A champion in the fight against "pork-barrel" spending, McCain had voted against funding that would have gone to a breast cancer program in the North Shore Long Island Jewish Health System because it was contained in an appropriations bill for the Department of Labor. He also voted against funding that would have gone to a women's cancer program at New York University because it was a part of an appropriations bill for the Department of Energy. McCain opposed the two bills for procedural reasons; he was not against funding women's health programs or research into breast cancer. In fact, the issue of breast cancer was unusually important to him: His sister, Sandy McCain Morgan—her given name was Jean but she now went by Sandy—suffered from the disease. If there was any government official in Washington who wanted doctors to find a cure for breast cancer, it was John McCain.

By Thursday, Bush and McCain were going at each other over the ad. Bush said McCain was becoming "increasingly . . . angry," an echo of the whisper campaign that had been launched against McCain before Christmas, and McCain said Bush needed to "get out of the gutter." In fact, McCain *was* angry—really angry—over the breast cancer research ad. When he charged that the ad was unfair, the Bush campaign pointed to McCain's own Web site, which featured a page that said: "As president, I would cut every one of the projects on the following list [because they are] garden-variety pork." The list did contain $1 million for a breast cancer research program at the North Shore Long Island Jewish Health System. But McCain argued that to take one example and say he was opposed to federal funding of breast cancer research and women's health issues was, at best, "a distortion" of his real views. Specifically, he voted against the bill in which the funding for the North Shore project was contained because the omnibus bill included millions of dollars for pet projects that McCain was against. "My message is," McCain said on the campaign trail, "'Governor Bush, get out of the gutter. Acknowledge the fact that I've been a strong supporter of breast cancer [research].'"

On Friday morning, on *The Today Show*, McCain was asked about the breast cancer research ads. "It is very unfortunate," he said. "It's not the first time or the last. They"—the Bush campaign—"have done nothing but run negative ads in state after state." During the day on Friday, the Bush campaign did much more than run ads. Wearing the pink ribbon that signifies the fight against breast cancer, Bush appeared at the Stony Brook University Health Sciences Center on Long Island accompanied by George Pataki, Rudolph Giuliani, and Elizabeth Dole. Also in attendance was Geri Barish, whom Pataki introduced as a research-funding lobbyist. To the 100 guests, Bush said: "A legitimate role of the federal government is to fund research to cure disease. It's not a matter of *if*, it's a matter of *when* we cure cancer." At a news conference after the event, Bush defended the ad he was running against McCain. "This is an issue," Bush said, somewhat defensively. "The ad came off the man's Web page. This is what he laid out. This is what he thought was important. . . . I don't think the senator should be squealing about pork and then squealing when somebody disagrees with one of the cuts he wants to make." Bush was just as defensive when he was confronted about the ad by Dean Reynolds for ABC's *World News Tonight*. Would Bush have run the ads if he'd known McCain's sister was in remission from breast cancer? Reynolds asked Bush, in an interview that was aired on Friday night. "All the more reason to remind him of what he said about the research that goes on there," Bush said flatly, not backing off at all.

Bush was not the only one being challenged in the drama surrounding the breast cancer research ad. Much to her amazement, Geri Barish suffered blistering attacks from members of the breast cancer research community, the colleagues she had worked with for years. Elsa Ford, president of the Brentwood/Bay Shore Breast Cancer Coalition, ridiculed Barish by saying: "She's usurping the power of the breast cancer movement and allowing it to be used for a candidate, and that's wrong." In fact, Barish was criticized so badly by so many people she ultimately regretted ever getting involved in the Bush campaign. "With all the controversy," she told *Newsday*, "I am sorry I did the radio spot and it's come out the way it did."

While the breast cancer research ad continued to play, another ad started airing at the end of the final week before Super Tuesday. This one questioned McCain's record on environmental issues. When McCain learned of the details of the television ad, he was furious. At a noontime rally on Wall Street on Friday, he referred to the new ad when he told the crowd, "Two million has come into this campaign"—again, the Bush campaign—"from a source we don't know, alleging things that are untrue."

The television ad was produced by Rob Allyn, a political consultant based in Dallas. His firm had worked for Bush during his campaign against Ann Richards for the Texas governorship in 1994. Allyn also worked for the Texas Republican Party. The ad was credited to a group identified in the spot as Republicans for Clean Air. The ad, which was running in New York, Ohio, and California, attacked McCain for his record on environmental issues while it praised Bush. In the ad, a picture of McCain was superimposed over smokestacks that were billowing black smoke. A narrator then said that McCain had voted against solar and renewable energy and Bush had "clamped down" on coal-burning electronic plants. In fact, just the opposite was true. As governor, Bush fought to keep loopholes in place so Texas plants would not have to comply with the Clean Air Act. During Bush's time as governor, Houston even surpassed Los Angeles as the city with the worst air quality in the country—another fact not mentioned in the ad. Nor did the ad reveal that a group called Republicans for Clean Air did not actually exist. It was a made-up organization intended to be a front for the wealthy Wyly brothers of Texas, Sam and Charles. Specifically, the Wylys had spent $2.5 million to run the ads on television in three states. The Wyly brothers were careful not to use the words "vote for" or "vote against," so the ad could be classified as an "issue" ad, and, as such, not be covered by existing campaign finance laws. This was just one example of the questionable advertising McCain wanted to regulate through campaign finance reform.

On Friday, as the debate over the environmental ad heated up, McCain accused Bush of trying to "hijack the campaign." McCain said: "It's clear this is a $2 million smear campaign. It's an attempt to derail this campaign. The people of New York and the country will reject it." On the other side, Bush denied knowing anything about Sam and Charles Wyly's paying for the ad, even though the brothers had given Bush $210,273 when he ran for governor in 1994 and 1998, and Charles was a Pioneer, which meant he had given $100,000 to Bush's presidential campaign. What's more, a company owned by the Wyly brothers had a state contract worth $1 million to handle the investments of the University of Texas, which ultimately reported to the governor of Texas, the position Bush currently held while he was running for president.

"In his 63 years," the *Los Angeles Times* said in a profile of McCain published on Friday, "the Arizona senator has survived three airplane crashes, a randy reputation even by fighter pilot standards, more than five years in a POW camp, a divorce of his own making, a career-threatening Senate scandal, a legislative record marked more by loss than victory and the outright animosity of many of his colleagues. And today [he] is running for president with that astonishingly fallible biography as his weapon." What had ended up damaging McCain more than anything in his own biography was the constant attack on him carried out by the Bush campaign and its surrogates.

Late on a Friday afternoon, McCain sat in the captain's chair in the back of the Straight Talk Express as it crept northward in Manhattan. McCain was on his way to another rally, this one at Sacred Heart University in Fairfield, Connecticut, but at the moment he was dejected and exhausted. He had arrived in New York at 1:30 in the morning, which meant he got very little sleep before beginning another long day on the campaign trail. Super Tuesday was only four days away. It would be the next day of reckoning in what had become a series of days of reckoning.

McCain was more than tired. He was weary of the assault that had been waged against him. In South Carolina, he had had to deal with a seemingly nonstop barrage of negative television ads, radio stops, push-poll calls, and surrogate attacks. Now, as Super Tuesday neared, he had to cope with the Wyly brothers' ad and an unfounded attack on his willingness to use federal money for breast cancer research. He was also still dealing with the fallout from the Virginia Beach speech. Some McCain supporters now openly questioned whether he should even have made that speech; Chuck Coughlin, president of a media relations group called High Ground, said the speech had "cost [McCain] the presidential election." And the speech's ultimate damage may not have surfaced yet; 40 percent of the Republican voters in California identified themselves as conservative Christians. All of these challenges were playing on McCain that afternoon as he sat on his bus. He was glad to have his daughter Sidney with him. He always liked having his children around, and he was especially close to Sidney, the child he had had with Carol. His caravan of four buses was moving slowly, mostly because his campaign planners underestimated the Friday afternoon rush-hour traffic.

"I was with McCain on the bus heading to Connecticut," Peter Rinfret says, "and they had the television on when the commercial came on about McCain being against breast cancer research. One senior staff said, 'We're going to kill them, we're going to absolutely kill them.' Cindy McCain looked at John and he sort of went white. He just sort of went ashen as he was watching it. Cindy started talking and he said, 'It's going to be okay.' And he got very quiet. This is a man they say has a vile temper, but he did not budge one inch. On that bus everybody was in a rage, but not McCain."

After a trip that seemed endless, McCain finally arrived at the Fairfield school. In the gym, 2,000 supporters had waited hours for his arrival. As the music pounded over the public address system and the crowd crushed in on either side, McCain, with Cindy beside him, moved along a wooden walkway that had been built through the middle of the gym. Shaking hands and signing copies of his book as he went along, McCain eventually reached the stage, where a huge American flag was the backdrop for the podium. McCain turned and faced the overflow and enthusiastic crowd. "There are four more days until Super Tuesday," McCain said between cheers, "and Connecticut will send a message—and you are the messengers! We're trying to get out of the death star, and they're shooting at us, and we're shooting at them . . . but we're going to get out of the death star because our cause is just! . . . There are too many McCainiacs in Connecticut for us to be stopped."

McCain needed to be worried about the Bush campaign's "shooting at us." Just that day, a new Bush flier had been mailed out to Connecticut Republicans. The flier called McCain a hypocrite who "attacks money in politics" but "solicits money from lobbyists with interests before his committee." The copy on the flier was a not-so-subtle reference to the Paxson Communications issue.

To the audience, McCain said that the onslaught of negative ads and negative phone calls was what "is evil and wrong in America today." But the line that got the biggest cheer in his 20-minute stump speech was one he included in almost every speech before the primaries: "I," McCain promised, "will always tell you the truth—no matter what."

On the Saturday before Super Tuesday, as he again sat in the back of the Straight Talk Express, McCain was asked by a reporter what he would do if he lost on Tuesday. In his now-trademark tongue-planted-firmly-in-cheek style, he said, "Actually I would contemplate suicide. We have some razor blades stashed in the back room." He made a loud slashing sound as he pointed one finger at his wrist. "Orson Swindle and I are thinking, in fact, of going back and establishing residence in Hanoi. They know us there. They don't bother us there. Good food, three squares, and a flop. We're always under watchful care."

Perhaps it was gallows humor—only three days were left until the showdown on Super Tuesday—or perhaps McCain was just that relaxed. "What struck me about McCain that weekend before the New York primary was that you would never have known that his political world was crumbling," says Congressman Peter King, who campaigned with McCain that weekend. "It seemed like he was going off to a weekend golf tournament. He was calm and relaxed. The only thing he ever seemed to get intense about was making sure there were enough Dunkin Donuts. He was just out there eating those doughnuts, talking away, the most calm guy in the world. You would never have known he was in the eye of the storm. The only anger I saw was when the Bush campaign in New York put out ads that John was against breast cancer research. It made him angry, but it was more of an inner rage. He didn't blow his top or have a temper tantrum. He didn't want to talk about it."

To be sure, McCain was doing all he could to win. On Saturday, he barnstormed New England in hopes of winning those states where polling indicated he was extremely competitive. On Saturday morning, 800 people came to a rally in Boston, where McCain attacked the ads being run against him in New York, Ohio, and California. "Where's the outrage?" he all but shouted at the crowd. "Are we going to allow Texas cronies of George W. Bush to hijack an election? Tell them to keep their dirty money in Texas, don't spread it all over New England and America." The audience, pumped up by McCain's inflated rhetoric, started chanting, "No New Texas! No New Texas!" Later in the day, during a television interview, McCain was asked if he still considered Bush a friend. Astonishingly, McCain allowed an agonizing 11 seconds to pass—*one, two, three, four, five, six, seven, eight, nine, ten, eleven*—before he said: "Yes."

On Sunday, campaigning from New York to Ohio to California, McCain kept up the offensive; at one point, he called Bush's campaign "Clintonesque." Obviously, McCain was furious over the Wyly ads. In a television interview on Sunday, McCain was as tough as he had ever been on Bush, who, he charged, was simply "not ready for prime time." Would McCain support Bush if McCain lost on Tuesday? "I expect Governor Bush to change," McCain said candidly. "I expect him to run an entirely different campaign than the kind that he's run in this primary. The scandal in Washington was the debasement of the institutions of government in 1996 by the Clinton-Gore campaign, which the Bush campaign is beginning to imitate right now as we speak. . . . It's so Clintonesque, it's scary. Raise the soft money. Run the attack ads. They're getting more and more like the Clinton campaign. They'll say anything."

In a high school outside Cleveland, Ohio, in the middle of McCain's campaign day, he declared: "Tell Governor Bush to stop his cronies in Texas from destroying the American political system." Late on Sunday night, at Diablo Valley College in Pleasant Hill, California, McCain spoke before an audience of 500 people. On Monday, he went up and down California, from Santa Clara to Los Angeles to Orange County to San Diego. McCain planned to be in Los Angeles for the results of Super Tuesday.

But first there was Monday. That day, after the McCain campaign had complained to the Federal Communications Commission about the Wyly ad—charging, in an emergency complaint, that there was no proper disclosure in the ad—McCain filed a complaint with the Federal Elections Commission against Charles and Sam Wyly of Texas. Even though Bush had said that he didn't know the Wyly brothers were going to run the ad and that he had no knowledge of how the ad was paid for, the McCain campaign argued that the Wyly brothers should be considered a part of the Bush campaign because they had given so much money to Bush. At a rally at Santa Clara University, McCain said: "We ask Governor Bush to do what he refused to do: Tell his sleazy Texas buddies to stop these negative ads and take their money back to Texas where it belongs, and don't try to corrupt American politics with your money." Earlier in the day, McCain had been more flip about Bush when he described him as "a combination of the cowardly lion, the tin man, and the scarecrow . . . and Karen Hughes is behind the curtain."

In San Diego, the last campaign stop before Super Tuesday, McCain told supporters: "I want to thank you for your love, for your affection, for your commitment, for allowing me to be part of one of the most exhilarating experiences of my life. The people we've known, the relationships we've had, the town hall meetings, the factory gates, all of the schools and universities that we've attended, all of the things that have been part of this is now going to be very decisive tomorrow."

As it turned out, Super Tuesday *was* decisive. Early in the day, as the results from exit polls began to come in from New York, Ohio, California, and other states, McCain and his staff saw the numbers were not going their way. It looked as if he would do well in New England, which was not surprising, but it began to appear that he might not win any other states. McCain was in Los Angeles, holed up at the Beverly Hilton Hotel, but he was ready to give what he hoped would be a victory speech that night, at the Pacific Design Center in West Hollywood. He spent the day doing a round of last-minute radio interviews by phone. Bush had returned to Texas; the media reported that he was happy to be back home in Austin. In the afternoon, before the polls had started to close, McCain made a remark that indicated how mean-spirited he felt the race had been. He ruled out the possibility that he would ever join a Bush ticket as the vice-presidential nominee. "Under no circumstances would I consider being vice president," McCain said, projecting an unusually strong sense of resolve. "I can serve the country and my family much better by being the Senator from Arizona."

By early evening, after the polls closed first on the East Coast and finally in California, McCain realized he was going to win four states: Connecticut, Massachusetts, Vermont, and Rhode Island. Connecticut was a bit of a surprise; Governor John Rowland and all the Republican members of the state's House and Senate had endorsed Bush, but that did not seem to sway the general population in the state. Then again, Jerry Brown had won the Democratic primary there in 1992, so the state had a tradition of being unconventional. In the final analysis, McCain had needed to win more than these four states to have a mandate to continue his campaign. Of the 13 states holding primaries on Super Tuesday, Bush had won nine: New York, California, Ohio, Maryland, Maine, Georgia, Missouri, Minnesota, and American Samoa.

When it was obvious what the night's results were going to be, McCain placed a congratulatory phone call to Bush in Texas before he headed to a private reception where Cindy presented him with a replica of the Straight Talk Express. It was as if she knew this was the end of her husband's run for the White House. Next, McCain proceeded to West Hollywood to make his speech. Across the country, another group of supporters had gathered at the Roosevelt Hotel in New York (in honor of McCain's hero, Teddy Roosevelt) to listen to what McCain had to say in his speech. Before an audience of 350 in the Pacific Design Center, with the television networks carrying his remarks live, McCain tried to put the best face he could on what had happened.

"We won a few and we lost a few today," McCain told his supporters, many of whom were crying. "And over the next few days, we will take some time to enjoy our victories and take stock of our losses. . . . Tomorrow, we will take a little time to reflect on the direction of our campaign. I want to assure you all that our crusade continues tonight, tomorrow, the next day, the day after that, and for as long as it takes to restore America's confidence and pride in our great institutions of democracy. . . . We will never give up this mission, my friends. I give you my word on that." Then, as confetti rained down from the ceiling, McCain and Cindy waved from the podium to a cheering crowd that did not want them to leave the stage.

McCain returned to Arizona the next morning and locked himself away in his cabin in Sedona with his family and staff. There, they debated what to do next. Much of their attention was focused on the future. At the moment, little energy was being spent on reliving the mistakes that had been made in the past. They had to decide what to do with a campaign that at one point looked like it could not be stopped. Only later would the questioning begin. When it did, one remark that seemed unusually pertinent came from the political consultant, Kieran Mahoney. "Looking back on it," Mahoney would say, "the day he'll rue in the campaign is when he went down and took on, in an inappropriate fashion, the Reverends Robertson and Falwell. If he had made those statements in sorrow and not in anger, it would have served him well. By being vitriolic, he raised more questions about himself than he did about them."

Looking back on the campaign, McCain had faced a number of problems. Some were of his own making, such as his apparent waffling on the politically sensitive issue of abortion. Others were clearly created by Bush, such as the sleazy campaigning in South Carolina. But, ultimately, McCain's biggest challenge was that the opposing team, as it were, was playing a different game. McCain may have been playing to win, but Bush was playing to win at any cost—any whatsoever. McCain had no strong institutional support from his own party, no link to organizations that had soft money to burn. On the contrary, he wanted to do away with soft money. McCain was handicapped financially, and that cramped his ability to respond to

Bush's attacks in a strategic and methodical fashion. Often, McCain's campaign seemed to be unfocused and unpredictable. Bush had the party's support and the best people in the business of politics to run his campaign. In the end, for McCain, "Faith in country" just wasn't enough.

"I am no longer an active candidate for my party's nomination for president," John McCain said on Thursday, March 9, as he stood on top of a cliff near Sedona, against, as one newspaper would describe it, "a spectacular backdrop of red rocks, snowcapped ridges, and white clouds stacked against a huge blue sky." He was standing outside in the state he loved, Arizona, in a tableau that was simply breathtaking in its beauty, and he had to say the words that he had hoped he would never have to say—*no longer an active candidate.* "I hoped," he continued in a soft, composed voice as Cindy once again stood beside him, "our campaign would be a source of change in the Republican Party, and I believe we have indeed set a course that will ultimately prevail in making our party as big as the country we serve."

McCain and his staff had debated throughout the day on Wednesday. Late in the afternoon, he had finally made up his mind, and his aides canceled McCain's travel plans to Colorado and Illinois. Leaving open the possibility that something strange might happen, McCain decided not to withdraw from the race but to suspend his campaign. "I am suspending my campaign," McCain said, being precise on what he was doing. "A majority of Republican voters made clear their preference for president is Governor Bush. . . . I congratulate Governor Bush and wish him and his family well. He may very well become the next President of the United States. This is an honor accorded to very few, and it is such a great responsibility that he deserves the best wishes of every American. He certainly has mine." McCain was careful, the press would duly note the next day in the front-page coverage McCain's suspension was afforded, not to endorse Bush. Then again, since he was only suspending his campaign, it would not have been appropriate for him to offer any endorsement.

Naturally, McCain talked about the McCainiacs, the millions of voters who had supported him and "ignited the cause of reform, a cause far greater and more important than the ambitions of any other candidate." While McCain talked to the wall of television cameras, off to the left, Murphy, Weaver, and other staffers wept. Finally, he had to address a subject that was sure to arise in the coming days: the possibility that he might bolt the Republican Party and run as an Independent. On this issue, McCain was unwavering. "I love my party; it is my home," he said. "Ours is the party of Lincoln, Roosevelt, and Reagan. That is good company for any American to keep." Still, a speech from McCain would not be complete, no matter what the occasion, if it did not have language in it about reform. This speech was no exception. "I am also dedicated," McCain said, "to the necessary cause of reform, and I will never walk away from a fight for what I know is right and just for our country. As I said throughout the campaign, what is good for my country is good for my party. Should our party ever abandon this principle, the American people will rightly abandon us and we shall surely slip into the mists of history, deserving the allegiance of none."

When McCain was finished, Howard Opinsky, who had fielded so many press calls for so long, walked over to the cliff and threw his pager over the edge into the ravine—to the applause of the press corps and McCain's staff. Then, without taking questions from reporters, McCain left. He had arranged for his staff to join him back at the cabin where he would grill pork ribs for everyone. Mostly, McCain, his friends, and his staff drank beer and whiskey sours and ate as the music from McCain's favorite oldies rock station played in the background. At some point, Bush called McCain to acknowledge his announcement that he was suspending his campaign. "We hadn't told the Bush campaign we were making the announcement," one McCain staffer says. "So we were back at the cabin enjoying ourselves when the phone rang. Cindy answered it. It was Bush. And he said, 'Is John there?' She knew it was Bush, so she said 'Sure' and gave the phone to John Weaver. Weaver said 'Hello,' and Bush said, 'It was a very nice speech you gave; my family is very honored.' And Weaver said, 'Who is this?' And Bush said, 'Weaver, is that you?' And Weaver said, 'Hold on a sec.' Then he handed the phone to McCain."

Ultimately, there would be a video about the McCain campaign. Naturally, it concluded with excerpts from McCain's speech before the Red Rocks near Sedona. But as McCain spoke the words that effectively ended his campaign, a phrase appeared on the video: "To Be Continued. . . ."

The next day, McCain said he was not prepared to endorse Bush until he studied how Bush was going to be able to advance his campaign goals. From his home in Arizona, McCain did talk by phone with a reporter from the *New York Times*. "I'm not bitter," he told the reporter for a story that ran on Saturday, "and I'm not going to indulge in recriminations. There is no point to it. The game's over. I could complain about the tactics, like the breast cancer ad, and I could agonize over my own tactical mistakes. But why do it? I'm a big boy, and he won."

This said, McCain went on a vacation abroad with his family. During the week or so he was away, Bush, who was still in Austin, had his own chat with the *New York Times*. In the one-hour interview, which ran in the newspaper on March 25, Bush was dismissive and cold when he talked about McCain. Did McCain change Bush's views on any subjects? "He didn't change my views." Did he enlighten any of his views? "No, not really." Didn't McCain help produce record voter turnout? "Well, then, how come he didn't win?" Did Bush have any regrets? "Like what? Give me an example. What should I regret?" And what about the negative tone of the campaign? "I didn't make the negative tone." It was a display of arrogance and condescension rarely seen in politics, but as Bush sat in his governor's office in Austin, he was as pompous and unapologetic as he had ever been. It was not a performance some members of the

Republican Party were happy to see in print, especially on the front page of the *New York Times*.

Back from his vacation, McCain, tanned and rested, returned to Capitol Hill on Monday, March 20—the day he approved the formation of a political action committee he named The Straight Talk Express PAC. The next day, after he had spent a quiet Monday catching up on paperwork in his office, McCain planned to return to the Senate chamber to give a speech—his first since he had ended his presidential run. The day started out with a meeting in his office, Room 241 of the Russell Senate Office Building, with the "Four Horsemen"—McCain and Senators Chuck Hagel of Nebraska, Fred Thompson of Tennessee, and Mike DeWine of Ohio, who served essentially as McCain's kitchen cabinet. Because McCain had announced to the press that he planned to make his first speech in the Senate since dropping out of the presidential race, his office was packed with reporters and camera crews, not to mention tourists, when the Four Horsemen arrived. "Oh my goodness," Thompson said as he tried to wend his way through the mob scene in the reception area to McCain's office. "What if we'd won."

After his powwow with the Horsemen, McCain met with reporters for three minutes outside his office. How does it feel to be back on the Hill? one reporter wanted to know. "Terrible! Depressing!" McCain quipped. "I'd much rather be on the Straight Talk Express." Logically, the subject of whether he would support the party's nominee came up. "I've always said that I will support the nominee of the party and I will do that," McCain said. "I look forward to discussions with Governor Bush as time goes on." As for McCain's reform agenda, he said: "I've also reiterated my unconditional commitment to those who voted for me in the name of reform. I will support the nominee of the party, but I also will not abandon my reform agenda and those millions of people who are relying on me to pursue it."

Then, he headed off to the Senate. Along the way, tourists gawked as camera crews struggled to keep up with him. Groups of strangers would stop, notice who it was, and spontaneously start to applaud. It was as if McCain was a Hollywood celebrity, not the senior senator from Arizona. When he arrived at the Senate, ready to make the speech that would be carried that night on the evening news, he walked into the chamber and found that it was empty. He was not surprised. Typical of McCain, he had announced to the media that he was making the speech, but he had failed—on purpose—to inform his colleagues. As he walked down the aisle to the Senate floor to make a speech that had been scheduled for 11:30 in the morning, the only other senator present was Barbara Boxer. As senators often do, she was making a speech to an empty chamber. When she saw McCain coming toward her, she stopped her speech to welcome him back.

After she departed, leaving the chamber empty, McCain made a speech about Kosovo—to no one. How ironic it was. Only days before, he was playing to rallies, many of them starting late at night, to find thousands of people had sometimes waited for hours to hear him give a stump speech. Today, his first day back in the Senate, he gave a speech to an empty room. There was no applauding, no cheering, no blaring music, no streamers. He was back to doing what he did before: working as a legislator. During his speech on Kosovo, he avoided any rehashing of the campaign, although he did end with a pronouncement about his supporters. "I intend to do what I can," he said, "working with my congressional colleagues, Republicans and Democrats, to help bring about the changes to the practices and institutions of our democracy that they want and deserve."

After the speech was delivered (his colleagues could later read it in the *Congressional Record*), McCain headed for the weekly luncheon of the Republican senate caucus. Because his attendance at the luncheon *had* been announced, his arrival there was so heavily anticipated the Capitol police had been called in to manage the crowd of media personnel and onlookers that had assembled. Behind closed doors, Trent Lott welcomed McCain back to the caucus, and the group of senators, many of whom had had their share of differences with McCain not only during his presidential run but at various other times in the past, rose to give him a standing ovation. In his brief remarks, McCain offered to take anyone present on a guided tour of New Hampshire. Later in the afternoon, McCain returned to the Senate floor to join a debate on whether Social Security recipients should lose their benefits if they worked.

During the next few days, events quieted down. The focus of much of the Bush campaign, if not the Republican Party, was to find a way to get McCain to endorse Bush. This would not be easy; the wounds from the primary campaign, especially after the mudslinging in South Carolina and the ugliness of the ads about breast cancer research and the environment, were severe and deep. But there was one power broker in Washington who had remained on good terms with both sides—Bob Dole, the former Senate majority leader and the 1996 Republican presidential nominee. Dole, who knew a thing or two about the rough and tumble of political campaigns, set up a lunch with McCain that took place on Tuesday, March 28. If there was anyone in Washington to whom McCain would listen, it was Dole. Dole had also maintained good relations with the Bush family, even though he had had his own spirited campaign against George H. W. Bush in 1988. At their lunch, Dole impressed on McCain that he should take a phone call from Bush. Finally, McCain agreed. When Dole communicated the good news on Tuesday afternoon, Bush called McCain right away, from Virginia. From all accounts, it was a pleasant enough conversation. Afterward, Bush spoke to reporters and, putting the best spin he could on the situation, proclaimed, "I think John and I both understand that the past is the past. It is time to move forward." John Weaver put it more bluntly: "The ice has been broken." The call had to be seen as a breakthrough, particularly because the admission came from Weaver, who, of all of the McCain insiders, was perhaps the most bitter toward the Bush camp.

The ice may have been broken, but McCain was not ready to make any moves to endorse Bush. He had other events planned for the month of April, and he saw no reason not to make the Bush campaign wait. On Friday, April 7, McCain appeared, along with Cindy, at the John F. Kennedy Library in Boston, where he held a book-signing before heading to Rhode Island and Connecticut to endorse Republican senate candidates. (Apparently, he was more than ready to endorse senate candidates, if not Bush.) "We lost the campaign," McCain told the crowd at the book-signing in Boston, "but we did not lose the crusade. The crusade will go on."

On Thursday, April 13, after much negotiation between the two staffs, Bush and McCain announced they would meet face-to-face for the first time since the end of McCain's campaign. But that meeting, scheduled to take place in Pittsburgh, would not happen until May 9, and even then, McCain would wait until his private meeting with Bush ended before he would decide whether to endorse Bush. Even so, Bush jumped at the chance to make a conciliatory gesture toward McCain. He told reporters in Austin: "I'm looking forward to it a lot."

Perhaps, but McCain would still make him wait. On April 19, the day after Bush announced he might consider putting McCain on the ticket as his running mate and would bring up the matter during their meeting in May, McCain returned to South Carolina for the first time since he had lost the primary. In a 30-minute speech before a conservative organization called the South Carolina Policy Council, McCain made a stunning revelation. In short, he admitted he had misled the voters of South Carolina. Revealing that during the campaign he "feared that if I [spoke] honestly I could not win the South Carolina primary . . . so I chose to compromise my principles [and] I broke my promise to always tell the truth," McCain said he felt the Confederate flag "should be removed" from the top of the statehouse in Columbia. "I believe the flag should be removed from your Capitol," he said, "and I am encouraged that fair-minded people on both sides of the issues are working hard to define an honorable compromise." Two months before, McCain had said his ancestors had "fought honorably" for the Confederacy during the Civil War, but now, before the Policy

Council, McCain declared his ancestors had "fought on the wrong side of American history." Still, the tone McCain struck that day was mollifying. "I am here," he said, "only to express my belated wish, my confidence, that you will resolve [the dispute] quickly." For McCain, the gesture of his coming to South Carolina to make such a speech was a matter of conscience, nothing more.

Also in mid-April, he was in New York. "I get a kick out of his deadpan sense of humor," Peter King says. "Around the middle of April, he ended up coming to my house on Long Island. He decided to get all the delegates on Long Island together and have an event at my house. He got a police escort onto the street. The neighbors were out waiting to see him. He came in and first thing he did was insult the two or three staff members with him. 'See my staff,' he said. 'I call them the "no-brains trust." If I had a better staff, I would be president.'"

Near the end of the month, McCain set out on his seventh trip to Vietnam since his release as a POW. The trip was being paid for by NBC, which had signed up McCain to be a guest on *The Today Show* on April 28, the date on which the United States had pulled out of Vietnam. In Vietnam, he would also conduct a town hall meeting for *Hardball.* On Tuesday, April 25, after flying into Vietnam that day, McCain, accompanied by Cindy and his family, returned to Truc Bach Lake, where he was shot down. After shaking hands with the local citizens along the way, he stopped to look at the memorial that had been built there to commemorate his rescue. Soon a crowd gathered around him. "I put the Vietnam War behind me a long time ago," McCain had said on his arrival in the country. "I harbor no anger, no rancor."

McCain was in Vietnam because Sunday, April 30, marked the 25th anniversary of the end of the war. As soon as he arrived there, he attended a repatriation ceremony at the airport. An 11-person military honor guard placed into silver-metal coffins six boxes of remains thought to be those of United States servicemen. Fifty U.S. military personnel and civilians were in attendance as the coffins were draped with American flags and carried into a C-17 cargo plane. From Vietnam, the coffins would be flown to Hickam Air Force Base in Hawaii, where the remains would undergo forensic analysis.

The next day, Wednesday, April 26, McCain was given a tour of Hoa Lo Prison, where he had been held during the war. Accompanied by Cindy and his son Jack, McCain seemed calm and unemotional as he walked about the prison grounds. "I put the war behind me when I left," McCain said stoically. "The memories I have are of the wonderful people I had the privilege of serving with." But when McCain was asked about the prison guards, he did not sound equally forgiving. "I still bear them ill will," he said, "not because of what they did to me but because of what they did to some of my friends, including killing some of them." He stated again, for the record, a reality he had noted (and written about) in the past: During the war, the North Vietnamese tortured POWs, himself included.

As if that statement was not controversial enough, McCain surpassed himself on Friday when he shocked his Vietnamese hosts by saying he believed the "wrong guys" had won the war. A strong proponent of a United States effort to rebuild economic and diplomatic relations with Vietnam, McCain was talking to reporters as he went on a walking tour of Ho Chi Minh City, the city known as Saigon during the war. "I think the wrong guys won," McCain said. "I think that they lost millions of their best people who left by boat, thousands by execution, and hundreds of thousands to re-education camps."

With the May 9 Bush-McCain summit approaching, Pat Robertson could not resist going on television (on Sunday, May 7) and taking yet another opportunity to minimize McCain. Appearing on *Meet the Press*, Robertson told Tim Russert he did not believe McCain would be a suitable running mate for Bush because the country needed "a balanced leader," a comment meant to echo the whisper campaign's innuendos, which had suggested that McCain was not mentally stable enough to be president. "We need somebody,"

Robertson continued, "with his hand on the nuclear trigger and on other levers of government. If Bush would like to have somebody screaming curses at him about three times a week at the other end of the White House, then McCain is his man."

Despite obstacles thrown in the way by people like Robertson, and despite more-or-less constant tension between their staffs, Bush and McCain met in person on May 9. Joe Albaugh, from Bush's staff, and John Weaver, from McCain's staff, had met for 45 minutes at the end of April to work out the details of the event. Bush had even phoned McCain on Sunday (no doubt having heard about Robertson's comments on television that day) to say he was looking forward to their meeting on Tuesday. Almost everything had been worked out and planned for when the two men met that May morning at the William Penn Hotel in Pittsburgh.

The first order of business was a private meeting between Bush and McCain in a fourth-floor conference room in the hotel. Bush sat on a green leather love seat, and McCain sat across from him in a matching chair. In their 80-minute meeting, which was 10 minutes shorter than had been planned, the two discussed a range of issues, among them taxes, education, campaign finance reform, and Social Security. McCain told Bush, point-blank, that he didn't want to be considered as a running mate. Next came the event for which Bush had been waiting: the press conference, where they would be photographed together. Bush entered the press conference first, followed by McCain. Standing next to one another, they volleyed some with the press. McCain said Bush had "the expertise" to lead the nation. But he added: "I want to emphasize one more time, I made it very clear to Governor Bush, I will continue to pursue the issue of reform. That is the agenda that drove me in my campaign and will drive me as long as I am in public service." McCain was asked if he would like a job in a Bush cabinet. Not surprisingly, McCain quipped, "Secretary of Reform."

When enough time had passed that it became obvious McCain was not going to say he endorsed Bush, a reporter put the question to McCain straight on.

"Are you endorsing the governor today?" the reporter asked.

"Yes," McCain said.

"Aren't you avoiding the e-word?" the reporter went on.

"I endorse Governor Bush," McCain said.

Then, as if he were trying to undercut the endorsement he just made, McCain repeated his statement six more times, not unlike a child reciting a nursery rhyme: *"I endorse Governor Bush, I endorse Governor Bush, I endorse Governor Bush, I endorse Governor Bush, I endorse Governor Bush, I endorse Governor Bush."*

Bush stood stiff as a rod next to McCain. No doubt furious at the flippant way McCain was performing the scene he had been brought here to play—The Endorsement of the Candidate—Bush was determined not to show his frustration. Instead, he put the best face he could on the situation. After several minutes passed and other subjects had been discussed, Bush offered, "By the way, I enthusiastically accept."

But the kicker to this awkward display was McCain's answer to the reporter's last leading question. Had McCain decided to "take the medicine now" and endorse Bush today instead of waiting until later? "I think your 'Take the medicine now' is probably a good description," McCain said, grinning.

On Saturday, May 13, at the convention of the state Republican Party in Arizona, the attendees elected Cindy McCain as the chairperson who would head the state's delegation to the Republican National Convention in late July and early August. This selection was not without conflict; traditionally, the governor headed the delegation, so it should have been headed by Jane Hull, an adversary of McCain and an endorser of Bush. It did not seem appropriate, to McCain and others, that his state delegation—a state he won in the primaries—should be headed by a woman who fought against him and, when interviewed by the *New York Times,* said he was mentally unfit to be president. So, after some discussions, Hull decided she would not challenge the convention's decision to name Cindy McCain chairperson.

On Monday, May 15, McCain had a fund-raiser for his Straight Talk Express PAC. The event, held in Washington at the Mayflower Hotel, cost $5,000 to attend the dinner and $1,000 to attend only an earlier forum and reception. In the solicitation letter, which served as an invitation, McCain wrote: "I am counting on you as one of our core group in the 'Straight Talk Crusade' to help me achieve the goals of STRAIGHT TALK AMERICA by making your maximum contribution. Your contribution of $5000 or $1000 respectively may be made from personal and PAC funds."

As he was raising money to continue his crusade, McCain was also busy advancing the issues that were important to him. On Wednesday, May 17, he addressed one topic Bush had used against him (by misrepresenting his record, McCain said) in the campaign: the environment. During hearings McCain held through the Senate Commerce Committee, he said there was "mounting evidence" for the existence of global climate change. While he was campaigning in New Hampshire, McCain had been hounded so much by one environmental group, he agreed to hold hearings on global warming. He was now fulfilling that promise by having six scientists testify, before the Commerce Committee, that the climate was getting warmer. Global warming was a sensitive issue with Bush—a fact that surely was not lost on McCain when he decided to hold these hearings during the weeks leading up to the national convention. In the past, Bush had gone out of his way to say he was not sure that conclusive evidence existed to prove global warming was taking place. This was an echo of the Republican majority position.

McCain continued to be troublesome for Bush. Later in May, the Arizona State Republican Party held a fund-raiser at the Arizona Biltmore. Jane Hull and Congressman Bob Stump chaired the $1,000-a-plate dinner, which Bush attended along with most of the Arizona congressional delegation, including Senator Jon Kyl, Congressman Matt Salmon, Congressman John Shadegg, Congressman J. D. Hayworth, and Congressman Jim Kolbe. But because Bush was there, some argued, McCain refused to attend. McCain's office said

McCain had a long-standing policy not to go to fund-raisers where soft money was raised. This event wasn't supposed to raise soft money for Bush, however; the funds were earmarked for statewide Republican candidates. Still, McCain did not show up, even though, the Bush campaign noted, he had been informed Bush would be attending.

As the month of May unfolded, the controversy surrounding Elian Gonzalez also played itself out. For months now, the country had debated over what to do with young Elian, whose mother had died at sea while she was trying to bring herself and Elian from Cuba to the United States. Elian had been cared for by his family in Miami only to have federal marshalls, under orders from the Clinton Administration, raid the family's home on Easter weekend and remove the child at gunpoint. Many Americans were horrified to see the front-page picture of a marshall, machine gun in hand, ripping Elian from the arms of the fisherman who had rescued him from the sea months before. Angered by the Clinton Administration's continued efforts to send the boy back to his father in Cuba—and to a communist regime—McCain released a statement at the end of May.

"The Clinton Administration's support for the Cuban government in pledging to return young Elian to Cuba—a fate that has befallen mainly Cuban criminals—should disturb all Americans who agree that life in Cuba as Fidel Castro's poster-child would be worse than the fate Elian's mother gave her life to escape," McCain said. "If Elian's father wishes to be reunited with his son, it should occur in a free country. U.S. policy on the future of Elian must be predicated on support for freedom for the father, not slavery for the son."

On Monday, June 5, McCain made his first public appearance in Arizona since dropping out of the presidential race. At a farewell breakfast for Mayor Sam Campana (Sam was a woman) at the Scottsdale Center for the Arts, McCain was upbeat and light-hearted as he spoke to the audience of 300. During his prepared speech, he did not mention Bush. In the question-and-answer session, the subject of Bush came up when McCain was asked about presidential ambitions. "It was one of the most uplifting experiences of my life to run a [presidential] campaign," McCain said. "It was a great ride. . . . I'm 63 years old, and in 2004 I will be campaigning for the reelection of President George W. Bush. As exhilarating as the experience was, the wear and tear and time away from my children, I'm not sure I would ever want to do it again."

During the week of July 17, McCain made headlines again as a result of a phone call he got from Governor Tom Ridge of Pennsylvania. On Tuesday, Ridge called McCain to tell him he knew that he, Ridge, was out of the running to be Bush's vice-presidential running mate. Because of that, he wanted McCain to put up *his* name. Ridge believed the Republicans could not lose with a Bush-McCain ticket. For some time, the Bush campaign had been vetting various potential running mates for Bush. The process was being conducted by Dick Cheney, an old friend of George H. W. Bush. (Cheney, who had never served in the military, was his secretary of defense.) Cheney had looked at a number of candidates for George W., including George Pataki, Tom Ridge, and Elizabeth Dole. Now that he had been excluded, Ridge wanted to start a draft-McCain movement. On Thursday, the day the Republicans in the House sent a letter to Bush urging him to pick McCain as his running mate, word was leaked to the Associated Press that, in a conversation with Ridge, McCain had said he "would serve" if called on. When Ridge had told the Bush campaign about the development, the news was treated coolly. Still, on Thursday night, when McCain appeared on CNN, he was asked about the developments. "It's a hypothetical," McCain said about his being Bush's running mate, "because I don't believe I'm in the process. But if Governor Bush called, I'd certainly like to talk to him about the weather and how things are going and how good a campaign he's running."

In the coming days, Bush shocked the political world by ignoring his list of possible vice-presidential candidates and selecting the man who had put the list together—Cheney. He was an odd choice for a number of reasons, not the least of which was the fact that he had a heart condition. Neither he nor Bush had served in the military, so the ticket would feature a pair who could be labeled "chicken hawks." Because Cheney ran Halliburton, the ticket could be seen as being too beholden to Big Oil. (Bush and his family had long been in the oil business.) In making his announcement of Cheney, Bush underscored what he felt was a comfort factor he had with Cheney. Apparently, in the long run, that was what was most important to Bush. With McCain, there certainly would have been no comfort factor. None. Loyalty was supremely important to Bush, who knew that McCain would never be truly loyal to him.

All of this political and human drama served as a backdrop for McCain's arrival in Philadelphia for the Republican National Convention late in the day on Saturday, July 29. McCain came in on the Straight Talk Express, which he had boarded earlier in the day in Arlington, Virginia, for the ride to Philadelphia. On board, McCain had with him 70 members of the press—almost as many as were covering Bush on the campaign trail. While on board the bus, McCain talked to reporters, just as he had during his presidential run. "I'm in step eight of a twelve-step presidential recovery program," McCain joked early on. "There [are] still some lingering animosities out there, but overall, our relationship—mine and Governor Bush—is very cordial." He also addressed the possibility of a future run for the presidency, especially if Bush should lose. "I really don't envision a scenario," he said, "but to say 'absolutely not'—I've never said 'absolutely not' to anything." With the chance for another run left open, McCain was asked if he often reflected back on the mistakes he made in the campaign. "I just force myself mentally . . . not to do that," he said candidly. "You just got to look forward." Finally, one reporter made the mistake of asking McCain if he had cleared this trip on the Straight Talk Express with the Bush campaign. "The last time I checked," McCain retorted without hesitation, "I'm a United States senator elected by the people of

Arizona." The implication was evident: McCain didn't have to clear anything with the Bush campaign.

The next day, Sunday, McCain appeared at an event organized by Arianna Huffington. Called the Shadow Convention, it was a sort of protest gathering that was being held in the Annenberg School auditorium at the University of Pennsylvania. During his speech, McCain said he "would urge all Americans to support my party's nominee, Governor George Bush of Texas." To this, the audience, made up of people who were discontented with, if not outright suspicious of, the current political system, began to hiss and boo loudly. Some even jeered. McCain paused, then continued by talking about "the candidate who offers change"—Bush. "He's for change, not the status quo," McCain said. When the auditorium was filled with more heckling, McCain said sternly, "If you like, I do not need to continue." The crowd settled down enough for McCain to finish.

"It's an amazing example of who John McCain is," Arianna Huffington says, "that he was willing to appear at the Shadow Convention despite extraordinary pressure being put on him by the Republican Party to cancel. The main reason why McCain appeared was because the convention was a direct challenge to the status quo on three issues, and one of the issues was campaign finance reform. For him not to appear would have implied campaign finance reform was not as important an issue as he said it was again and again. The other reason he appeared was, he told me he would and he is a man of his word. He wasn't going to allow pressure to make him change his mind. This is the kind of man he is, the kind of leader he is."

Afterward, McCain headed for a ballroom in the Sofitel Hotel, where he met with the 240 delegates who were assigned to him as a result of his winning seven states during the primaries. It was, to say the least, an emotional moment for McCain. Here was the end result of the long and exhausting process he had put himself and his family through: 240 people who were willing to vote for his nomination for president. McCain got up on a small stage to speak to his delegates. Technically, he was going to release them so they could vote for Bush. So he made it official by saying, "It was a good fight, my friends. I release all of these delegates." But, more important, McCain wanted to thank the delegates, and when he did, for the first time since it had all come to an end on March 9 before Red Rocks, he choked up. "I am very very grateful to the people in this room who spent their blood, sweat and tears on behalf of this campaign," he said. "I will always be grateful." Then his voice caught and it was all he could do to keep from crying.

Some delegates wept openly, as did Cindy, who stood beside him as she had so often during the campaign. For the longest time, McCain couldn't speak. With one finger, he dabbed his eye. He had come so far from those agonizing days as a POW in Vietnam, so far for a man who should not even be alive, and now it was over. "I will never be able," McCain finally uttered, "I will never be able to thank you." There was a pause; then he tried to change the mood. "This is a time for celebration," he said. "This is a time for happiness." But it wasn't, for as the confetti rained down on them, many of the people in the room that night knew in their heart that, as far as the 2000 Republican presidential nomination was concerned, the best man had not won. Bush might even go on to beat the Democrats' nominee, Al Gore, in November, but still the best man had not won.

M cCain's night at the Republican National Convention was Tuesday, August 2. Early in the evening, the convention honored three former Republican presidents—Gerald Ford, Ronald Reagan, and George Bush. Ford and Bush were in the hall, and Reagan was represented, as he often was these days, by the former first lady, Nancy Reagan. Also speaking that evening were Bob Dole, the party's presidential nominee in 1996; General H. Norman Schwarzkopf, who had overseen the U.S. troops during the Persian Gulf War; and Jim Kolbe, the Arizona congressman who, because he is openly gay, was greeted with a silent protest by members of the Texas delegation who bowed their heads in prayer as he delivered his speech on international trade.

Next came the evening's main speakers—first, Condoleezza Rice; then, Elizabeth Dole. Finally, as the *Star Wars* theme blasted over the hall's sound system, McCain entered the stage. The Bush campaign had banned all posters for other candidates—namely, McCain—but the Connecticut delegation had snuck some in anyway, so throughout the audience there was a smattering of placards with McCain's name on them. In a speech written mostly by Mark Salter, McCain spoke directly of Bush. "I support him," he said. "I am grateful to him. I am proud of him." Then he noted the interwoven history of the Bush and McCain families. "He is a good man from a good family that has, in good times and bad, dedicated themselves to America," McCain said. "Many years ago, the governor's father served in the Pacific with distinction under the command of my grandfather. Now it is my turn to serve under the son of my grandfather's brave subordinate." He next addressed the larger issue of the Greatest Generation, saying, "They fought for love, for love of an idea that America stood for something greater than the sum of our individual interests. Let us take courage from their examples. And from the new world they built, build a better one."

Finally, McCain got back to the reason why he was speaking— the candidacy of George W. Bush. Bush "wants nothing to divide us into separate nations," McCain said, as if to negate somehow the charges he had made during the primaries that Bush had associated with people who were anti-Catholic. "Not our color. Not our race. Not our religion. Not our politics." Referring to himself as "a distant runner-up" in the race, McCain said in summary: "Unless we restore to the people sovereignty over government, renew their pride in public service, reform our public institutions [and] reinvigorate our national purpose, then America's best days will be behind us. . . . If you believe patriotism is more than a sound bite and public service should be more than a photo opportunity, then vote for Governor Bush."

Near the end of the speech, McCain included an odd passage. "I will not see what is over America's horizon," he said. "The years that remain are not too few, I trust, but the immortality that was the aspiration of my youth has, like all the treasures of youth, quietly slipped away." It seemed surreal for a man as active and outgoing and driven as McCain to be talking about his mortality and his distant youth—the passage also had a strangely elegiac tone to it—so the easy way to read what McCain was saying was to conclude he was trying to put his goals and ambitions into historic perspective. When he finished, the packed auditorium gave McCain a warm ovation.

On Wednesday, because he had been bothered by a spot on his left temple, McCain departed Philadelphia and returned to Washington so he could go to the Bethesda Naval Hospital. There, doctors gave him a complete physical and removed not one but two spots: one from his left temple, the other from his left arm. Because the spots were skin cancers, the doctors sent them off to be biopsied. Whatever the results, the spots could not have been too advanced; McCain had been seeing a doctor regularly ever since his first cancer episode in 1993.

By Thursday, August 4, McCain was back in Philadelphia to be on stage, at Bush's side, during the closing ceremony of the convention. That night, little was made of the fact that McCain had a bandage on his temple. In fact, all seemed well when on Thursday, August 10, Bush and McCain started campaigning together. Appearing with Bush at the John Steinbeck Museum in Salinas, California, McCain called Bush "a good and decent man [who] is going to lead this nation." Earlier, several thousand people showed up at the Salinas Amtrak station to see Bush and McCain. McCain spoke to the crowd. Calling himself a "guy from Arizona," he said: "Barry Goldwater of Arizona ran for president. Mo Udall of Arizona ran for president. Bruce Babbitt of Arizona ran for president. And, as you know, I ran for president. Arizona may be the only state in America where mothers don't tell their children they can grow up to be president."

Later, as McCain was getting on a train in Lodi, he was asked by reporters about the bitterness of the primaries. "When you're in a tough primary, a lot of things are said," he reasoned. "The bottom line is, Governor Bush and I are in agreement on the themes that are common to our party." The two men planned to campaign together on Friday and Saturday in Oregon and Washington. To make up for any snubs in the past, McCain made a point of attending two fund-raisers with Bush as well: one in Stockton on Thursday and one in Seattle on Friday night.

McCain also seemed to be doing fine when he and Bush, along with their wives, flew to Arizona to spend the weekend at McCain's cabin. On Saturday morning, after having spent the last three days campaigning in California, Oregon, and Washington, Bush and McCain had posed for pictures aboard an aircraft carrier in Everett, Washington. Next, Bush and McCain flew to Prescott, Arizona, a small town located 100 miles northwest of Phoenix, so Bush could speak at a midafternoon rally on the steps of the Yava-pai County Courthouse, where Barry Goldwater had started his ill-fated presidential campaign 36 years before, on September 3, 1964. Finally, they headed for Sedona and there, on a six-and-a-half-acre estate named Hidden Valley, which features orchards of apple, apricot, peach, cherry, pecan, and almond trees, as well as cottonwood and sycamore groves, the Bushes and the McCains spent a quiet Saturday night, the McCains in the main house and the Bushes in the guest house. The property, owned by the Cindy Hensley McCain Family Trust and acquired in three parcels since 1990, also features a caretaker's cottage.

McCain may have seemed normal during the campaign swing with Bush, but in fact he wasn't. On Thursday, August 10, he had been told by doctors that the biopsies that had been taken at Bethesda had tested positive for melanoma. The entire time he was on the campaign trail with Bush, he and Cindy had to deal with the reality that he now had a form of skin cancer that could be deadly. For McCain, this news made the trip an unusually difficult one to deal with. Not only was he having to travel with someone who had just defeated him in one of the ugliest campaigns in recent political history, not only did he have to sound enthusiastic as he campaigned for him, but he also had to cope with the fact that his future was now uncertain. As a way of coping with the medical news, as soon as the Bushes left Sedona on Sunday, McCain took Cindy and his children to a houseboat on Lake Powell for a family vacation.

On Wednesday, August 16, McCain released a statement through his office. It read: "During a routine examination, two unrelated spots were discovered on Senator John McCain: One on his left temple, the other on his left arm. The spots were confirmed to be melanomas." The news put a different spin on the passage near the end of his speech at the Republican National Convention where he talked about his own mortality and his youth, which was now in the distant past. Did McCain suspect something his doctors had confirmed only later? Were his remarks prophetic or simply eerie?

On Thursday, back in Phoenix, McCain underwent a battery of tests at the Mayo Clinic to determine how far the melanoma had spread. Besides a complete blood workup, he was given a chest X ray, an electrocardiogram, an MRI, a CAT scan, and an echocardiogram. It was standard procedure for him to have these tests for this condition. When the tests were done, he consulted with his doctors, as he did again on Friday morning. On Thursday night, he had canceled an appearance at a fund-raiser for a local state senator; he also canceled a trip to Ohio. In the Friday morning meeting, which lasted for three hours, the doctors told him the test results were encouraging, though there had been a change in his condition. After a biopsy of his left temple in 1996, the results were negative. Now the skin cancer was malignant. Returning from the Mayo Clinic, McCain met with reporters at his house. There, he and Cindy took out to the reporters a wheelbarrow full of bottled water and a basket of sunscreen. When one reporter asked Cindy if she was scared, McCain took charge, saying, "I woke up late last night and I did see her thumbing through the insurance policies." That night, McCain and Cindy went to a baseball game at One Ballpark to see the Arizona Diamondbacks play the Chicago Cubs.

On Saturday, having checked into the Mayo Clinic early that morning, McCain was in surgery for five and a half hours, under a general anesthesia, to remove the malignant skin cancer from his left temple and left upper arm. Removal of the cancer from the arm required only a simple excision. However, the operation on the left temple was much more extensive; it included removal of lymph nodes from his face and his neck. Luckily for McCain, doctors determined that the cancer had not spread to the lymph nodes. If it had, his chances for survival would have been drastically reduced. Because doctors had caught the disease in time, McCain's prognosis was good. During recovery, when McCain was asked by his doctor, John Eckstein, if he wanted him to meet with the press and say anything on his behalf, McCain, able to muster his quick sarcastic wit, looked up at the doctor and said, "Call Trent Lott. I know he'll be on pins and needles." When the doctor did meet with reporters, he provided a straightforward description of McCain's status, noting that the cancer had not spread to the lymph nodes and declaring, "All melanoma was removed during the surgery." Speaking to reporters, Cindy was much more emotional. "I have said many prayers this week, as you can imagine," she said. "And all my prayers have been answered."

By Sunday, McCain was walking around his wing of the Mayo Clinic and having guests. On Monday, he was released from the clinic and returned to his home in Phoenix. The operation on his arm had been simple, so the pain in that area was minimal, but to remove the cancer from his temple had required deep surgery, which left him with severe pain in the days afterward.

Not surprisingly, throughout much of September, McCain took it easy and concentrated on making a full recovery. By October, he was ready to get back to politics. He did so in two ways. First, he continued to campaign for Bush and the Republican Party; second, he focused on issues important to him. In October, he appeared on television in ads he had recently cut to endorse the passage, in Oregon and Colorado, of ballot initiatives that would effectively close the gun-show loophole in those states. Under current regulation, a buyer did not have to submit to a background check if he or she bought a gun at a gun show. McCain wanted to require *all* gun buyers, even those purchasing guns at gun shows, to submit to a background check. In the 30-second ad, which started airing in Denver on October 4, McCain looked straight into the camera and said: "I'm John McCain with some straight talk. Convicted felons have been able to buy and sell thousands of guns at gun shows because of a loophole in the law. Many were later used in crimes. That's wrong."

In the past, McCain and the National Rifle Association had been friendly; with this ad, that relationship came to a complete end. The ads were paid for by Americans for Gun Safety—a not-for-profit organization with chapters in 28 states. The organization was set up in July by Andrew J. McKelvey, the CEO of TMP Worldwide, which owned, among other companies, Monster.com. McKelvey, a Republican, put up $8 million for the ad campaign. Earlier, McCain had voted against legislation that would have closed the gun-show loophole, but, he said, the massacre at Columbine High School (a gun bought at a gun show was used in the tragedy) made him rethink his position. He tried to get at the push-pull nature of the controversy with this line of thought: "I believe law-abiding citizens have the right to own guns. But with rights come responsibilities."

On Friday, October 20, McCain reteamed with Bush. Originally, the two were supposed to reunite in New Hampshire for the first time since McCain had trounced Bush in the primary there, but McCain didn't make it. Bush went through with the appearance at St. Anselm College in Manchester and explained McCain's absence by saying, "I know some of you might be here to see him"—that, no doubt, was an understatement—"but he ate some rotten crawfish in Mississippi last night, and he's not feeling very well." In fact, McCain *had* gotten food poisoning the night before in Laurel, Mississippi, when he ate catfish and shrimp at a fund-raiser for Republican congressional candidate Dunn Lampton. He stopped in Washington to see his doctor, and when he was pronounced to be in good shape, he continued to New England and met up with Bush in Bangor, Maine.

There, in front of an audience of thousands who had gathered in an airport hangar, McCain addressed the Bush versus McCain battle in the primaries by quoting Vince Lombardi, the legendary head coach of the Green Bay Packers. "Show me a good loser," McCain reminded the audience Lombardi once said, "and I'll show you a loser." As the audience laughed, McCain went on. "The campaign that Governor Bush and I waged," he said, "was good for us, it was good for America, and I believe that I can best help Governor Bush in this campaign by telling the American people of my firm commitment and belief the country will be in very good hands with the next president of the United States, Governor George W. Bush." McCain mentioned the debate appearances Bush had made with Gore during the presidential campaign. He called Bush "calm, assured . . . and fully prepared to restore integrity and respect to the White House. On the other side, we saw three different people." It was a not-so-subtle slap at Gore who, many believed, changed so dramatically from debate to debate that he actually seemed to be different candidates.

Specifically, McCain said, Bush was "prepared to restore the morale, the respect, the dignity and the lifestyle of the men and women in the military. I say to our men and women in the military, help is on the way." In fact, in their appearance together, McCain played up how he felt Bush would be able to handle military matters. "We found out with the USS Cole," McCain said (referring to the American battleship that was hit on October 12 while it was refueling in Yemen by what turned out to be a suicide bombing attack carried out by an Al Qaeda cell, an assault that killed 17 American sailors and almost sank the ship), "that we live in a dangerous world. It is unpatriotic not to talk about military readiness." On this issue, McCain said he believed Bush was "fully prepared" to be commander-in-chief of the United States armed forces. When Bush spoke, he focused on the politics of the moment. "I'm counting on you," he told the crowd, "in the next nearly two weeks to find a neighbor, convince a friend to go to the polls, and don't be afraid if they're an open-minded Democrat or an Independent either, because you know what? Open-minded Democrats and Independents want to change Washington, D.C. They're tired of what's going on." Bush had once criticized McCain for appealing to those very same voters.

One gaffe took place during their appearance. Well before Bush had finished speaking, a confetti cannon went off, which signaled the release of the balloons. In mid-sentence, Bush stopped to watch the balloons float slowly up into the air as the confetti rained down on the stage.

The next day, Saturday, McCain joined Cheney to campaign in Michigan; on Monday, Cindy traveled with Bush through Wisconsin. On Wednesday, October 25, McCain joined Bush and his brother Jeb as they barnstormed Florida. Then, at the end of the month, McCain accompanied Bush on a campaign swing through California. Bush told a crowd at an airport hotel in Burbank that he wanted to win California, a wish that ultimately did not come true. Ironically, at the same time that McCain was campaigning with Bush in California, an ad was running on television on cable stations in Los Angeles, San Francisco, San Diego, and Sacramento advancing McCain's signature issue, campaign finance reform. Appearing in the spot with Warren Beatty, one of the most liberal members of the notoriously liberal Hollywood community, McCain attacked a campaign finance reform proposal sponsored by the California legislature. In the ad, McCain and Beatty, sitting beside each other, nodded their approval as the voice-over announcer said that "Prop 34" was "disguised as campaign finance reform." Beatty declared, "It's written by people already in office to benefit people already in office." He was followed by McCain who said, "And what it actually does is wipe out real reform, Prop 208, which was passed overwhelmingly by the voters." That legislation was passed in 1996; now the California legislature was trying to overturn that proposition with a weaker one. The campaign to defeat Prop 34 was being funded by Max Pavelsky, a

Los Angeles millionaire, who put up $600,000 of his own money. The television ad campaign alone cost $250,000.

When McCain finished his campaign appearances with Bush in California, he was done. He had paid his dues to the party, not to mention to Bush. Then, as the November election rolled around and the subsequent electoral crisis unfolded in Florida, McCain watched quietly. The Republicans controlled the House by six seats and the Senate was divided 50–50 (for the first time in American history), but the presidency was in limbo. More than a few critics in the Republican Party—and certainly more than a few McCainiacs—believed that, had McCain been the party's nominee, the election would not have been close at all. Some even felt that, if McCain had decided to run as an Independent, he could have won the three-way race. Simply put, many saw McCain as the best man for the job. Ultimately, these scenarios would remain what they were—fantasies. The reality was: Gore may have gotten more of the popular vote, but, in the end, George W. Bush would be sworn in as president. And despite the gestures McCain had made to help Bush get elected, he would soon find out that, in the "Bush" world, once one is viewed as an enemy, one is always viewed as an enemy. In the early days of the Bush Administration—and in the weeks and months to come—McCain would know firsthand how it felt to be an enemy of the Bushes.

II "I think," John McCain says, "in general, the Bush campaign did very well. Bush won. Obviously, they made some tactical mistakes. I think they showed some overconfidence near the end that was clearly not warranted—when Karl Rove was touting they had it in the bag. You gotta remember Yogi Berra's adage, 'It ain't over till it's over.' Overall, I think they ran an effective campaign. I think that it was one which appealed to a certain stability back in the White House. I don't want to say 'honor and decency'—you know, as was their phraseology. But I think Americans are very schizophrenic about Bill Clinton. I think they appreciate the incredible skills that he had. At the same time, they were not happy with his personal behavior. And I think President Bush, to a degree, appealed to that. He said, 'What you see is what you get with me.' And I think that was effective."

But McCain believed there were lessons to be learned from the 2000 presidential election. "I think the first thing we learned is, there's a compelling requirement for electoral reform," McCain says. "Not just in Florida, but all over America, there are groups of Americans who are underrepresented because their votes were not counted. I think that's the first lesson we learned. There is a second lesson. In a healthy economy and a pretty good record over eight years, Al Gore did not maximize his opportunities to be elected President of the United States. A seminal aspect of that was the three debates. I think his biggest problem was that he never clearly identified himself to the American people: 'Here's who I am and what I stand for.' That's why the three debates are sort of the quintessential aspect of it, because he was three different people in three different debates. The American public tuned in and saw three different guys and they went: 'What's this?'

"What the American people want is a person who can articulate a vision of the future to them. This is why great Americans such as Scoop Jackson and John Glenn were never able to secure the nomination of their party. And, for whatever reason, Al Gore was never able to articulate a vision of the future of America to the American people."

11

MAN OF THE PEOPLE

"I realized when we were about to organize for the new session," says Senator Thad Cochran, a Republican from Mississippi, "that John needed another vote for campaign finance reform [CFR]. He had 59 votes to invoke closure to get the bill to the floor, to the motion to proceed to consider the bill, and I thought, 'If we are going to be able to write a bill that is fair to both parties and also the interests that are going to be reflected in the Congress, what better time than when you have 50 Republicans and 50 Democrats.' While I didn't agree with everything in McCain-Feingold, I did agree that we needed to start. So I walked up to John while we were at an organizational luncheon, sat down, and told him just what I thought. I could tell by his expression that he was ecstatic. He was really fired up over the fact that I would be willing to get on board."

This was all McCain needed. Bush had not even been sworn in as president when, on January 4, 2001, McCain and Feingold held a press conference on Capitol Hill—accompanied by their new supporter, Thad Cochran—to announce their intention to introduce McCain-Feingold on January 22, with Cochran as a cosponsor. The importance of the addition of Cochran was clear in the news conference; he represented the 60th vote, the number needed to prevent a filibuster.

With Feingold and Cochran at his side, McCain addressed the reason why he was not going to delay in introducing his bill, an act in defiance of key Republicans who wanted him to wait to bring up campaign finance reform so as not to embarrass one of the main opponents of that reform, George W. Bush, the new president. "To say that we shouldn't take it up right after the inauguration because of some legislative agenda is simply nonsense," McCain said. "Everyone knows that the longer you delay bringing up the issue, the less likelihood of its passage. I mean, that's just a political reality. . . . I promised millions of Americans, when I ran for president of the United States, that I would not give up on this crusade of reform, the gateway to which is CFR. I cannot and will not in good conscience give up on the effort."

On Saturday, January 13, Bush, one week away from being inaugurated, called McCain and spoke to him on the phone for 20 minutes. McCain and Feingold planned to reintroduce their bill on January 22, two days after Bush was sworn in as president, and Congressmen Christopher Shays and Marty Meehan had said they intended to introduce the House version of the bill at the same time, so Bush was calling to send McCain a signal. He may have told McCain he wanted to settle their disagreement over campaign finance reform, but what he really wanted McCain to do, what surrogates of Bush had talked about openly in the press, was to get McCain to hold off reintroducing his legislation so that Bush could have the political stage to himself in the initial months of his presidency.

Because of the election crisis, many Bush supporters worried about whether he could start his time in office from a position of power, unity, and resolve. To have his main challenger from the primary campaign reintroduce so soon a piece of legislation that Bush had so publicly argued against might make Bush appear weak, and if McCain succeeded in advancing his own political agenda, the initial balance between Congress and the new administration in the White

House was in jeopardy. McCain was determined to do whatever he wanted to do, regardless of the wishes of the new president, but he tried to put the best spin he could on the disagreement when he appeared on CBS's *Face the Nation* on Sunday, January 14. "He wants to get this issue [campaign finance reform] resolved," McCain said. "He and I have some disagreements, but we are, again, in agreement that we ought to take up and address the issue." McCain skirted the fact that the Bush camp wanted him to wait until later to address the issue—a request he was going to ignore.

On January 22, as he had said he would, McCain introduced in the Senate a bill to reform campaign finance laws. McCain-Feingold would ban unlimited, unregulated soft money contributions, beef up rules on ads run by advocacy groups, and make unions get permission from nonunion members to use their fees for political contributions. At a news conference after his introduction of the bill, McCain—surrounded by Senators Feingold, Fred Thompson (Republican from Tennessee), James Jeffords (Republican from Vermont), Carl Levin (Democrat from Michigan), and Congressman Christopher Shays (Republican from Connecticut)—told reporters, "After one of the closest elections in our nation's history, there's one thing the American people are unanimous about: They want their government back." McCain's bill was similar to one he and Feingold had proposed in 2000. That bill had passed in the House but never got to the Senate because the Republican leadership opposed it.

Soon, Bush had set up a meeting with McCain. It took place at the White House on Wednesday, January 24. McCain wanted an early vote in the Senate on campaign finance reform. Now Bush was transparent, if he had not been earlier: He wanted McCain to hold off on pushing for McCain-Feingold so that he—Bush—could advance his own legislative agenda first. The Senate was evenly divided, 50–50, for the first time ever, so neither party controlled the body outright, but if McCain agreed to stand out of the way of the new president, Bush would not have to use any of his clout to try and block McCain's efforts. By the end of the meeting, during which campaign finance reform and legislative timetables were discussed at length, no resolution had been reached. From Bush's point of view, the matter was simple: McCain had not agreed to back off. This meant the meeting had been a failure.

After the meeting, McCain emerged from the West Wing to talk to reporters. Trying to put the best face on what had happened, he told them he looked forward to having additional conversations with Bush concerning campaign finance reform since he did not feel optimistic that the present meeting had resolved their disagreements. "I believe," McCain said, choosing his words carefully, "I came away with the distinct impression that he's favorably disposed toward continued discussions on this issue and seeing if we can't work out something with the belief that both of us hold that this system needs to be fixed."

As if to underscore the fact that McCain was now playing on turf with which he was much more familiar than Bush, McCain watched a week later as a group called the House Centrists Coalition—five Democrats and five Republicans—sent a letter to Speaker of the House Dennis Hastert in which they announced: "We urge you to establish an expeditious timetable for consideration of true campaign finance reform. We want to avoid delay." It was not a letter the White House would have wanted sent.

On February 6, McCain made another move that angered the Bush Administration: He joined with the Democrats to announce his cosponsorship of a patient's bill of rights. The bill was being sponsored in the Senate by one of the icons of American liberalism: Ted Kennedy. Lincoln Chaffee, the Republican senator from Rhode Island, intended to support the bill, as did Senator John Edwards of North Carolina, a Democrat. The bill would be called McCain-Kennedy-Edwards. "What happened was," John Edwards says, "McCain and Kennedy and Tom Daschle—all three—stopped me one day and asked me to work on the bill with John. We had a series of meetings over several months, working on the bill, drafting the bill together. John McCain is a person of great strength and character. He stands up for what he believes in, whether it's popular or unpopular. He is a breath of fresh air to work with."

The White House was worried about the patient's bill of rights, so much so that on February 5 the Bush Administration sent aides to meet with two key advocates of the bill in the House—Congressmen Charlie Norwood, a Republican from Georgia and a dentist, and Greg Ganske, a Republican from Iowa and a doctor—to try to persuade them not to advance the bill in the House. It looked as if the White House was going to have some luck with Norwood, if not Ganske. Norwood—a cosponsor of the bill with John Dingell, a Democrat from Michigan—seemed to buckle from pressure put on him over the weekend at a Republican congressional retreat. By McCain's coming out publicly to support the bill in the Senate at the same time the White House was trying to kill it in the House, McCain was sending another signal to the Bush camp that, at least as far as his legislative agenda was concerned, he could not be controlled.

Indeed, by March, some political observers were starting to point out that Washington had not seen this kind of political feud shaping up, with two powerhouses in the same party going at it, since the 1960s, when the Democrats engaged in an openly bitter battle that played out between Lyndon Johnson and Robert Kennedy. "Bush allies believe," the *Los Angeles Times* noted on March 17, "McCain is trying to broaden his national power base by systematically opposing the administration on several high-profile subjects: health care, gun control, and, most prominently, campaign finance reform, the volatile issue the Senate will begin debating Monday." Pointing out that McCain had met with Bush only once since the inauguration, the paper quoted an unnamed source close to McCain who openly broached a subject that had started to make the gossip rounds in Washington: the possibility that McCain would become so fed up with the Republican Party that he would bolt it to become either a Democrat or an Independent. "If you close every door in the party," the McCain source said, "at some point he has to come to a hard decision about what he's going to do. He's less and less bound by any residual loyalties to the party."

In fact, after being in Washington for nearly two decades, McCain now found himself taking positions that were consistently in opposition to those taken by the majority of members of his own party. The issues were vital: campaign finance reform, gun control, health care, and taxes. On these matters, McCain was in favor of campaign finance reform (his party was not); in favor of limited gun control—specifically, closing the gun-show loophole (his party was not); in favor of a patient's bill of rights (his party was not); and in favor of a tax cut that benefited the working class, not the rich (his party was not). He was becoming, political observers could argue, a candidate who could claim he was a true populist—a man of the people. At some point, McCain had to reach the hard but inevitable conclusion that, at least as far as legislative issues were concerned, he was siding with the Democrats much more than he was with the Republicans. The question was obvious: How much more time would pass before he got fed up with fighting his own party and leave it?

During February and March, McCain and Feingold had appeared in a series of town hall meetings across the country to discuss the issue of campaign finance reform and try to generate support for their bill. The sixth—and last—meeting took place at St. John's College in Annapolis on March 16. The two senators got a long standing ovation, which contributed to the event's feeling more like a rally than a town hall meeting. "We are challenging every single special interest that buys influence in Congress," McCain told the audience. "We are doing this for the next generation of Americans. . . . We are optimistic. This is not the end, but only the beginning of legislation to reform many aspects of government. But we don't believe we can achieve these [other reforms] until we have campaign finance reform." To that end, Feingold added: "Current campaign financing laws are making a joke of the idea of one man, one vote. It's not $1 million, one vote."

For the last two weeks in March, the Senate debated McCain-Feingold. On Thursday, March 22, in the middle of that debate, McCain spent a good part of the day not on Capitol Hill lobbying his fellow senators but on the campus of the boarding school he once attended. The year before, Episcopal had established an honor named after Allen C. Phillips, a member of the faculty for 42 years: the Allen C. Phillips Lecture on Integrity in Action. McCain had been asked to give this year's annual lecture, and he had accepted with gratitude.

McCain had often wanted to go back to Episcopal to see the campus where he had spent three years getting ready for the Naval Academy. After his return from Vietnam, he was driven by a desire to see William B. Ravenel, who had had a lasting impression on him when he was a student at Episcopal. McCain had wanted to discuss the subject of honor with his former mentor, but he discovered, when he got back to Washington, that Ravenel had died while McCain was in Vietnam. Now, at least McCain would be able to return and speak to today's student body, which had changed enormously since McCain was a student there. Significantly, in 1991, the school had admitted women. At present, of the 400 or so students, 40 percent were women.

As soon as McCain arrived on campus, he noticed how different the place looked. The buildings appeared new and modern, and naturally, of the students rushing from building to building, a large number were young women, a sight he would have never seen when he was an Episcopal student. He was greeted by the headmaster, Rob Hershey, and taken into an administrative building where he met with a group of honor students. They treated him like what he was—the school's most famous alumnus, the unexpected student-made-good who had come home to receive an admiring welcome.

Later, in Callaway Chapel, before a standing-room-only crowd of students, faculty, and guests, McCain looked out from the podium onto an audience made up mostly of alert, young faces, and spoke in the simple, honest style for which he had become known. "I have very fond memories of this place," McCain said, "and some of the best memories of my life. And to be recognized by this school for my small contribution to public service is an honor I will long remember and treasure." McCain then addressed the issue of honor. "I think that the great strength of this institution is its adherence to an honor code. It's both a privilege and a burden because, forever, you will have the obligation and the burden that if you do something in your life that is a violation of the honor code, you're not going to be able to get around it, you're not going to be able to rationalize it away, you're not going to be able to excuse it."

Obviously, McCain was referring, at least in part, to his years as a POW, and, despite whatever mixed feelings he had had about his conduct in the Hanoi Hilton in the past, he could point with unqualified pride to one decision he made in Vietnam. "You may know that, at one point, because my father was a very high-ranking admiral in the navy," McCain told his mostly young audience, "[the North Vietnamese] offered me the opportunity to come home early because it would have been a propaganda show that they released the admiral's son. And I guarantee you that one of the reasons why I had the strength to refuse that offer was that I hoped that I could come back here some day. And I couldn't have come back here if I had accepted that offer and left behind my fellow prisoners . . . a number of them had been there several years before I had."

Eventually, McCain turned to the subject about which he spoke in almost every talk he gave these days—whether it was before a caucus of his colleagues in the Senate or a group of high school students in northern Virginia. The topic was his efforts "to reform the institutions of government." That a key part of that reform process was unfolding in the Congress even as he spoke was a detail not lost on McCain. "The so-called soft money," he said, "the unregulated, undisclosed money that pours into American political campaigns influences and affects the way that we conduct our public lives and the course of our legislative agenda. Until we reform that, then we will not be able to reform the other institutions of government."

As the debate over McCain-Feingold was playing out, McCain challenged Bush on another issue. Recently, Bush had appeared in Orlando, Florida, where he vowed never to sign a bill that would regulate HMOs, which was exactly what the patient's bill of rights being worked on by McCain and others would do. McCain responded to Bush's pronouncement by saying he wanted the bill voted on by Memorial Day, a move that could require Bush, within the first six months of his presidency, to veto a bill that would be popular with the public.

As this conflict hit the newspapers, the larger drama of the debate over campaign finance reform continued to play out in the Senate. As a way to try to shoot down McCain-Feingold, Chuck Hagel, a Republican from Nebraska who was so close to McCain he had been a national cochair of McCain's presidential campaign, introduced an alternate version of campaign finance reform that had the backing of the White House—a bill that, in McCain's estimation, did not provide true reform but created the illusion of reform. Actually, Hagel's version maintained the status quo. "But recognizing both the Senator's hard work and sincere concern, I must oppose this amendment," McCain said on the Senate floor as he led an effort that ultimately shot down Hagel's bill. "I must oppose it because it preserves—indeed, it sanctions—the soft-money loophole that has made a mockery of current campaign finance law."

On Wednesday, the Senate voted to raise the limit for the amount of money an individual can contribute to a candidate—that is, "soft money"—from $1,000 to $2,000. The Senate raised the hard money limit as well, from $25,000 to $37,500. This was the first change in the campaign finance laws since 1974, when many campaign laws were rewritten to offset the Watergate scandal. The current changes, which were included in an amendment that grew out of a compromise of amendments sponsored by Senators Fred Thompson and Diane

Feinstein, passed by an overwhelming margin: 84 to 16. The passage of this amendment, especially by such a wide margin, indicated one important fact: It now looked as if campaign finance reform had a good shot of passing. It was, in short, a stunning, even historic, development.

On Thursday, March 29, the Senate voted down the last amendment that could have blocked McCain-Feingold—more evidence, it appeared, that the Senate would approve campaign finance reform. After the defeat of that amendment, McCain and Feingold walked out of the Senate chamber and, as onlookers applauded, hugged Granny D, an elderly citizen-activist who had walked across much of the country to protest the corrupt political system. As Granny D watched, McCain and Feingold met with reporters. Feingold said of the legislation that was expected to be voted on in Monday's session: "We're almost there!"

As expected, on Monday, the Senate voted 59 to 41 for McCain-Feingold. On the floor of the Senate, McCain spoke before the vote. "I asked at the start of this debate for my colleagues to take a risk for America," he said. "In a few minutes, I believe we will do just that. I will go to my grave deeply grateful for the honor of being a part of it." With the passage of the bill in the Senate, the focus of the debate shifted to the House, where the Republicans, especially those closely associated with the White House, had vowed to shoot it down.

"Have you seen Siegfried and Roy?" John McCain said to no one in particular as he stood outside at the foot of a stairwell on the grounds of a high school in Phoenix. Clear and sunny, it was still unusually temperate for an April day in Arizona. McCain was about to do something he had done countless times before—shoot a commercial, this one a public service announcement. A cheerful and pleasant young woman named Kathy was applying makeup to McCain's face. An old pro at this, McCain joked with her in a playful, lighthearted manner. As she worked, Kathy had to be careful with the left side of McCain's face because, earlier in the week, he had undergone plastic surgery to lessen the six-inch vertical scar running from the top of his temple to his jawbone. The scar was a harsh reminder of the major operation he had undergone to remove the cancerous melanoma. So far, five separate follow-up tests had shown no signs of skin cancer, so this recent surgery was done purely for cosmetic reasons.

Kathy dabbed away, gingerly. McCain changed the subject, recalling with studied satisfaction his recent trip to Las Vegas. He and Cindy had had an excellent dinner at the Bellagio Hotel before they took in Siegfried and Roy's famous magic show. "I mean," McCain continued, talking to Kathy or anyone else from the commercial crew standing nearby who happened to be listening, "it's flashy, it's glitzy, it's Las Vegas." He stopped, pausing for dramatic effect. "But they make an elephant disappear!"

Before long, McCain was joined by Greg Stevens, his media consultant during the presidential campaign. Stevens had produced McCain's "biography" commercial, the 30-second spot that had caused members of the Bush campaign such consternation since it underscored the dramatically different lives Bush and McCain had lived. On this day, Stevens was overseeing the filming of the public service announcement because the nonprofit organization producing the spot was one of his clients.

"We're ready for you, John," Stevens said.

McCain followed Stevens to a makeshift soundstage constructed on the school's quadrangle. As McCain stood below a boom mike, students milled around in the background. Their movements had been carefully coordinated by the director so that, in the final commercial, McCain would appear to be standing in the middle of a busy schoolyard. Dressed in a gray suit, blue shirt, and red tie—a far cry from the faded blue jeans and cowboy boots he often wore in Arizona—McCain looked the very part of the politician.

"Here we go," Stevens said, standing behind the cameraman.

"Action!" the director yelled.

Then, as the cameraman slowly dollied the camera along a set of tracks laid out in front of him, McCain stared into the eye of the camera and spoke.

"In this great country, owning a gun is a right that carries responsibilities," McCain said in an understated but authoritative tone. "Yet, every year, tens of thousands of kids bring guns to school. As adults, we owe it to our children to be responsible—by keeping our guns locked up. And kids, if someone is talking about using a gun, do the right thing. Tell a parent or teacher. What you do today may save a friend's life tomorrow."

McCain stopped. He had shot so many commercials through the years that he had read his lines from the camera's teleprompter with a polished, professional delivery on the first take.

"Now let's do it again before the sun goes behind a cloud," the director said, concerned about getting as many good takes as he could. The commercial, sponsored by the Americans for Gun Safety Foundation, would be shown as a trailer in some 2,500 theaters during the summer. Before the shoot was wrapped, McCain had filmed a dozen or more takes.

Moments later, back at the makeup table, McCain stood patiently as Kathy removed his pancake makeup with a wet miniature sponge. A journalist who had watched the filming of the commercial asked McCain a question that had often been posed to him since the 2000 presidential race: Would he ever run for president again?

"It was the greatest experience of my life," McCain said. "It was wonderful. But I cannot envision running again. We captured a magic moment. There was an outpouring of affection. I'm 64. I'd be 68 if I ran again."

"Even in eight years, you'd only be 72," the journalist noted.

"Ugh," McCain said.

"How old was Ronald Reagan when he was first elected?"

"Seventy something," McCain said.

Later, when the public service announcement shoot was finished, McCain sat in the front seat of his new sedan as his state political director, Lawrence Pike, drove him to the next stop on his crowded schedule—a dentist appointment. The journalist sat in the back seat.

En route, the journalist asked McCain what he thought about being labeled a maverick. "I'm sure in some ways I deserve that label," McCain said as the car wound its way through the streets of Phoenix, "because I've taken some positions that are at best independent and sometimes in contradiction to the majority of my party. My view is, I really am of the party of Abraham Lincoln and Teddy Roosevelt. Roosevelt was the Great Reformer, the Great Environmentalist. I think that I adhere closer to these principles than some of my colleagues."

"How do you respond when people describe you as an American hero?"

"My great privilege was to serve in the company of heroes," McCain said. "I was able to observe a thousand acts of courage and compassion and love. That's the great privilege of my life. I've made many, many mistakes in my life both in prison and out of prison. I'm far from a perfect individual. I'm far from a hero in my view because of the many failings I have shown from time to time."

"You mean you don't consider your life heroic?"

"No," McCain said. "Not in the slightest."

"So how do you feel when someone says you're a hero?"

"Embarrassed. Slightly embarrassed."

The car stopped in the parking lot of the dentist's office.

"How would you describe your relationship with President Bush?"

"I think it's cordial," McCain said, "and I will do everything in my power to work with him as President of the United States, recognizing that my first obligation is to the American people."

"Did you want the vice presidency?"

"No. If Bush had sat down and said, 'I need you as vice president in order to run the country,' of course I would have said yes. But I made it clear to him that I didn't want to be vice president. So I pretty well ensured the question would never be asked, and it was never asked."

"Did you want to be named secretary of defense?"

"No," McCain said. "I'm very happy in the Senate. I think that's where the action is. That way, I can always speak my mind."

In May, McCain continued his assault on the White House. On May 2, he criticized Bush for killing the Kyoto Treaty at the end of March—the treaty, originally endorsed by Vice President Al Gore in 1997, proposed to curb the global greenhouse effect by strictly controlling carbon dioxide emissions. "I wouldn't have done that," McCain said about Bush's decision to remove the United States from the long list of nations worldwide that had agreed to sign it. "I don't agree with everything in the Kyoto Protocol, but I think it is a framework we could have continued to work with. We could have fixed it." The implication was all too apparent: Bush should have found a way to have the United States sign on to the treaty but didn't. The back story was implied: Because the treaty was championed by environmentalists and opposed by Big Oil, Bush caved in to pressure from the energy industry and came out against the treaty.

McCain's remarks about Kyoto were still fresh when on Tuesday, May 15, McCain and Senator Joseph Lieberman of Connecticut introduced a bill that would close the gun-show loophole. This was yet another piece of legislation the White House didn't want, so it was only a matter of time before rumors again started to circulate that McCain was leaving the Republican Party. Bush set up a private dinner at the White House with himself and McCain and their wives. It was supposed to take place on May 24, but McCain canceled it at the last minute because he was working late in the Senate, trying to defeat the Bush tax cut—yet another example of the ongoing conflict between Bush and McCain. Just two Republicans would vote against the Bush tax plan. McCain was one.

Rumors of McCain's leaving the party were certainly not helped when, in early June, an article in the *Washington Post* speculated that

McCain was going to leave the Republicans so he could mount a third-party challenge to Bush in 2004. On Thursday, May 31, John Weaver (McCain's political guru), Daniel McKivergan (McCain's legislative director), William Kristol (of the *Weekly Standard*), and Marshall Wittman (of the Hudson Institute) met for lunch to discuss whether McCain should leave the party—or so it was reported. On what McCain planned to do next, Kristol was quoted as saying, "I think McCain honestly doesn't know what he's going to do but is open to all possibilities." The extensive coverage of the *Post* story served to fan the flames of the controversy surrounding McCain's continued membership in the only political party to which he had ever belonged.

But another source of tension was driving these rumors. On May 24, after a series of disagreements with Bush and his administration over its legislative agenda, dating all the way back to the early days of the Bush presidency, Senator James Jeffords of Vermont, a Republican, had announced his decision to leave the party to become an Independent. When he made this move, the Senate was no longer going to be divided evenly at 50–50. He had shifted control of the Senate to the Democrats. In the media firestorm following Jeffords' announcement that he was going to leave his party, which culminated with Jeffords appearing on the cover of *Newsweek*, McCain released a statement that itself would attract attention, mostly for its biting tone toward the Republican Party: Republicans must learn "to respect honorable differences among us, learn to disagree without resorting to personal threats, and recognize that we are a party large enough to accommodate something short of strict unanimity on the issues of the day. Tolerance of dissent is the hallmark of a mature party, and it is well past time for the Republican Party to grow up."

"Jim and I are good friends," McCain says. "I think the first thing that happened was that Jim Jeffords was bypassed as chairman of the Labor and Education Committee on the education bill. The Republican leadership and the White House basically gave it to the next guy down the line, Judd Gregg, and bypassed Jim. I think that upset him. But let me back up a bit. I think there was a fundamental failure to understand that Jim Jeffords represents a state that elects a socialist as . . . congressman, a state that is very proudly liberal. So Jim Jeffords' voting record is very different from that of Trent Lott and Richard Shelby. So that fundamental misunderstanding was there. Then they passed him up on the education chairmanship.

"Then they threatened—the White House threatened, the Senate leadership threatened—the Northeast Dairy Compact, which is huge in Vermont because they have so many of these small dairy farmers. There was a fundamental intolerance that, I think, clearly just drove Jim Jeffords to say: 'Okay.' It was immature behavior to threaten a senator—which, by the way, they weren't capable of—unless you want to drive him out of the party. And that's exactly what they did."

What few people at the time knew was this: In the six weeks before Jeffords made his move to leave the Republican Party, the Democrats were lobbying McCain to do what Jeffords ended up doing first. Using the meetings about the patient's bill of rights as cover, the Democrats met with McCain in hopes of talking him into leaving the Republican Party and shifting the power of the Senate. It would have been the ultimate insult to Bush. "I believe Chris Dodd approached him first," says a McCain confidant. "Before long, Kennedy, Edwards, and Harry Reid were also involved. They were all communicating back to Daschle. McCain knew they were also talking to Jeffords, but Jeffords didn't know they were talking to McCain. Essentially, the Democrats were going down both paths to see which one panned out. They were already to the point of discussing committee assignments with John who had decided that he actually didn't want any committee chairmanship because it would make him look power-hungry. Then Jeffords went public and John didn't need to do anything. For him to have changed after that, it would have been redundant. But was he ready to go? I believe, yes, he was ready to go."

In fact, the Jeffords camp did hear gossip at the time that McCain was thinking about leaving the party. "I heard rumors to that effect," a Jeffords staffer says. "I didn't hear about it from Daschle's office or Reid's office. I did hear the rumors, though."

The shift of power in the Senate was scheduled to take place on June 6, and when it did, the new majority leader would be Tom Daschle of South Dakota. As it happened, Daschle and McCain had planned for Daschle to visit the cabin in Sedona on the weekend of June 2 and 3. The confluence of these events—the lunch-cum-planning-session concerning McCain's going to a third party, which was reported in the *Washington Post;* Jeffords' announcing his intentions of leaving the Republican Party; and Daschle's visit to Sedona—created such a strong buzz that it led to what could only be described as a media feeding frenzy. Generally assuming that Daschle had traveled to Sedona to iron out the final details of McCain's departure from the Republican Party, the media covered the face-to-face meeting in Arizona as if it was a wedding of a celebrity superstar couple. Helicopters hovered over the McCain cabin; their passengers were television cameramen and still photographers who hoped to get a shot of the two men while they met. No one seemed to care that McCain's representatives described the Daschle visit as purely social. It had been on both senators' calendars for months, and their wives had even come along. The press scrutiny was so intense that McCain canceled all of his media appearances and had his office in Washington release a statement on Saturday.

McCain hoped the statement, direct and candid and not filled with deniable assertions or half-truths, would stop the explosion of media coverage of him. It read: "I have not instructed nor encouraged any of my advisors to begin planning for a presidential run in 2004. I have not discussed running for president again with anyone. As I have said repeatedly, I have no intention of running for president, nor do I have any intention of, or cause to, leave the Republican Party. I hope this will put an end to future speculation on this subject."

Still, the fascination with McCain and his intentions did not die. Even Daschle's moves were studied. Observers were puzzled by his attendance, on Sunday night, at a private political dinner at the Royal Palms Hotel, and, on Monday, at a $1,000-a-plate lunch at the University Club in downtown Phoenix. Only 25 to 30 people showed up at the fund-raiser for DASHPAC, but the event itself raised questions. Just what was Daschle up to?

Finally, on the evening of Tuesday, June 5, McCain had his dinner at the White House. No doubt fearful that McCain was meeting with Daschle to talk about leaving the Republican Party, Bush called McCain on Saturday night and invited him and Cindy to dinner. That dinner led to McCain's making a number of jokes about the evening. One was a joke he told over and over: *Yeah, Cindy and I had dinner at the White House with Laura, the President—and the two food tasters!* The dinner did not facilitate any rapprochement between the two men. Indeed, the feud between them was becoming impossible to miss. This fact was made undeniably clear when, on June 7, Congress passed Bush's tax cut, the one political victory Bush wanted more than any other, but McCain voted against it. On Tuesday, June 19, Ron Hlavinka of Scottsdale wrote to the *Arizona Republic* about a development that had taken place: the creation of a recall movement, which had virtually no chance of succeeding, to try and remove McCain from his Senate seat. "Senator John McCain lately has demonstrated an astounding indifference to his main constituency," Hlavinka wrote, "particularly with his incredible vote against the tax cut and his blatant schmoozing with the most extreme liberals in Congress. . . . I don't realistically expect the recall movement to proceed very far, but I will sign the petition if only to send a message to Senator McCain—'Don't turn your back on the people who voted you into office' and 'If you really want to change parties, become a Republican.'"

On that same day, the *Los Angeles Times* ran a similar piece questioning McCain's Republicanism. Under the title "McCain—Democrat in GOP Clothing?" Ed Ranger, who ran against McCain on the Democratic ticket in 1998, pondered in an editorial just how much of a Republican McCain was anymore. "John McCain might have saved my friends and me a lot of time, effort, and money," Ranger wrote. "If he had only let me know he was going to be a centrist Democrat in his third U.S. Senate term, I would never have become the Democratic nominee against him in 1998. . . . I thought I was running against a fellow who voted with Newt Gingrich and Trent Lott 95 percent of the time. How was I to know he'd been playing possum all that time? This was a guy with ratings of zero from the American Federation of Teachers and the United States Student Association; eleven percent from moderate environmental groups and the public interest research group; five percent from the national women's political caucus; fourteen percent from the AFL-CIO. . . . I could go on and on, but my point is not to criticize our newfound friend. I'm just trying to remind myself why the heck I spent twelve months, one hundred and fifty thousand dollars of my own money and more than one hundred and fifty thousand miles on the road telling Arizonans what a rightwinger McCain was. Perhaps it is a good thing I lost (actually I was trounced). I might have deprived the country of a valuable Democratic leader."

McCain, still a star, ended the month, on June 22, by appearing on *The Late Show with David Letterman*. It was not the kind of media attention usually afforded a senior senator from a Western state.

B y the first week in July, the controversy over whether McCain was leaving the Republican Party had become so overwhelming that McCain felt the need to issue, to the Republican precinct chairmen in Arizona, a four-page letter that explained his recent actions. To clarify why he broke ranks with his party and voted against the Bush tax cut, he wrote: "I voted against the final bill, not because I suddenly stopped supporting tax cuts after a lifetime of support for lower taxes but because those who needed it most were getting the least." In short, McCain couldn't support the Bush tax cut because it didn't give enough of a break "to the middle and lower classes." (Never mind that the sentiment could have come from any number of conservative Democrats; McCain felt it justified his willingness to refuse to support Bush on the touchstone issue of both his campaign and his presidency.) On the attention-grabbing visit Tom Daschle recently made to Sedona, McCain wrote: "He is my friend. We don't agree on many issues, but someone very important to me taught me long ago that honorable political disagreement should not make personal enemies of people. I have many friends who are Democrats and many friends who are Republicans." Underscoring the reason he wrote the letter, McCain noted that "[d]espite occasional differences on some issues," he remained "a proud member of the party of Reagan, Goldwater, Roosevelt, and Lincoln." To that end, he reminded the precinct chairmen that he was completely in line with the Republican Party on issues like school vouchers (he was in favor of them), private retirement accounts (he was for them as well), free trade, and missile defense.

The letter was supposed to quash the now widely circulated rumors that McCain was getting ready to bolt the Republican Party and go the way of his political hero Teddy Roosevelt and start a third party—an organization that would be equivalent to the Bull Moose Party, which caused the Republican candidate, William Howard Taft (the sitting president), to lose to the Democrat, Woodrow Wilson, in the presidential election of 1912. It was also intended to kill the fledgling recall effort that had grown out of the discontent some Arizona Republicans felt over McCain's failure to support the Bush tax cut and his eagerness to be friendly with Democrats like Daschle, a man disliked not only by Republicans but also by many conservative Democrats. Recall may have been a long shot—the recall movement had to get a certain number of signatures, then run a candidate against McCain, then convince McCain to resign because the law allowed the governor to pick between McCain and a challenger only if

McCain agreed to step down first—but McCain wanted to try to quell the effort, if for no other reason than to avoid the negative publicity a recall effort was bound to generate.

The letter may have been intended to reassure both voters and party insiders that McCain was not ready to leave the Republican Party, but at the very time McCain's letter was circulating through the party in Arizona, as well as the local and national press, he all but totally undermined the argument by inviting a group of visitors to Sedona for the Fourth of July weekend. Not only did he have Warren Beatty and his wife, Annette Bening, he also hosted Joseph Lieberman, Al Gore's running mate and the man who most helped Gore try to defeat Bush for the presidency. What did this group have in common? Beatty and McCain may have teamed up to do an ad to support authentic campaign finance reform—Beatty had even given McCain an unofficial endorsement during the presidential campaign—and Lieberman and McCain may have joined efforts to try and close the gun-show loophole, but the three men were united in that, at one time or another, they had all been in strong opposition to George W. Bush.

By mid-July, the Recall McCain Committee was in full swing. With its headquarters in a small office on the second floor of a building in Phoenix—small as in 286 square feet—the committee, a handful of people who were determined to do their best to drive John McCain out of office, was working feverishly to get 349,269 valid signatures by October 16. Actually, they needed to get a number in the neighborhood of 420,000 because the validity of many of the signatures would be challenged. When a reporter from the *Arizona Republic* dropped by to check out the committee, he happened upon a room jammed with volunteers who were busily opening envelopes stuffed with checks and answering phones that were constantly ringing. He also discovered Marcia Regan, whom the paper would later describe as "a softspoken Phoenix homemaker leading the recall." She was upset with McCain mostly, it seemed, because his national political ambitions had taken up any time he might have had for Arizona, or so Regan appeared to think. "If Senator McCain chooses to not take us seriously, that's his choice," Regan told the *Republic*. "He's elected by the people. He should be able to be recalled by the people. Obviously he doesn't have time for Arizona."

Specifically, the committee was angry with McCain because of his associations with Democrats and because he was now advancing a legislative agenda they found repugnant, particularly bills like McCain-Feingold, McCain-Lieberman, and McCain-Kennedy-Edwards (the patient's bill of rights). They also hated that he voted against the Bush tax cut, especially since he had voted *for* the Reagan tax cuts. For these reasons, the committee felt, McCain should be recalled, and what was remarkable about the recall effort, which had virtually no chance of succeeding, was that the local media in Arizona, or at least some of them, were taking the committee seriously.

In early August, McCain again angered the right-wing Republican base when he and Lieberman took on the issue of global warming by proposing a piece of legislation that would impose mandatory limits on greenhouse gases. Voluntary limits, which the Bush Administration was proposing, would not work because companies would not comply. "The current situation demands leadership from the United States," McCain said. Voluntary compliance "will not be enough to meet the goal of preventing dangerous effects on the climate system."

At the end of August, McCain had another medical scare. On August 17, during a routine physical examination at the Mayo Clinic in Phoenix, doctors discovered he had an enlarged prostate gland. Although it was probably benign, surgery was recommended nevertheless. But first McCain decided to proceed with a five-day trip, as part of a congressional delegation, to Estonia, Latvia, Bulgaria, and the Czech Republic. He returned on August 28. On the next day, his 65th birthday, he checked into the Mayo Clinic to undergo surgery that day for the enlarged prostate gland. Under a general anesthesia, he was operated on for 70 minutes in what turned out to be a routine procedure for a benign prostate-gland enlargement, the kind that affects between 15 and 20 percent of men in the country. At the same time, doctors removed stones from his bladder, another common disorder. McCain stayed in the hospital Wednesday and Thursday nights—during which time Bush called him to wish him well—and checked out of the clinic to go home on Friday. In his self-deprecating style, McCain said of the operation on his prostate gland, "It's a fairly routine thing for an old guy like me." Undeterred by these medical problems, McCain spent the weekend at home in Phoenix, then flew to Washington for the opening session of the Senate on Tuesday.

"As of the fall of 2001, what will be the legacy of John McCain?" a journalist had asked one day in August while McCain was home in Phoenix.

"Oh, I think a footnote somewhere in the history books," McCain said. "He ran, for a while, a surprisingly good campaign for president. He motivated a lot of young people. And he was one who was not afraid to take on issues, even though he was going to lose, because he tried to do the right thing."

"Do you think that legacy might be different five years from now?"

"You don't know how history will judge you, and you don't know how you'll behave because you don't know what lies ahead, but I hope it doesn't change too much."

"Are there any events that could take place that would allow you to run for the presidency again?"

"I don't envision that scenario. I mean, you know, all kinds of things could happen, but I don't envision any likely scenario that would call for that."

"But you would never say 'never.'"

"I'm not sure how you say 'never,'" McCain said, "when life is full of those twists and turns."

"A year from now, we could be in a completely different place in American history."

"Yup."

"And your whole vision of your place on the political landscape may change."

"Oh, well, that's true, yeah. But I continue to believe that we're the noblest experiment in the history of the world. My job is to do what little I can to see that that dream continues. All nations through-out history have fallen; they've risen and fallen. And someday Amer-ica will fall. But I want that day to be put off as long as possible."

As it happened, the country was in a completely different place much sooner than a year from that August. That "different place" was created by the attacks on September 11.

"I was in my office in Washington," McCain says about the morn-ing of September 11, "and I had the television set on. I saw it on television. My first thought [when the first airplane hit] was, 'Maybe it's just an accident.' Then I began to think about it: 'That'd be very unusual for that kind of thing to happen.' Of course, all doubts were removed when the second plane hit.

"I felt shock followed by anger. I concluded quickly that it was an act of terror. Then, obviously, I connected it with the embassy bombings in Africa, the attack on the USS Cole, and other incidents, going all the way back to the bombing of the marines in Beirut."

On the morning of Monday, September 17, McCain appeared at the Chaparral High School in Scottsdale. In the one-hour question-and-answer session he held with students in the school gymnasium, he was asked about the attacks on the World Trade Center and the Pentagon. "This is as serious a threat as we, in our nation, have ever faced," he said. "I promise you the United States of America will win. And we will never allow this kind of thing to happen again." Afterward, he met with firefighters at Firestation 17 who were about to leave for New York. Then, that night, he appeared on *The Tonight Show with Jay Leno*. At the end of the week, on Friday, he traveled to New York to view the disaster area firsthand.

Throughout October, McCain was outspoken, both privately and publicly, about the need for a nonpartisan commission, in the vein of the one that studied the Japanese attack on Pearl Harbor, to conduct a study and issue a report that would describe what occurred on September 11, why it occurred, and how the government failed to prevent it from happening. He was extremely vocal, again both privately and publicly, about the importance of an American military response to the attacks. When Bush ordered the attack on Afghanistan on October 7, McCain was in full support. In fact, by the end of the month, he was urging the Bush Administration to use "all the might of United States military power"—including ground troops—to crush the Taliban and Al Qaeda fighters in Afghanistan. "It's going to take a very big effort," McCain said on CNN Late Edition on Sunday, October 28, "and probably casualties will be involved and it won't be accomplished through air power alone."

On Friday, December 21, McCain made his view official when he and Lieberman introduced a bill in the Senate to establish a commission to examine what happened on September 11. "If there were serious failures on the part of individuals or institutions within the government or the private sector," McCain said in putting forth the bill, "we have the right to know, indeed the need to know." McCain and Lieberman wanted a 14-member bipartisan commission, the National Commission on Terrorist Attacks Upon the United States, that would be fashioned after the commissions that investigated the attack on Pearl Harbor and the assassination of President Kennedy. President Roosevelt had appointed a commission 11 days after the attack on Pearl Harbor; 71 days had passed since the attacks on the World Trade Center and the Pentagon, and President Bush had made no move whatsoever to set up a similar commission.

At the time McCain was proposing a commission to investigate September 11, he put into writing some of his thoughts about how Bush had handled the attacks and the aftershock. In late December, Human Events magazine published remarks about Bush solicited from the eight people who had challenged him for the Republican presidential nomination; among them were Steve Forbes, Pat Buchanan, Elizabeth Dole, and Orrin Hatch. The conservative magazine had named Bush Man-of-the-Year, and, in his 500-word tribute to Bush and others connected to September 11—and to the American response—McCain saluted "the countless acts of heroism and leadership by so many Americans who have well earned the distinction of men and women of the year." McCain made a list of the people too: the firefighters, the police officers, the members of the military, Rudolph Giuliani, Colin Powell, Donald Rumsfeld, Condoleezza Rice. Then there was this about Bush: "And there's no doubt that President Bush . . . has provided the leadership for this moment." Indeed, according to McCain, Bush "rallied our nation and much of the world in this righteous cause to defend . . . our liberty, and our very lives."

Eventually, McCain became reflective. "For all the terrible suffering they caused," McCain would say in May at Wake Forest University, "the attacks of September 11 did have one good effect. Americans remembered how blessed we are, and how we are united with all people whose aspirations to freedom and justice are threatened with violence and cruelty. . . . We instinctively grasped that the terrorists who organized the attacks mistook materialism as the only value of liberty. They believed liberty was corrupting, that the right of individuals to pursue happiness made societies weak. They held us in contempt. . . . Spared by prosperity from the hard uses of life, bred by liberty only for comfort and easy pleasure, they thought us no match for the violent, cruel struggle they planned for us. . . . They badly misjudged us."

On March 27, 2002, the House of Representatives had voted into law Shays-Meehan, the House version of McCain-Feingold, by a margin of 240 to 189. The bill had been passed in the House in 1998 and 1999, but now there was an equivalent piece of legislation that had been passed by the Senate. In fact, on March 20, the Senate voted on the exact version of the House bill, passing it 60 to 40. This meant the bill could be submitted to the president to be signed into law and McCain would realize his dream of passing meaningful campaign finance reform—*if* the House had passed Shays-Meehan. It did. "We had preconferenced the bill," says Congressman Christopher Shays. "We had agreed to take up the same bill in the House and the Senate. This is what a lot of people didn't understand—the fact that we actually passed campaign finance reform without a conference. It's unheard of. So when it passed in the Senate, I was hopeful it would pass in the House, but we knew it was going to be nip and tuck because there's a hundred ways to kill it. If someone wanted to make one little change, that would mean our preconference would result in the bill going to conference, where it would have been killed."

As soon as the bill passed, it was obvious that the principals— McCain, Feingold, Shays, Meehan—had produced, after many years of work, a piece of legislation that could have a profound effect on the American political system. "I believe that you have to ask yourself," Shays says, "'What would happen if we didn't pass this legislation?' You can't say, 'Compare what it is today to what it will be.' You have to say, 'If it hadn't passed, what would it have become, compared to what it *has* become?' A few years ago, $10 million was a big fund-raiser—huge. Then it was $20 million. After that, $20 million became $30 million. Frankly, without campaign finance reform, you could have had a major soft-money fund-raiser that could have probably tipped $50 million—and then ultimately $100 million. It's unbelievable."

As for working with McCain, Shays says: "When you've been locked up for five years in a North Vietnamese prison, you can draw a line in the sand and not be so inclined to compromise. But we did good. We passed meaningful legislation. We did it as partners, and I'm pretty impressed with what we accomplished."

As the Bush presidency proceeded, the animosity between the Bush and McCain camps remained strong. The passage of campaign finance reform and the way Bush chose to sign it into law—in the quiet of the Oval Office one morning, with no White House ceremony—only made the rift worse. That resentment had been there a year ago. "I'll tell you a small example," McCain says about an incident that took place around April 2001. "Larry Eagleburger, the former secretary of state, was asked by General Scowcroft to be on the Intelligence Advisory Group to the President of the United States. And Eagleburger told Scowcroft he'd like to serve. Scowcroft called him and said, 'No, you can't be on it, because you backed McCain.' To be very honest with you, if President Bush knew that Larry Eagleburger, a former secretary of state, was nominated, he'd say, 'Absolutely. It'd be great.' But somewhere in that hierarchy it was blocked. And numerous others have been, also. So there remains bad feelings. People invest their hearts and souls—and blood, sweat, and tears—into a political campaign."

A year later, that resentment was still there, and it was personal. "I can see the intensity of the animosity between the president and John," Thad Cochran says about a meeting of the two that occurred in the early summer of 2002. "President Bush was in a meeting of all the Republican senators in the Capitol. I happened to be seated by John McCain. The president was sort of working the crowd after his speech, and I was close to the aisle where the president was shaking hands with senators and stopping to exchange greetings and pleasantries. He got to me, looked at me, shook hands with me, and did not even look at John, who was standing right there beside me. He had to see him. I glanced, kind of out of the corner of my eye, after the president turned away, to see what John was doing. John was looking straight ahead. He would not look at the president. They would not even look at each other. They did not acknowledge each other's presence."

In his mid-60s, McCain remained a maverick. At Episcopal, he was a high-strung teenager who never backed down from a fight. In Vietnam, he fought his captors with every ounce of energy he had in his badly damaged body; only those who died there were able to give more. As a politician, he fought for what he believed was right—no matter what the consequences. It should not have been surprising that his relationship with Bush would become so vitriolic. Bush represented another enemy to fight, another obstacle to battle along the way.

Through the years, McCain has been relatively guarded about his private life, although he identified his favorite actor as Marlon Brando, his favorite Brando picture as *Viva Zapata!*, his favorite author as Ernest Hemingway, his favorite novel as *For Whom the Bell Tolls*, and his favorite color as blue. He liked *American Graffiti*—one of his favorite pictures—in part because of its soundtrack. Growing up, he loved the music of Elvis Presley and Roy Orbison. Between the Beatles and the Rolling Stones, he preferred the Beatles, but perhaps that was because "The Rolling Stones," he says, "really came into their own after I got shot down." On the whole, however, McCain has focused his life less on private pursuits (except for his devotion to his family) and more on public service.

"John is a person who has basically committed his life to serving his country as a public servant," says Everett Alvarez, who maintained a friendship with McCain after their days as POWs in Vietnam. "He's done this as a military officer and a public servant. He is close to his family; he's close to his kids. Even Carol's boys that John adopted from Carol's previous marriage, those boys have always called him 'Dad.'

"John refers to us as his 'good friends.' He doesn't have a lot of friends. He has Orson and Bud, who are probably his closest because they basically saved his life. He's close to his own family, and he has a few close friends that he shares time with—and he's committed to them—but, beyond that, it's politics and serving the country. Sometimes I'll call his staff and they'll say, 'Can you at least take him out and get him a decent meal?' He's possessed."

In future years, the McCain legacy will continue. John Sidney McCain IV, McCain's oldest son with Cindy, has announced his intentions to apply to the U.S. Naval Academy. If accepted, he will be the fourth John Sidney McCain to attend that institution.

"**I** remain a conservative: less spending, less government, lower taxes," John McCain says about his transformation as a politician, an evolution that has taken him from the far right to the center of the American political spectrum. "You know, lower taxes under certain circumstances. But what I believe, and fervently hope, is happening is that I have broadened my views, that my experiences have taught me and matured me. I also hope that I have become someone who understands better the hopes and dreams and aspirations of average citizens. That's what I hope has happened to me.

"My basic fundamental beliefs are, I still think, appropriate to America. But many of the issues that existed in 1982, when I came to Washington as a member of the House of Representatives, either do not exist or have changed. In 1982, we were in the middle of the Cold War—very different times.

"I can remember in the middle of the 1980s that aid to the Contras was a big issue. You know, the issues change, but my principles, I hope, have remained the same because I think they are valid, well-thought-out principles. Again, I hope my experiences, my reading, my ability to listen and learn, have all made me a person who is more sensitive to and attuned to average citizens. For example, I'm pro-life, but over the years I've become more and more convinced that the Republicans should have a plank in our platform that says, 'We're a pro-life party, but we not only tolerate, but embrace, those individuals in our party who hold a different opinion on this specific issue.' In 1982, I probably wouldn't have said that.

"I also say this to the right wing, 'Your great hero and icon is Ronald Reagan. Ronald Reagan continuously espoused the big-tent theory. The reason why the Republicans were able to have a majority under President Reagan was because he got the so-called "Reagan Democrats." He reached out and became an inclusive party—a majority party.'"

EPILOGUE

"Patriotism in this country is not, nor should it ever be, merely a sentimental attachment to blood and soil," John McCain said on July 11, 2002, in a noontime address to a packed audience at the National Press Club in Washington. "Our love of country is a love of ideals. The values of freedom inspire our patriotism: government derived from the consent of the governed; an economic system that is an open market for creativity, innovation, competition, and self-improvement."

Dressed in a gray business suit and fully made up for the dozen or more television cameras focused on him, McCain looked every bit the presidential candidate. "Americans have proved beyond a shadow of a doubt that a nation conceived in liberty will always be stronger, wealthier, more just, and happier than any nation that rations liberty to exalt the few at the expense of the many." His voice was sure and clear; his understated delivery was carefully modulated for broadcast. "We are the greatest nation in history because we trust freedom. We trust that . . . people who are free to act in their self-interest will perceive their interest in an enlightened way and use their wealth and power to create a civilization in which all people can share in the opportunities and responsibilities of freedom."

McCain's speech, which had been heavily hyped in the media, was billed as a major address on corporate corruption. That issue had dominated the public's imagination in the spring and summer of 2002 as Wall Street responded, usually unfavorably, to a litany of corporate scandals involving Enron, Arthur Andersen, Global Crossing, WorldCom, Tyco, and others. What McCain was really doing, however, was reminding the press—and ultimately, the public—that he was still a formidable force on the American political stage. In many ways, his appearance was purely political, and much of his core presidential campaign staff—not to be confused with his Senate office staff—had reassembled for the occasion. Present were Herb Allison, a key member of McCain's fund-raising operation, who had helped to write the speech; Rick Davis, McCain's presidential campaign manager; Orson Swindle, McCain's friend from Vietnam who had traveled with McCain throughout much of his presidential bid; and John Weaver, McCain's equivalent to Karl Rove who, fed up with the Republicans, had changed parties not too long ago to become a Democrat and work for the Democratic Congressional Campaign Committee. Before and during the speech, Weaver crept about the room studying the way the reporters—maybe as many as 100 had shown up—were responding to his candidate.

To understand fully the context of the event, one had to have been present at a lunch that took place weeks before. At the luncheon between a journalist and a McCain staffer, the subject of whether McCain might change parties came up. "Here is what I believe is going on," the journalist said. "McCain is waiting to see what happens in the midterm election in November before he decides what to do. If the control of the Senate returns to the Republicans by one seat, McCain could change parties and reclaim the power in the Senate for the Democrats. That way, if he decides to run for president as a Democrat or as an Independent, he could also affect the control of the Senate at the same time. No matter what, he won't do anything before the midterm election. After that, he has to make up his mind by January or February. Otherwise, he won't have enough time to put together a presidential campaign." To this, the McCain staffer said: "That's it exactly. Only here's the thing: McCain has no idea, really, what he's going to do." There was this, though: Members of McCain's presidential campaign inner circle, the staffer revealed, had already been approached for their availability.

That group was there at the National Press Club on July 11, and their candidate seemed to know exactly what he was doing. Few speeches by senators at National Press Club functions had sounded so presidential. "I am a supporter of the free enterprise system to the marrow of my bones," McCain said. He then detailed the changes he believed were needed to protect the investor community, moves that would shore up the economy. He favored harsh penalties for securities fraud. He supported the growing belief that accounting firms should not be allowed to provide consulting services to their clients. He advocated having companies claim stock options as operating expenses. He said he believed that "top corporate officers should be required to certify personally to the SEC that the company's financial reports are accurate and that all information material to the health of the company has been disclosed."

All in all, it was an involved, well thought out, almost intellectual speech—a visionary edict, nothing like the talks routinely delivered on the Senate floor. It achieved its purpose. It delivered the message that John McCain had not gone away. Should the economy not improve, or should the public come to understand the full meaning of the failure of Tora Bora—when the American military's top brass wanted to send ground troops into Afghanistan to destroy 4,000 Al Qaeda fighters, probably including Osama Bin Laden, only to have Bush, fearful of massive U.S. casualties, refuse to order the troop movement, which allowed the Al Qaeda fighters to flee from Afghanistan into Pakistan—George W. Bush could become vulnerable, as his father did before him. McCain would then be ready to challenge Bush for the White House, this time fully prepared for the fight.

"Some will counsel that this crisis in corporate governance is not so grave that it requires decisive government intervention," McCain said, summing up with remarks that could have been directed at members of the Bush Administration. "I disagree. What is at risk in this series of unfolding corporate scandals is the trust that investors, employees, and all Americans have in our markets and, by extension, in the country's future. To love the free market is to loathe the scandalous behavior of those who have betrayed the values of transparency, trust, contract and faith that lie at the heart of a healthy and prosperous free enterprise system, and the patriotism that sustains an aspiring and confident free society."

At the end of his speech, McCain held a brief question-and-answer session, not unlike the countless ones he had conducted during his presidential campaign. Then, surrounded by some members of his campaign staff—his *presidential* campaign staff—he left. In the wake of his departure, as the reporters milled about the room, one woman journalist quipped, loud enough for others to hear: "So where's the bus?" She meant the Straight Talk Express.

"It's outside on the street," Herb Allison said without missing a beat, alluding to a bus that, of course, was not there. "Didn't you see it when you came in? It's just sitting there, waiting."

Going forward from July, just where might this phantom bus travel? In August, to Arizona, where McCain would celebrate his sixty-sixth birthday at the time his Washington office would confirm that he had just hired as his legislative director Christine Dodd, who had previously worked for the eight-term Ohio congressman Tom Sawyer—a liberal Democrat. In September, to Tennessee, where McCain would join Congressmen Harold Ford, a Democrat, and Tom Osborne, a Republican, at a town hall meeting on public service. In the early fall, to Sedona, where McCain would have a tête-a-tête with John Kerry at the cabin. In mid-October, to New York, where McCain would host NBC's *Saturday Night Live*—a gig rarely offered to a politician. Could all of this change at a moment's notice? As McCain said: "Life is full of those twists and turns."

SOURCE NOTES

Prologue

Page 1 "Just before eight o'clock . . ." The prologue is based on information and quotes contained in the following articles: "Hooray! President Wafflehouse Signs the Campaign 'Reform' Bill," the *Union Leader* (Manchester, New Hampshire), April 3, 2002; "Constitution Slips Bush's Mind As He Signs Bill," the *Desert News* (Salt Lake City, Utah), March 31, 2002; "Campaign Finance: As Bush Quietly Signs Limits, Opponents Swing into Action," the *Atlanta Journal-Constitution*, March 28, 2002; "Bush Signs Campaign Reform Legislation," the *Augusta Chronicle* (Augusta, Georgia), March 28, 2002; "Bush Quietly Signs Finance Reform Bill," the *Austin American-Statesman*, March 28, 2002; "Campaign Finance Law Signed Without Ceremony," the *Boston Globe*, March 28, 2002; "W Signs Reform Law, Then Pursues Funds," the *Daily News* (New York), March 28, 2002; "Bush Signs Campaign Finance Bill Despite His Misgivings," the *Dallas Morning News*, March 28, 2002; and "Bush Signs Finance Reform Bill, Turns to Fund-Raising," the *Los Angeles Times*, March 28, 2002.

Admiral McCain

Page 5 "He had commanded . . ." The official biography of John Sidney McCain was supplied to me by the Department of the Navy.

Page 5 "Task Force 38's motto . . ." Some details in this paragraph come from *John McCain: An Essay in Military and Political History* by Jack Karaagac (Landham, Maryland: Lexington Books, 2000).

Page 6   "In the last six months of the war . . ." From the official naval biography of John Sidney McCain.

Page 6   "He refused to back off—ever." Admiral J. S. McCain Died on Coast at 61," *New York Times*, September 7, 1945, pp. 1 and 23; the article was based on information supplied by the Associated Press.

Page 6   "That same day, he also made his point . . ." The information in this paragraph comes from "War Strain Kills Adm. McCain as He Gets Home," *New York Herald Tribune*, September 8, 1945.

Page 7   "The last year of the war . . ." The information in this and the next two paragraphs concerning the typhoons comes from the *USA Today* Web site.

Page 8   "He was born on August 9, 1884 . . ." From the official naval biography of John Sidney McCain.

Page 8   "When he graduated on February 12, 1906 . . ." The yearbook citation of John Sidney McCain was supplied to me by the U.S. Naval Academy.

Page 9   "The couple had three children . . ." The official naval biography of John Sidney McCain Jr. was supplied to me by the Department of the Navy.

Page 9   "In 1918, the year World War I ended . . ." The information in this paragraph comes from John Sidney McCain's official naval biography. The quote comes from an interview with John Sidney McCain Jr. conducted by John T. Mason Jr. on January 6, 1975, for the U.S. Naval Institute. The interview, "The Reminiscences of Admiral John S. McCain Jr., U.S. Navy (Retired)," was published in phamplet form by the Naval Institute in December 1999.

Page 9   "'My father,' he would say, 'was a great leader' . . ." The quote comes from the Naval Institute interview with John Sidney McCain Jr. conducted by John T. Mason Jr.

Page 10   "In September 1927 . . ." The information in this paragraph comes from the naval biography of John Sidney McCain Jr.; the quotes come from the Naval Institute interview with John Sidney McCain Jr. conducted by John T. Mason Jr.

Page 10   "When he graduated on May 1, 1931 . . ." The yearbook cita-
          tion for John Sidney McCain Jr. was supplied to me by the
          U.S. Naval Academy.

Page 11   "'The only thing I say to you' . . ." The quote comes from the
          Naval Institute interview with John Sidney McCain Jr. con-
          ducted by John T. Mason Jr.

Page 11   "Roberta and her twin sister . . ." The information in this
          paragraph comes from *Faith of My Fathers* by John McCain
          with Mark Salter (New York: Random House, 1999) and
          "McCain's Chiefs of Distaff; Think 'Auntie Mame' Rolled
          into Two, and You'll Get the Picture" by Ken Ringle, *Wash-
          ington Post*, March 6, 2000.

Page 11   "In July 1933 . . ." The information in this paragraph comes
          from the naval biography of John Sidney McCain Jr. as well
          as "McCain's Chiefs of Distaff" by Ken Ringle.

Page 12   "Slew McCain remained . . ." From the naval biography of
          John Sidney McCain.

Page 13   "During World War II . . ." From the naval biography of John
          Sidney McCain Jr.

Page 13   "As for Slew, he served . . ." From the naval biography of
          John Sidney McCain.

Page 15   "Admiral Charles Lockwood gave the luncheon . . ." From
          the Naval Institute interview with John Sidney McCain Jr.
          conducted by John T. Mason Jr.

Page 15   "McCain's body was flown . . ." The information in this and
          the next two paragraphs comes from the obituaries of John
          Sidney McCain published in the *New York Times* and the *New
          York Herald Tribune*. Certain facts were also confirmed with the
          Office of John McCain in Washington, D.C.

Page 17   "'They brought me back and put me in charge' . . ." From the
          Naval Institute interview with John Sidney McCain Jr. con-
          ducted by John T. Mason Jr.

Page 17   "McCain held that post . . ." From the naval biography of
          John Sidney McCain Jr.

Page 17   "'We were all steeped in the tradition' . . ." This unpublished
          quote comes from my interview with Thad Cochran, June
          2002.

Anchors Away

Page 19   "As a young boy, Johnny exhibited . . ." The information about John McCain's temper emerging at an early age comes from *Faith of My Fathers* by John McCain with Mark Salter.

Page 20   "In the early years of his life, Johnny's parents . . ." The information in this paragraph comes from my interview with John McCain, August 2001.

Page 20   "Founded in 1944, only two years . . ." The information about St. Stephen's comes from documents supplied to me by the school and from my interview with Charles Hooff, March 2002.

Page 21   "Malcolm Matheson, another . . ." This unpublished quote comes from my interview with Malcolm Matheson, March 2002.

Page 21   "'Episcopal was one of the better prep schools' . . ." This unpublished quote comes from my interview with Dick Thomsen, March 2002.

Page 22   "Jack and Roberta were enrolling Johnny . . ." The information in this and the next two paragraphs comes from various documents supplied to me by the Episcopal High School.

Page 23   "'In a word, it was brutal' . . ." This unpublished quote comes from my interview with Charles Hooff, March 2002.

Page 24   "'We lived in curtained alcoves' . . ." This quote comes from "The School with a Southern Accent" by Ken Ringle, *Washington Post*, November 11, 1989.

Page 24   "'It had been used by the Union' . . ." This unpublished quote comes from my interview with Ken Ringle, June 2002.

Page 24   "Before long, the brash . . ." The information in this paragraph comes from documents supplied to me by Episcopal. The unpublished quote comes from my interview with Ken Ringle, June 2002.

Page 25   "'As headmaster, I actually saw' . . ." This unpublished quote comes from my interview with Dick Thomsen, March 2002.

Page 25   "'That was another subculture, being a waiter' . . ." This unpublished quote comes from my interview with Ken Ringle,
June 2002.

Page 26   "By his senior year, McCain had gotten in line . . ." Senior
yearbook entries were supplied to me by Episcopal.

Page 26   "'They called my uncle' . . ." This unpublished quote comes
from my interview with Robert Whittle, March 2002.

Page 27   "'William Ravenel was a leader' . . ." This unpublished quote
comes from my interview with Robert Whittle, March 2002.

Page 28   "'It was three fateful years ago' . . ." The senior yearbook citation of John McCain.

Page 28   "'Following his first summer at the Naval Academy' . . ." The
incident in which McCain returned to Episcopal from the
Naval Academy was told to me by Dick Thomsen when I interviewed him in March 2002.

Page 29   "'I was basically told when I was young' . . ." This unpublished quote comes from my interview with John McCain,
August 2001.

Page 29   "'He had a little bit of internal conflict' . . ." The quote by
Frank Gamboa comes from the *Boston Globe*, January 23, 2000.

Page 30   "'He just wouldn't back down' . . ." The quote by Jack
Dittrick comes from "McCain's Course Hasn't Been Straight
Or Narrow," the *Los Angeles Times*, March 3, 2000.

Page 30   "'The plebe will be barked at' . . ." This quote comes from
John McCain: An Essay in Military and Political History by John
Karaagac.

Page 31   "'The next four days' . . ." This quote comes from *John
McCain: An American Odyssey* by Robert Timberg (New York:
Touchstone Books, 1999), page 52. This book was taken, for
the most part, from *The Nightingale's Song* by Robert Timberg
(New York: Simon and Schuster, 1995).

Page 31   "McCain's yearbook citation . . ." The yearbook citation was
supplied to me by the U.S. Naval Academy.

Page 32   "For the next two-and-a-half years . . ." The incident of the
airplane crash comes from *American Odyssey* by Robert
Timberg.

Page 33   "McCain continued to fly himself . . ." The incident of the airplane crash comes from *American Odyssey* by Robert Timberg.

Page 34   "On November 9, 1958, McCain's father . . ." From the naval biography of John Sidney McCain Jr.

Page 34   "'When Admiral McCain was commander' . . ." This unpublished quote comes from my interview with Tom Arrasmith, June 2002.

Page 35   "On May 1, 1967, Jack McCain was named . . ." From the naval biography of John Sidney McCain Jr.

Vietnam

Page 37   "For Lieutenant Commander John McCain . . ." The description of the *Forrestal* episode comes from articles that appeared in the *New York Times* in July and August 1967.

Page 41   "'I was first in Vietnam' . . ." This quote comes from an essay written by John McCain included in *The Soldiers' Story* edited by Ron Steinman (New York: TV Books, 1999).

Page 42   "'It was dumb the way we were doing it' . . ." This unpublished quote comes from my interview with Robert W. Smith, June 2002.

Page 43   "'I was an aide to a general' . . ." This unpublished quote comes from my interview with Paul Vallely, June 2002.

Page 45   "Four days after the March on the Pentagon . . ." John McCain first wrote about his shoot-down over Hanoi in his article "Inside Story: How the POWs Fought Back," *U.S. News & World Report*, May 14, 1973.

Page 47   "This day, On had left work . . ." The description of and quotes about the rescue of John McCain by Mai Van On come from "McCain's Vietnam Rescuer Recalls 32-Year-Old Event," an Associated Press article that appeared in, among other newspapers, the *Los Angeles Times* on February 24, 2000.

Page 48   "Once On and Lua had pulled McCain . . ." "Inside Story" by John McCain, *U.S. News & World Report*.

Page 49   "'I was taken into a cell' . . ." John McCain first described the incident with an interrogator and a Vietnamese doctor in "Inside Story" in *U.S. News & World Report* and his essay in *The Soldiers' Story*.

Page 51   "Men soon came and took . . ." "Inside Story" by John McCain, *U.S. News & World Report*.

Page 51   "When the doctor finished . . ." Ibid.

Page 52   "Before long, it became evident . . ." "Hanoi Says McCain's Son Terms U.S. 'Isolated,'" *New York Times*, November 11, 1967.

Page 53   "Two weeks after the surgery on his right arm . . ." From "Inside Story" by John McCain, *U.S. News & World Report*.

Page 53   "That night, McCain was taken . . ." The facts in this paragraph come from "Inside Story" by John McCain, *U.S. News & World Report*, and McCain's essay in *The Soldiers' Story*.

Page 54   "'When they brought John in' . . ." This unpublished quote comes from my interview with George ("Bud") Day, July 2002.

Page 54   "'When Overly left, John and I were alone' . . ." Ibid.

Page 55   "One day in mid-June, McCain was taken . . ." John McCain first described the episodes involving the Vietnamese's attempt to release him in "Inside Story" in *U.S. News & World Report*.

Page 56   "'I was in a cell that was catty-corner' . . ." This unpublished quote comes from my interview with Jack Van Loan, July 2002.

Page 57   "Three days after the earlier meeting . . ." "Inside Story," *U.S. News & World Report*.

Page 59   "In August 1968, the North Vietnamese decided . . ." Ibid.

Page 60   "In August of that year, Navy Lieutenant Robert F. Frishman . . ." "Ex-POWs Charge Hanoi with Torture," *New York Times*, September 3, 1969.

Page 61   "One morning during Christmastime, the guards came . . ." The description of the episode at Christmas 1969 comes from the essay by John McCain in *The Soldiers' Story*.

Page 62   "'the hotel where they didn't leave a mint' . . ." John McCain often made this remark during his speeches on the campaign trail during his run for the presidency.

Page 62   "'He had landed in that Ho Chi Min pond' . . ." This unpublished quote comes from my interview with James Stockdale, June 2002.

Page 63   "'My first encounter with John McCain' . . ." This unpublished quote comes from my interview with Orson Swindle, June 2002.

Page 63   "At the time, the Hanoi Hilton . . ." The description of the prison comes in part from *P.O.W.* by John G. Hubbell (New York: McGraw Hill, 1976).

Page 64   "'In late 1970,' McCain later wrote, 'there was a change' . . ." This quote comes from the essay by John McCain in *The Soldiers' Story*.

Page 65   "'Once we engaged in a little bit' . . ." This unpublished quote comes from my interview with Orson Swindle, June 2002.

Page 66   "'Finally,' Swindle says, 'in November 1971' . . ." Ibid.

Page 66   "'Believe it or not,' McCain would write . . ." *The Soldiers' Story*.

Page 66   "'We had hours upon hours of time' . . ." This unpublished quote comes from my interview with Orson Swindle, June 2002.

Page 66   "In 1971, the POWs were finally able to have a proper church service . . ." *The Soldiers' Story*.

Page 68   "As McCain was enduring his fifty-sixth month . . ." The description of Jane Fonda's trip to North Vietnam comes from *Jane Fonda: An Intimate Biography* by Bill Davidson (New York: Dutton, 1990).

Page 69   "'The day before, these guys were cleaned up' . . ." This unpublished quote comes from my interview with William Haynes, April 2002.

Page 70   "'We were absolutely dismayed' . . ." This unpublished quote comes from my interview with Jack Van Loan, July 2002.

Page 70 "The years 1971 and 1972 . . ." "Inside Story," *U.S. News & World Report.*

Page 71 "'We had a loudspeaker in the cell' . . ." This unpublished quote comes from my interview with John McCain, August 2001.

Page 72 "'John is very competitive' . . ." The episode about the bridge game comes from my interview with Orson Swindle, June 2002.

Page 74 "'[A]fter I got back,' McCain would write . . ." "Inside Story," *U.S. News & World Report.*

Page 74 "'When I read your name off' . . ." Ibid.

Page 74 "'I think history will judge the Vietnam War' . . ." This unpublished quote comes from my interview with John McCain, August 2001.

Page 75 "'We had time to analyze what we perceived to be' . . ." This unpublished quote comes from my interview with Orson Swindle, June 2002.

Page 75 "As for John, 'He was' . . ." Ibid.

Page 75 "'John was a hero' . . ." This unpublished quote comes from my interview with Jack Van Loan, July 2002.

Page 75 "Paul Galanti, another American POW, adds . . ." This unpublished quote comes from my interview with Paul Galanti, July 2002.

Page 76 "'His father may have been commander-in-chief' . . ." This unpublished quote comes from my interview with Everett Alvarez, July 2002.

Coming Home

Page 77 "'Other guys would have snapped' . . ." This unpublished quote from Richard Nixon was provided to me by Monica Crowley who interviewed Nixon repeatedly during the four years prior to his death when she worked as his aide.

Page 77 "'That night at the White House' . . ." This unpublished quote comes from my interview with George ("Bud") Day, July 2002.

Page 78   "Paul Galanti remembers . . ." This unpublished quote comes from my interview with Paul Galanti, July 2002.

Page 78   "'When Nixon held his' . . ." This unpublished quote comes from my interview with Monica Crowley, June 2002.

Page 78   "'It took me about 40 minutes to adjust' . . ." This unpublished quote comes from my interview with John McCain, August 2001.

Page 79   "'Carol had taken the kids to her parents' house' . . ." *Faith of My Fathers.*

Page 79   "'The outpouring on behalf of us' . . ." "Inside Story," *U.S. News & World Report.*

Page 80   "'They said, "You're never going to fly again"' . . ." This unpublished quote comes from my interview with Carl Smith, June 2002.

Page 81   "At the end of 1973 . . ." The quote and facts in this paragraph come from "One POW's Fresh Appraisal of U.S.: Interview with Cdr. John S. McCain III," *U.S. News & World Report,* December 31, 1973, pp. 47–48.

Page 81   "Finally, in the article . . ." Ibid.

Page 82   "'During this period,' says Senator John Warner . . ." This unpublished quote comes from my interview with John Warner, June 2002.

Page 83   "'I had heard legendary stories' . . ." This quote comes from the foreword John McCain wrote to *Glory Denied: The Saga of Jim Thompson, America's Longest-Held Prisoner of War* by Tom Philpott (New York: W.W. Norton, 2001).

Page 84   "'At the time, VA-174' . . ." This unpublished quote comes from my interview with Carl Smith, June 2002.

Page 86   "'I'll never forget' . . ." This unpublished quote comes from my interview with Chuck Nash, August 2002.

Page 87   "'The Senate Liaison Office had been a backwater office' . . ." This unpublished quote comes from my interview with Carl Smith, June 2002. Certain facts about the Senate liaison office contained in this section of the chapter were confirmed by the Office of John McCain.

Page 87   "'In the late 1970s,' Carl Smith says . . ." Ibid.

Page 87   "McCain was also asked to perform . . ." The facts and quotes in the paragraph come from my interview with Ken Ringle, June 2002.

Page 88   "Mostly, in those years . . ." The facts and quote in this paragraph come from my interview with Gary Hart, June 2002.

Page 88   "'Senator "Scoop" Jackson and his party' . . ." This unpublished quote comes from my interview with Frank Gaffney, May 2002.

Page 89   "When he was not traveling . . ." The facts and quote in this paragraph come from my interview with Carl Smith, June 2002.

Page 89   "While McCain was making more and more new friends . . ." Ibid.

Page 90   "'As the senate liaison for the navy' . . ." This unpublished quote comes from my interview with Thad Cochran, June 2002.

Page 92   "Some onlookers criticized McCain for divorcing Carol . . ." The unpublished quote in this paragraph comes from my interview with Carl Smith, June 2002.

Page 92   "As his separation from Carol . . ." The information and quotes about the Hensley family in this paragraph come from "Beer Baron Father-in-Law Key McCain Funds Source" by Pat Flannery, the *Arizona Republic*, February 17, 2000.

Page 92   "Hensley had served as a bombardier in Europe . . ." Ibid.

Page 94   "Years later, McCain would focus . . ." The unpublished quote in this paragraph comes from my interview with John McCain, August 2001.

The Congressman from Arizona

Page 95   "'When John married Cindy' . . ." This unpublished quote comes from my interview with Thad Cochran, June 2002.

Page 95   "'I think something happened in the late 1970s' . . ." This unpublished quote comes from my interview with Gary Hart, June 2002.

Page 96   "John was a dark, dark horse . . ." "McCain's Complex Quest: Campaign Must Deal with Many Paradoxes" by David Broder, the *Washington Post,* May 23, 1999.

Page 97   "'We were both big fans of Felix the Cat' . . ." This unpublished quote comes from my interview with Orson Swindle, June 2002.

Page 97   "(Congressional committee assignments . . ." Information about how Congress functions comes from my interview with Gordon Hamel, August 2002.

Page 98   "During the 98th Congress . . ." All facts and quotations in this and the next two paragraphs come from the official Congressional record.

Page 100   "But, on one issue . . ." Details in this paragraph were confirmed in my interview with John McCain, August 2002.

Page 101   "In the 99th Congress . . ." All facts and quotations in this paragraph come from the official Congressional record.

Page 101   "One highlight of his second session in Congress . . ." Facts and quotations about McCain's trip to Vietnam included in this and the next four paragraphs come from "Inside Vietnam: What a Former POW Found," *U.S. News & World Report,* March 11, 1985.

Page 103   "In the autumn of 1985 . . ." The information in this paragraph about legislation comes from the official Congressional record.

Page 104   "On May 2, 1986 . . ." Certain biographical facts about McCain and his family were confirmed by the Office of John McCain.

Page 104   "On October 10, McCain enjoyed . . ." The information in this paragraph about legislation comes from the official Congressional record.

Page 105   "'The night before the election' . . ." McCain often told this anecdote about Barry Goldwater during stump speeches while on the campaign trail as he ran for the presidency in 1999 and 2000.

Page 105   "'It was a cakewalk' . . ." This unpublished quote comes from my interview with Tim Meyer, August 2002.

Page 106   "'President Nixon watched McCain' . . ." This unpublished quote comes from my interview with Monica Crowley, June 2002.

Page 106   "'Everything in him told him to fight' . . ." This unpublished quote from Richard Nixon was provided to me by Monica Crowley who interviewed Nixon repeatedly during the four years prior to his death when she worked as his aide.

One Hundred Kings

A general note: Through a source, I approached Dennis DeConcini in mid-2002 on two separate occasions and asked him to give me an interview for this book; the coversation could have been conducted either on or off the record, at his discretion. DeConcini declined.

Page 108   "A week later, on April 9 . . ." the *Arizona Republic,* July 7, 1989.

Page 109   "In short, DeConcini argued . . ." Ibid.

Page 110   "Keating came to my office . . ." "McCain Repays Keating Firm for Trips," the *Washington Post,* October 12, 1989.

Page 111   "'The Reagan Administration plan to reflag' . . ." the *Arizona Republic,* June 21, 1987.

Page 112   "'There is no doubt in my mind' . . ." the *Arizona Republic,* August 22, 1987.

Page 113   "'Clearly, the United States should give the Central Americas' . . ." the *Arizona Republic,* September 27, 1987.

Page 114   "The year 1988 . . ." Certain facts in this paragraph were confirmed with Joyce Campbell.

Page 115   "In mid-July, McCain met with Bush . . ." the *New York Times,* July 22, 1988.

Page 115   "On Wednesday, July 22, McCain addressed . . ." In this and the next paragraph, the comments made by Jane Fonda were taken from *Jane Fonda* by Bill Davidson. The comments made by McCain were taken from the *Congressional Record.*

Page 117   "On August 14, the *Arizona Republic* ran . . ." the *Arizona Republic,* August 14, 1988.

Page 120   "No sooner had the name 'Dan Quayle' . . ." Certain facts in this paragraph were confimed with John Batchelor, the author of *Ain't You Glad You Joined the Republicans?*, a history of the Republican Party.

Page 120   "Immediately, so much criticism . . ." Information about the military records of George W. Bush and Lloyd Bentsen Jr. comes from my article "All Hat, No Cattle," *Rolling Stone*, July 1999.

Page 121   "McCain himself called the choice . . ." the *Arizona Republic*, August 19, 1988.

Page 122   "Because all politics are local . . ." the *Arizona Republic*, August 22, 1988.

Page 122   "'One reason we went through' . . ." the *Arizona Republic*, August 26, 1988.

Page 122   "In early October . . ." the *Arizona Republic*, October 6, 1988.

Page 124   "On the local front . . ." the *Arizona Republic*, November 14, 1988.

Page 128   "'Here were people pointing fingers' . . ." This unpublished quote comes from my interview with Alan Simpson, July 2002.

Page 131   "The ordeal could not wait. . . ." the *Arizona Republic*, July 9, 1989.

Page 136   "Through the fall . . ." The quotes from this and the following four paragraphs are available in the *Congressional Record*.

Page 139   "At the end of 1990, McCain continued . . ." the *Arizona Republic*, December 9, 1990.

Page 140   "With this as backdrop, now came an episode involving Roger Stone . . ." The information and quote in this paragraph come from my interview with Roger Stone, February 2002.

Page 141   "On January 4, 1991 . . ." The quotes from this and the next seven paragraphs are available in the *Congressional Record*. The events were also covered by the major daily newspapers, including the *Washington Post*, the *Los Angeles Times*, and the *New York Times*.

Page 144   "Four days before the cutoff date . . ." The comments made by McCain were taken from the *Congressional Record*.

Page 148   "In July, only weeks after his return . . ." Information in this and the following paragraph was supplied to me by John McCain; I also used "A Friendship That Ended the War" by James Carroll, *The New Yorker*, October 21, 1996.

Page 148   "'Our differences occurred when we were kids' . . ." This unpublished quote comes from my interview with John Kerry, February 2002.

Page 149   "'It is hard to overstate how profoundly' . . ." the *Arizona Republic*, March 8, 1992.

Page 150   "'I have huge affection and respect for John McCain' . . ." This unpublished quote comes from my interview with John Kerry, February 2002.

Page 152   "On January 13, 1993, just as Bill Clinton . . ." The information in this paragraph comes from my interviews with John McCain and John Kerry as well as "A Friendship That Ended the War" by James Carroll.

Page 152   "'By the end of 1992, Kerry had suggested' . . ." This passage was taken from *Nixon in Winter* by Monica Crowley (New York: Random House, 1998).

Page 153   "'In the late 1980s and early 1990s' . . ." This quote comes from my interview with John McCain, November 2001.

The Senator from Arizona

Page 156   "The group he chose was the Oregon Citizens Alliance . . ." The description of the event and the quotes from McCain's speech come from the *Arizona Republic*, September 5, 1993.

Page 157   "'All Americans deserve the opportunity' . . ." the *Arizona Republic*, October 13, 1993.

Page 158   "'Every day in Arizona' . . ." the *Arizona Republic*, December 16, 1993.

Page 159   "'The greatest challenge to U.S. security' . . ." the *Arizona Republic*, January 9, 1994.

Page 159   "'There are some who have characterized' . . ." the *Arizona Republic*, April 21, 1994.

Page 160 "McCain was not willing to reform . . ." The facts about his Sense of the Senate resolution concerning parking in Washington area airports come from the *Arizona Republic*, April 21, 1994. The definition of what a Sense of the Senate resolution is comes from Gordon Hamel.

Page 161 "That summer, McCain experienced . . ." *Arizona Republic,* July 3, 1994.

Page 162 "On August 22, 1994, Cindy McCain . . ." The information in the section dealing with Cindy McCain's addiction to prescription drugs comes mainly from the reporting of the *Arizona Republic* (and *Phoenix Gazette,* its sister publication), particuarly articles published by John Kolbe on August 22, 1994, Bill Hart on August 24, 1994, and Martin Van Der Werf and Susan Leonard on August 23, 1994. I also used information from the Stanton Peele Addiction Web site and an article called "The Next First Lady?" by Toby Harnden, which appeared on the Web site The Age, February 25, 2000. "How Cindy McCain Was Outed for Drug Addiction" by Amy Silverman, which appeared on October 18, 1999, on Salon.com, was helpful as well.

Page 167 "'Late in the year, McCain and I appeared' . . ." This unpublished quote comes from my interview with Gary Ackerman, June 2002.

Page 168 "On May 23, McCain and Kerry . . ." "Time to Open an Embassy in Vietnam" by John McCain, the *Washington Post,* May 23, 1995.

Page 170 "On Tuesday, July 11, McCain joined up . . ." "A Friendship That Ended the War" by James Carroll.

Page 170 "There were, however, other Americans . . ." The *U.S. Veteran Dispatch* has a Web site with the address usvet@icomnet.com; the home base of the publication is located in Kinston, North Carolina.

Page 172 "On Thursday morning, September 7, McCain and Alan Simpson . . ." The information in this and the following paragraph comes from articles published in the *Washington Post;* the unpublished quote comes from my interview with Alan Simpson, July 2002.

Page 173 "'There was a debate in the Senate' . . ." This unpublished quote comes from my interview with John McCain, August 2001.

Page 174 "'Before I close, I would like to offer' . . ." This quote by John McCain comes from the *Congressional Record.*

Page 175 "'I went to the funeral' . . ." This unpublished quote comes from my interview with Eliot Engel, July 2002.

Page 177 "'This bill will not cure public cynicism' . . ." This quote by John McCain comes from the *Congressional Record.*

Page 178 "'Ultimately, the short list' . . ." This unpublished quote comes from my interview with Joyce Campbell, April 2002.

Page 179 "'Before long, Dole was getting' . . ." Ibid.

Page 179 "'Dole was getting really frustrated' . . ." Ibid.

Page 180 "'McCain was loyal to Dole' . . ." This unpublished quote comes from an anonymous source.

Page 180 "'The common bond of their friendship' . . ." This unpublished quote comes from my interview with Joyce Campbell, August 2002.

Page 180 "During this trip, McCain met . . ." The Associated Press article that appeared in, among other places, the *Los Angeles Times,* February 24, 2000.

Page 181 "'As Republicans prepare to begin' . . ." the *Arizona Republic,* November 27, 1996.

Page 182 "'I was at the British Embassy' . . ." This unpublished quote comes from my interview with Peter King, June 2002.

Page 187 "In the first weeks of 1999, McCain cast . . ." McCain's vote on the impeachment of Bill Clinton is documented in the *Congressional Record.* Certain facts in this paragraph were confirmed with John Batchelor.

Page 188 "In January, in his office on Capitol Hill, McCain . . ." Details about McCain's meeting with Mike Murphy included in this and the next two paragraphs were confirmed in my interview with John Weaver, June 2002.

Page 194 "In late August, Random House . . ." Details in this paragraph were confimed with an anonymous source.

Presidential Politics

Page 197   "On Monday, September 27, 1999 . . ." McCain's announcement was covered by the major daily newspapers; certain details about the event were confimed with Peter Rinfret.

Page 205   "Near the start of the whisper campaign . . ." Details about the editorial published in the *New York Times* on November 26, 1999, as well as his unpublished quote about the matter come from my interview with James Stockdale conducted in June 2002.

Page 206   "'There's a difference between anger and irritation' . . ." This unpublished quote comes from my interview with Alan Simpson, July 2002.

Page 208   "On Sunday, December 5, McCain . . ." Details of the fundraiser in Pentagon City were confirmed with Ken Ringle, Dick Thomsen, among others.

Page 210   "That night, on board the *Intrepid* . . ." Facts of the award ceremony on the *Intrepid* were confirmed with Bill White. As with many of these events, I was also in attendance.

Page 212   "'They basically shook hands and talked about it' . . ." This unpublished quote comes from my interview with Christopher Shays, August 2002.

Page 218   "The Dole endorsement . . ." This unpublished quote comes from my interview with Joyce Campbell, August 2002.

Page 231   "On Thursday night, as he waited . . ." Details of the fundraiser at the home of John Billock were confirmed with Peter Rinfret.

Page 231   "'A woman there asked him about abortion' . . ." This unpublished quote comes from my interview with Ben Davol, February 2002.

Page 240   "That day, Bush had *not* been out there . . ." The details come from the *Washington Post,* January 2000.

Page 242   "By midafternoon on February 1 . . ." Details in this and the following paragraph were confirmed with an anonymous source as well as the Office of John McCain.

Page 243   "'I went up to the suite' . . ." This unpublished quote comes from my interview with Peter Rinfret, February 2002.

Page 244   "Not long after Bush finished . . ." The comment made by McCain to Peter Rinfret was confirmed by Rinfret.

Page 244   "'He was very pumped in the elevator' . . ." This unpublished quote comes from my interview with Ben Davol, February 2002.

Page 244   "'When I tell you the ballroom' . . ." This unpublished quote comes from my interview with Peter Rinfret, February 2002.

Page 245   "'It was just very electric' . . ." This unpublished quote comes from my interview with Phil Paluzzi, February 2002.

Page 245   "'I am on that door where John is to come in' . . ." This unpublished quote comes from my interview with Orson Swindle, June 2002.

Page 245   "'I was standing, looking at the TV' . . ." This unpublished quote comes from my interview with Ben Davol, February 2002.

"The Dirtiest Race I've Ever Seen"

Page 252   "The McCain campaign may have had . . ." The article "The Manchurian Candidate" was downloaded from the Web site.

Page 253   "On February 4, Kerry, Max Cleland . . ." The letter organized by John Kerry was supplied to me by the Office of John Kerry.

Page 254   "'The first indication we got that things' . . ." This unpublished quote comes from my interview with Orson Swindle, June 2002. In his quote Swindle refers to "John McCain and Russell Feingold" by Albert R. Hunt, *Profiles in Courage for Our Time*, edited by Caroline Kennedy (New York: Hyperion, 2002).

Page 254   "'What a farce Burch was' . . ." This unpublished quote comes from my interview with Everett Alvarez, August 2002.

Page 264   "'It was a black child' . . ." This unpublished quote comes from an anonymous source.

Page 264   "'In South Carolina,' Frank Rich wrote . . ." This editorial by Frank Rich appeared in the *New York Times* on February 23, 2000.

Page 266   "As McCain looked out onto the huge gathering of reporters . . ." The details in this scene were confirmed with Peter Rinfret.

Page 275   "McCain might have quibbled . . ." This document was downloaded from the Web site LewRockwell.com.

Page 276   "'One of the entertaining vignettes' . . ." This unpublished quote comes from my interview with John McCain, August 2001.

Page 276   "On February 19, the polls would be open . . ." The details of Primary Day were confirmed by Peter Rinfret as well as coverage in the *Washington Post,* the *Arizona Republic,* the *New York Times,* and other newpapers.

Page 277   "As he had in New Hampshire . . ." Details in this paragraph were confirmed with an anonymous source.

Page 278   "'He got off the bus that day at the hotel' . . ." This unpublished quote comes from my interview with Peter Rinfret, February 2002.

Page 278   "As McCain, Murphy, Weaver, Salter, and Davis . . ." The details of this and the next three paragraphs were confirmed with John Weaver.

Page 280   "'Cindy had always been with me' . . ." This unpublished quote comes from my interview with John McCain, August 2001.

The Best Man

Page 282   "'I endorsed McCain the day after he lost South Carolina' . . ." This unpublished quote comes from my interview with Peter King, June 2002.

Page 288   "'In Virginia, we had no' . . ." This unpublished quote comes from my interview with Paul Galanti, August 2002.

Page 291   "'They sent out a press release' . . ." Ibid.

Page 301   "'I was with McCain on the bus' . . ." This unpublished quote comes from my interview with Peter Rinfret, February 2002.

Page 301   "After a trip that seemed endless . . ." Details about the scene at Sacred Heart University were confirmed with Ben Davol.

Page 302   "'What struck me about McCain that weekend' . . ." This unpublished quote comes from my interview with Peter King, June 2002.

Page 307   "'I am no longer an active candidate' . . ." Certain details about McCain's speech at Sedona near the Red Rocks were confirmed by John Weaver and an anonymous source.

Page 308   "At some point, Bush called McCain . . ." The information concerning the telephone call from George W. Bush to John McCain was supplied to me by an anonymous source.

Page 309   "Ultimately, there would be a video . . ." The John McCain video was supplied to me by Ben Davol.

Page 314   "'I get a kick out of his deadpan sense of humor' . . ." This unpublished quote comes from my interview with Peter King, June 2002.

Page 316   "Despite obstacles thrown in the way . . ." Details about the McCain-Bush meeting in Pittsburgh were confirmed by the Office of John McCain.

Page 319   "'The Clinton Administration's support' . . ." This quote comes from a press release issued by the Office of John McCain on May 31, 2000.

Page 320   "During the week of July 17 . . ." The information in this paragraph was confirmed for me at the time by a confidential source to whom McCain said he would join the Bush ticket as the vice-presidential nominee if asked.

Page 322   "'It's an amazing example' . . ." This unpublished quote comes from my interview with Arianna Huffington, August 2002.

Page 322   "Afterward, McCain headed for a ballroom . . ." The details in this and the following paragraph were confirmed by the Office of John McCain.

Page 332   "'I think,' John McCain says . . ." This unpublished quote comes from my interview with John McCain, August 2001.

Page 333   "But McCain believed there were lessons . . ." Ibid.

Man of the People

Page 335   "'I realized when we were about to organize' . . ." This unpublished quote comes from my interview with Thad
Cochran, June 2002.

Page 341   "For the last two weeks in March . . ." The episode of
McCain's return to Episcopal High School comes from "Senator John McCain Comes Home," an article published in the
spring 2001 issue of *The High School,* the alumni magazine of
Episcopal High School. A copy of the journal was supplied
to me by the school.

Page 344   "'Have you seen Siegfried and Roy?' . . ." The two scenes—
on the school grounds and in the car—resulted from the re-
porting I did on John McCain in Phoenix in April 2001.
Shorter versions of the scenes were included in "John
McCain's War on the White House," which appeared in
Rolling Stone, June 7, 2001.

Page 349   "In the media firestorm . . ." The quote from John McCain,
released from his Capitol Hill office, was widely quoted in
the press.

Page 349   "'Jim and I are good friends' . . ." This unpublished quote
comes from my interview with John McCain, August 2001.

Page 350   "What few people at the time knew . . ." The information in
the paragraph, as well as the quote, comes from my interview
with an anonymous source in June 2002.

Page 351   "In fact, the Jeffords camp . . ." The information in the paragraph, as well as the quote, comes from my interview with an
anonymous source in May 2002.

Page 351   "The shift of power in the Senate . . ." Details in this paragraph were confirmed by the Office of John McCain.

Page 351   "McCain hoped the statement . . ." The statement was released by Nancy Ives from McCain's Capitol Hill office.

Page 352   "Still, the fascination with McCain . . ." Details about
Daschle's visit with McCain come from the *Arizona Republic,*
June 5, 2001.

Page 352   "On Tuesday, June 19, Ron Hlavinka . . ." the *Arizona Republic,*
June 19, 2001.

Page 357   "'As of the fall of 2001' . . ." The exchange took place between John McCain and me in Phoenix in August 2001. A
portion of it was published in "The *Rolling Stone* Interview
with John McCain," which appeared in the magazine in September 2001.

Page 358   "'I was in my office' . . ." This unpublished quote comes from
my interview with John McCain, August 2002.

Page 360   "On March 27, 2002 . . ." The information about the passage
of McCain-Feingold and Shays-Meehan was confirmed by
the Office of John McCain.

Page 361   "'We had preconferenced the bill' . . ." This unpublished
quote comes from my interview with Christopher Shays, August 2002.

Page 361   "As the Bush presidency proceeded . . ." The unpublished
quote in this paragraph comes from my interview with John
McCain, August 2001.

Page 362   "A year later, that resentment . . ." The unpublished quote in
this paragraph comes from my interview with Thad Cochran,
June 2002.

Page 363   "Through the years, McCain has been . . ." The information in
this paragraph comes from my interview with John McCain,
August 2001.

Page 363   "'John is a person' . . ." This unpublished quote comes from
my interview with Everett Alvarez, July 2002.

Page 363   "In future years, the McCain legacy . . ." The information in
this sentence comes from my conversation with John Sidney
McCain IV, August 2001.

Page 364   "'I remain a conservative' . . ." This unpublished quote comes
from my interview with John McCain, August 2001.

Epilogue

Page 365   "'Patriotism in this country' . . ." The text of McCain's speech
at the National Press Club was supplied to me by the Office
of John McCain. I was present for the speech in Washington
as well as for the luncheon with an anonymous source, which
took place in the early summer.

INDEX